Quantum International Relations

Quantum International Relations

A Human Science for World Politics

Edited by

JAMES DER DERIAN AND ALEXANDER WENDT

OXFORD
UNIVERSITY PRESS

OXFORD
UNIVERSITY PRESS

Oxford University Press is a department of the University of Oxford. It furthers
the University's objective of excellence in research, scholarship, and education
by publishing worldwide. Oxford is a registered trade mark of Oxford University
Press in the UK and certain other countries.

Published in the United States of America by Oxford University Press
198 Madison Avenue, New York, NY 10016, United States of America.

Library of Congress Control Number: 2021925622
ISBN 978–0–19–756821–7 (pbk.)
ISBN 978–0–19–756820–0 (hbk.)

DOI: 10.1093/oso/9780197568200.001.0001

1 3 5 7 9 8 6 4 2

Paperback printed by LSC Communications, United States of America
Hardback printed by Bridgeport National Bindery, Inc., United States of America

Contents

Foreword: Setting the Stage
Stephen J. Del Rosso

When asked in the early post–Cold War years what to make of the continued tur-
bulence that had dashed the promise of a new era of peace and stability in world
affairs, the astute diplomat, political scientist, and social philosopher Harland
Cleveland told this author that "everything is related to everything else, only
more so now than ever."[1] The first half of this seemingly unremarkable but deceptively insightful statement had become increasingly apparent in the international
relations (IR) field, where the acceleration of interactions across time and space
was attributed to the inexorable forces of globalization. It also held true within
certain branches of physics, but for different reasons. In quantum physics, the
microscopic world under examination was inextricably interconnected in ways
that conformed to an elegant and unerring mathematical logic that lent solidity
and structure, however "weird," to an otherwise inscrutable level of analysis.

It is the second half of Cleveland's sentence where basic understandings of IR
and quantum physics diverge and where *perceptions* of reality come further into
play. While the IR specialist of that era could point to phenomena in the macroscopic world—ethnic conflict, "failed states," resource scarcity, and new forms of
nuclear danger—that appeared to overlap and connect with increased frequency,
these did not represent a step change in world affairs. Rather, the end of the bi-
polar Cold War standoff that had attracted most of the attention within the field
had made more visible developments that had long been unfolding. Similarly,
in commenting on 9/11 two decades later, German publisher and editor Josef
Joffe noted, "Cataclysmic as it was, that event was more like a bolt of lightning
that illuminated the essential contours of the international landscape than like
an earthquake that reconfigured it."[2] Observed perturbations in the world were
becoming more noticeable, even if empirically no more numerous.

For the quantum physicist, there was no disjuncture between perception and
reality within the well-ordered contours of the quantum world. Everything that
had related to everything else remained so, with no apparent intensification
or upturn in interactions. While the many interpretations of quantum physics
spurred debate and disagreement within the field, these internecine wrangles did
not detract from the *true* step change that occurred over the preceding century
that had upended classical, Newtonian notions of the inner workings of the universe. Instead of a rational, mechanical system governed by natural laws of cause
and effect, quantum posited a far more complicated and less intuitive notion of

reality. In a quantum system, the visible world reveals only a sliver of what is going on beyond our gaze: there is no certainty; all is potentiality. Reality is not independent of the observer; both are intertwined and constitutive of each other, and subjectivity is a feature, not a bug of the system.

It is not surprising, then, that quantum mechanical terminology and concepts, however rudimentarily understood, if at all, would become analogized to describe the seeming new world disorder that no longer conformed to Newtonian conceptions of separable, billiard ball states and rational actors bumping up against one another in ways that "classical" IR theory presumed to explain and sometimes predict. Key quantum concepts—however abstruse in their scientific meaning—such as "entanglement," "superposition," and, perhaps above all, "the uncertainty principle" appeared to offer an apt vocabulary for trying to make sense of a world that increasingly defied ready explanation. On an even more superficial level, references to quantum that had spiked in popular culture during the first quantum revolution of the early twentieth century made a comeback in the later decades of the century and the beginning of the next as Madison Avenue affixed the term to all manner of products, from dishwasher detergent to motorcycle parts, for connoting something exceptional and powerful.

Long mired in the paradigm wars that rehashed stale debates between contending theories, dominated by the twin poles of neorealism and liberal internationalism, and sporadically challenged by upstart critical theorists and other thinkers who rejected both their ontology and epistemology, the IR field was ripe for change. So too was the world of foreign policy practice. Echoing the late US secretary of state George Shultz's earlier invocation of "quantum diplomacy" to describe an international system in which "true reality is hard to record,"[3] Armenian president (and theoretical physicist) Armen Sarkissian more recently called for "a reassessment of modern politics guided by the principles of quantum physics [to] make sense out of trends that baffle and undermine the establishment."[4]

Paralleling the ideational ferment in diplomacy and a major branch of the social sciences, and building on the cumulative insights of earlier eras, quantum advances in the natural sciences presented tantalizing possibilities for ushering in a new revolution in the practical application of theory to practice. While the cognoscenti within the physics field had long understood that quantum theory provided the insights leading to the development of a host of technologies, including transistors, lasers, LEDs, GPS, mobile phones, and, more consequentially, predating these innovations, the atomic bomb, for most, quantum's connection to everyday life remained largely unknown or too distant and abstract to matter. But beginning in the second decade of the twenty-first century, popularized by a receptive media, corporate marketing, and growing national security concerns that America was losing a quantum race to a newly formidable

China, quantum re-emerged as a matter of serious inquiry among experts and the attentive public.

Much of this renewed interest was focused on the eye-popping potential of quantum computing, which, if realized, could perform calculations in minutes that would take classical computers hundreds of years to complete. As breathlessly reported, this revolutionary advance could lead to "unhackable" communications systems and military sensors that could render stealth technologies obsolete. Beyond the hard security realm, quantum advances were touted as processing "big data" in mindboggling ways that could mimic huge chemical reactions, for example, to create new medicines and materials. And, among other innovations, they could be used to address world hunger by increasing the production of fertilizers, tackle climate change by boosting the extraction of carbon dioxide from the air, and vastly accelerate improvements in the resilience and efficiency of power grids.

Separating the hype from reality whenever quantum is invoked remains an ongoing challenge. Critiques of inflated and false quantum claims have been particularly pointed among certain voices within physics itself. A profane and biting Twitter account[5] created by an anonymous group of contrarian physicists punctured reports of purported breakthroughs in quantum computing touted in academic publications and more popular media. Even more dispassionate and civil adherents in the field cautioned against eruptions of irrational exuberance over the near-term applicability of quantum developments that are still in their early stages.

And yet, from outside the world of physics, the hype over quantum served a larger purpose. The fact that corporate behemoths such as Google, Microsoft, and IBM, as well as the US government, had decided to cumulatively invest billions in the promise of quantum (paralleled by even greater investments in China, and lesser but still considerable ones from Canada, Australia, France, Japan, India, Russia, Singapore, and India, among others), helped validate the exuberance—irrational or otherwise—of the nonscientific layperson. Such sparks of interest, or less charitably, flights of fancy, helped loosen the intellectual bolts on rusty doctrines and worldviews in need of repair or replacement.

As suggested previously, beyond the technological potential of quantum developments, perhaps the most intriguing bolts to be loosened lie in the social sciences, where quantum theory is already making inroads, for example, in studies of cognition and decision theory. It also offers promising alternatives to concepts borrowed from Newtonian physics, like market equilibrium in economics. The "quantizing" of IR that is reflected in this volume and pioneered by renowned political scientist Alexander Wendt and the forward-thinking, IR theorist and filmmaker James Der Derian, along with a new breed of expansive thinkers, is perhaps its most bold extrapolation. Wendt's *Quantum Mind and*

Social Science,[6] which followed by a decade and a half his award-winning book pioneering the constructivist school in political science,[7] challenged the basic ontological, epistemological, and normative tenets undergirding traditional IR theory.

Whether grounded in analytical hubris, reflexive defensiveness, or lack of understanding or creativity, Wendt's apostasy predictably provoked objections within the cloistered guild of the field from left, right, and center. His audacious but methodically reasoned supposition that human consciousness—a phenomenon whose explanation remains a lacuna in classical social science—is itself a quantum process, entangling all beings and the universe across distance and time, smacked for some of intellectual overreach. By speculating that human beings are "walking wave functions," Wendt created a ready foil for the naysayers zealously guarding IR's dominant disciplinary parapets. Perhaps still chafing from the missteps of the science envy that animated the behavioral turn that first riled political science in the 1950s and 1960s and still reverberates today, the sentinels of the status quo can be forgiven (somewhat) for casting a skeptical eye toward this new paradigm-shifting aspirant and refusing to take the leap, quantum or otherwise, that it entails. While even quantum technologists may be dismissive of the notion of quantum minds, and quantum social scientists may, in turn, reject the more fanciful claims of the technologists, their two literatures are currently so distinct and lacking in references to each other that the potential benefits of a united front against the doubters in each camp remain an alluring but distant goal.

For IR, the difficulty in introducing quantum concepts into the established canon relates to a puzzle inherent in the nature of the subject matter. Although quantum theory has been applied to solve problems for about a century, beyond the logic of mathematical formalism, even quantum physicists do not know how it works. Unlike classical physics, for those who reject Wendt's conjecture about quantum human beings, there is nothing in the observable world that appears to duplicate quantum behavior. This presents a daunting communication challenge when making the case for greater adoption of quantum perspectives within IR and, indeed, throughout social science. IR theorists can readily visualize how opposing armies can fight each other, and, irrespective of any deep knowledge of nuclear fission, the catastrophic consequences of a breakdown in nuclear deterrence as vividly captured in the iconic image of the mushroom cloud. Even more esoteric threats to international peace and security from emergent technologies such as artificial intelligence and cyber—which are increasingly linked to, even reliant upon, quantum developments—can at least be imagined in the form of thinking robots or villainous computer hackers. Quantum's potential disruptive impact is much harder to envision; it lacks a mushroom cloud equivalent.

How might philanthropy help overcome this conceptual hurdle? Grantmakers are by and large unburdened by the press of current events that limit policymakers' ability to think strategically and add to their store of intellectual capital amassed outside of government, and the disciplinary strictures that often stymie intellectual pathbreakers in the academy. In principle, foundations can look beyond the horizon to invest philanthropic venture capital in ideas that challenge hoary shibboleths and may someday prove consequential. Well-established foundations, especially in the expansive field of international peace and security, are continually searching for ways to become more relevant and cutting edge, while the so-called New Philanthropists, with their funding largely derived from profitmaking in the information technology sector, seem to be on a constant quest for the next shiny new thing. Quantum would appear to fit the bill for both.

Chastened by two attempts in the pages of the *Chronicle of Philanthropy*[8] to exhort peers at other foundations to join with the Carnegie Corporation of New York in its initial exploratory efforts to better understand the potentially profound and far-ranging implications of the emergent quantum revolution, I empathize with the reluctance of other philanthropies to follow our lead. There is a dizzying array of more urgent threats on the broad international peace and security agenda to command their attention and dollars, and even this agenda has received less foundation consideration and funding in recent years.[9] Since the corporation's own investment in quantum is modest compared with its funding of work in more traditional areas of international peace and security, such as nuclear nonproliferation, great power competition and cooperation, peacebuilding in Africa, and regional conflicts, among others, I had no reason to expect that my quantum evangelism would result in a windfall of grantmaking support. But, despite the crowding out by so many competing concerns, I harbored some hope that there might be other intrepid believers who would join in my conversion to the cause. So how did I come to enlist in the quantum crusade?

This deliberate resort to religious terminology reflects the epiphany I had on my own road to Damascus, or, more precisely, on a twenty three-hour plane ride to Australia to—attend my first Project Q symposium in 2016, organized by the aforementioned James Der Derian, the director of the University of Sydney's Centre for International Security Studies. The event, which deepened my newfound faith in quantum, brought together an eclectic mix of scientists, philosophers, diplomats, soldiers, scholars, writers, artists, and futurists to tease out some of quantum theory's most important implications for both good and ill. The underlying premise of this avowedly interdisciplinary gathering—another feature that foundations purport to encourage but too rarely succeed in advancing—was to get ahead of quantum's technological curve to anticipate and help steer its eventual social effects. As one informed observer of this endeavor explained to me, "Most social scientists spend their time trying to explain past events, in the hopes that this will shed light on future ones. That might make sense in a deterministic and linear world, but the kinds of social effects that quantum is likely to have will be hard, if not impossible, to understand in this way. Thus, in this case, it is absolutely essential for social scientists [and others] to get out of their usual reactive mode into a pro-active one, even if that entails a good deal of speculation."[10]

At this event and subsequent Q project symposia supported by the Carnegie Corporation, Der Derian and his diverse invitees explored some of the most probing speculative questions posed by the latest quantum revolution, however protracted and tentative may be its unfolding: What inspiration, ideas, and concepts can we draw from quantum physics? How can we prepare for the emergent quantum revolution when its trajectory and implications are not yet known? How might quantum advances interact with other technologies? Will quantum developments ultimately lead to sentient computer programs and feral algorithms? To what extent will quantum applications be weaponized? Are social media and data mining already producing quantum effects in world politics? What new kinds of scientific inquiries will make it possible? And what are the philosophical and ethical implications?

The chapters that follow in this volume are a fitting coda to these expansive and thought-provoking discussions and a tangible deliverable in philanthropic terms. The authors delve into some of the most penetrating and beguiling aspects of what might be described as an incipient but promising quantum turn in social science, especially within IR. With contributions that examine the comparisons between quantum and systems theorizing, the philosophical roots of quantum thinking, the contextualization of the hype surrounding quantum, the potential of quantum pedagogy, and a quantum ontology for validating ethical choices, among others, the authors collectively stake their claim for breaking new intellectual ground and paving the way for further analysis and discourse. The cumulative insights reflected in these chapters represent just the kind of forward-looking, exploratory thinking that, as noted, foundations are ideally positioned to support.

But however well intended and diligently pursued, the broader and lasting effects of a grant-funded project such as this cannot be conclusively determined or predicted. Philanthropic efforts to promote positive social change are inherently complicated given the multifaceted causal chains involved, the difficulty in discerning macro developments from micro interventions, and the often-extended time required before any shoots appear from seeds once planted. Despite the many thoughtful attempts to overcome these challenges, evaluative metrics in the field remain a work in progress. As even the bumptious New Philanthropists have discovered, measuring grantmaking impact is not as clear-cut as calculating price-earnings ratios. The great industrialist and philanthropist Andrew Carnegie had earlier come to the same realization. He established his namesake grantmaking foundation in 1911 with an abiding belief in the power of ideas to change the world for the better. His most ambitious idea was the abolition of war. While he and this philanthropic progeny may have fallen short in reaching this lofty goal, the Carnegie Corporation's many investments to both limit war's effects and curb its frequency continue apace, notwithstanding the difficulty involved in proving a negative.

Although the ability of even the most generously endowed and capable foundations to move the needle on the most pressing problems of our age is necessarily limited and imperfectly measured, this should not prevent efforts to get ahead of the curve on developments with potentially profound, if distant, effects—or, as Albert Einstein famously implored at the dawn of the atomic age, "to change our modes of thinking."[11] Among the abiding challenges of contemporary life is what Carlos Fuentes once identified as the need to "transform information into knowledge."[12] This challenge has increased exponentially in an age of information overload marked by a pronounced noise-to-signal ratio between what is accessible and what is useful. As knowledge becomes more specialized and fragmented, its transformation into practical application, to say nothing of wisdom, becomes more elusive.

It is perhaps predictable that quantum ideas—as specialized and fragmented as any in the natural sciences—would provoke pushback from those social scientists who fail to appreciate or perceive the embedded wisdom contained in these ideas and their applicability well beyond the metaphorical. Classical, Newtonian conceptions of the world, however refuted and transcended by quantum physics, provide a simple and comforting, if also inadequate, refuge from the messiness and indeterminacy of contemporary affairs. If, in an age marked by a global pandemic, endless (and ignominiously ended) wars, and the increasingly harmful effects of climate change, the magnitude of the relational dynamic that Harland Cleveland cited decades ago seems truly "more so now than ever," philanthropy has an obligation to advance new thinking that might offer novel insights for addressing old and new threats and evolving notions of security. What is a grant proposal, after all, if not, in quantum terms, a potentiality that is unknown until observed and measured? The foundation grant that funded the proposal on which this volume is based represents a potentiality whose merit and promise now await the observation and measurement of its readers.

Notes

1. Harland Cleveland, quoted in Stephen Del Rosso, "The Insecure State: Reflections on 'the State' and 'Security' in a Changing World," *Daedalus, What Future for the State,* Spring 1995, p. 175.

2. Josef Joffe, "Of Hubs, Spokes, and Public Goods," *National Interest*, October 30, 2002, https://nationalinterest.org/article/hubs-spokes-and-public-goods-2159.
3. George Shultz, quoting Sydney Drell, "Diplomacy, Wired," *Hoover Digest*, January 30, 1998.
4. Armen Sarkissian, "We Need an Era of Quantum Politics," *Financial Times*, August 28, 2020, https://www.ft.com/content/be19ce7e-bb88-4127-9496-6c9e492d52aa.
5. https://twitter.com/BullshitQuantum
6. Alexander Wendt, *Quantum Mind and Social Science*, Cambridge University Press, 2015.
7. Alexander Wendt, *Social Theory of International Politics*, Cambridge University Press, 1999.
8. Stephen Del Rosso, "The Quantum Age Beckons: Philanthropy Should Help Us Understand It," *Chronicle of Philanthropy*, February 7, 2017; and Stephen Del Rosso, "The Quantum Revolution Rolls On and Philanthropy Is Falling Behind," *Chronicle of Philanthropy*, October 2, 2018.
9. David Callahan, "You Never Give Me Your Money: Big Funders Neglect Peace and Security in a Dangerous Era," *Inside Philanthropy*, June 12, 2018, https://www.insidephilanthropy.com/home/2018/6/12/you-never-give-me-your-money-big-funders-neglect-peace-and-security-in-a-dangerous-era.
10. Stephen Del Rosso, Carnegie Corporation of New York, private e-mail with anonymized reviewer, November 10, 2014.
11. Albert Einstein, quoted in "Atomic Education Urged by Einstein," *New York Times*, May 25, 1946, p. 13.
12. Carlos Fuentes, quoted in Vartan Gregorian, "Colleges Must Reconstruct the Unity of Knowledge," *Chronicle of Philanthropy*, June 4, 2004, https://www.chronicle.com/article/colleges-must-reconstruct-the-unity-of-knowledge/. A former career diplomat, Stephen Del Rosso directs the International Peace and Security program at the Carnegie Corporation of New York.

Contributors

Mathias Albert is Professor of Political Science at Bielefeld University. He works on the theory, history and sociology of world politics and has published numerous books and articles, among them *A Theory of World Politics* (Cambridge, 2016). He has a second academic identity in youth research, particularly through the German Shell Youth Surveys (Shell Jugendstudien) and has more recently also become active in polar research.

Badredine Arfi is the University of Florida Research Foundation Professor of International Relations and Political Science. He has a PhD in theoretical physics and a PhD in political science/international relations. His interests include theories of international relations, social science methodologies including machine learning and artificial intelligence, philosophy of social theory, and deconstruction. He is the author of *International Change and the Stability of Multi-ethnic States* (2005), *Linguistic Fuzzy Logic Methods in Social Sciences* (2010), and *Re-Thinking International Relations Theory via Deconstruction* (2012).

Felix Maximilian Bathon studied Sociology, Politics, and Economics at Zeppelin University Friedrichshafen and Sociology in Bielefeld. He is entangled in the practice and logic of doing theory while writing his PhD thesis on small group theory grounded in systems theory.

Thomas Biersteker is Gasteyger Professor Honoraire at the Graduate Institute, Geneva, and a Global Fellow at the Woodrow Wilson International Center for Scholars in Washington, DC. Author, editor, or coeditor of eleven books, his next book, coedited with Oliver Westerwinter and Kenneth Abbott, is *Informal Governance in World Politics* (Cambridge, forthcoming 2022). His research interests include global governance, international relations theory, and international sanctions, and he is the principal developer of UNSanctionsApp. He received his BA from the University of Chicago and his MS and PhD from MIT.

Stephen J. Del Rosso directs the International Peace and Security Program at the Carnegie Corporation of New York. A former US career diplomat, he also served as Director of Programs at the Chicago Council on Foreign Relations and managed The Pew Charitable Trusts' Global Security Program. Earlier, he was a Presidential Management Fellow at NASA, news producer at the Voice of America, and staff assistant to a British Member of Parliament. He holds a PhD in political science from the University of Pennsylvania and an MA in Law and Diplomacy from Tufts University's Fletcher School.

James Der Derian is the Michael Hintze Chair of International Security at the University of Sydney, where he directs the Centre for International Security Studies and Project Q: Peace and Security in a Quantum Age (funded by the Carnegie Corporation of

New York). He was born quantum in the United States, was classically trained in the United Kingdom, and now decoheres in Australia. He is currently working on a new documentary film and book, *Project Q: War, Peace and Quantum Mechanics.*

K. M. Fierke is Professor of International Relations in the School of International Relations at the University of St. Andrews, Scotland. Her most recent book, *Snapshots from Home: Mind, Action and Strategy in an Uncertain World* (Bristol, 2022), explores the relevance of the parallel between quantum physics and Eastern philosophy for navigating the uncertainty of the pandemic and postpandemic world. Along with Nicola Mackay, she is co-investigator of a quantum project, funded by the Human Family Unity Foundation in the United States, titled *Mapping the Empire: The Contemporary Legacy of Historical Trauma and Forced Displacement.*

Shohini Ghose wanted to be an explorer like Rakesh Sharma, the first Indian to go to space. She hasn't made it to space yet, but she did become an explorer of the quantum world as a Physics Professor and the NSERC Chair for Women in Science and Engineering at Wilfrid Laurier University, Canada. She examines how quantum physics can transform computing and communication. She and her colleagues were the first to observe a connection between quantum entanglement and chaos theory. She aims to create an inclusive physics community as the Director of the Laurier Centre for Women in Science.

Jairus Victor Grove is Chair of the University of Hawai'i at Mānoa Department of Political Science where he also directs the Hawai'i Research Center for Futures Studies. He is the author of *Savage Ecology: War and Geopolitics at the End of the World* (Duke, 2019). He is currently working with Antoine Bousquet on a book tentatively titled *Between Oblivion and Forever: A Critique of Nuclear Reason.*

Nicholas Harrington is a final-year PhD candidate through the University of Sydney. He is currently employed as a research assistant for Project Q, a transdisciplinary and interdisciplinary unit specializing in the application of quantum physics across the social sciences, domiciled at the University of Sydney. Harrington's dissertation concerns a quantum interpretation of political philosophy. Harrington was awarded the University Medal in 2019 for his honors thesis on European Union integration.

Jon R. Lindsay is an Associate Professor at the Georgia Institute of Technology, School of Cybersecurity and Privacy, with a cross appointment in the Sam Nunn School of International Affairs. He is the author of *Information Technology and Military Power* (Cornell, 2020) and editor of volumes on *Cross-Domain Deterrence* (Oxford, 2019) and *China and Cybersecurity* (Oxford, 2015). He has served in the US Navy with operational assignments in Europe, Latin America, and the Middle East.

Nicola Mackay is a clinical physicist turned systemic constellation therapist and researcher. She has been in private practice for twenty years and has a busy therapy practice and teaching school based in Western Europe and the United States. She is the author of several books on systemic therapy. She, in collaboration with K. M. Fierke, is currently focusing on exploring the influence of collective memory on the transgenerational inheritance of trauma through a quantum lens.

Manjana Milkoreit is a Postdoctoral Researcher at the University of Oslo's Department of Sociology and Human Geography with a background in global environmental governance and public policy. Integrating cognitive theories into social environmental science, her research focuses on the role of future thinking in climate change politics and deliberate sustainability transformations. She is the author of *Mindmade Politics: The Cognitive Roots of International Climate Governance* (MIT Press, 2017).

Michael P. A. Murphy is SSHRC doctoral fellow in International Relations and Political Theory at the University of Ottawa, and the author of *Quantum Social Theory for Critical International Relations Theorists* (Palgrave, 2021). He serves as an elected school board trustee, Editorial Assistant at *Security Dialogue*, and an associate member of the uOttawa Scholarship of Teaching and Learning Research Unit. He has published over two dozen articles, appearing in *International Relations, Contemporary Security Policy, Millennium, Journal of International Political Theory, Critical Studies on Security*, the *Journal of Political Science Education*, and elsewhere. His work can be found at http://bit.ly/37NJMkZ.

Karen O'Brien is a Professor of Human Geography at the University of Oslo, Norway, and co-founder of cCHANGE, an organization that supports transformations to sustainability. Her research focuses on the social and human dimensions of climate change, and she finds quantum social science fascinating. Her recent book, *You Matter More Than You Think: Quantum Social Change for a Thriving World*, explores what quantum paradigms mean for climate change and social change.

Leonardo Orlando is an Affiliate Junior Researcher at the Center for International Studies of Sciences Po (Paris). He holds a PhD in political science and international relations (Sciences Po) and bachelor's and master's degrees in philosophy (Université Paris 1 Panthéon-Sorbonne). Convinced that social science without Darwin is like astrophysics without general relativity or physics without the laws of thermodynamics, he analyzes political phenomena through the lens of evolutionary psychology and neuroscience.

David Orrell is an applied mathematician and writer. He obtained his DPhil in mathematics from Oxford University and has worked in diverse areas including weather forecasting, cancer biology, and quantum economics. He is the author of many books on science and economics including *Quantum Economics and Finance: An Applied Mathematics Introduction*, and *Money, Magic, and How to Dismantle a Financial Bomb: Quantum Economics for the Real World*. He lives in Toronto.

Mark B. Salter is a Professor of Political Studies at the University of Ottawa and Editor-in-Chief of *Security Dialogue*. He is the editor of *Making Things International 1* (Minnesota, 2015), *Making Things International 2* (Minnesota, 2016), *Research Methods in Critical Security Studies* (Routledge 2nd edition forthcoming), and *Politics at the Airport* (Minnesota, 2008), among others.

Michael Schnabel is a Research Assistant Professor at the University of Chicago Harris School of Public Policy. He has a PhD in theoretical physics and applies methods from physics and neuroscience to model collective decision-making and information processing in social systems. His current research topics include opinion formation, deliberative democracy, quantum cognition, and cognitive models of decision-making.

Frank L. Smith III is a Professor and Director of the Cyber and Innovation Policy Institute at the US Naval War College. He is also Non-Resident Fellow with the United States Studies Centre at the University of Sydney. His interdisciplinary research examines how ideas about technology—especially bad ideas—influence national security and international relations. He has a PhD in political science and a BS in biological chemistry, both from the University of Chicago.

Jayson Waters is a Doctoral candidate with the Centre for International Security Studies at the University of Sydney. He became entangled with *Project Q: Peace and Security in a Quantum Age* in 2014 and has been a passionate advocate for quantum approaches to international relations ever since. His thesis interrogates the historical, theoretical, and technological linkages between international relations and quantum mechanics, with the auxiliary purpose of identifying new avenues for inquiry and theoretical development.

Alexander Wendt is Mershon Professor of International Security and Professor of Political Science at The Ohio State University. Author of several well-known early articles, in 1999 he published *Social Theory of International Politics* (Cambridge), which won the "Best Book of the Decade" award from the International Studies Association in 2006. Wendt then realized it was all wrong and spent ten years rewriting it as *Quantum Mind and Social Science* (Cambridge, 2015).

Laura Zanotti is a Professor of Political Science at Virginia Tech. After spending ten years as a peacekeeper at the United Nations, and subsequently writing about it in her 2011 book *Governing Disorder*, she realized it was necessary to explore the ontological assumptions of policy practices. Her quantum-inspired ontological critique appears in *Ontological Entanglements, Agency and Ethics in International Relations* (Routledge, 2019), in several journal articles, as well as in a recent *Millennium* forum on her book.

INTRODUCTION

1

Quantum International Relations

The Case for a New Human Science of World Politics

James Der Derian and Alexander Wendt

Everything in the future is a wave, everything in the past is a particle.
—Sir William Lawrence Bragg, Nobel Prize in Physics, 1915

Epiphanies figure large in the story of quantum mechanics. Within a single momentous year, Heisenberg's fever-induced vision of the act of observing altering the reality observed provided the missing piece for the principle of uncertainty. Bohr's Taoist-inflected yin-yang of a single object sharing opposing attributes of wave and particle opened the doors of perception for his holistic principle of complementarity. Schrödinger's ecstatic dalliance in Davos inspired the wave equation that he thought would "save the soul" of classical mechanics by showing how a packet of waves could create the illusion of a single particle.

As with the wave that becomes particulate, so too comes the passage of this book. An epiphany serves as a catalyst for a radical break from the past, which then becomes an origin story for an indeterminate future.

One epiphany takes place in Berlin, when a controversy erupts over the naming of a street after a dead American president, Ronald Reagan. Under the gaze of global media, ideological interests become entangled, negotiations shift from city to state to the world stage, and a local event becomes an international incident. The superposition of the author as observer-participant collapses into a bit player of what former secretary of state George Shultz and physicist Sidney Drell first identified as "quantum diplomacy."[1]

The other epiphany comes with the discovery of *The Quantum Society: Mind, Physics, and a New Social Vision* in a Chicago bookstore remainder bin. Danah Zohar and Ian Marshall present the radical hypothesis of consciousness as a macroscopic quantum mechanical phenomenon, a "quantum self," with profound and potentially revolutionary implications for society. Even if highly speculative and not intended for an academic audience, *what if* the book was right? Given the failure of the classical philosophical and scientific orthodoxy to make any progress on the mind-body problem, the idea surely warrants further investigation. One reversal of perspective and fifteen years later, the other author comes up with a response to the question of a quantum mind.[2]

These epiphanies of course pale in significance to the revelations that gave rise to quantum mechanics. But they produce a similar effect: a willingness to break with outdated worldviews to enable new modes for comprehending reality.[3] Our shared epiphanies gave us cause to shed past differences and to undertake a collaborative inquiry into the societal and geopolitical implications of quantum theory, science, and technology, a convergence that interprets quantum as a *new human science* for International Relations (IR).[4] Linking a natural science like physics to the human sciences, and both then in turn to IR, might in some quarters elevate an interdisciplinary misdemeanor to an academic felony. We believe, however, there to be epistemic affinities that go back to shared origins and a break from natural philosophy, followed by coeval modes of inquiry that were empirical, relational, and observer dependent. As we learn from chapters by rising quantum IR scholars Nicholas Harrington and Jayson Waters, physicists literally shared university hallways with philosophers, and key thinkers regularly exchanged views about new discoveries in quantum physics, continental philosophy, and psychology that defied classical explanations. Similarly, just as a radical break from divine cosmology gave rise to the diversity of the early human sciences, quantum's emergence in physics and extension into IR have produced pluralist, one might even say profane, interpretations of the world, as Badredine Arfi and Michael Murphy richly demonstrate in their chapters. A quantum human science celebrates this unity in diversity.

In this book a body of international scholars coalesce around a singular intent, to "quantize IR." Quantizing IR is sure to trigger mixed responses, an effect multiplied by the complex and indeterminate nature of quantum theory itself. Since its inception at the turn of the last century, quantum seems to have generated almost as many interpretations, schools, and cosmologies as there are religious sects. And yet physicists have found a way to live and let live, largely because they have come to acknowledge the empirical validity of quantum mechanics. The same cannot (yet) be said in IR. Caught in what looks to be a preparadigmatic moment, and with no equivalent of a Peace of Westphalia in sight, differences— in a field of knowledge already known for a narcissism of petty differences—are unlikely to be resolved anytime soon. Hence, we have chosen a less-than-grand strategy that follows the irregular path of early quantum mechanics itself, which from its inception has been marked by a series of fitful dialogues within and between the human sciences and the positive sciences but still managed to find a common way forward.[5]

The chapters in this book are drawn from a series of presentations made at workshops, international symposia, and annual professional meetings.[6] They share, in a manner similar to the *Gedankenexperimente* of the 1920s, an exploratory collective effort to find a better mode of comprehending world politics in transformation. We note that these early thought experiments were followed by laboratory and other proofs that made quantum mechanics the most successful theory in the history of physics, even if one narrowly measures success by technologies derived from quantum mechanics, like transistors, televisions, lasers, laptops, mobile phones, and, somewhat more ambiguously, the atomic bomb. Indeed, our effort to quantize IR is compelled by an apprehension, going back to Einstein's fear of atomic weapons changing everything except our modes of thought, that the next revolution in quantum technology will outstrip conventional theories and practices in world politics.

As the fundamental theory of physical reality, quantum is not going away; the trickier question is how well it will travel outside of physics.[7] The idea of a quantum IR could well be received as just another short-lived "turn" in the discipline's long and winding road. We believe, however, that the consilience of transdisciplinary approaches combined with technological drivers presents the opportunity and, indeed, the necessity for a new human science of IR with quantum at its core. We introduce three forces of change, which the following chapters take up in greater detail, that most profoundly call into question traditional approaches and endorse a new human science of IR: *quantum technology*, *quantum theory*, and *quantum science*.

Quantum Technology

The most concrete stimulus for a quantized IR is technological—in particular, an accelerating global race to build the advanced quantum systems for computing, communications, control, and artificial intelligence.[8]

There are currently at least four different pathways to the development of quantum computers: superconducting, trapped ion, silicon dot, and topological. Fundamental to all is the quantum bit or "qubit," which, entangled in all possible states of superposition, provides an exponential advantage over classical computers based on digital bits in binary states of either 0 or 1. The almost unimaginable increase in computational power—one quantum computer with 300 qubits could perform more calculations than there are atoms in the universe—would provide profound advantages in strategically vital areas, including encryption and decryption; radar and sensors; navigation and targeting; simulation and data mining; machine learning and pattern recognition. Google, IBM, Microsoft, and other major high-tech giants have been in competition over the past several years to achieve "quantum supremacy," the somewhat hyperbolic term coined by theoretical physicist John Preskill to describe the moment when a quantum computer proves capable of executing tasks impossible for the most powerful supercomputer, like large-number prime factoring (the basis of most classical encryption), multivariable optimization (like the "traveling salesman problem"), or the simulation of complex many-body systems (like astronomical bodies).[9]

For better or worse, the number of players in this game is limited by the staggering cost of developing quantum technologies, which commonly involves supercooling, shielded facilities, rare materials, and considerable financial as well as intellectual capital. This leaves the geopolitical field primarily open to superpowers like the United States and China. However, the European Union and middle powers like Australia, Canada, India, Japan, and Singapore, pursuing comparative advantages through collaborative research and development projects, are clearly in pursuit of a step change through quantum technology that might well register as an increase in geopolitical status. Alongside, and in some cases out ahead of the US tech firms, Alibaba, Baidu, and Quantum CTek in China are pouring billions into quantum computation and communication, often in concert with state-financed initiatives based at leading universities.[10]

If history is to be the judge, new asymmetries will result with the emergence of new "quantum haves" and "quantum have-nots"; and, as with every new powerful technology, funding on how best to weaponize quantum, especially in the application of quantum artificial intelligence to intelligence, surveillance, and reconnaissance (ISR), has already begun. Deep in defense departments and under the darkness of classified programs in spy agencies, memos are probably already circulating about the coming "RQMA" or "Revolution in Quantum Military Affairs."[11]

It remains uncertain which corporation, state, university, or synergy thereof will achieve the first major breakthrough and come out on top in the quantum race (not always, as we learned from the digital revolution, one and the same). Nor is it clear who will benefit and who will be harmed from a "quantum revolution"—or even that the correlation of social, strategic, and technological forces will amount to a true revolution. In his timely chapter, international security expert Jon Lindsay suggests the worries are overblown, and that even the most vaunted threat, to RSA-protected communications, is unlikely to result in a "cryptocalypse."

Timelines are key. At the moment, two to twenty years have been mooted for the building of a universal quantum computer with—and this is a key qualification—adequate error correction to overcome the natural tendency of qubits to decohere in noisy environments. Nonetheless, given the enormous investments committed and progress achieved so far, we consider it better to pose cautionary questions *now*, rather than *after* quantum technologies go online; and if not by concerned scholars, who else? The networked vulnerabilities, potential accidents, and ethical challenges of new quantum technologies are unlikely to be high on the agenda of profit-driven corporations, polarized political elites, and short-term governmental regimes.

Key Concepts of Quantum Theory

As part of making the case for the relevance of quantum mechanics to IR, we wish to highlight the multifold approaches shared by most of the contributors to this book: a quantum worldview (from multiple perspectives); a conceptual heuristic (to "quantize" everything); and a pragmatic attitude (what value added does quantum bring to IR?). Although we do not pretend this amounts to a grand or unified field theory of IR, we do believe this assemblage of quantum approaches has a comparative advantage over others that are largely derived, often un-self-consciously, from Newtonian or classical physics and Hobbesian or mechanistic political theories. Because of the inherent complexity as well as the oft-mentioned "weirdness" of all things quantum, we do feel obligated to introduce the central concepts that inform quantum IR, many of which may be unfamiliar or appear paradoxical for those coming from a classical worldview (i.e., most of IR). A fuller account is provided in two chapters by physicists: Michael Schnabel, who presents the basic linear algebra and probability theory of key quantum principles to develop a formal as well more intuitive sense of how quantum differs from classical approaches, and Shohini Ghose, who then takes the next step, to show how the application of those quantum principles in computing, encryption, and communication could surpass classical limitations on how we understand and redress pressing global issues, including pandemics and climate change.

This raises the question of how or even if quantum concepts should "travel" outside physics, a concern that seems to grow with every theoretical leap and technological innovation inspired by quantum mechanics. During quantum's originary moments, from Max Planck's coinage of "quantum" in 1900 to the breakthrough gathering of the leading theorists at the Solvay Conference in 1927, physics was only just divorcing from its disciplinary cohabitation in universities as a subfield of natural philosophy (Victor Frankenstein was an early if aberrant example of an experimental natural philosopher who got carried away by the new science of electricity). Disruptive ideas crossed disciplines with an alacrity now lost—Martin Heidegger to Werner Heisenberg, Søren Kierkegaard to Niels Bohr, Alfred North Whitehead to David Bohm, Carl Jung to Wolfgang Pauli—that served to inspire, inform, and reform a shared worldview that burned brightly if briefly in the interwar period.[12] Physicists also cited the influence of holistic Eastern philosophies on the early formulations of quantum mechanics.[13] During this period, even the nascent field of political science at the authoritative level of the president of the American Political Science Association acknowledged the significance of the new discoveries in quantum theory.[14] In his provocative chapter, Jairus Grove presents a revisionist history of this febrile period, upending the traditional version of philosophy as secondary or epiphenomenal to physics and, in the process, subverting the critique that quantum IR represents the latest instance of "science envy" in the social sciences.

Seeking to explain phenomena that were considered nonsensical and counterintuitive in classical terms, the early quantum physicists realized that their findings, proven through mathematical formalism, would not be easily translatable into everyday language. Bohr, Heisenberg, and most of their peers considered this good reason to reach out to other disciplines of learning rather than to quarantine quantum to physics. Bohr's papers on the philosophical implications of quantum theory fill, literally, volumes; a short quote from Heisenberg captures the essence of their argument:

> The positivists have a simple solution: the world must be divided into that which we can say clearly and the rest, which we had better pass over in silence. But can anyone conceive of a more pointless philosophy, seeing that what we can say clearly amounts to next to nothing? If we omitted all that is unclear we would probably be left with completely uninteresting and trivial tautologies.[15]

What follows is our attempt to recapture in a new human science for IR something like the transnational, transdisciplinary, even transcendent moment of quantum mechanics at its inception. We offer in this book "traveling documents" for key quantum concepts, to visit and we hope to stay awhile in IR. We are fully aware from our previous transgressions of traditional IR that there will be opposition to this effort, from scientists on the grounds that quantum concepts cannot possibly scale up to the macrophysical level as well as from social scientists who belittle quantum concepts as mere metaphors, or worse. We and other quantum IR scholars deal in depth with the scaling problem; as for the metaphorical issue, our short answer is: too late to worry *and* too soon to say. Quantum effects once thought confined to the subatomic level have already been shown to scale up to the biological, cognitive, and human behavioral levels. Even at the metaphorical level, as when former US secretary of state George Shultz speaks of a new "quantum diplomacy" or the current president of Armenia Armen Sarkissian (who happens to be a theoretical physicist) of a globalizing "quantum politics," they attest to the superior heuristics of quantum theory to understand quantum-like phenomena.[16] Or put another way: when observational practices and visual imagery transmitted in near simultaneity through densely networked systems of multiple media produce powerful superpositional *effects* as well as entangled *affects*, the heuristic advantage of quantum over classical approaches becomes increasingly difficult to refute. And to pre-empt the predictable retort: come the day of a quantum convergence between human and artificial intelligence, shall we deem it "quantum-like" or "human-like"?

These are admittedly speculative propositions but with potentially revolutionary outcomes. *If* quantum technology goes online, quantum science continues to scale up, *and* quantum consciousness proves measurable at the macrophysical level, a quantum approach could well become the *most realist* of social scientific theories. It will then fall upon those in the social sciences upholding worldviews based on the motions of planets, pulleys, and billiard balls to defend their concepts—or to recognize them as metaphors whose metaphorical nature has been forgotten. At this emergent stage, we believe it best to practice an open pluralism on the critical question of when, how, and at what scale quantum behavior is actual, potential, or "merely" metaphorical. Practically all of the investigations undertaken in the book directly address this issue; and, we believe, they do a good job of demonstrating how networked, complex, or emergent aspects of *human* systems can be quantum in their own right, giving quantum theory a heuristic advantage over classical approaches. Several authors use the observer-dependent nature of quantum to de-familiarize IR, forcing us not just to rethink the classical concepts of the discipline but to reconsider the objective reality of its primary referents and subjective powers of its multiple actors. In a powerful revisionist history of Canada's relationship to its Indigenous people, Mark Salter applies the mechanism of measurement with quantum principles of superposition and entanglement to challenge one of IR's most sacrosanct concepts, state sovereignty. David Orrell reinterprets money as a nonclassical object in superposition that only takes on distinct value through authoritative and institutional acts of measurement or observation. Similarly, K. M. Fierke and Nicola Mackay identify hidden quantum effects of trauma on security practices that become observable when toxic political entanglements collapse as speech acts. Karen O'Brien and Manjana Milkoreit present three case studies on the social and environmental benefits to be gained from a complementarity of quantum and cognitive approaches to climate politics. We would not be the first to say such quantum investigations can sound weird—right up until the moment they make better sense than classical explanations.[17]

We cannot in this introduction explicate every strange concept or adjudicate every controversial element of quantum. We do believe the book as a whole makes a credible case for applying quantum concepts to IR (as well as to other social science disciplines).[18] Our task, at the risk of mimicking the bias of the Nobel Prize for the discoveries of select individuals, is to elucidate what we believe to be the primary quantum concepts that are most adaptive to IR. We try to stick as close as possible to the "show-don't-tell" style of documentary film, as we conceive of this introduction as a short teaser for the full features that follow.

Let us start with a long take of a brief version of quantum mechanics, which emerged from a series of conceptual breakthroughs by Albert Einstein, Niels Bohr, Max Born, Werner Heisenberg, Wolfgang Pauli, Louis de Broglie, Paul Dirac, Erwin Schrödinger, and a handful of other physicists who would intuit, posit, model, debate, and not all agree but eventually prove both mathematically and experimentally that quanta in the form of atoms, photons, and electrons exist as both waves and particles until the point of collapse or observation; that their position and velocity could not be simultaneously measured; that they could correlate nonlocally across vast distances; that they could pass through seemingly impermeable barriers; and yes, that, Schrödinger's cat could potentially, simultaneously, and absurdly be both alive and dead at the same time—until we opened the box.

These principles, such as complementarity, uncertainty, entanglement, tunneling, teleportation, superposition, and wave function, form the fundaments of quantum mechanics. The new quantum formulation of atomic behavior, subsequently confirmed by experiments, repudiated much of Newtonian physics at the microphysical level. It challenged classical conceptions of space and time at the macrophysical level. And it cast into doubt philosophical assumptions about causality, determinism, prediction, and an observer-independent reality at the cosmological level.

Rather than attempt a comprehensive exegesis of *all* of the concepts that revolutionized physics, we have picked out those that have been particularly significant in the quantum revolution and figure centrally in quantum IR: entanglement, superposition, uncertainty and the measurement problem, and the collapse of the wave function.

At the macro or classical level, the elementary parts of any science are assumed to be "fully separable." By that, scientists mean that nothing about those parts logically or ontologically presupposes any other parts; every part is what it is by virtue of its own physical make-up, and only that. Of course, parts can interact causally with each other to produce emergent effects, like the motion of a car, but the parts of an engine do not depend *constitutionally* on each other to be what they are, and as such can be removed from the engine without changing their identity; the whole can always be broken down into self-subsisting parts.

On the surface, this seems to be true of human beings—the elementary parts of social science—as well. Even though living in society we are deeply dependent upon each other in a causal sense for survival, in a constitutive sense we seem to be fully separable "individuals," clearly demarcated by our skins. After all, even if every other human being suddenly vanished, your body would still be there alive and well, completely unchanged. As for your mind, if you are a materialist—which is the ontology of classical physics and the orthodoxy (if increasingly embattled) in philosophy—then it is nothing more than your brain, which is also

encased in your skin and thus seemingly separable from other minds. An assumption of separability is therefore the ontological foundation of the doctrine
of atomism in philosophy, and of methodological individualism in social science
(and from there on to liberal political theory and all the rest).

One of the greatest and still most puzzling discoveries of quantum physics
is that at the subatomic level, at least, this assumption does not hold, that the
elementary parts of reality are not fully separable but *entangled* (in which
two particles remain correlated over large distances). Although philosophers
might disagree in their metaphysical interpretations, everyone agrees on the
basic physical facts, which are that the behavior and properties of entangled
particles exhibit correlations ("nonlocal causation") that have no causal explanation and are inexplicable in classical terms. Indeed, it is now problematic to
speak of elementary "parts" at all, since the tiny but hard and separable atoms
imagined to lie at the bottom of the classical universe dissolve subatomically
into ghostly "wave functions," which, following the principle of uncertainty,
represent merely the probability of finding classical particles at a given location *should* we look there (and if we don't look, there is no certainty for saying
any particles are there at all). In short, entanglement makes quantum theory
fundamentally holistic: the properties, even existence, of the parts depend in
top-down fashion on the whole, rather than the other way around as in the
classical worldview.

Precisely because it contradicted both classical physics and our everyday experience of material objects, the holism of entanglement was something of a
scandal among early quantum physicists, with Einstein leading the first-wave
charge of scientific realism against the second-wave formulations of the so-called
Copenhagen or instrumentalist school of quantum mechanics. In contrast, practically all physicists today have not only come to terms with superposition, entanglement, and nonlocal causation but also are exploiting them to build quantum
computers based on spin-up/spin-down orientations of entangled qubits. Yet
most would still argue that although universal in some broad sense, quantum
has no significant effects at the macrophysical level and as such does not scale
up to IR.

It is ironic, therefore, that despite the strong intuitions that sustain methodological individualism, in the social sciences holism has long been supported
by strong intuitions of its own, and as such was never eliminated as a social
ontology in the way it was as a physical ontology by the classical worldview.[19]
The intuitions that sustain social holism revolve heavily around language and
the seemingly irreducible relational quality of meaning and practices. Consider
two famous examples. One is Hegel's analysis of the "master/slave relation"—
a person literally cannot *be* a master unless there are slaves around to "make"
them one, again not in a causal sense (though that matters for reproducing

slavery over time), but constitutively. As such, it is not just the physical states of brains encased safely inside skins that make certain people masters, but whether other people, especially slaves (*sic*), mutually *recognize* them as such. The other is Jaegwon Kim's analysis of what happened to Xantippe when her husband Socrates was forced to commit suicide—she became a widow, but not, in Kim's analytic philosophical treatment, because of a causal process, but a noncausal one.[20] While hardly ever discussed this way, these examples sound a lot like descriptions of entities that are distinct (masters and slaves; husbands and wives) but not fully separable (can't have one without the other), and between which there can be nonlocal causation (changing one instantly changes the other). In short, in contrast to the material world, where it indeed seems "spooky" and counterintuitive, in the social world, by virtue of language, entanglement seems to be given and entirely commonplace.

Although individualism nevertheless remains the default ontology in most social science, holism is dominant in mainstream philosophy of language (and those branches of social science indebted to it). However, in the past, social or linguistic holists have never felt a need for quantum foundations, on the belief that it was enough to show that linguistic meaning is irreducibly relational. But like everything else language is physical too, and so either it is classical or quantum—but if it is classical and as such trapped in brains, then how could it be holistic?[21] There is in our view a tension or even contradiction here, the resolution of which could depend on the mind-body problem. If the ontology of consciousness, as we suggest later, also turns out to be quantum rather than classical, then it might not be trapped within brains, but could be the manifestation of our entanglement with the world and with each other. That would provide a completely different basis for social theorizing, both positive and normative, than the orthodoxies today, one in which there is a real (if limited) sense in which quite literally—which is to say physically—"I am You."[22]

In the classical worldview, all objects and their properties are always in well-defined and noncontradictory states. Objects are of course also always in process, eroding, decaying, growing, and so on, and thus constantly changing (however slowly). However, classical logic tells us that at any given instant, the musical chairs are stopped and everything is in either state A or not-A—there are no "in-between" states, nor overarching ones that could encompass both possibilities. Note that this says nothing about our ability fully to *know* objects and their properties, especially as complexities rapidly mount the deeper inside them we probe; the point here is ontological, about what objects can *be*, not epistemological. And given the materialism of the classical worldview, it should hold equally for mental objects and their properties as for material ones, since according to the materialists the mind is nothing but the brain. While a subjective experience like "ambivalence" might *feel* like we are in state A and not-A simultaneously, in fact each of the zillions of brain states that cause and/or constitute that feeling is in one state or the other. After all, as material objects, how could they not be?

Quantum theory provides an answer with the concepts of superposition and wave function. One of the most fundamental findings of quantum physics is that at the subatomic level the familiar, well-defined objects of classical physics dissolve into wave functions, which as we have seen describe only the probability of finding classical objects (particles) when we look for them, not the objects themselves. Moreover, and crucially, unlike the back of a house, which we have no reason to doubt is there when we are not looking at it, we have no warrant for such a claim in the quantum world. A wave function describes only potentialities, not actualities—a "super"-position of different actual "positions." While from a classical perspective that might make it less than perfectly real, the wave function is clearly real in some sense, and it has the virtue of being able to encompass in a unitary description not just possibilities that never end up happening, but even mutually exclusive ones, both A and not-A.

If reality ultimately consists of superpositions, then a key question is how it gets from many possible worlds to the one actual world we observe in the physics lab—from ghostly wave functions to well-defined, material particles hitting a screen. Known most commonly (if not precisely) as the "collapse" of the wave function, how and why this process occurs is one of the deepest mysteries in the debate over the interpretation of quantum theory.[23] Of what we do know and generally agree on, however, three related points stand out in the present context.

First[24], wave functions collapse, following the uncertainty principle, whenever we try to measure them. That might suggest the world would not exist but for us humans, but most interpreters resist such hubris and draw the opposite conclusion, that measurement is a highly general process, which is somehow ubiquitous in nature. Second, it is not just that wave functions collapse when they are measured, but where—where particles actualize on the screen in the famous double-slit experiment—depends on the details of the measurement. This has led some interpreters to argue that in quantum physics measurement is "creative" or in some related way "causes" collapse in a certain direction. However, that is contested by others, so the most one can safely say here is that in an experimental setting there is an entanglement between the observer and the observed, and the final result is "elicited" by their unfolding relationship. Finally, wave function collapse is nondeterministic, having no apparent external (or internal) cause; given the probabilities, where a particle will actually land is anyone's guess. Although consonant with our intuitions about free will, this quantum "leap" is problematic for physicists because it means they are forced to bolt together two unrelated mathematical formalisms to describe the entire process. One, the Schrödinger equation, models the (deterministic) evolution of a wave function in the absence of measurement, and then the other, von Neumann's "projection postulate," models (after the fact) what happened in the collapse from measurement: surely a clunky, unsatisfactory state of affairs for physicists who crave an elegant theory of everything, but this is where we are—for now.

Quantum Science

While it is natural that a race for quantum supremacy would transport and elevate quantum ideas into fields beyond physics, a skeptic might plausibly argue that we do not need anything as radical as a human science of quantum IR to analyze it. After all, a technology race is a technology race, and security scholars have a whole host of classical concepts for comprehending complex emergent phenomena, from game to complexity to chaos theories. Frank Smith's timely chapter injects a healthy note of skepticism along these lines, reminding us of how the quantum race, like all powerful new technologies caught in the securitization web, is subject to rational expectations and performative perspectives that might take on a hyperreal quality but still can (perhaps) be explained in classical terms. Conversely, Mathias Albert and Felix Barton suggest that systems might have nonclassical attributes that do not necessarily require quantum approaches, although they identify a range of striking similarities between systems and quantum theories.

We believe, however, that new developments in *quantum science* call even advanced forms of classical and nonclassical (but not quantum) thinking into question. Quantum science is conventionally understood as the application of quantum mechanics to scientific fields adjacent to and outside of physics, including quantum biology, quantum chemistry, quantum information, and quantum cognition.

The first and most immediately significant implication for quantum IR is the appearance of quantized models of cognition and decision theory, which after rigorous empirical testing seem to account for all of the irrational, "Kahneman-Tversky" anomalies that psychologists have consistently observed using classical rationality as a normative baseline. The empirical success of quantum decision theory is in our view extraordinary (quantum game theory is probably next) and has helped create a thin but rapidly growing layer of highly mathematical quantum theorizing across the social sciences.[25] The second development is the unexpected birth of a new discipline, quantum biology, based on the discovery that an ever-growing number of organisms use quantum processes in nontrivial ways for survival.[26] If birds (for navigation) and plants (for photosynthesis) can exploit quantum processes to their benefit, then it seems unlikely that evolutionary pressures would select *against* such a remarkable ability in the human case. And third, there has been at least slow progress on the most controversial question of all: whether the brain is a quantum computer, in which case human beings would literally be "walking wave functions."[27] Their hands still full of skeptics in their own fields, most quantum biologists and decision theorists today want little to do with such a speculative idea; but if their work continues to bear fruit, it makes quantum brain theory (see later) an ever more natural inference.

So far, this is about what is going on at a very micro-level; the question facing IR scholars and social scientists more generally is whether superpositions and wave function collapse can be found at the human or macroscale, not just by analogy, but *really*. Most physicists would still say no because of the decoherence problem, where microscopic quantum effects "wash out" in large, wet, and warm environments like the brain.[27] However, that opposition is clearly challenged by the emergence of quantum biology and especially quantum decision theory.

Classical decision ("rational choice") theory assumes that people have a portfolio of preferences and beliefs in their minds, which ideally obey the rules of classical logic and thereby make their holders rational. Moreover, although rarely explicit, it seems clear that a tacit assumption of this model is that the brains behind the human mind are classical. If they were quantum, why would the standard of rationality be classical, given the vastly greater, almost "superrational" computational powers of a quantum brain? All of this is to say, according to the rationalist orthodoxy, the contents of our mind/brains— our "types" in the jargon—will always be in well-defined states. If they are rational, then actors can be assumed to know their *own* types, but often not those of others; as classical states, others can be assumed to *have* types, but they are hidden away in other brains. Thus, the primary strategic problem facing rational actors in such a world is trying to determine others' types so that interaction will be optimal (think security dilemma theory).

A very different picture emerges from quantum decision theory, best explained by Ariane Lambert-Mogiliansky and coauthors in an essay suggestively entitled "Type Indeterminacy: A Model of the KT (Kahneman-Tversky)-Man."[28] Playing off "Harsanyi Man," the ideal Bayesian rational actor operating under uncertainty, Lambert-Mogiliansky et al. represent a person's "state" as a superposition of all their potential types relevant to a given situation, each of which is modeled as a distinct vector in an n-dimensional decision space. The superposition of these vectors does not collapse into an actual type until a measurement (interaction) occurs, whether on one's own or someone else's initiative. At that point, depending on the context, one vector will become what is called "preferred" and a single type will emerge in the collapse of their wave function (manifested as "behavior"). Note that this is the exact opposite of the standard, classical view. Rather than being an expression of underlying, well-defined preferences and beliefs, the latter *become* well defined only through the act of measurement itself. Thus, whereas Harsanyi Man's problem is merely uncertainty about others' types, KT "Man" (*sic*) does not even know her *own* type until she makes a choice. Perhaps the feeling of ambivalence is more genuine than classical metaphysics would have us believe.

Quantum IR builds on the resonances between Lambert-Mogiliansky's highly mathematical quantum model of human beings as collapsing superpositions and Judith Butler's performative model of agency (which figures centrally in Karen Barad's approach to quantum social theory as well).[29] Although as a feminist theorist Butler's foil is identity theory more than rational choice, her critique of the former is similar to what we have just seen. Namely, gendered performances are not enacted by an intrinsically gendered subject with pre-existing desires and beliefs; rather, they make someone a gendered subject with those desires and beliefs in the first place. We would not want to overstate the affinities between these theorists, but it is striking to us that two approaches that—at least on the surface—could hardly be more different epistemologically or methodologically would arrive at such similar pictures of the human being. At the very least, a consilience of quantum theory and IR into a new human science presents the opportunity for a fresh and potentially very fruitful interparadigmatic dialogue not just about social ontology but epistemology as well.

We acknowledge (once more) that all of these new bodies of research challenge a fundamental but completely implicit assumption of the social and natural sciences: that quantum theory is only relevant at the subatomic scale, above which quantum effects decohere and classical physics takes over. In different ways, a new human science accommodates suggestive evidence that far from washing out above the molecular level, in living organisms quantum effects might actually get *amplified*, right on up to the human scale.

Proving all of this is another matter. Science, ultimately, is a measurement problem, indeed, the crux of the problem in quantum science. At the quantum macrocosmic level, Albert Einstein was considered by many of his peers to be an upstart patent clerk with a dubious theory of relativity—until Sir Arthur Eddington developed an irrefutable method to measure gravitational lensing during the 1919 solar eclipse. It is not without irony that at the microcosmic level many scientific realists shared Einstein's dismissal of the quantum principle of entanglement as "spooky action at a distance"—until a loophole-free Bell test conclusively measured quantum entanglement in 2015. In quantum, the measurement problem is further complicated if not upended by the uncertainty principle, which elevates an epistemological problem into an ontological paradox: until observed (or measured) we cannot know if Schrödinger's famous cat is dead, alive, or getting a quadrillion hits on YouTube across the multiverse.

The history of quantum science suggests *so far* there are good reasons to be skeptical about the positivist value of a quantum approach to IR. But there are other reasons not to be dismissive. There might not yet be objective scientific evidence to make the leap from a micro- to a macroquantum theory; but we strongly believe there are now compelling subjective reasons to engage quantum IR in the kind of thought experiments that first set quantum mechanics in motion. This obviously can have implications for not just scientific but political practices, as demonstrated by Laura Zanotti in her chapter, in which she uses a quantum ontology of agency to critique the repeated failure of a universalist ethics in IR. The absence of laboratory proofs or sufficient measurement tools should not impede an inquiry into the most perplexing questions of the human condition; indeed, a quantum human science combining the most advanced subjective and objective approaches might well provide the best possible answers.

We have in mind—literally—a vexing problem that is so often glossed over in the social sciences and ignored by almost everyone in IR but for a few feminist theorists, the hard problem of consciousness undertaken by Wendt (Wendt 2015) and now advanced in this book by Leonardo Orlando (as well as K. M. Fierke and Nicola Mackay), who ventures deep into neuroscience and the philosophy of mind to explore how a quantum approach to social ontology and consciousness revalorizes the holistic aspects of human action in international politics. More precisely, these investigations seek to explain conscious actions in a way consistent with what quantum physics tells us about the nature of reality. The materialist orthodoxy—which social science has followed since Hobbes— has always assumed that the relevant physics is classical, because the brain is a macroscopic material object. Unfortunately, after centuries of hard work, this starting point has proven incapable of generating a theory of consciousness that even most materialists could agree on, and now some have drawn from their explanatory failure the only "logical" conclusion: that consciousness is an illusion. In contrast to this unproven and wildly counterintuitive claim, quantum theory is only mildly counterintuitive, and at least has room for consciousness to play a crucial role in the collapse of the wave function, which has generated growing interest in "quantum consciousness theory" as a potential solution to the mind-body problem.[30]

This might seem far from the world of IR, though our own disciplinary debates between positivists and interpretivists are but localized manifestations of the mind-body question.[31] There is also a growing recognition—in some quarters an apprehension—as quantum artificial intelligence labs are set up by tech giants as well as by aspiring and existing superpowers that quantum consciousness will soon cease to be a merely *human* question. When consciousness becomes a chimera of the human and the artificial, not only new scientific but also new philosophical and spiritual cosmologies of a quantum bent might well be needed if we are to be "at home in the universe."[32]

The Last Epiphany?

After a transdisciplinary inception followed by a long confinement in physics, quantum theory is breaking out, engaging with other natural and social sciences, and forming a new human science for IR. As a fundamental worldview, theory of reality, and enabler of new technologies, quantum touches everything, in theory and increasingly in practice. It remains to be seen how far it will go in IR; perhaps nowhere fast if blindly opposed or blithely ignored. However, if the effect of quantizing IR is anything like the effect of quantum theory in physics and now in biology, chemistry, engineering, computer science, and philosophy, then this will not be just another "turn" but the start of a permanent revolution that warrants our close attention. There is possibly as much peril as promise in such a revolution, and, as said of war and generals, quantum is just too important to be left to scientists alone.

The other characteristic of a theory that touches everything is that there are no obvious limits to how it might relate to IR. We call for a new human science in recognition of the need for transdisciplinary approaches that can respond comprehensively to diverse questions for IR in troubled times, that range from physical to metaphysical, empirical to theoretical, and explanatory to normative. Although this might lead to a degree of conceptual eclecticism or even philosophical incommensurability, this inchoateness in our view is not surprising or necessarily detrimental to the early stages of a critical inquiry.

This is also why we offer multiple approaches rather than a single grand theory of quantum IR. Our title intentionally if ironically invokes Hedley Bull's noted essay in which he forcefully challenged the scientific-behavioralist approaches to IR then emanating from the United States to make the case for a "classical approach" of philosophical, historical, and juridical inquiry.[33] We obviously do not seek to retrieve a classical Newtonian science, in which states interact like billiard balls, humans reductively behave as rational choice actors, and power is reduced to unitary objective interests. Nor is this a call for another "great debate" or a polemical attack on other theoretical approaches. It is, rather, the beginnings of a holistic effort to revive, update, and apply quantum ideas that will advance a new human science of quantum IR.

A final epiphany closes this book, reminding us that the quantum journey has never been a purely academic exercise. It comes from Stephen Del Rosso, director of the Peace and Security Program at the Carnegie Corporation in New York, whose philanthropic support made possible this inquiry into a new quantum human science for IR. After submitting the preface to this book, in which he writes about his own quantum epiphany, Del Rosso shared in an email what he "can only believe is an omen."[34] It came at the end of a sermon, zoomed during the COVID-19 pandemic, by his local Unitarian-Universalist minister.

Invoking Bell's theorem on nonlocality, the minister explained to his virtual flock how quantum demonstrates "human interdependence and cosmic interconnectedness." The minister concluded, as he does every Sunday, "and now the service truly begins...."

Amen to that.

Notes

1. See Der Derian (2011).
2. See Zohar and Marshall (1994); Wendt (2015); and Kripal (2019) for an illuminating discussion of how epiphanies (including Wendt's) can lead to reversals of perspective, or "flips."
3. See Katzenstein, ed. (2022) for a comprehensive account of how Newtonian worldviews have informed and continue to dominate the study and practice of world politics.
4. "Human science"—from its early proponents like Dilthey, Wildebande, and Tarde to later revivalists like Foucault, Bourdieu, and Latour—carries a fair share of Eurocentric and gendered baggage, but we believe it better expresses than "social science" the potential for a quantum convergence of subjective and objective modes of inquiry.
5. The first encounter between quantum mechanics and the social sciences came early, only to largely disappear: see later and essays by Harrington and Waters on William Bennett Munro's Presidential Address to the American Political Science Association in 1927, "Physics and Politics—An Old Analogy Revised" (Munro, in Becker 1991). For later quantum forays into the social sciences by the authors, see Der Derian (2001, 2011, 2013, 2019) and Wendt (2006, 2010, 2015, 2018).
6. Early versions of the essays were first presented at the annual Project Q Symposia held at Q Station in Sydney, Australia (2014–2019, with the support of the Carnegie Corporation of New York and the University of Sydney); an interdisciplinary conference in Columbus, Ohio (2018, with the support of the Mershon Center at Ohio State University); and over a dozen roundtables and panels at recent International Studies Association annual meetings (2015–2019). An initial selection of papers was published in *Security Dialogue* (2020). In spite of concerted efforts to redress gender, ethnic, and national imbalances in IR and physics, both in the organization of events and the publications of papers, we have fallen short. There are, however, promising signs in personal communications as well other publications of rising interdisciplinary interests among a new generation of scholars representing greater diversity than currently exists in either discipline.
7. Attempts to maintain disciplinary boundaries can often entail misrepresentations, satires, and even hoaxes perpetrated on those seeking a dialogue. Most notorious is "Transgressing the Boundaries: Towards a Transformative Hermeneutics of Quantum Gravity" by Allan Sokal, published in the 1996 "Science War" issue of *Social Text*, which put a chill on the science-humanities dialogue for close to a decade (full disclosure: Der Derian published on unrelated topics in *Social Text*). For a rigorous

critique of sloppy reasoning as well as unprofessional conduct in the hoax, see a response by mathematician Gabriel Stolzenberg (http://math.bu.edu/people/nk/rr/).

8. On the implications of quantum innovation for international security see in particular interviews (www.projectqsydney.com) and articles by presenters from the Project Q Symposia (2017, 2018, 2019), including Michael Biercuk (Biercuk and Fontaine 2017), Jon Lindsay (Lindsay 2018), and Elsa B. Kania (Kania 2018).

9. In October 2019 Google claimed experimental realization of quantum supremacy when its 53-qubit Syracuse processor calculated in 200 seconds a complex circuit problem that would take a classical supercomputer 10,000 years to accomplish. Shortly after IBM asserted that a paradigmatic breakthrough for quantum computing had not been reached and, somewhat predictably, claimed to be closer: "Quantum computing is on the verge of sparking a paradigm shift. Software reliant on this nascent technology, one rooted in the physical laws of nature, could soon revolutionize computing forever. Bear in mind, however, that it took classical computing many decades to go from individually programmed logic gates to the sophisticated cloud-based services of today—and we hope to see quantum computing take that same leap in just a few short years." See Arute et al. (2019), Pednault et al. (2019), and Wehden et al. (2021). The new holy grail of "quantum advantage" was claimed as early as December 2020 by Chinese scientists. See Zhong et al. (2020).

10. For instance, the Chinese University of Science and Technology at Hefei has several research sites dedicated to quantum systems, including a complex of newly constructed buildings and labs outside of Shanghai dedicated solely to quantum communications, which one of the editors visited shortly after a ribbon-cutting ceremony with President Xi and other leading corporate and government officials.

11. The national security imperative to pursue quantum research—as well as to conduct surveillance on other powers seeking to get there first—was leaked by Edward Snowden in January 2014 (see Der Derian 2014).

12. It should be noted that disruption was not always productive, as in the case when Einstein dismissed Bergson's views in the famous 1922 (non)debate in Paris. See chapters 2 and 3; Jimena Canales (2015); and Arthur I. Miller (2009).

13. Perhaps the most influential overview of Eastern cosmologies and its similarities with quantum physics was the best-selling book, *The Tao of Physics: An Exploration of the Parallels between Modern Physics and Eastern Mysticism*, by the physicist Fritjof Capra (Capra, 1975).

14. See Wendt (2015), and Waters (2022).

15. Werner Heisenberg (1971).

16. See Der Derian (2011, 2013) on "quantum diplomacy" and "quantum war"; see Thornhill (2018, 2019) on the "quantum politics" of former theoretical physicist and current president of Armenia, Armen Sarkissian

17. "The difference between classical and quantum physics is that quantum physics is weird," Freeman Dyson (2007).

18. Some noteworthy, cross-disciplinary books include, in queer theory, Barad (2007); cognitive science, Busemeyer and Bruza (2012); philosophy, Ney and Albert (2013), Lewis (2016), and Maudlin (2007); biology, Al-Khalili and McFadden (2014); economics, Orrell (2018); and race theory and creative arts, Phillips (2015).

19. See, for example, Pettit (1993).
20. See Kim (1974).
21. See Wendt (2015: 250–255) on the contradictions between social holism and the classical ontology its advocates usually take for granted.
22. The phrase is Daniel Kolak's; for discussion, see Wendt (2015: 242).
23. This raises questions (with substantial relevance for IR) about indeterminacy, causation, and the ontology of potentiality, topics debated in a growing body of philosophical literature on the wave function. For example, see Lewis (2016), Maudlin (2007), and Ney and Albert (2013).
24. See, for example, Haven and Khrennikov, eds. (2017).
25. For an accessible introduction see Al-Khalili and McFadden (2014).
26. See Wendt (2015: chapter 5) for a brief introduction and references to further reading.
27. See Waldner (2017).
28. See Lambert-Mogiliansky et al. (2009) and Wendt (2015: 162–163).
29. See Butler (1990), the embryonic text on queer identity and performativity; and Barad (2007).
30. See Penrose, S Hameroff and S Kak, eds. (2017) on the recent state of play regarding the quantum consciousness hypothesis.
31. See Wendt (2018) for further discussion.
32. The expression is taken from Stuart Kauffman, who works across the disciplines of physiology and psychology as well as philosophy and physics to find answers to persistent ontological and cosmological questions that he believes only an expanded application of quantum mechanics can provide. See Kauffman (2016).
33. See Bull (1966).
34. In addition to Stephen Del Rosso and the Carnegie Corporation of New York, we gratefully acknowledge the support of Ohio State University, University of Sydney and the Project Q team (see www.projectqsydney.com).

References

Al-Khalili, J and J McFadden (2014) *Life on the Edge: The Coming of Age of Quantum Biology.* London: Bantam Press.

Arfi, B (2005) Resolving the Trust Predicament in IR: A Quantum Game-theoretic Approach. *Theory and Decision*, 59(2), 127–174.

Arute, F, K Arya, R Babbush, et al. (2019) Quantum Supremacy Using a Programmable Superconducting Processor. *Nature*, 574, 505–510.

Barad, K (2007) *Meeting the Universe Halfway: Quantum Physics and the Entanglement of Matter and Meaning.* Durham, NC: Duke University Press.

Becker, T, ed. (1991) *Quantum Politics: Applying Quantum Theory to Political Phenomena.* New York: Praeger.

Biercuk, M J and R Fontaine (2017) The Leap into Quantum Technology: A Primer for National Security Professionals. *War on the Rocks*, https://warontherocks.com/2017/11/leap-quantum-technology-primer-national-security-professionals.

Bull, H (1966) International Theory: The Case for a Classical Approach. *World Politics*, 18(3), 361–377.

Busemeyer, J and P Bruza (2012) *Quantum Models of Cognition and Decision*. Cambridge: Cambridge University Press.

Butler, J (1990) *Gender Trouble: Feminism and the Subversion of Identity*. New York and London: Routledge.

Canales, J (2015) *The Physicist and the Philosopher: Einstein, Bergson, and the Debate That Changed Our Understanding of Time*. Princeton, NJ: Princeton University Press.

Capra, F (1975) *The Tao of Physics: An Exploration of the Parallels between Modern Physics and Eastern Mysticism*. New York: Random House.

Der Derian, J (2001, 2009) *Virtuous War: Mapping the Military-Industrial-Media-Entertainment Network*. New York: Perseus/Westview Press (2001) and Routledge (2009).

Der Derian, J (2011) Quantum Diplomacy, German-US Relations and the Psychogeography of Berlin. *Hague Journal of Diplomacy*, 6(3–4), 373–392.

Der Derian, J (2013) From War 2.0 to Quantum War: The Superpositionality of Global Violence. *Australian Journal of International Affairs*, 6(5), 570–585.

Der Derian, J (2014) Director's Letter. https://sydney.edu.au/arts/arts/ciss/news/index.shtml?id=2421.

Der Derian, J (2019) A Quantum of Insecurity. *New Perspectives*, 27(9), 13–27.

Der Derian, J and Wendt, A (2020) Quantizing International Relation. *Security Dialogue*, 51(5), 399–413.

Dyson, F (2007) *The Scientist as Rebel*. New York: New York Review of Books.

Giles, M and W Knight (2019) Google Thinks It's Close to "Quantum Supremacy." Here's What That Really Means. *MIT Technology Review*, March 9, https://Quantum IR.technologyreview.com/s/610274/google-thinks-its-close-to-quantum-supremacy-heres-what-that-really-means/.

Haven, E and A Khrennikov, eds. (2017) *The Palgrave Handbook of Quantum Models in Social Science*. London: Palgrave Macmillan.

Heisenberg, W (1971) *Physics and Beyond: Encounters and Conversations*. New York: Allen and Unwin.

Kania, E B (2018) China's Quantum Future: Xi's Quest to Build a High-Tech Superpower. *Foreign Affairs*, https://Quantum IR.foreignaffairs.com/articles/china/2018-09-26/chinas-quantum-future.

Katzenstein, P J, ed. (2022) *Uncertainty and Its Discontents: Worldviews in World Politics*. New York: Cambridge University Press.

Kauffman, S (2016) *Humanity in a Creative Universe*. New York: Oxford University Press.

Kim, J (1974) Noncausal Connections. *Nous*, 8(1), 41–52.

Kripal, J (2019) *Flip: Epiphanies of Mind and the Future of Knowledge*. New York: Bellevue Literary Press.

Lambert-Mogiliansky, A, S Zamir, and H Zwirn (2009) Type Indeterminacy: A Model of the KT (Kahneman-Tversky)-Man. *Journal of Mathematical Psychology*, 53(5), 349–361.

Lewis, P J (2016) *Quantum Ontology: A Guide to the Metaphysics of Quantum Mechanics*. New York: Oxford University Press.

Lindsay, J (2018) Why Quantum Computing Will Not Destabilize International Security: The Political Logic of Cryptology. https://ssrn.com/abstract=3205507 or http://dx.doi.org/10.2139/ssrn.3205507.

Marin J M (2009) "Mysticism" in Quantum Mechanics: The Forgotten Controversy. *European Journal of Physics*, 30, 807–822.

Maudlin, T (2007) *The Metaphysics of Physics*. New York: Oxford University Press.

Miller, A I (2009) *Deciphering the Cosmic Number: The Strange Friendship of Wolfgang Pauli and Carl Jung*. New York: W.W. Norton.

Ney, A and D Z Albert, eds. (2013) *The Wave Function: Essays on the Metaphysics of Quantum Mechanics*. Oxford: Oxford University Press.

Orrell, D (2018) *Quantum Economics: The New Science of Money*. London: Icon Books.

Pednault, E, J Gunnels, D Maslov, and J Gambetta (2019) On "Quantum Supremacy." https://Quantum IR.ibm.com/blogs/research/2019/10/on-quantum-supremacy/.

Penrose, R, S Hameroff and S Kak, eds. (2017) *Consciousness and the Universe: Quantum Physics, Evolution, Brain and Mind*. Cambridge, MA: Cosmology Science Publishers.

Pettit, P (1993) *The Common Mind*. Oxford: Oxford University Press.

Phillips, R, ed. (2015) Black Quantum Futurism: Theory and Practice. https://www.black quantumfuturism.com/.

Project Q: Peace and Security in a Quantum Age (2014–2021) https://projectqsydney.com/.

Thornhill, J (2018) Quantum Politics and a World Turned Upside Down. *Financial Times*, October 6.

Thornhill, J (2019) Lunch with the FT: Armen Sarkissian. *Financial Times*, June 15/16.

Waldner, D (2017) Schrödinger's Cat and the Dog That Didn't Bark: Why Quantum Mechanics Is (Probably) Irrelevant to the Social Sciences. *Critical Review*, 29(2), 199–133.

Waters, J (2022) Estranged/Entangled: A Genealogy of Quantum Mechanics and International Theory (PhD Dissertation, University of Sydney).

Wehden, K, et al. (2021) IBM's Roadmap for Building an Open Quantum Software Ecosystem. https://www.ibm.com/blogs/research/2021/02/quantum-development-roadmap/.

Wendt, K (2006) *Social Theory* as Cartesian Science: An Auto-Critique from a Quantum Perspective. In Stefano Guzzini and Anna Leander, eds., *Constructivism and International Relations: Alexander Wendt and His Critics*. London: Routledge, 181–219.

Wendt, K (2010) Flatland: Quantum Mind and the International Hologram. In Mathias Albert, Lars-Erik Cederman, and Alexander Wendt, eds., *New Systems Theories of World Politics*. London: Palgrave, 279–310.

Wendt, A (2015) *Quantum Mind and Social Science*. Cambridge: Cambridge University Press.

Wendt, A (2018) The Mind-Body Problem and Social Science: Motivating a Quantum Social Theory. *Journal for the Theory of Social Behaviour*, 48, 188–204.

Zhong, H-S, et al. (2020) Quantum Computational Advantage Using Photons. *Science*, 370(6523), 1460–1463.

Zohar, D and I Marshall (1994) *The Quantum Society: Mind, Physics, and a New Social Vision*. New York: Morrow.

PART 1.
HISTORY AND THEORY

2

Quantum Mechanics and the Human Sciences

First Encounters

Nicholas T. Harrington

This chapter investigates the efforts made by the founders of quantum theory to transfer the insights of their revolutionary new physics into the human sciences—an intellectual enterprise I term *quantum transposition*.[1] Since there is renewed interest in finding ways of enriching the contemporary social sciences with the findings of quantum physics, it is worthwhile to understand how those individuals responsible for discovering this new field of knowledge approached such a transfer or synthesis, and the prospect of interdisciplinarity. The following pages reveal the degree to which the quantum founders—physicists such as Niels Bohr (1885–1962), Max Born (1882–1970), Albert Einstein (1879–1955), Werner Heisenberg (1901–1976), Wolfgang Pauli (1900–1958), Erwin Schrödinger (1887–1961), and the mathematician John von Neumann (1903–1957)—attempted such a maneuver in their time, and how they expected the application of quantum insights to be most fruitful beyond physics.

Unsurprisingly, it will be shown that with respect to quantum transposition (as with much else besides), the quantum founders did not possess a unified position. To make sense of the early landscape, I suggest a four-category typology that communicates the distinct forms of approach to quantum transfer attempted during the period—i.e., during the 1930s and 1940s. Each quantum founder can be associated with one of these four categories, although, notably, two founders straddle boundaries. The four distinct forms of approach are *epistemic*, *ontological*, *formalist*, and *rejection*. To the first category, epistemic, belong those founders who believed the applicable lessons quantum offered the human sciences were principally epistemological. In other words, founders who adhered to the epistemic form believed quantum physics revealed something unique about the construction and sharing of human knowledge, and felt the human sciences would benefit from this perspective. This chapter shows that Niels Bohr, Wolfgang Pauli, and Max Born were all proponents of the epistemic form of quantum transfer. The second category, ontological, houses the founder who believed quantum physics had revealed something profoundly different about how reality was constituted and that, therefore, the quantum revolution should stimulate an ontological shift within and across the human sciences. The ontological form of transfer is distinguished particularly from the epistemic insofar as the concern was not merely with reorienting *how* reality was understood. Rather, emphasis was placed on a perceived revolution in *the nature of reality* itself. This chapter shows that Werner Heisenberg alone dared to advance such convictions. The third category, formalist, describes the founder who believed quantum's unique and highly effective mathematical formalism represented an important contribution to the human sciences. In other words, the formalist believed the relations between human and social phenomena could be expressed mathematically, leading to probabilistic explanations and predictions concerning human behavior in society. Max Born is the founder who can be described as advocating the formalist form of quantum transfer. The fourth and final category, rejection, is associated with those founders who did not believe quantum physics served any value for the human sciences. In essence, they rejected the proposition that there was any necessary connection between the revolutionary findings of quantum physics (be that epistemic, ontological, or formal) and future progress and development in the human sciences. Albert Einstein, John von Neumann, and, generally speaking, Erwin Schrödinger are the founders associated with a rejection of quantum transposition (albeit for very different reasons).

In adopting this typology, it is important to recognize that the founders themselves never used the term *quantum transfer* or *transposition*, let alone ascribed one of the four categories to themselves. Indeed, the founders would likely have resisted such easy classification. This observation, however, does not render the designations unjustified, since contemporary scholarship supports these distinctions through the broad association of Bohr with an epistemological interpretation[2] of quantum theory; Heisenberg with an ontological interpretation[3] of quantum physics; Born and von Neumann with quantum mathematical formalism[4]; and Einstein with a general rejection[5] of quantum physics.

In addition to the variety of approaches the founders advocated—as represented by this chapter's typology—there was variation between the early quantum physicists concerning the human science disciplines they felt would most benefit from the influence of quantum physics. The most ambitious program was that envisaged by Niels Bohr, who advocated his theory of complementarity to distinguished audiences of anthropologists, ethnologists, biologists, chemists, psychologists, and theologians. If there was one field, however, where all the founders (bar Einstein) saw some correlation, it was psychology. In many ways, they considered the gap in knowledge between the physical description of the brain and the existence of consciousness similar to the epistemic situation with which they themselves were confronted in the 1920s. To this extent, there was an underlying desire on the part of the founders to see the human sciences undergo a kind of "revolution" comparable to the one they had driven in their own field, so that the mysteries of consciousness, and even the nebulous notion of "life" itself, would be better understood.

It is notable that the *patterning* of quantum transposition, as it applies to the various quantum founders, was mirrored in the degree and manner in which they respectively felt quantum had revolutionized the field of physics per se. In other words, the more disruptive and transformative the physicist believed quantum to be, the more they tended to advocate for its deployment outside of physics. Conversely, the less revolutionary, or indeed, the less complete a theory the physicist believed quantum to be, the less inclined that scientist was to see quantum applied outside of physics. Therefore, the spectrum of quantum transposition in the 1930s and 1940s in many ways reflected the spectrum of quantum interpretation per se—with Niels Bohr on one end of the spectrum and Albert Einstein on the other. Niels Bohr, the progenitor of the Copenhagen interpretation, believed quantum to be a complete theory and radical departure from the conceptual framework of classical physics. And Albert Einstein, the somewhat inadvertent and reluctant quantum contributor, considered quantum's incommensurability with strict relativity theory to demonstrate its incompleteness.

Physics and the Human Sciences

Although a full treatment is well beyond the scope of this chapter, it is worth situating the efforts the founders made to extend quantum beyond the borders of natural science in their broader context. To paraphrase Peter Manicas's pithy thought experiment, if we took a time machine back to Harvard in the 1870s, we would feel quite out of place, with nothing like the social science departments with which we are now familiar. If we then zapped ourselves to 1925, however, we would find ourselves quite at home, enjoying a neat assortment of sociology, psychology, and anthropology departments. Manicas, therefore, concludes, "the practices which define what may be called 'mainstream' social science…were largely settled" in the last quarter of the nineteenth and the first quarter of the twentieth centuries. He goes on to say that since this time, "these practices have changed surprisingly little" (Manicas 1988, 5).

Of special concern for this chapter, however, is that during this taxonomical period (i.e., the period when the divisions between the human science disciplines were being established), the epistemological and ontological underwriting for the human sciences became that of classical physics. In other words, at the same time as the disciplines themselves were being born, they were being given a distinctly classical physics form. According to Philip Mirowski, the contemporary disciplines known as economics and political economy can be traced to the 1870s, when a "physics/economics synergy" emerged that was based upon the "slavish imitation of physics" (Mirowski 1989, 9, 393). Mirowski explains that from the late nineteenth century onward, "metaphors of motion and of the physical world were a primary rhetorical resource" that shaped the contours and trajectory of these social science disciplines (Mirowski 1989, 9). In his painstaking 1991 work, *The History and Philosophy of Social Science*, Scott Gordon demonstrates that the "discipline of political science contains few general theories of politics." Specifically, Gordon goes on to say, "political scientists borrow most of their theories from economics and sociology" (Gordon 1991, 409). The human sciences, therefore, with which the founders of quantum physics were confronted were the product of two entangled historical impulses. The first was the desire to categorize, enclose, and draw boundaries around distinct "disciplines." The second was the inexorable use of classical physics metaphors and concepts to underwrite the methods and practices of these newly departmentalized human sciences.

Given what Mirowski tells us about classical physics metaphors and the construction of economics as a discipline, and what Gordon tells us about economics and the conceptual impoverishment of political science as a discipline, it's easy to see why William Bennett Munro wrote his 1928 essay.[6] Munro, a Harvard political scientist, published an article titled "Physics and Politics." It was a direct appeal for change in his discipline. Munro's objective was to "release political science from the old metaphysics and juristic concepts" (Munro 1928, 10). These old concepts were those of classical physics. Munro bemoaned the fact that

> the science of government is still...in bondage to eighteenth-century deification of the abstract individual man. Both the science and the art of government still rests upon what may be called the atomic theory of politics. (Munro 1928, 3)

Munro's essay has a clear thesis: "A revolution so amazing in our ideas concerning the physical world must inevitably carry its echoes into other fields of human knowledge" (Munro 1928, 2). If political science was based on classical physics and classical physics had been revolutionized by quantum theory, then political science necessarily awaited the self-same revolution—or, so Munro believed. Interestingly, however, the *kind* of quantum transfer Munro demanded was not one that any of the quantum founders advocated. Munro saw physics as a heuristic font. That is to say, Munro believed physics provided the human sciences with a battery of conceptual metaphors and systemic analogies. Munro saw parallels between the conceptual models of classical physics and those of government, society, and politics. Therefore, since the conceptual models in physics underwent evolution, so too, believed Munro, ought the conceptual models of his political science.

Importantly, despite what appears a perfectly justified use of quantum theory—and, indeed, given Mirowski's thesis, would seem a superficially suitable corrective—not one of the early quantum physicists argued for this kind of quantum transfer. The idea that quantum physics was simply a metaphorical larder from which other disciplines could pick and choose was not one the quantum founders ever endorsed. Instead, the founders believed, when it came to the question of human sciences, quantum physics either presented a profound epistemological challenge, overturned prior metaphysics, provided useful mathematical formalism, or served little purpose at all.

Epistemic Quantum Transfer

Niels Bohr was the first quantum founder to suggest its application outside physics. Perhaps this was to be expected from a man Max Born called the "deepest thinker in physical science" (Born 1936, 42). In 1933, Bohr gave a lecture to the Second International Congress of Light Therapists in Copenhagen. Bohr's address, titled "Light and Life," argued that biologists had "more or less intuitively" (Bohr 1933, 421) adopted the attitude physicists had been forced to assume when confronted with the overwhelming complexity of natural phenomena. The diversity of life—a constellation of variety "far beyond the grasp of scientific analysis" (Bohr 1933, 421)—compelled the reduction to "simple concepts" that permit scientific explanation. This reduction, however, was, to a certain extent, fraught. Bohr argued the practice of conceptual reduction necessarily generated epistemic paradoxes since instances arose frequently wherein two pictures of the same phenomenon presented mutually exclusive descriptions. Bohr claimed this kind of limitation was "first recognised through a thorough study of the interaction between light and material bodies, which disclosed features that cannot be brought into conformity with demands hitherto made to a physical explanation" (Bohr 1933, 421). It should be noted that this early attempt, although short on specifics of how quantum might aid biology, nevertheless represents what can be considered the epistemic (or Bohrian) "form" of quantum transfer. Simply put, Bohr recommended complementarity be adopted in any field where complex phenomena were described using more simple concepts. The logic underpinning the epistemic form of quantum transfer was relatively straightforward: any field that reduces the complex to simple conceptual pictures will necessarily encounter incommensurable paradoxes. These conceptual paradoxes can only be accommodated or overcome through the theory of complementarity since complementarity represents an epistemic paradigm (or perspective) where mutually exclusive pictures are considered the necessary constituents of a more complete description of the phenomenon under investigation. In other words, according to Bohr, any form of science (be it human, natural, physical, political, or social) that relied on simplified concepts to describe complex phenomena would benefit from the quantum insight he considered most important—that is, the epistemic strategy he termed the *principle of complementarity*.

In 1938, Bohr addressed the International Congress of Anthropological and Ethnological Sciences and clarified he was in no position to "contribute in any direct way" (Bohr 1939, 268) to specific problems in the field of anthropology. The purpose of his talk, however, was to "give an impression of a general epistemological attitude which we have been forced to adopt in a field as far from human passions as the analysis of simple physical experiments" (Bohr 1939, 271). Again, in 1949, when giving a radio address to Danish students on the threshold of entry into university, Bohr emphasized it was possible to "trace complementarity" to "all spheres of cultural life" (Bohr 1949, 70). In this speech, Bohr providing an example of extra-physical complementarity. Bohr explains to his audience:

> We need only to think of the complementary way in which we use two such words as "thoughts" and "feelings" in order to describe the situations which every human being experiences every day. These words refer precisely to aspects of our inner experiences, each of which is equally important but excludes the other in the sense that even our warmest feelings completely lose their character when we try to clarify them along the path of cold logical thought. (Bohr 1949, 70)

Pauli's Complementarity

Niels Bohr was not the only quantum founder who endorsed the epistemic form of quantum transfer. Wolfgang Pauli and Max Born, contemporaries and close associates of Bohr's, both advocated for quantum's deployment in the human sciences through the application of complementarity. Pauli penned an article in 1949 titled "The Philosophical Significance of the Idea of Complementarity," wherein he restated Bohr's general thesis but restrained any impulse he might have had to expand upon it or provide application specifics. Pauli, in a manner echoing the style and substance of his dear friend Bohr, writes:

> This situation in regard to complementarity within physics leads naturally beyond the narrow field of physics to analogous situations in connection with the general conditions of human knowledge. (Pauli 1949, 41)

Pauli refers in particular to the field of psychology, where he claims the "concept of consciousness in fact demands a cut between subject and object, the *existence* of which is a logical necessity, while the *position* of the cut is to a certain extent arbitrary" (Pauli 1949, 41). Pauli believed the subject/object dichotomy of personal identity to reflect necessarily complementary features. Thus, Pauli recommended an epistemic form of quantum transfer for the discipline of psychology. Five years later, Pauli made a very similar series of arguments in a separate article titled "Ideas of the Unconscious from the Standpoint of Natural Science and Epistemology." This article is a unique enterprise in that it attempted a synthesis between prevailing ideas in quantum physics and those of psychology. Specifically, Pauli compared considerations of the unconscious in the human sciences and the physical paradoxes encountered within quantum theory. Pauli explained:

> The "unconscious" itself has a certain analogy with the "field" in physics, and both are brought into the realm of the irrepresentable (*Unanschauliche*) and paradoxical through a problem of observation. In physics however we do not speak of self-reproducing "archetypes," but of "statistical laws of nature involving primary probabilities"; but both formulations meet in their tendency to extend the old narrower idea of "causality (determinism)" to a more general form of "connections" in nature, a conclusion to which the psycho-physical problem also points. (Pauli 1954, 164)

There is no doubt that Pauli's emphasis on the synergy between quantum physics and psychology was greatly influenced by his long-running personal relationship with psychoanalyst Carl Gustav Jung (1875–1961). In one of the earliest extant correspondences between the two men, Jung thanks Pauli for sending him "the Bohr article 'Licht und Leben' (Light and Life)" (Jung 1933, 4). This intellectual exchange represents material evidence of Pauli's efforts to propagate quantum physics into the human sciences. In a letter the following year, Pauli confronts Jung with the thesis, in question form, that motivated all Pauli's subsequent psychological writings:

> Might it not be preferable to advocate the view that the unconscious and the conscious are complementary (i.e., in a mutually exclusive relationship to each other), but not that one is part of the other? (Pauli 1934, 6)

It is noteworthy that in Jung's detailed reply letter of October 1934, the term *complementary* is conspicuously absent, as is any mention of mutual exclusivity (Jung 1934). We can perhaps surmise that Jung's disinclination to pursue—or even respond to—Pauli's thesis of "complementary consciousness" compelled Pauli to take this work up for himself. Almost two decades later, in the essay he wrote for their joint publication, titled *The Interpretation of Nature and the Psyche*, Pauli restated the thesis he had first put to Jung almost two decades prior:

> The general problem of the relation between psyche and physis, between the inner and the outer, can, however, hardly be said to have been solved by the concept of "psychophysical parallelism."...It would be most satisfactory of all if physis and psyche could be seen as complementary aspects of the same reality. (Pauli 1952, 211)

In the final analysis, however, Pauli proceeded similarly to Niels Bohr before him: (1) the connection is made between the epistemic limitations inherent in classical physics and those of the particular human sciences discipline under discussion, and (2) the application of the epistemic insights generated by the quantum revolution is recommended.

Ontological Quantum Transfer

While Pauli can be seen as a straightforward advocate of Bohr's form of quantum transfer, Werner Heisenberg presents something (albeit tentatively) altogether different. Reading Heisenberg's philosophical writings, it soon becomes apparent that he believed quantum theory indicated more than a mere "problem of knowledge" (as Bohr termed it[7]). Heisenberg took quantum theory to have ontological implications. In particular, Heisenberg believed quantum physics greatly weakened materialist claims. He writes:

> The elementary particles are certainly not eternal and indestructible units of matter, they can actually be transformed into each other.... [M]odern physics takes a definite stand against...materialism. (Heisenberg 1958, 71)

Indeed, Heisenberg appears to adopt a form of "substance monism," whereby he argues that the fundamental property of the universe—the *prima materia* (to borrow Aristotle's formulation)—is "energy." Following a discussion of what takes place when elementary particles collide, Heisenberg concluded, "all particles are made of the same substance: energy" (Heisenberg 1958, 71). Heisenberg's ontological commitments led him to a particular form of quantum transfer: ontological. According to Heisenberg, it was not simply our *understanding* of the substance of the human sciences that was subject to revision following the quantum revolution—the *substance* of the human sciences itself was up for renegotiation. Heisenberg stated:

After the experience of modern physics—our attitude toward concepts like mind or the human soul or life or God will be different from that of the nineteenth century, because these concepts belong to the natural language and have therefore immediate connection with reality.... [M]odern physics has perhaps opened the door to a wider outlook on the relation between the human mind and reality. (Heisenberg 1958, 200–202)

As a general formulation, what Heisenberg anticipated was a form of "synthesis," where the ontological challenge presented by quantum physics would be incorporated into *all* the human sciences insofar as the metaphysics underpinning the subjects under investigation were shifted away from strict materialism. This sentiment is enshrined in the closing words of Heisenberg's principal work on philosophy, *Physics and Philosophy* (1958):

In the final state of unification many different cultural traditions may live together and may combine different human endeavors into a new kind of balance between thought and deed, between activity and meditation. (Heisenberg 1958, 206)

Although (as with all the quantum founders) the precise manner in which quantum theory was to affect the human sciences remained at best promissory, Heisenberg was a determined advocate of quantum transfer, or what he referred to as the "process of expansion of modern physics" (Heisenberg 1958, 188).

Formalist Quantum Transfer

Although Max Born should also be considered an adherent to the Bohrian form of quantum transfer insofar as he was a staunch advocate of complementarity in the human sciences,[8] Born distinguished himself insofar as he saw a role for quantum mathematical formalism in the human sciences. In the introduction to a series of lectures Born gave in 1948, he expressed his desire to "explain how physics may throw some light on...the behaviour of man" (Born 1951b, 3). In particular, Born was invested in explicating *cause* and *chance*. Most importantly, however, Born interpreted these concepts statistically—that is, "in the mathematical theory of probability" (Born 1951b, 1). According to Born, due to the clarity and abstraction of quantum formalism, "only in physics has a systematic attempt been made to use the notions of cause and chance in a way free of contradictions" (Born 1951b, 1). In addition, Born can be credited as the only quantum founder to make a specific connection between quantum and political theory. In 1951, in the editorial postscript to an earlier essay titled "The Restless Universe," Max Born writes:

> The new philosophical ideas developed by science during these 100 years may help towards a deeper understanding of social and political relations. Indeed, we find two systems of thought which deal with the same structure, the state, in completely different, apparently contradictory ways. (Born 1951a, 232)

To some extent, the parallels Born drew between the "state" of political theory and the "state" of quantum physics are similar to the approach offered by Pauli, when he compared the "unconscious" in psychology with the "field" in physics. Where the two physicists part ways, however, is on account of Born's explicit use of quantum formalism. Although frustratingly underdeveloped, Born offers a tantalizing glimpse of what might have been an entirely new discipline. According to Born, social governance could be interpreted as the interaction between two opposing limits: freedom and regulation. Therefore, to describe the prevailing state of society, Born believed there "must exist a relation between the latitudes of freedom Δf and of regulation Δr, of the type $\Delta f. \Delta r \sim p$, which allows a reasonable compromise" (Born 1950, 108). Born refused to provide a value, formula, or derivative for "'political constant' p," instead eschewing responsibility and leaving this opportunity to those prepared to develop a "future quantum theory of human affairs" (Born 1950, 108).

Paradoxical Schrödinger

Schrödinger does not fit neatly into any of the four typological categories; nor does he warrant his own. One might argue that Schrödinger possessed a preference for the formalist form of quantum transfer—that is, if Schrödinger saw a role at all for quantum in the human sciences, it was its statistical mathematics. Schrödinger acknowledged that "from all we have learnt about the structure of living matter, we must be prepared to find it working in a manner that cannot be reduced to the ordinary laws of physics" (Schrödinger 1944, 76). However, when pressed to resolve the strangely "orderly" and "dynamical" features of life, Schrödinger merely hinted at some governing "law" of "Nature." Without offering particulars, Schrödinger suggested this governing "law" was "nothing else than the principle of quantum theory over again" (Schrödinger 1944, 81). In other words, when nature would not conform to a classical explanation, it was better handled using the kind of statistical explanation that addressed the apparent discontinuity of quantum. Given this very discontinuity was what so frustrated Schrödinger about quantum per se, his conclusion reads more like an admission of defeat than a well-formed hypothesis.

Schrödinger's abiding interest in philosophy further complicates the picture we have of him as a founder invested in the human sciences. To be a vocational physicist and a hobby philosopher was not unique to Schrödinger. Indeed, Pauli, Heisenberg, Bohr, Born, and Einstein all opined upon philosophy. What was unique about Schrödinger's philosophy, however, was that he didn't mingle quantum physics with his philosophizing, despite touching upon many areas that might appear suitable terrain. Across the entire length of his 1964 philosophical publication, *My View of the World*—which includes two essays separated by twenty-five years of personal reflection—Schrödinger does not mention physics, let alone quantum physics, once. On the other hand, Schrödinger did engage with a range of topics the other founders appear to deliberately avoid: the esoteric and the mystic.

Although Schrödinger does not use the term *panpsychism* (i.e., the philosophical perspective that at a fundamental level everything in the universe contains consciousness, that reality is mind/consciousness "all the way down" [Wendt 2015, 5]), his fundamental solution to the question of existence strongly intimates this metaphysics. In his essay "What Is Real?," Schrödinger pursues the Cartesian thought experiment to test the philosophical boundary between experience and consciousness—between mind and matter—and concludes:

> If we decide to have only one sphere, it has got to be the psychic one, since that exists anyway (*cogitat—est*). And to suppose that there is an interaction between two spheres involves something of a magical, ghostly sort; or rather, the supposition itself makes them into one single thing. (Schrödinger 1960, 52)

According to Schrödinger, the reason the suggestion of a mind-matter interaction resolves in favor of mind is that

> danger arises if we forget that the causal nexus ["between psychical" and "physical events"] is situated in our *idea* of the external world—if we insist on locating it in a self-supportingly "existent" external world not dependent on our psychic experience. (Schrödinger 1960, 53)

Schrödinger, therefore, is a paradoxical figure insofar as he tacitly conceded to the application of quantum theory to address the mysteries of "life," while simultaneously adhering to a strict personal philosophical separation between the human and natural sciences. Schrödinger was a philosopher who wholeheartedly embraced the mysterious and the mystical, but without making any recourse whatsoever to the form of physics that, if nothing else, certainly merits the appellation "mysterious."

Rejection of Quantum Transfer

Albert Einstein is the figure that best represents a rejection of quantum transposition. Einstein did not believe quantum physics had any great capacity to illuminate the human sciences, in no small part because he held a jaundiced view of quantum theory in general. In a notorious 1935 paper, given the shorthand the "EPR paper," Einstein, Boris Podolsky, and Nathan Rosen asked the titular question, "Can Quantum-Mechanical Description of Physical Reality Be Considered Complete?" Their answer was no, "the description of reality as given by a wave function is not complete" (Einstein, Podolsky, and Rosen 1935, 777). Ironically, the thought experiment Einstein devised in the EPR paper to refute claims to quantum completeness, instead of revealing a "contradiction" (Einstein, Podolsky, and Rosen 1935, 777), became the basis for a later proof by John Stewart Bell for the concept of quantum entanglement (cf. Bell 1964). Due to the considerable inspiration Einstein's objections provided for the refinement and advancement of quantum theory, he should be considered an inadvertent and reluctant founder. The prospect of entanglement—that a change of state in one system could simultaneously and instantaneously effect a change of state in a system separated by space-time—remained for Einstein sufficient cause to reject quantum theory. More than ten years after the EPR paper, in a private letter to Max Born, Einstein maintained his rejection of quantum theory on the basis that "the theory cannot be reconciled with the idea that physics should represent a reality in time and space, free from spooky actions at a distance" (Einstein 1947, 158).

The best evidence we have for Einstein's rejection of the value of quantum transposition is his complete silence on the matter. This is not to say that the absence of positive proof is proof of the negative case. However, the degree to which Einstein discussed social, political, and philosophical issues throughout his lifetime afforded him constant and ample opportunity to suggest even the most modest of connections between quantum theory and the human sciences. The Born-Einstein letters, which span almost forty years (February 1916–January 1955), are littered with Einstein's informal opinions on the politics of his time: from his view that the "Bolsheviks do not seem so bad" (Einstein 1920, 22) to his assertion that he "never had a particularly favourable opinion of the Germans (morally and politically speaking)" (Einstein 1933, 114). In a short essay he wrote in 1934, titled, *The World as I See It*, Einstein put forward his political philosophy:

> My political ideal is that of democracy. Let every man be respected as an individual and no man idolized. (Einstein 2014, 5)

Einstein also wrote essays on pacifism, the accumulation of wealth, the meaning of life, economic crisis, culture, minorities, and geopolitics.[9] Therefore, the fact that a connection between quantum theory and the social world was not made, even once, suggests that either this idea never occurred to Einstein or he had no interest in pursuing this avenue. Given that many of his contemporaries (especially his long-time interlocutor Niels Bohr) were making public pronouncements and publishing articles concerning quantum transposition, the suggestion that quantum transfer never occurred to Einstein is inconceivable. Consequently, we are left to conclude that Einstein denied any role for quantum theory in the human sciences.

Von Neumann's Silence

It may surprise some readers, given this chapter's typology of quantum transposition, not to find John von Neumann listed alongside Max Born under the section dedicated to the formalists. This surprise suggests the question: why was it that the mathematician "par excellence"—to borrow Leon van Hove's compliment (van Hove 1958, xi)—of quantum mechanics did not deploy quantum formalism in the human sciences? Our puzzlement is further compounded given that von Neumann *did* make significant mathematical contributions to the human sciences—that is, in the fields of economics, sociology, and neurology—although, critically, the formalism was distinctly classical rather than quantum. An answer is suggested by remarks von Neumann and Oskar Morgenstern made in the introduction to their landmark 1944 work, *Theory of Games and Economic Behaviour*. When justifying the transfer of mathematical models into economics, they write:

> One would misunderstand the intent of our discussions by interpreting them as merely pointing out an analogy between these two spheres. We hope to establish satisfactorily, after developing a few plausible schematizations, that the typical problems of economic behavior become strictly identical with the mathematical notions of suitable games of strategy. (von Neumann and Morgenstern 1990, 2)

In other words, von Neumann and Morgenstern were not operating on the basis that economic behavior "appears" mathematical, or that economic actors should be rendered as mathematical objects. Rather, von Neumann and Morgenstern argued that the dynamics that emerge as a result of economic interaction, and thereby the economic "problems" requiring a solution, are substantively mathematical in nature. The corollary is that *the form of mathematics required to solve economic problems is specific to the particular dynamics observed*. In the case of "strategic interaction between rational economic actors," von Neumann and

Morgenstern considered game theory—that is, the mathematical formalism of classical *logic*—the most appropriate form of mathematics. Their explanation necessarily implies that von Neumann and Morgenstern *did not believe* the observable dynamics of economic interaction were best represented by quantum models. Von Neumann did not consider economic interaction to be "quantum" in nature.

In 1955, von Neumann wrote a series of lectures intended for presentation at Yale, under the heading *The Computer and the Brain*. Von Neumann intended to provide an "understanding of the nervous system from the mathematician's point of view" (von Neumann 1986, 1). Despite describing the human nervous system as having a "*prima facie* digital character," and that the "message-system" used in the brain was "of an essentially *statistical* character," von Neumann was careful to establish he was *not* attempting a description of "consciousness" or "the Understanding" (von Neumann 1986, 40, 79, 1). The key distinction is that von Neumann remained resolutely invested in only describing and explaining the "physical" operation of the brain using mathematics. The lectures conclude with a discussion of phenomena in the brain that escape physical explanation. Instead of providing a formal hypothesis, von Neumann conceded that "whatever the system is, it cannot fail to differ considerably from what we consciously and explicitly consider as mathematics" (von Neumann 1986, 82). Once again, we must acknowledge that von Neumann simply did not believe neurology was a suitable domain for quantum formalism. Von Neumann did not consider the brain "quantum" in nature.

In a letter to Garrett Birkhoff in 1935, von Neumann provides an enigmatic statement concerning the issue of whether their paper should make claims concerning the "physical reality" of quantum mechanics. Von Neumann cautions:

> I wanted to avoid discussing this rather touchy and complicated question, and withdraw to the safe—although perhaps narrow—position of dealing with "causal statements" only. Do you propose to discuss the question fully? It might become too philosophical, but I would not say that I object absolutely to it. But it is dangerous ground—except if you have a new idea, which settles the question more satisfactorily. (von Neumann 1935, 49)

In the end, we can't be sure if von Neumann rejects the transfer of quantum formalism into the human sciences because he didn't think it was useful, didn't think the social world reflected quantum dynamics, couldn't develop satisfactory quantum social mathematics, or didn't want to become entangled in "dangerous philosophy." What we do know, however, is that of the founders in this chapter, von Neumann was the only one not to write a book of philosophy, while simultaneously being the only founder to make a substantive contribution to the human sciences—albeit a *nonquantum* contribution.

Reverse Correlation

So far, this chapter has only considered the correlation between quantum theory and the human sciences in one direction: the influence quantum theory might have on the human sciences. What has not been discussed—despite being a significant area of scholarship—is the influence the human sciences had on quantum physics. Broadly speaking, we enter the domain of the sociology of science and the well-established principle that science never emerges ex nihilo. Instead, scientific practices arise within specific historical, social, cultural, political, and material contexts—all of which act to establish the epistemic and ontological contours of a science per se. Indeed, the constitutive reality of scientific practice is associated as much with its birth in the seventeenth century as with its later development into subdisciplines such as quantum physics. Pioneering this form of research, Steven Shapin contributed significantly to establishing this thesis. In his 1996 work, *The Scientific Revolution*, Shapin writes:

> Science is a historically situated and social activity and … it is to be understood
> in relation to the *contexts* in which it occurs.… There is as much society inside
> the scientist's laboratory, and internal to the development of scientific know-
> ledge, as there is outside. (Shapin 1998, 9–10)

Michel Foucault is another thinker who contributed to this field of study. Although the term *discourse* does not appear in his 1966 work, *The Order of Things*, Foucault's description of the circumstances under which scientific practices emerge and evolve certainly comports with his later writing in this area. Foucault concluded that the "epistemological field, the *episteme* in which knowledge … manifests" represents, for scientific practice, its "conditions of possibility" (Foucault 2002, xxiv).

Returning our attention to quantum physics, Alexei Kojevnikov demonstrated that a physicist's choice of concepts and theoretical framework may be conditioned by their ideological preferences. In his 1999 article, "Freedom, Collectivism, and Quasiparticles," Kojevnikov described the influence Soviet socialism had on the formation of distinct quantum concepts for specific physicists in the early and mid-twentieth century. Kojevnikov explains that because Yakov Frenkel, Igor Tamm, Lev Landau, and David Bohm were "all socialists of various kinds" and cared about "politics almost as much as about science," they introduced "collectivist terminology and models into quantum physics" (Kojevnikov

1999, 299–300). In his follow-up 2002 article, "David Bohm and the Collectivist Movement," Kojevnikov describes how David Bohm (1917–1992) deployed "collectivist notions in his attempts to understand the behavior of particles in dense physical systems," resulting in Bohm's discovery of "collective-individual plasma" (Kojevnikov 2002, 163, 191).

Quite aside from scholarship within the sociology of science, it is worth noting that the influence of philosophy, politics, and the culture of their time had not escaped the physicists themselves. Werner Heisenberg, who in 1971 wrote the introduction to the published collection of the Born-Einstein letters, noted that all "scientific work is, of course, based consciously or subconsciously on some philosophical attitude; on a particular thought structure which serves as a solid foundation for further development" (Heisenberg 1971, x). According to Heisenberg, the disagreements between Born and Einstein about the "correct interpretation of atomic phenomena" were ineluctably infused with "human, political and ideological problems" (Heisenberg 1971, vii). Evidence for this hypothesis—that is, that a position on philosophy and human affairs can play a decisive role in the formulation of physical sciences—is provided by Einstein, who writes to Born in 1919:

> May a hard-bitten x-brother and determinist be allowed to say, with tears in his eyes, that he has lost his faith in humanity? The impulsive behaviour of contemporary man in political matters is enough to keep one's faith in determinism alive. (Einstein 1919, 11)

The extent to which Einstein's worldview wedded him to the idea of determinism, and thus a rejection of the kind of discontinuity implied by quantum theory, is well beyond the scope of this chapter. Suffice to say, however, Einstein's determinist social and political worldview predated the quantum revolution of the 1920s and 1930s, and nothing that he read or encountered during that period changed his view that humankind existed in a deterministic system. Notably, the reverse position was held by Max Born, who was also able to conceive of discontinuity in the field of physics. Born writes to Einstein some twenty-five years after Einstein's first assertions of determinism:

> To me a deterministic world is quite abhorrent—this is a primary feeling. Maybe you are right, and it is as you say. But at the moment it does not really look like it in physics—and even less so in the rest of the world. (Born 1944, 155)

We see, therefore—at least in the case of Einstein and Born—that just as there is a relationship between a founder's views on quantum theory and their attitudes toward quantum transposition, there is also a patterned relationship between a physicist's worldview and their perspective on quantum theory per se.

Conclusion

The question of how the founders of quantum physics felt about deploying their findings outside the natural and into the human sciences receives an answer as multifarious and nuanced as their interpretations of quantum theory per se. Broadly speaking, the physicists associated with the Copenhagen interpretation—that is, Niels Bohr, Werner Heisenberg, Wolfgang Pauli, and Max Born—consistently and confidently advocated for quantum's role outside of physics. On the other side of the spectrum were Albert Einstein, John von Neumann, and, generally speaking, Erwin Schrödinger, who, while enjoying much personal philosophizing, maintained a strict separation between quantum physics and the human sciences.

This chapter has suggested a four-form typology for the early advocacy of quantum transposition, as advanced by the pioneers of quantum physics: *epistemic, ontological, formalist,* and *rejection.* Niels Bohr, Wolfgang Pauli, and Max Born argued that the lessons of quantum physics that bore upon the human sciences were epistemic in nature. Werner Heisenberg argued that quantum physics necessitated a shift in the ontologies underwriting all the human sciences. Max Born (and, to a lesser extent, Erwin Schrödinger) alluded to the practical deployment of quantum mathematical formalism in the human sciences. Albert Einstein, John von Neumann, and, generally speaking, Erwin Schrödinger rejected the idea that quantum theory had a role to play in the human sciences. Interestingly, Bohr felt that quantum physics revealed a "problem of knowledge" (epistemology), Heisenberg believed quantum had distinct metaphysical implications (ontology), Born was responsible for an essential component of quantum mechanics (formalism), and Einstein didn't hold much truck with quantum theory at all (rejection). Therefore, it is not unreasonable to suggest that the approach particular founders of quantum physics took to deploying their findings into the human sciences was in many ways patterned to their interpretation of quantum theory per se.

Notes

1. I am aware that *transpose* has a specific meaning in quantum mechanics, that is, the act of exchanging the position of indices within a matrix along the main diagonal. However, I have appropriated this term due to its broader, conceptual, meaning. Transposition conveys "what the quantum founders were doing" when they shared their ideas with the human sciences. The term encapsulates both a sense of "intention" (wanting to pursue this objective) and the "act" (the efforts aimed at achieving their objective). The underlying dynamics of this effort are (1) the act of taking, or the intention to take, the ideas, theories, concepts, methods, epistemology, ontology, and

cosmology of quantum physics into a separate discipline; (2) the act of using, or the intention to use, the ideas, theories, concepts, methods, epistemology, ontology, and cosmology of quantum physics outside the natural sciences; (3) to move something from its natural/native/typical/familiar/emergent domain; *and* (4) to suggest the use of something in an unnatural/foreign/novel/unfamiliar domain.

2. The idea that Niels Bohr offered an epistemological interpretation of quantum theory is well supported by Michel Bitbol and Stephano Osnaghi (cf. Bitbol and Osnaghi 2013). Indeed, since Bohr considered complementarity his great contribution to quantum physics, while complementarity is quite clearly an epistemic principle, the burden of proof is on those who would argue against the epistemic interpretation. Even those who do make ontological claims based on Bohr's quantum physics are compelled to acknowledge these claims are inferences, extensions, and/or elaborations. Karen Barad succinctly describes this predicament: "Bohr's philosophy-physics contains important and far-reaching ontological implications, but unfortunately he stays singularly focused on the epistemological issues and does not make this contribution explicit or explicate his views on the nature of reality" (Barad 2007, 31).

3. The assertion that Heisenberg pursued an "ontological" project and believed quantum physics had overturned the "materialist-mechanical" worldview is supported by Patrick Heelan. Heelan wrote an authoritative account of Heisenberg's thinking in his 1970 book, *The Observable: Heisenberg's Philosophy of Quantum Mechanics*. Heelan writes that Heisenberg believed "physics was a quest for a better understanding of what nature is *really* like" (Heelan 2016, 8). Two considerations weigh heavily in Heelan's favor: (1) the two men were well acquainted and frequently discussed philosophy, *and* (2) Werner Heisenberg reviewed and approved Heelan's work prior to publication.

4. Max Born referred to his interpretation of quantum physics as a "statistical interpretation" (Born 1951b, 122). In addition, Florian Boge confirms that Max Born's principal contribution to quantum theory was a "thoroughly 'statistical' interpretation" (Boge 2018, 47), exemplified by what is known as *Born's rule*, a key component of quantum mechanics that enables probabilistic calculation of wave function collapse, that is, the realization of eigenvalues within an eigenstate. In 1932, von Neumann quite literally "wrote the book" on quantum mathematical formalism: *Mathematical Foundations of Quantum Mechanics* (von Neumann 2018).

5. The idea that Albert Einstein rejected the completeness of quantum theory is universally acknowledged. Theoretical physicist A. Douglas Stone confirms Einstein "rejected the new quantum theory as the ultimate description of reality" (Stone 2013, 316). Indeed, Stone notes that "Einstein himself never applied the quantum formalism to a specific physics problem for the rest of his career, except in the context of a famous critical paper written in 1935" (Stone 2013, 316). Stone refers of course to the EPR paper, wherein Einstein deploys quantum formalism for the sole purpose of refuting the completeness of quantum theory.

6. Munro's early encounter with quantum physics is noted by Becker (1991) and Wendt (2015); Munro's failure to impact International Relations is investigated in Jayson Waters's chapter that follows.

7. Niels Bohr often stated his belief that quantum theory had revealed the "general problem of knowledge" (Bohr 1929, 5). Indeed, there is a strong argument to be made that, for Bohr, quantum physics was primarily an epistemic enterprise. That is to say, Bohr's experimental work in physics, quite aside from the insights into the operation of nature at a subatomic level, had revealed something fundamental about how human beings construct and share knowledge.

8. In a lecture given by Born in 1936 to demonstrate that "physics, besides its importance in practical life, as the fundamental science of technical development, has something to say about abstract questions of philosophy" (Born 1936, 54), he gave a detailed explanation of complementarity and credited Bohr with discovering a principle that "may help to solve fundamental difficulties in biology and psychology" (Born 1936, 52). In the final chapter of his published series of 1948 lectures, *Metaphysical Conclusions*, Born makes clear the intellectual debt he owes to Bohr's theory of complementarity and his persistent acceptance of the same: "Science has undoubtedly two aspects: it can be regarded from the social standpoint as a practical collective endeavour for the improvement of human conditions, but it can also be regarded from the individualistic standpoint, as a pursuit of mental desires, the hunger for knowledge and understanding, a sister of art, philosophy, and religion. Both aspects are justified, necessary, and complementary" (Born 1951b, 128).

9. Albert Einstein wrote several philosophical essays and social commentaries, varying in length from short aphorisms to numerous pages. Their titles are given as: "The Meaning of Life," "The World as I See it," "The Liberty of Doctrine," "Good and Evil," "Society and Personality," "Of Wealth," "Education and Educators," "Paradise Lost," "Religion and Science," "The Religiousness of Science," "The Plight of Science," "Fascism and Science," "The Pacifist Problem," "The Question of Disarmament," "Women and War," "Thoughts on the World Economic Crisis," "Culture and Prosperity," "Minorities," and "The Jews." See Einstein (2014).

References

Barad, Karen. 2007. *Meeting the Universe Halfway: Quantum Physics and the Entanglement of Matter and Meaning*. London: Duke University Press.

Becker, Theodore L. (ed.). 1991. *Quantum Politics: Applying Quantum Theory to Political Phenomena*. New York: Praeger.

Bell, John. 1964. "On the Einstein Podolsky Rosen Paradox." *Physics* 1, no. 3: 195–200.

Bitbol, Michel, and Stefano Osnaghi. 2013. "Bohr's Complementarity and Kant's Epistemology." In *Niels Bohr, 1913–2013*, edited by Olivier Darrigol, Bertrand Duplantier, Jean-Michel Raimond, and Vincent Rivasseau, 199–221. Cham: Springer International Publishing.

Boge, Florian. 2018. *Quantum Mechanics: Between Ontology and Epistemology*. Cham: Springer International Publishing.

Bohr, Niels. 1929. "Introductory Survey." In 1961. *Atomic Theory and the Description of Nature*, edited by Niels Bohr, 1–24. London: Cambridge University Press.

Bohr, Niels. 1933. "Light and Life." *Nature* 131, no. 1 (March 25): 421–423.

Bohr, Niels. 1939. "Natural Philosophy and Human Cultures." *Nature* 143, no. 1 (February): 268–272.

Bohr, Niels. 1949. "Manuscript of Radio Talk to Gymnasium Students: Atoms and Human Knowledge." In 2006. *Volume 12: Popularization and People (1911–1962), Niels Bohr Collected Works*, edited by Finn Aaserud, 63–70. London: Elsevier.

Born, Max. 1936. "Some Philosophical Aspects of Modern Physics." In 1956. *Physics in My Generation: A Selection of Papers*, edited by Max Born, 37–54. London: Pergamon Press.

Born, Max. 1944. "Born Letter to Einstein: 10th October." In 1971. *The Born-Einstein Letters: Correspondence between Albert Einstein and Max and Hedwig Born from 1916 to 1955*, translated by Irene Born, edited by Paul Atkins, 155–157. London: Macmillan Press.

Born, Max. 1950. "Physics and Metaphysics." In 1956. *Physics in My Generation: A Selection of Papers*, edited by Max Born, 93–108. London: Pergamon Press.

Born, Max. 1951a. "From the Postscript to 'The Restless Universe.'" In 1956. *Physics in My Generation: A Selection of Papers*, edited by Max Born, 225–232. London: Pergamon Press.

Born, Max. 1951b. *Natural Philosophy of Cause and Chance: Being the Waynflete Lectures 1948*. Oxford: Clarendon Press.

Einstein, Albert. 1919. "Einstein Letter to Born: 4th June." In 1971. *The Born-Einstein Letters: Correspondence between Albert Einstein and Max and Hedwig Born from 1916 to 1955*, translated by Irene Born, edited by Paul Atkins, 11. London: Macmillan Press.

Einstein, Albert. 1920. "Einstein Letter to Born: 27th January." In 1971. *The Born-Einstein Letters: Correspondence between Albert Einstein and Max and Hedwig Born from 1916 to 1955*, translated by Irene Born, edited by Paul Atkins, 20–23. London: Macmillan Press.

Einstein, Albert. 1933. "Einstein Letter to Born: 30th May." In 1971. *The Born-Einstein Letters: Correspondence between Albert Einstein and Max and Hedwig Born from 1916 to 1955*, translated by Irene Born, edited by Paul Atkins, 113–114. London: Macmillan Press.

Einstein, Albert. 1947. "Einstein Letter to Born: 3rd March." In 1971. *The Born-Einstein Letters: Correspondence between Albert Einstein and Max and Hedwig Born from 1916 to 1955*, translated by Irene Born, edited by Paul Atkins, 157–158. London: Macmillan Press.

Einstein, Albert. 2014. *The World as I See It*. Translated by Alan Harris. New York: Open Road Integrated Media.

Einstein, Albert, Boris Podolsky, and Nathan Rosen. 1935. "Can Quantum-Mechanical Description of Physical Reality be Considered Complete?" *Physical Review* 47, no. 1 (May): 777–780.

Foucault, Michel. 2002. *The Order of Things: An Archaeology of the Human Sciences*. London: Routledge.

Gordon, Scott. 1991. *The History and Philosophy of Social Science*. New York: Routledge.

Heelan, Patrick. 2016. *The Observable: Heisenberg's Philosophy of Quantum Mechanics*. New Yok: Peter Lang.

Heisenberg, Werner. 1958. *Physics and Philosophy: The Revolution in Modern Science*. Edited by Ruth Nanda Ashen. New York: Harper & Brothers.

Heisenberg, Werner. 1971. Introduction. In 1971. *The Born-Einstein Letters: Correspondence between Albert Einstein and Max and Hedwig Born from 1916 to 1955*, translated by Irene Born, edited by Paul Atkins, vii–x. London: Macmillan Press.

Jung, Carl. 1933. "Jung Letter to Pauli: 2nd November." In 2000. *Atom and Archetype: The Pauli/Jung Letters, 1932–1958,* edited by C. A. Meier, translated by David Roscoe, 3–4. Princeton, NJ: Princeton University Press.

Jung, Carl. 1934. "Jung Letter to Pauli: 29th October." In 2000. *Atom and Archetype: The Pauli/Jung Letters, 1932–1958,* edited by C. A. Meier, translated by David Roscoe, 3–4. Princeton, NJ: Princeton University Press.

Kojevnikov, Alexei. 1999. "Freedom, Collectivism, and Quasiparticles: Social Metaphors in Quantum Physics." *Historical Studies in the Physical and Biological Sciences* 29, no. 2: 295–331.

Kojevnikov, Alexei. 2002. "David Bohm and the Collectivist Movement." *Historical Studies in the Physical and Biological Sciences* 33, no. 1: 161–192.

Manicas, Peter. 1988. *A History and Philosophy of the Social Sciences.* Oxford: Basil Blackwell.

Mirowski, Philip. 1989. *More Heat Than Light: Economics as Social Physics, Physics as Nature's Economics.* New York: Cambridge University Press.

Munro, William. 1928. "Physics and Politics—An Old Analogy Revisited." *American Political Science Review* 22, no. 1: 1–11.

Pauli, Wolfgang. 1934. "Pauli Letter to Jung: 26th July." In 2000. *Atom and Archetype: The Pauli/Jung Letters, 1932–1958,* edited by C. A. Meier, translated by David Roscoe, 5–6. Princeton, NJ: Princeton University Press.

Pauli, Wolfgang. 1949. "The Philosophical Significance of the Idea of Complementarity." In 1994. *Writings on Physics and Philosophy,* edited by Charles P. Enz and Karl von Meyenn, translated by Robert Schlapp, 35–42. Berlin: Springer-Verlag.

Pauli, Wolfgang. 1952. "The Influence of Archetypal Ideas on the Scientific Theories of Kepler." In 2012. *The Interpretation of Nature and the Psyche,* edited by Marvin Jay Greenberg, 147–212. New York: Ishi Press International.

Pauli, Wolfgang. 1954. "Ideas of the Unconscious from the Standpoint of Natural Science and Epistemology." In 1994. *Writings on Physics and Philosophy,* edited by Charles P. Enz and Karl von Meyenn, translated by Robert Schlapp, 149–164. Berlin: Springer-Verlag.

Schrödinger, Erwin. 1944. "What Is Life?" In 2013. *What Is Life? With Mind and Matter & Autobiographical Sketches,* edited by Canto Classics, 1–92. Cambridge: Cambridge University Press.

Schrödinger, Erwin. 1960. "What Is Real?" In 1964. *My View of the World,* translated by Cecily Hastings, edited by Erwin Schrödinger, 49–81. Cambridge: Cambridge University Press.

Schrödinger, Erwin. 1964. *My View of the World.* Translated by Cecily Hastings. Cambridge: Cambridge University Press.

Shapin, Steven. 1998. *The Scientific Revolution.* Chicago: University of Chicago Press.

Stone, Douglas. 2013. *Einstein and the Quantum: The Quest of the Valiant Swabian.* Princeton, NJ: Princeton University Press.

van Hove, Léon. 1958. "Von Neumann's Contributions to Quantum Theory." In 2018. *Mathematical Foundations of Quantum Mechanics,* edited by Nicholas A. Wheeler, translated by Robert T. Beyer, xi–xv. Princeton, NJ: Princeton University Press.

von Neumann, John. 1935. "Von Neumann Letter to Garrett Birkhoff: 15th January." In 2005. *John Von Neumann: Selected Letters,* edited by Miklós Rédei, 49–50. Providence, RI: American Mathematical Society.

von Neumann, John. 1986. *The Computer and the Brain.* New Haven, CT: Yale University Press.

von Neumann, John. 2018. *Mathematical Foundations of Quantum Mechanics*. Edited by Nicholas A. Wheeler, translated by Robert T. Beyer. Princeton, NJ: Princeton University Press.

von Neumann, John, and Oskar Morgenstern. 1990. *Theory of Games and Economic Behaviour*. Princeton, NJ: Princeton University Press.

Wendt, Alexander. 2015. *Quantum Mind and Social Science: Unifying Physical and Social Ontology*. Cambridge: Cambridge University Press.

3

Mind, Matter, and Motion

A Genealogy of Quantum Entanglement and Estrangement

Jayson C. Waters

Introduction

In the late 1920s, Alfred North Whitehead (1985: 6) noted that it "is a re-markable characteristic of the history of thought that branches of mathematics, developed under the pure imaginative impulse, thus controlled, finally receive their important application [in the natural sciences]....In more recent years, the theory of probability, the theory of tensors, the theory of matrices are cases in point." The extent to which formal scientific ideas have inspired, guided, and constrained international and political theory is similarly remarkable. The Newtonian analogy of states as billiard balls is the obvious example, but there is a rich history of other analogies such as states as superorganisms (Lemke, 2011) and fields (Wright, 1955; Rummel, 1975), not to mention the role of game theory in modeling conflict and theorizing nuclear deterrence (Schelling, 1960). In recent years, a number of international scholars have suggested that quantum mechanics offers a valuable set of tools and strategies to address many of the in-tractable problems, as well as new challenges, faced by International Relations (Der Derian and Wendt, 2020; Wendt, 2015). However, despite several inter-national symposia, panels and roundtables at professional conferences, and a special journal issue dedicated to "quantizing" International Relations (IR), it re-mains difficult to say whether we are on the verge of a "quantum wave" or merely witnessing another instance of ideas bouncing off each other to little collective effect (of course, this depends on how one measures the phenomenon).

Part of this difficulty arises from the way quantum is represented as "cutting edge," as a moniker to be casually applied to our finest computers, satellites, sensors, dishwashing tablets, and running shoes. With all the current hype, it is easy to forget that quantum's roots go back well over a hundred years. This line can be drawn earlier or later, but it is generally accepted that quantum mechanics nominally began with Max Planck in 1900, was further developed by Albert Einstein and Niels Bohr early in the twentieth century, and came into its modern form in the mid-twenties with the pioneering work of Werner Heisenberg, Erwin Schrödinger, Max Born, Bohr, and others. So, where does quantum theory sit in the rich tapestry of intellectual cross-fertilization? Is the consideration of quantum's crossover into IR an untimely worry, or is it long overdue?

This chapter attempts an answer by presenting a genealogy of the entanglements and estrangements of quantum mechanics and IR.[1] Tracked and traced back through the decades, these entanglements and estrangements illuminate how we arrived at the present, some missed opportunities along the way, and some dark roads we might wish to avoid. In examining the origins of quantum International Relations—when entanglements occurred, why they ceased, when and why they re-emerged—we are presented with a complex web of competing histories and interpretations of the emergence of both fields of thought.[2] For example, the "international" in IR is not an old category, and the boundaries of IR have shifted considerably over the last century. Further, during its naissance, IR was an "interdiscipline" and proudly proclaimed to be "the crown, the summit, of a general education" (Anonymous, 1929: 201). While this facet of the discipline's history was later obscured and forgotten (Alker and Biersteker, 1984), it is impractical to discuss early IR without reference to other related, and constitutive, disciplines. Accordingly, this genealogy has been broadened to include aspects of political science and other relevant social sciences.

The Quantum Interwar

In October 1927, at the fifth Solvay Conference, Max Born and Werner Heisenberg (2009: 398) declared "quantum mechanics to be a closed theory [*geschlossene theorie*], whose fundamental physical and mathematical assumptions are no longer susceptible of any modification." Quantum theory continued to develop in the months, years, and decades that followed this pronouncement, but by 1927 the core of quantum mechanics was established, and later developments built upon this foundation. Along with the general acceptance of quantum theory, there was an emerging awareness that this scientific revolution was of importance beyond the domain of physics. Attempting to forestall premature extrapolations of quantum mechanics, A. S. Eddington (1929: 211) cautioned that it "would be wiser to nail up over the door of the new quantum theory a notice, 'Structural alterations in progress—no admittance except on business,' and particularly to warn the door keeper to keep out prying philosophers." Eddington's refrain was not heeded.

A mere two months after the fifth Solvay Conference, the first entanglement between political science and quantum mechanics occurred at the annual meeting of the American Political Science Association. The association's president, William Bennett Munro (1928: 2), called upon political scientists to engage with quantum mechanics and to borrow by analogy from the new physics, citing that through "no jugglery of words can we keep Mind and Matter and Motion in watertight compartments." A revolution, Munro (1928: 2–3) continued, "so amazing in our ideas concerning the physical world must inevitably carry its echoes into other fields of human knowledge," and it is "inconceivable that a greatly changed point of view, or a series of far-reaching discoveries, in any one science can be wholly without influence upon the others, even upon those which are not closely allied."

Munro even provided a preliminary quantum model—thereby satisfying his own call to arms—in which the individual, like the atom, has a nucleus (a habit-system) that controls an individual's actions. Ideas were conceived as the electrons of the social universe and the "social atmosphere, like the physical universe, is filled with these invisible units of energy...gaining lodgement [sic] here and there, or departing from some human atom where they have been weekend guests" (Munro, 1928: 5). Ultimately, Munro (1928: 10–11) believed that by adopting the objectivity, methods, and ideas of the physicists, we could "discover the true purposes and policies which should direct human action in matters of government."[3]

Despite coming from the authoritative level of the president of the association, Munro's call for a quantum politics was largely ignored. In the subsequent two decades his address was only cited a handful of times, and in most cases these references were critical. However, Munro's was not an isolated plea. It emerged from within the context of a larger, and older, positivist discourse. Munro's speech was entitled "Physics and Politics—An Old Analogy Revised." The analogy he wished to revise was provided fifty-five years earlier by Walter Bagehot in his book *Physics and Politics: Or, Thoughts on the Application of the Principles of "Natural Selection" and "Inheritance" to Political Society* (1873). As the subtitle suggests, Bagehot's book was primarily concerned with the application of biology to politics and in many ways foreshadowed social Darwinism and the later "biopolitics" of Johan Rudolf Kjellén and Jakob von Uexküll (Lemke, 2011: 9–11). Like Munro, Bagehot sought to understand the hidden physical mechanisms by which societies were directed and thereby could be controlled. Bagehot hypothesized a mechanism of inherited traits like Munro's but based on a Darwinian analogy rather than an atomic one (1873: 8–11). Leaving the particulars of these analogies aside, this desire to discover the laws of social dynamics, and the mechanisms by which societies may be actuated and controlled, is a continuation of Auguste Comte's earlier call for a positivist social physics.

Munro was also situated within a contemporary positivist discourse that called for a "new politics." According to R. K. Gooch (1928: 254), "More than one ex-president of the same learned association, as well as large numbers of articulate 'authorities' through out [sic] the country, look hopefully to the 'exact' sciences as models for and aids to the new science of government." Proponents of the "new politics" argued that "metaphysics is useless and dangerous; idealism has no touch with reality; rationalism and analysis yield only empty abstractions; deduction is sterile; and the realm of the *a priori* is dubbed a 'sublime cloud-land'" (Gooch, 1928: 256). Political scientists were at a crossroads and it was widely argued that they should turn away from the overly juristic and philo-sophical methods of the past and toward the objective methods of the natural sciences, methods that appeared to yield predictability, certainty, and security (Ellis, 1927). Consequently, there were calls for political scientists to engage sci-ences such as anthropology, sociology, social psychology, eugenics, and statistics (Merriam and Barnes, 1924; Merriam, 1925; Ogburn and Goldenweiser, 1927; Catlin, 1927). Charles Merriam (1925: 237–238) provided the most articulate and expansive conception of this "new politics" in his 1925 book, *New Aspects of Politics*. Merriam envisioned a politics that would

> look forward as well as backward, it would supplement traditional lore with experiment...it would create and control habits, as well as utilize those that are handed down. It would use the mechanisms of education and eu-genics for political and social organization and control. It would explore the recesses of human nature, of human political nature, uncontrolled by authority or tradition. The new politics would not be unmindful of history or tradition or of the "subconscious," but it would also consider inheritance and environment as science unfolds them rather than as power or privilege portrays them for personal advantage. The new politics would endeavor to substitute ascertained fact and observed relations for mere opinion, and ex-periment for unfounded belief.

While Munro's quantum model did not take off, his plea was heard insofar as political scientists increasingly engaged with the physical sciences and "scien-tific methods" from the 1930s onward. Munro's own romance with quantum was short lived and he soon turned to social psychology. While his interest in "scien-tific methods" and his positivist bent never completely faded, he conceded that (1934: 6) "Politics is not an exact science, like physics or mathematics. In politics 2 and 2 do not necessarily make 4, as in arithmetic. They may make 22.... [Y]ou deal very largely with variable and unknown quantities.... Adding one unknown factor to another merely gives you a guesswork result." Almost fittingly, this first brief entanglement with quantum begins and ends with Munro, a man who was both quantum and classical, heard and unheard, heeded and ignored. For now, at least, the "jugglery of words" kept mind, matter, and motion in separate, if not in completely watertight, compartments.

Science and International Relations

While American political science was at a disciplinary crossroads in the twenties, IR was still in its naissance and its relationship with "science" was of a different character. In interrogating why quantum mechanics failed to have an impact on IR at this juncture, it is necessary to examine the discursive and material conditions that shaped, constrained, and homogenized the emerging discipline. A brief review of early textbooks, technical manuals, articles, and conference proceedings is instructive in this matter and demonstrates subtle but significant variations in the role of science in the constitution of the discipline.

The first foundational text considered is D. P. Heatley's *Diplomacy and the Study of International Relations* (1919). Heatley did not offer a definition of what he meant by IR, but it is implied that the study of IR entails the study of diplomacy, ethics, and international law, and it is suggested that IR is the study of "the relations of State to State" (1919: 86). Heatley liberally applied the label of "science" to European public law, diplomacy, international jurisprudence, and politics and even discusses a "Science of Right"—a science of ethics aimed at the establishment of peace (1919: 207). Heatley's contemporary, James Bryce (1922: 1), wrote that IR was the study of "the relations of States and peoples to one another" and was "closely connected with nearly every branch of the principle human sciences— Ethics, Economics, Law and Politics." Beyond the "principle human sciences," Bryce held that (1922: vii–viii) "history is the best—indeed the only—guide to a comprehension of the facts as they stand" and thus played an integral role in the study of IR. Like Heatley, Bryce also referenced the "sciences" of diplomacy and statecraft (1922: 15, 148). Heatley and Bryce's mobilizations of the category of "science" should not be construed as an attempt to constitute the fields to which it is applied as exact sciences. "Science" was used here in the European tradition, meaning structured and rigorous knowledge, and served to differentiate the study from the practice—for example, Heatley (1919: 32) described diplomacy as "the art and daily application of the science" of international politics. Alfred Zimmern (1931: 5), another influential author of the interwar period, characterized IR as "the study of the structure and the philosophical, political, and economic principles of Modern Society. The International Relations with which we are concerned are not the special relations between scholars, nor the general relations between nations throughout the past—neither academic policy on the one hand nor world history on the other—but the relations between peoples at the present time." These three characterizations of the discipline provide subtly different images of the structure, purpose, and constitution of the discipline. In doing so they each constrain and discipline IR in different ways and toward slightly different ends.

Early IR departments—if they existed separately to politics or political science departments—operated largely independently of one another. This began to change with the formation of international organizations and conferences that served to guide and standardize the discipline. In 1928, the League of Nations' Institute of Intellectual Co-operation (IIC) formed the Conference of Institutions for the Scientific Study of International Relations (ISSIR)—which later became the International Studies Conference—as a medium for institutions involved in the teaching and study of IR to cooperate and coordinate. Thus, the ISSIR, along with the IIC, formed the global social infrastructure of the discipline and thus served to guide, inform, and constrain the structure, scope, and teaching of the discipline. The name of the ISSIR was chosen as there was a sense at the first conference that "there was something important in common to us, and we had to find a name for it" (Anonymous, 1929: 190). "Scientific" was chosen as the appropriate term and merely signified that the institutions involved "all had certain standards of work" (Anonymous, 1929: 190). The ISSIR envisioned creating a new science of International Relations by harmonizing "political science, international law, economics, history, sociology, and…geography," thereby allowing them to exercise their rightful influence on global affairs (Anonymous, 1929: 201). Unlike the proponents of "new politics," the ISSIR and its members were not seeking to make IR a science via mimicry, analogy, or the adoption of the standards and practices of another discipline. Indeed, the idea of being scientific in that sense was viewed as being "rather dull" (Anonymous, 1929: 190).

According to A. J. Toynbee (Anonymous, 1929: 191), the ISSIR was guided by a great fear and a great hope. The fear (Anonymous, 1929: 191) was "that the forces of disorder which were let loose fifteen years ago may be let loose again (or, rather, that we may let them loose), and the great hope is that the terrible and now quite fatal institution of war may be removed from our horizon through fair-minded common study of international questions by masses of men and women in all the countries concerned." Zimmern (Anonymous, 1929: 202) further highlighted the importance of peace to IR, stating, "in seeking peace—which, after all, was the thought in the minds of the founders of this Institute, and, I think, in the minds of the founders of most of the other institutions represented at our Conference—we have found something even more valuable; we have found something in the intellectual and even in the spiritual realm." This "spiritual dimension" and the existence of the ISSIR is a historical peculiarity that speaks to the constraints placed upon the nascent discipline. In one sense the discipline was free to constitute itself as it saw fit, and in another the discipline was constrained institutionally and politically—at an international level—in that it had a purpose: the promotion and maintenance of peace.

The images of early IR drawn from Heatley, Bryce, Zimmern, and the ISSIR all share a common orientation in which the discipline was already considered "scientific." This was not "science" in the same sense as one finds in contemporary natural and social sciences, but it did not need to be. Unlike the positivist sciences that pursued objectivity, nascent IR sought a science of justice, morality, and peace. To be scientific here was not to collect "facts for facts' sake" (Anonymous, 1929: 191); it was an active, normative science.

Had IR sought congress with the physical sciences, as those of the "new politics" movement in political science did, it is unlikely it would have chosen a revolutionary science such as quantum mechanics. In the twelve months following the publication of Heisenberg's 1925 paper, quantum went "through three distinct phases associated with the names Born and Jordan, Dirac, and Schrödinger" (Eddington, 1929: 206–207). This anarchy remained for a decade, and in the conclusion to *The Restless Universe*, Max Born (1935: 277) reflected that "we have sought firm ground and found none. The deeper we penetrate, the more restless becomes the universe, and the vaguer and cloudier." This state of flux in atomic physics rendered quantum an unappealing object for integration or imitation for nascent IR compared to the established, and more easily comprehensible, sciences of biology, eugenics, geography, psychology, or classical physics—sciences that all provided a more familiar description of reality and were all eventually incorporated. After all, what is the strangeness in an "Oedipus complex" or "superorganisms" when compared to the idea that matter is composed of neither waves nor particles, but something else altogether: *wavicles*?[4]

Razed Ontologies

Jimena Canales (2015) has argued that an ill-fated debate between Einstein and the philosopher Henri Bergson initiated the split of physics from philosophy. Whitehead, however, placed the origin of this split a century earlier, arguing that (1968: 44) "as science grew, minds shrank in width of comprehension. The nineteenth century...failed to produce men of learning with a sensitive appreciation of varieties of interest." Regardless of the temporal location of this split, the relationship between philosophy and physics was not the same in the 1920s as it had been in previous decades and centuries. However, this split can only have been partial in nature. The philosophy of science of Alfred North Whitehead (1985), Bertrand Russell (1927), Michael Polanyi (1946: 14ff), and Hans Reichenbach (1944) all demonstrate the continued engagement of the two disciplines. Many physicists also remained deeply engaged with philosophy, and according to Born (1938: 2), "the physicist remembers that all this [experimentation] is done for a higher task: the foundation of a philosophy of nature." There are two philosophies that emerged coeval, and in dialogue with, quantum mechanics that are of relevance: Russell's neutral monism and Whitehead's philosophy of organism.

In light of quantum mechanics, Russell (1927: vii) and Whitehead (1985: 116) developed philosophies that were consistent with quantum mechanics, relativity, and human experience. Of the two philosophies, Whitehead's is the more complex in that it presented an entirely new cosmology. Unfortunately, Whitehead (1985: xii) took measures to make his arguments general and to avoid the explicit details of developments in physics. Nonetheless, Michael Epperson (2004) has conclusively shown that Whitehead's philosophy of organism demonstrates an intimate fluency with both the new quantum mechanics of the Copenhagen school and the old quantum theory of Planck, Einstein, and those seeking to maintain an objectivist science. According to Russell (1927: 138) both philosophers were, in essence, attempting to achieve the same philosophy, but Russell was attempting to chart a less metaphysical, and more "logically simple," route. Indeed, their two philosophies are remarkably similar. Both adopt what may be described as ontologies of movement—for Russell this was a neutral monist event ontology, and for Whitehead this was a process ontology—and both chart a middle path between materialism and idealism, arguing that fundamental reality is composed of neutral entities, the philosophical equivalent of *wavicles*, that are neither mental nor physical.

While a full explication of these philosophies is impractical here, it is pertinent to note that both philosophies have had a reciprocal relationship with the sciences. Russell's neutral monism has been particularly influential in consciousness studies (Holman, 2008; Persson, 2006; Chalmers, 2015), and Whitehead's philosophy has had a wide impact on the natural and social sciences, most notably helping to shape David Bohm's (2002: 61ff) reformulation of quantum mechanics. Whitehead and Russell have not been influential in IR; however, Whitehead is being gradually introduced by William Connolly (2013), Jairus Grove (2019), and other "new materialists." More broadly, traces of quantum can additionally be found in the work of Heidegger—he and Heisenberg were close friends—and Wittgenstein's philosophy represents a parallel, although unrelated, construction to Bohr's quantum philosophy (Stenholm, 2015). All of this serves to illustrate that philosophy is a vector through which quantum ideas have been absorbed and transmitted to other disciplines, including IR. We need to ask to what extent the scholars who mobilize these philosophies may be, albeit unknowingly, implicitly quantum. The scope of these orthogonal entanglements, although difficult to discern, may be broader than we might imagine.

The Radiance of a Thousand Suns and the Destroyer of Worlds

Atomic weapons radically and permanently altered the course of IR and physics (both as disciplines and practices). For the first time human action controlled subatomic processes in a way in which they acted on a macroscopic scale. Physics entered World War II as the "quiet, pure science of old" and emerged "a decisive factor in the power politics of nations" (Born, 1956: 233). The science of minuscule became the source of ultimate power; atoms transitioned from abstract to absolute, and what was once incomprehensible in a conceptual sense became unfathomable and omnipresent in a tragic sense. In the postscript to the second edition of *The Restless Universe*, Born (1951: 279) reflected that "the dance of atoms, electrons and nuclei, which in all its fury is subject to God's eternal laws, has been entangled with another restless Universe which may well be the Devil's: the human struggle for power and domination, which eventually becomes history."

Physics and politics have long been interrelated; however, the atomic era entangled the two in an unprecedented manner. Political theorists, philosophers, world leaders, and the general public scrambled to learn about atomic weapons. Many prominent physicists became active in political movements and began urging politicians and the public to learn from the other messages of atomic physics and to work toward peace and cooperation. Another subset of physicists took up postwar positions in government as "scientific advisors" or switched their focus entirely from physics to fields as diverse as biology, chemistry, and IR. Additionally, there were several significant interdisciplinary conferences such as the American Philosophical Society's Symposium on Atomic Energy and Its Implications (Smyth, 1946; Oppenheimer, 1946; Shotwell, 1946) and Raymond Aron's Colloques de Rheinfelden (Aron et al., 1960).[5] However, while historically notable, these conferences failed to leave a lasting impression on IR or the other disciplines concerned. Ultimately, while IR and quantum became tacitly entangled through atomic weapons, the discipline remained largely wedded to the Cartesian-Newtonian paradigm, and few considered the deeper connections between quantum mechanics and IR.

The first significant exploration of this relationship occurred in Hans Morgenthau's (1965 [1946]) *Scientific Man vs. Power Politics*. Morgenthau argued (1965 [1946]: 132) that the social and political sciences modeled themselves after the mechanistic physics of Galileo, Descartes, and Newton. However (Morgenthau, 1965 [1946]: 132), quantum theory had "transformed causation into statistical probability and replaced determinism by the principle of indeterminacy" and thereby rendered classical physics obsolete. IR and the other social and political sciences were emulating "a ghost from which life has long since departed" (Morgenthau, 1965 [1946]: 132). The new physics, Morgenthau boldly asserted (1965 [1946]: 144), "shows...that there exists a close correspondence between the human mind...and nature and society." Modern science had unified the social and physical worlds; however, "the common element of which mind, nature, and society partake is no longer reason pure and simple but reason surrounded, interspersed, and underlaid with unreason, an island precariously placed in the midst of an obscure and stormy ocean" (1965 [1946]: 144–145).

In critiquing the philosophic foundations of "science" in the social sciences, Morgenthau was arguing for a quantum reformulation of IR. Unfortunately, Morgenthau's discussion of quantum only occupied a small portion of *Scientific Man* and was quickly forgotten.

Morgenthau's critique, although inspired by quantum, was positioned within a larger critique of IR's rationalism and idealism that emerged in the forties (Carr, 2016; Wright, 1942a; Morgenthau, 1965 [1946]). The fifties saw the "resolution" of these critiques via the "behavioral revolution," which purported to "fix" IR by excising the moral and ethical dimensions that were central to the early discipline and introducing "scientific objectivity" and empirical methods in their place. However, for all the talk of "scientific theories" and "scientific methods," quantum mechanics was almost completely overlooked. Ignoring Morgenthau's criticisms, the "behavioralist revolution" continued to model itself after Newtonian physics—variously paired with evolutionary biology, game theory, statistics, and other sciences—and the discipline once again refused to "give up the ghost."

The late fifties and early sixties witnessed the arrival of a critique of behavioralism and an evolving awareness, and criticism, of the role of Cartesian-Newtonian ideas in the social sciences. For example, James Robinson (1957) and Martin Landau (1961) published articles demonstrating the role of Newtonian physics in political theory. However, it is with Hannah Arendt that quantum tentatively re-entered discourse.

While not principally concerned with quantum, Arendt reintroduced quantum to philosophico-political discourse in *The Human Condition*. In the last section, Arendt (1958: 248–325) provides a phenomenological analysis of the relationship between physics—including quantum mechanics—and human agency. However, counter to Munro's call for engagement, Arendt engages in a devastating critique of the role of science in the fracturing of the modern world. It is inspired by the new physics, but it is equally a reaction against it. Following Arendt, Floyd Matson developed upon this critique in *The Broken Image* (1966). Drawing on quantum mechanics, psychotherapy, and psychobiology, Matson developed a detailed critique of the Cartesianism and scientism of the social sciences. Arguing against positivism, behavioralism, and scientific humanism, Matson proposed a "humane science," a quantum-inspired political theory that took the principles of Heisenberg's *uncertainty* and Bohr's *complementarity* seriously (1966: 113ff, 229) and made whole the fractured "image of man." While quantum inspired, it is important to note that Matson drew on a large body of other discourses including the quantum-like gestalt psychology. Unfortunately, Matson's book was a solitary insurgency, like Munro's before him, and did not leave a lasting impact upon IR or political science. Nonetheless, Arendt and Matson represent important orthogonal entanglements between quantum mechanics and IR. For the next entanglements we must turn to social field theory.

Social Field Theory

Although it is not immediately obvious, social field theory is another vector through which quantum infiltrated IR. Social field theory originated with the gestalt psychologist Kurt Lewin in the 1930s. Lewin hoped to transition psychology away from what he viewed as an antiquated Aristotelian science of dichotomous classifications to a modern Galilean science of continuous and dynamic fields, tensions, and forces (Rummel, 1975: 35ff). Lewin "borrowed by analogy" from physical field theories (electromagnetism and relativity) to develop a model in which mind was characterized as a dynamic field. This dynamic field consisted of various tensions, forces, and needs—coexisting in an evolving *quasi-equilibrium*—and was situated within a larger environmental field (a *life space*). Lewin's theory was rapidly adopted, expanded upon, and generalized into other disciplines (Brown, 1936; Mannheim, 1940), ultimately arriving in IR in the fifties through the work of Quincy Wright (1955), who is better known for his influential study of war (Wright, 1942a, 1942b). Wright considered the shift to a field theoretical analysis as a necessary and inevitable step in the development of IR (1955: 531). Graphically, Wright proposed a field model of international politics that consisted of six dimensions of capabilities and six dimensions of values that he vividly described (1955: 546) as a "twelve-dimensional semi-opaque cheese, within which maggots crawl around, the larger ones representing states with the government at the head and the people at the tail." Many followed Wright's example in developing field theories of IR, but it is with R. J. Rummel that this larval field theory emerged from its chrysalis, not as a moth but as a quantum-like analytic tool and theory of IR.

Rummel began his work on social field theory in the mid-sixties as a part of his work on the Dimensionality of Nations Project (DON)—first commenting on its likeness to quantum mechanics in 1967 (459)—and continued to expound upon his field method, theory, and philosophy into the mid-eighties. Rummel sought to create a joint "mathematical and substantive theory" that enabled the study of war in a scientific and empirical manner (1977: 9). Rummel (1970: 28–29) described his resultant method—which was an improved version of factor analysis—as entailing a "mathematical formalism departing from the formalism of classical physics" and approaching the formalism "of quantum theory." There were also parallels in how Rummel's model treated uncertainty in political behavior. For example, according to Rummel (1970: 106), "we may not be able to measure the characteristics well (characteristics such as nationalism, ideology, and democracy) that we feel might be closely related to United Nations voting.... We are thus in a dilemma similar to that faced by the nuclear physicist... and, like him, we resort to an untraditional mathematical approach."

It is important to emphasize that Rummel's engagement with quantum was convergent, not emergent. Rummel's (1975: 7) field model "grew from social analyses (of International Relations) and only after full conceptual, mathematical, and operational elaboration, was convergence with physical field theories sought." Rummel's (1975: 4) accompanying "realist" philosophy, while similarly convergent with some interpretations of quantum mechanics, integrated a "variety of theoretical and philosophical approaches to war and violence" and served as a "phenomenological framework for analyzing whether war is inevitable and what might be done about it." The two defining aspects of this philosophy were *organicism* and *intentional humanism*. Rummel's (1975: 307) organicism is a form of holism that was "opposed to both the mechanistic and vitalist interpretations of life and the universe." Rummel's intentional humanism, on the other hand, was partly based on Dewey's "transactional" philosophy and posited that man and nature are inextricably interwoven. According to Rummel (1977: 483), the combination of this philosophy and method represented

> a shift from a Newtonian approach to man scientifically and quantitatively to a quantum theory perspective; from an emphasis on known variables and determinate observations and functions to unknown variables and indeterminate observations and functions; from an emphasis on absolute characteristics and fully specified functional relations to a view of the whole, the interrelatedness of men, groups, and characteristics.

Upon the publication of all five volumes of *Understanding Conflict and War* in 1981, James Ray (1982: 185) anticipated that the series would "not have the immediate impact... that one might otherwise expect from a work of such scope written by one of the more famous names in the field." Indeed, despite Rummel being well regarded and recognized in the discipline, Ray's pessimistic prediction was proven right and Rummel's social field theory has been largely ignored by the discipline.

Entanglement

In September 1982, the political scientist Glendon Schubert (1983) presented a paper at the meeting of the Association for Politics and the Life Sciences that argued the case for a "quantized" social theory. Unlike Rummel, Schubert drew directly from the quantum mechanics of Heisenberg, Bell, and Bohr, as well as a broad spectrum of behavioral and psychobiological sciences. Reflecting upon the new quantum and biological sciences, Schubert (1983: 108) contended that "our political world...inescapably represents a highly indeterminate complex of events regarding which great and continuing uncertainty is bound to continue," and "we ought to be constructing models of politics and political behavior in which *chance* plays a major part in explaining what is happening and why." In short, he called for models of politics that renounced the Newtonian ideas of causality, objectivity, and determinism, all the while embracing indeterminism, interconnectivity, and uncertainty. While Schubert (1989: 303; Russell, 1977) was interested in quantum mechanics, this curiosity was motivated by a larger concern in creating a new science of "psychobiological politics."

Schubert's article inspired the formation of a "quantum politics study group" at the University of Hawaii in the early eighties.[6] According to Dator (2006: 201), participants included "Glen Schubert, Rudy Rummel, Dick Chadwick, Ted Becker, Christa Slaton, Chris Jones, Sharon Rodgers, Kenn Kassman, Tim Dolan, Jim Dator, and...others." Their respective attraction to quantum stemmed from numerous sources. As mentioned earlier, Rummel noted parallels between his theory and mathematical apparatus and those of quantum theory; Schubert was drawn to quantum via biophysics and psychobiology, for its superior heuristic and explanatory value; Dator (1984: 53) was enticed by Schubert's views as well as Jack Burnham's examination of the relationship between quantum mechanics and aesthetics in *Beyond Modern Sculpture* (1968); and the others were variously captivated by the popular writings of physicists such as Heisenberg, Bell, Bohm, and Capra. This group thus represented a range of interests, from those who were drawn to the "methods" and those who were drawn to the "message" of quantum. The follow-on efforts of this study group were substantial. Dator (1984) published a paper on quantum politics and political design, Schubert (1989) further expanded upon his quantum-inspired "psychobiological politics" in *Evolutionary Politics*, and the quantum politics group presented their work at the 1987 American Political Science Association conference (Dator, 1992). Additionally, many involved in this study group later collaborated on a collected volume entitled *Quantum Politics* (Becker, 1991). In a short but intense period this group published a significant, if neglected, body of literature, applying quantum mechanics to political phenomena in novel ways.

While *Quantum Politics* may be considered the acme of the "quantum wave" at the University of Hawaii, other works were to follow. Becker and Slaton published another "quantum" book, *The Future of Teledemocracy*, in 2000, and Dator promoted quantum politics as recently as 2006. A decade of work by the group in the eighties, and Rummel's contributions throughout the late sixties and seventies, have left a rich archive of a "second wave" of entanglements. Their quantum work may not be well remembered now, but most of the scholars involved—particularly Becker, Dator, Rummel, Schubert, and Tribe—were prominent scholars in their respective fields. Alexander Wendt (2015: 12) does make note of the quantum politics of Becker et al. but states that "they were not cumulative and are little known today." They may not have been cumulative in the sense that they had differing approaches to quantum and were not interested in creating a single school of thought; however, many other past insurgencies in IR have had a significant regional impact without ever enjoying global recognition. Nonetheless, Wendt is correct in saying that these quantum entanglements are "little known today." These quantum modes of inquiry failed to gain disciplinary traction, and ultimately, the lack of institutional support, funding, and interest led to one more forgotten discourse and yet another disciplinary estrangement.

Collapse

Any genealogy needs to keep in mind how the contemporary era gives cause to re-evaluate the "origins" of the modern quantum IR movement. Der Derian's earliest reference to quantum mechanics appears in his introduction to *The Virilio Reader* (1998) and relates to Paul Virilio's extensive use of quantum mechanics in *Polar Inertia* and later works. Two years later, Der Derian (2000) explicitly linked his "virtual theory" to quantum mechanics and reiterated this connection in *Virtuous War* (2001). Der Derian's (2001: 217) mobilization of quantum mechanics was motivated by a critique of what he refers to as the "Baconian-Cartesian-Newtonian mechanistic model." A decade later Der Derian returned to quantum and provided quantum-inspired studies of late modern forms of diplomacy (2011) and war (2013). "Subject to constant observation, intervention, manipulation and even production by a pervasive and diffuse global media," diplomacy had, according to Der Derian (2011: 377), "become a phase-shifting, level-jumping, distance-traversing, volatile superposition between states of being and becoming, occupied one moment by a pin-striped representative of the state, de-localized the next by a pixellated [*sic*] representation of the global event." Der Derian similarly provided a "quantized" analysis of war (2013: 574) in which he describes warfare as having transitioned from scripted, classical warfare (War 1.0), to image-based violence (War 2.0), to "an indeterminate, probabilistic, and observable-dependent form that defies fixation by word, number, or image" (Quantum War). To keep pace with these changes, Der Derian (2013: 571) argues for a "transdisciplinary approach to global conflicts."

In the same period, Wendt (2005) began the process of "quantizing" his social theory of international politics. As a prelude of things to come, Wendt (2005) presented a detailed "autocritique" in which he carefully repudiated much of his earlier approach to IR theory. In 2015 Wendt delivered on his intent to systematically reformulate his social theory of international politics from *quanta* up. His overall argument is of considerable depth and nuance, but as he states in the preface to *Quantum Mind and Social Science*, his thesis is deceptively simple (2015: 37): human beings are literally "walking wave functions." In place of the Newtonian ideals of objectivity, causality, and determinism, Wendt introduces a deep sense of entanglement, probability, and indeterminacy and a vision of reality as holistic and holographic.

Considered together, Der Derian and Wendt mobilize quantum in markedly different ways. Der Derian is responding to the increasing "interconnectivity of everything" as well as the emergent enhancements and difficulties we will face when quantum technologies become operational. His arguments thus fall, broadly, among the phenomenological approaches to quantum. On the other hand, Wendt is arguing for a fundamentally different philosophy of mind and nature. Both are averse to Cartesian-Newtonian modes of theorizing but draw from different catalysts to justify their calls to radically transform how we see, think, and act in IR. While there are superficial similarities between Der Derian's and Wendt's proposals and the earlier arguments of Matson, Rummel, and Schubert, it would be incorrect to see them as a continuation of the aforementioned. Wendt and Der Derian approach quantum from a distinct philosophical context, and Wendt offers a far more radical vision for quantum in IR and the social sciences than any that has come before.

Nonetheless, it is noteworthy, though hardly a peculiarity of quantum IR, that many scholars, including Der Derian and Wendt, seem unaware of the full scope of prior contributions of quantum entanglements between politics and physics. Der Derian and Wendt (2020) both reference *Quantum Politics*, but only do so in passing. This oversight is not surprising given the long history of IR discourses operating within geographically, disciplinary, and temporally bounded "siloes." We have seen from this genealogy how easy it is for transdisciplinary insurgencies, such as the quantum politics group, to be largely ignored in their day and quickly forgotten. It does, however, raise the question—one that deserves its own sociology of knowledge—of whether disciplinary resistance and discursive amnesia will recur in contemporary efforts to quantize IR.

Giving Up the Ghost

Alfred North Whitehead (1967: 72) cautioned that in "the study of ideas, it is necessary to remember, that insistence on the hard-headed clarity issues from sentimental feeling, as it were a mist, cloaking the perplexities of fact. Insistence on clarity at all costs is based on sheer superstition as to the mode in which human intelligence functions. Our reasonings grasp at straws for premises and float on gossamers for deductions." If we risk clarity for a moment, we can safely say that the past and current deployments of quantum theory in IR—and the other related social sciences—all arise from a dissatisfaction with the "ghost" of the Cartesian-Newtonian paradigm. Munro's approach was rather simplistic in that he saw a new physics, understood it to be superior, and sought to adopt it. However, he failed fully to comprehend the "new physics" and he remained within an existing lineage of positivism. Fundamentally, Munro stayed classical while calling for a "quantum politics." However, to expect Munro to be "fully quantum" in 1927 is to ask for an impossibility. While the theory was "complete" in the minds of its originators, universal acceptance was far from complete both within and outside the world of physics; energetic debates persist to this day regarding the nature, interpretation, closure, and even mere possibility of comprehending quantum mechanics.

Twenty years after Munro, Morgenthau saw through the Cartesian-Newtonian paradigm, declared it a "ghost," and argued for a quantum basis for IR and the other social sciences. While Morgenthau's critique of idealism and rationalism was widely heeded, the most radical aspect was overlooked, and the Cartesian-Newtonian "ghost" persisted. Later applications of quantum, such as Arendt's and Matson's, arose again from a dissatisfaction with Cartesian-Newtonian ideas, but this time from a phenomenological perspective. Both lamented how the world, "man," and reality had been fragmented and contorted by classical mechanics. Arendt and Matson are both clearly interested in quantum mechanics, but their interest arose more from a desire to debunk existing ideas and philosophies. Nonetheless, both Arendt's and Matson's entanglements are of historical value, even if they did not directly impact the discipline. This cycle of disenchantment and discovery recurred with Rummel, Schubert, Dator, Becker, Der Derian, and Wendt. The mechanistic Newtonian paradigm has been shown to be inadequate time and time again, and yet we cling to it.

Perhaps, rather than asking why quantum has not flourished in the discipline, it is more prudent to ask why the discipline has fought off, and otherwise neglected, theories and models that offer superior heuristic value and force us to see the world as it is, quantum. After all, we have always lived in a quantum world. Our world was never only Newtonian in the same way that our solar system was never governed by the Ptolemaic system of cycles and epicycles. This fact has only become more obvious as technology (particularly atomic weapons, lasers, and modern computers) has advanced, and "quantum effects" have encroached upon the macroscopic. Our mobilizations of quantum have not been driven by fads, but by necessity. To "quantize" IR is merely to attempt to better understand our world and ourselves in line with our best physical theories.

If we further pursue the development of a quantum IR, we would do well to engage not only with the physicists but also with philosophers, mathematicians, biologists, legal scholars, psychologists, and anyone else who is willing to take quantum in new directions (as pursued for the past six years with the Project Q symposia).[7] Transdisciplinarity should be the default when it comes to quantum. IR has always been transdisciplinary, even when it sought to declare its own independence (Alker and Biersteker, 1984). A second mode of transdisciplinarity should be reclaimed through the rediscovery of quantum approaches that have come before. The quantum models of the sixties, seventies, and even eighties may seem outmoded today, but they represent significant intellectual progress and should be treated accordingly.

In closing, we may return to the question of whether quantum IR is a "particular" moment, an uncertain wave, or perhaps a coming tsunami? In surveying historical interactions, we can see that the disciplines have been periodically drawn together and apart. These entanglements and estrangements may be construed as peaks and troughs in various ways, and the groupings presented here are not the only available options. Dependent upon our modes of observation, this history can be viewed as one long slow wave, as an interference pattern of many smaller ripples, or simply as an accumulation of "particular" moments. Regardless of the constitution and distribution of these "quantum waves," we can see that quantum mechanics is an old companion to IR. Perhaps a better question would be to ask why we divide up reality in the ways that we do? If reality is fundamentally quantum, and by all accounts this is the case, it seems unlikely that IR can afford to be anything other. Words can only keep mind, matter, and motion separate for so long. At some point we have to give up the Cartesian-Newtonian ghost.

Notes

1. This genealogy is an abridged version of a significantly larger genealogy that will appear in my thesis.
2. The contemporary separation of political theory and international theory poses a conceptual challenge for this genealogy at the outset. While the two discourses are presented as separate today, they assume the existence of the other (Walker, 1993).
3. It is worth noting that the metaphors and analogies proposed by Munro suggest that he was referring to the "old quantum theory" of Planck, Einstein, and Bohr (in his classical stage). Thus, an argument could be made that this was not the first entanglement. However, such an argument would neglect to note that Heisenberg's quantum theory incorporated the "old quantum theory" rather than replacing it entirely. It was a renovation rather than a replacement.

4. The term "wavicle" enjoyed a brief period of usage before physicists decided its utility was outweighed by the confusion it elicited.

5. Interestingly, the Colloques de Rheinfelden were funded by the Congress for Cultural Freedom, which was the front for a covert Central Intelligence Agency program designed to discredit Communism and promote American political ideals (Saunders, 2000).

6. Much of the information in this section was gleaned from James A. Dator, to whom I owe a great debt of gratitude.

7. Project Q is a sustained effort to entangle IR and quantum mechanics at workshops and annual symposia at the Q Station in Sydney, Australia. Project Q began in 2014 with support from the Carnegie Corporation of New York; a virtual symposium was held in 2021. Further information can be found at http://www.projectqsydney.com.

Bibliography

Alker, Hayward R. and Thomas J. Biersteker. 1984. "The Dialectics of World Order: Notes for a Future Archeologist of International Savoir Faire." *International Studies Quarterly* 28 (2): 121–142.

Anonymous. 1929. "The Conference of Institutions for the Scientific Study of International Relations." *Journal of the Royal Institute of International Affairs* 8 (3): 185–202.

Arendt, Hannah. 1958. *The Human Condition*, Chicago: University of Chicago Press.

Arendt, Hannah and Karl Jaspers. 1992. *Hannah Arendt/Karl Jaspers Correspondence, 1926–1969*, New York: Harcourt Brace Jovanovich.

Aron, Raymond, George Kennan, Julius Robert Oppenheimer, et al. 1960. *Colloques de Rheinfelden,* Paris: Calmann-Lévy.

Bagehot, Walter. 1873. *Physics and Politics: Or, Thoughts on the Application of the Principles of "Natural Selection" and "Inheritance" to Political Society*, London: Henry S. King & Co.

Becker, Theodore L. (ed.). 1991. *Quantum Politics: Applying Quantum Theory to Political Phenomena*, New York: Praeger.

Becker, Theodore L. and Christa Daryl Slaton. 2000. *The Future of Teledemocracy*, Westport, CT: Praeger.

Bohm, David. 2002. *Wholeness and Implicate Order*, London: Routledge Classics.

Born, Max. 1935. *The Restless Universe*, translated by Winifred M. Deans, London: Blackie & Son Limited.

Born, Max. 1938. "Some Philosophical Aspects of Modern Physics." *Proceedings of the Royal Society of Edinburgh 57* (1): 1–18.

Born, Max. 1951. *The Restless Universe,* translated by Winifred M. Deans, 2nd rev. ed., New York: Dover.

Born, Max. 1956. *Physics in My Generation* , London: Pergamon Press.

Born, Max and Werner Heisenberg. 2009. "Quantum Mechanics." In *Quantum Theory at the Crossroads: Reconsidering the 1927 Solvay Conference*, trans. and ed. Guido Bacciagaluppi and Antony Valentini, Cambridge: Cambridge University Press.

Brown, R. F. 1936. *Psychology and Social Order*, New York: McGraw-Hill.

Bryce, James. 1922. *International Relations: Eight Lectures Delivered in the United States in August, 1921* , New York: Macmillan.

Burnham, Jack. 1968. *Beyond Modern Sculpture: The Effects of Science and Technology on the Sculpture of This Century*, New York: George Braziller.

Canales, Jimena. 2015. *The Physicist and the Philosopher: Einstein, Bergson, and the Debate That Changed Our Understanding of Time*, Princeton, NJ: Princeton University Press.

Carr, E. H. and Michael Cox. 2016. *The Twenty Years' Crisis, 1919–1939 Reissued with a New Preface from Michael Cox*, London: Palgrave Macmillan UK.

Catlin, George Edward Gordon. 1927. *The Science and Method of Politics*, New York: Kegan Paul.

Chalmers, David, 2015. "Panpsychism and Panprotopsychism." In *Consciousness in the Physical World. Perspectives on Russellian Monism*, ed. Torin Alter and Yujin Nagasawa, pp. 246–276, Oxford: Oxford University Press.

Connolly, William. 2013. *The Fragility of Things*, Durham, NC: Durham University Press.

Dator, James A. 1984. "Quantum Theory and Political Design." In *Changing Lifestyles as Indicators of New Cultural Values*, ed. Rolf Homann, pp. 53–65, Zurich: Gottlieb Duttweiler.

Dator, James A. 1992. "Thought Experiments in Politics—Quantum Politics: Applying Quantum Theory to Political Phenomena Edited by Theodore L. Becker." *Futures 24* (3): 297–281.

Dator, James A. 2006. "Civil Society and Governance Reform." In *Fairness, Globalization, and Public Institutions*, ed. Jim Dator, Richard C. Pratt, and Yongseok Seo, pp. 178–216, Honolulu: University of Hawaii Press.

Der Derian, James. 2000. "Virtuous War/Virtual Theory." *International Affairs 76* (4): 771–788.

Der Derian, James. 2001. *Virtuous War: Mapping the Military-Industrial-Media-Entertainment Network*, Boulder, CO: Westview Press.

Der Derian, James. 2011. "Quantum Diplomacy, German-US Relations and the Psychogeography of Berlin." *Hague Journal of Diplomacy 6* (3–4): 373–392.

Der Derian, James. 2013. "From War 2.0 to Quantum War: The Superpositionality of Global Violence." *Australian Journal of International Affairs 67* (5): 570–585.

Der Derian, James (ed.) and Paul Virilio. 1998. *The Virilio Reader*, Malden, MA: Blackwell Publishers.

Der Derian, James and Alexander Wendt. 2020. " 'Quantizing International Relations': The Case for Quantum Approaches to International Theory and Security Practice." *Security Dialogue 51* (5): 399–413.

Eddington, Arthur Stanley. 1929. *The Nature of the Physical World*, New York: Macmillan Company.

Ellis, Ellen Deborah. 1927. "Political Science at the Crossroads." *American Political Science Review 21* (4): 773–791.

Epperson, Michael. 2004. *Quantum Mechanics and the Philosophy of Alfred North Whitehead*, New York: Fordham University Press.

Gooch, Robert Kent. 1928. "Government as an Exact Science." *Southwestern Political Science Quarterly 9* (3): 254.

Grove, Jairus. 2019. *Savage Ecology: War and Geopolitics at the End of the World*, Durham, NC: Duke University Press.

Heatley, D. P. 1919. *Diplomacy and the Study of International Relations*, Oxford: Clarendon Press.

Heisenberg, Werner. 1925. "Über quantentheoretische Umdeutung kinematischer und mechanischer Beziehungen." *Zeitschrift für Physik 33*: 879–893.

Holman, Emmett. 2008. "Panpsychism, Physicalism, Neutral Monism and the Russellian Theory of Mind." *Journal of Consciousness Studies 15* (5): 48–67.

Landau, Martin. 1961. "On the Use of Metaphor in Political Science." *Social Research 28* (3): 331–353.

Lemke, Thomas. 2011. *Bio-Politics: An Advanced Introduction*, New York: New York University Press.

Mannheim, Karl. 1940. *Man and Society in an Age of Reconstruction*, New York: Harcourt, Brace & Co.

Matson, Floyd. 1966. *The Broken Image: Man, Science and Society*, New York: Anchor Books.

Merriam, Charles Edward. 1925. *New Aspects of Politics*, Chicago: University of Chicago Press.

Merriam, Charles Edward and Harry Elmer Barnes (eds.). 1924. *History of Political Theories, Recent Times: Essays on Contemporary Developments in Political Theory*, New York: Macmillan Company.

Morgenthau, Hans. 1965 [1946]. *Scientific Man vs. Power Politics*, 6th ed., Chicago: University of Chicago Press.

Munro, William Bennett. 1928. "Physics and Politics—An Old Analogy Revised." *American Political Science Review 22* (1): 1–11.

Munro, William Bennett. 1934. *Personality in Politics: A Study of Three Types in American Public Life*, New York: Macmillan Company.

Ogburn, William Fielding and Alexander Goldenweiser (eds.). 1927. *The Social Sciences and Their Interrelations*, London: Allen & Unwin.

Oppenheimer, J. Robert. 1946. "Atomic Weapons." *Proceedings of the American Philosophical Society 90* (1): 7–10.

Persson, Ingmar. 2006. "Consciousness as Existence as a Form of Neutral Monism." *Journal of Consciousness Studies 13* (7–8): 128–146.

Polanyi, Michael. 1946. *Science, Faith, and Society*, London: Oxford University Press.

Ray, James Lee. 1982. "Understanding Rummel." *Journal of Conflict Resolution 26* (1): 185.

Reichenbach, Hans. 1944. *Philosophic Foundations of Quantum Mechanics*, Berkeley: University of California Press.

Robinson, James. 1957. "Newtonianism and the Constitution." *Midwest Journal of Political Science 1* (3–4): 252–266.

Rummel, Rudolf J. 1967. "Understanding Factor Analysis." *Journal of Conflict Resolution 11* (4): 444–480.

Rummel, Rudolf J. 1970. *Applied Factor Analysis*, Evanston, IL: Northwestern University Press.

Rummel, Rudolf J. 1975. *Understanding Conflict and War: Volume 1*, London: John Wiley & Sons.

Rummel, Rudolf J. 1977. *Field Theory Evolving*, London: Sage Publications.

Russell, Bertrand. 1927. *The Analysis of Matter*, London: Kegan Paul, Trench, Trubner & Co.

Russell, Peter H. 1977. "Human Jurisprudence by Glendon Schubert." *University of Toronto Law Journal 27* (3): 364–368.

Saunders, Frances S. 2000. *The Cultural Cold War: The CIA and the World of Arts and Letters*, New York: New Press.

Schelling, Thomas C. 1960. *The Strategy of Conflict*, Cambridge, MA: Harvard University Press.

Schubert, Glendon. 1983. "The Evolution of Political Science: Paradigms of Physics, Biology, and Politics." *Politics and the Life Sciences 1* (2): 97–110.

Schubert, Glendon. 1989. *Evolutionary Politics*, Carbondale: Southern Illinois University Press.

Shotwell, James T. 1946. "The Control of Atomic Energy under the Charter." *Proceedings of the American Philosophical Society 90* (1): 59–64.

Smyth, H. D. 1946. "Fifty Years of Atomic Physics." *Proceedings of the American Philosophical Society 90* (1): 1–6.

Stenholm, Stig. 2015. *The Quest for Reality: Bohr and Wittgenstein; Two Complementary Views*, Oxford: Oxford University Press.

Walker, R. B. J. 1993. *Inside/Outside: International Relations as Political Theory*, Cambridge: Cambridge University Press.

Wendt, Alexander. 2005. "Social Theory as Cartesian Science: An Auto-critique from a Quantum Perspective." In *Constructivism and International Relations: Alexander Wendt and His Critics*, ed. Stefano Guzzini and Anna Leander, pp. 178–235, New York: Routledge.

Wendt, Alexander. 2015. *Quantum Mind and Social Science*, Cambridge: Cambridge University Press.

Whitehead, Alfred North. 1967. *Adventures of Ideas*, New York: Free Press.

Whitehead, Alfred North. 1968. *Modes of Thought*, New York: Free Press.

Whitehead, Alfred North. 1985. *Process and Reality: An Essay in Cosmology: Corrected Edition*, ed. David Ray Griffin and Donald W. Sherburne, New York: Free Press.

Wright, Quincy. 1942a. *A Study of War: Volume I*, Chicago: University of Chicago Press.

Wright, Quincy. 1942b. *A Study of War: Volume II*, Chicago: University of Chicago Press.

Wright, Quincy. 1955. *The Study of International Relations*, New York: Appleton-Century-Crofts.

Zimmern, Alfred. 1931. *The Study of International Relations: An Inaugural Lecture Delivered Before the University of Oxford on 20 February 1931*, Oxford: Clarendon Press.

4

A Quantum Temperament for Life

A Dialogue between Philosophy and Physics

Jairus Victor Grove

What if Quantum isn't the Right Kind of Weird?

—Jairus Grove, 2016

The only laws of matter are those which our minds must fabricate, and the only laws of mind are fabricated for it by matter.

—James Clerk Maxwell. 1877

Introduction

This chapter is inspired by four recurrent criticisms levied against quantum thinking in the social sciences: (1) science envy; (2) colonization by the natural sciences; (3) metaphorical misappropriation; and (4) redundant insights already gleaned from poststructuralism, critical realism, and complexity theory. Rather than refute each claim specifically, I take a more oblique strategy, targeting the narrow perspective of science—in particular, of the quantum event—that informs these criticisms.[1]

By "quantum event" I refer not only to the beginnings of quantum mechanics but also the enabling intellectual ethos that continues to hold great value for contemporary research in the social sciences and International Relations. Philosophers and physicists, displaying a humility and spirit of adventure held in tension, engaged throughout the interwar period in a provocative, sustained, and yet forgotten dialogue about quantum. Philosopher Alfred North Whitehead might not have been capable of performing the double slit experiment, but he could debate its significance with interlocutors across both fields. Likewise, physicist Niels Bohr did not possess the depth of philosophical knowledge to *be* a philosopher, but he possessed sufficient interest and knowledge to engage and challenge contemporaries like Arthur Bentley and John Dewey in ways that pushed everyone involved beyond what their own experience could have produced.

I want to argue that mutual willingness amid the vulnerability of reaching out beyond one's expertise, while also bringing the virtue of one's own expertise to bear on shared questions, offers promise for the interdisciplinary collaboration we need today. We face not just another quantum revolution, but also challenges from artificial intelligence, climate change, nuclear weapons, global govern-ance, and many other multisector complexities that demand of us expertise *and* the risk of dilettantism if we are to respond to the world in any meaningful way. Taking up within the social sciences an ethos of intellectual adventure similar to that of the interwar is needed now more than ever.

The persistent and most pressing question is how to position quantum thinking among other kinds of and claims to knowledge: what happens when we flatten scientific and philosophical inquiry, and what does this broader under-standing of quantum offer the social sciences?

In the first section I sketch the major contributions of quantum physics and relational philosophy side by side to demonstrate overlapping concerns and also the independence of philosophy to pursue these questions. In the second sec-tion I make the case for an ethos of adventurous humility for engaging quantum theory. Alongside this ethos, I want to present a nonprogressivist view of the "purpose" of theory. What if the value of the social sciences is not progress at all? What if the value of the social sciences is to work out the most important philosophical and scientific tasks or problems from within each context, era, and point of inquiry?

An Outline of the Quantum Event

What was the quantum event? Was it only in physics, or was it a more funda-mental crisis in the nature of reality for which every discipline had to reckon? If the latter, then what role did philosophy play in giving the world its due in a com-plex and chancy cosmos? The contribution of quantum physics can be under-stood along four lines of inquiry: discreteness, scale, space/time, and causality.

Discreteness is a key feature of a Newtonian or mechanical worldview. For things to be made of parts, and for those parts to enter into an efficient causal relationship, they must be separate. Quantum experiments challenged many of the assumptions about the presumed boundaries between people and things. Different examples from quantum theory include the observer problem (acts of measurement and observation produce phenomena); entanglement (communi-cation between particles despite spatial distance and no apparent relation); and nonlocality (electrons as probabilities rather than objects at particular coordi-nates). All of these examples complicate how we understand relationality and substance. In the words of an editorial from the *New York Times* in response to quantum theory, "It is like matter is now a wraith" (Crease and Goldharber, 2014). According to Bohr, words like "inside" and "outside" are arbitrary after quantum insights. Speaking of the problem of the observer's body in an experiment, he writes: "It was by no means necessary that this limit should coincide with the geometrical limits of the physical body of the individual who observes" (Bohr, 1998: 120).

Contrary to the common assumption that all quantum effects "wash out" in the macro world, scale was from the start and remains a concern of quantum theorists. In addition to the ways in which entanglement questioned our spatial understandings of distance and matter, we also have Heisenberg and Schrödinger's work in biology as evidence that quantum phenomena had a longer reach into the micro- and macroscopic world. Heisenberg in particular was curious about the role of quantum phenomena in genetics. One of the examples he gives of how quantum phenomena cross scales is the way radiation causes changes to evolutionary history. When a particular gene gets knocked out sometimes but not at other times, then what? It changes the whole course not just of an individual animal but of the entire species: "In such cases the statistical laws of quantum theory assume a direct practical importance for the behavior of a living being" (Heisenberg, 1979: 91).

Discreteness and scale are particular ways in which the conception of reality changed after the popularization of Albert Einstein's theories of relativity. Beyond the average person's grasp of the theory itself, the point taken was that perceived reality did not conform with empirical testing. The idea, for instance, that gravity could change time or that speed and position altered the nature of space suggested that reality was in some very basic sense not intuitive. That we now had to speak of space/time and the fact that reality was "relativistic" was a shock to political and social theories that rested on the providence and elegance of a clock-like universe.

Bohr's concept of complementarity was much more radical in that it challenged the very logic of causality. Complementarity questions whether reality is strictly contingent or if novelty can emerge semiautonomously from initial conditions. According to Prigogine and Stengers, Bohr's insight into Planck's constant is that the "wave collapse" is only describable as an interaction between the measurement apparatus and the light being measured. The "value" assigned is not assigned to the light packet but to the interaction, that is, the measurement itself (Prigogine and Stengers, 1985: 226). According to Bohr, "This novel feature is not only entirely foreign to the classical theories of mechanics and electromagnetism, but is even irreconcilable with the very idea of causality" (Bohr, 1998: 141–142). One of the most basic characteristics of empiricism, the observation of cause and effect, is at some level, according to Bohr, an illusion.

Very much parallel to these scientific insights, but historically prior to the experiments of quantum physics, there are, broadly speaking, four corresponding clusters of contributions from relational philosophies: monism, the continuity of relations, panpsychism, and a shift to process over efficient causality.[2]

Monism, the theory that everything in the world is made of one substance rather than the dualism of mind and body or some other division, goes back to the very beginnings of ancient thought but made a distinct comeback at the end of the nineteenth century. Some of the most well-known thinkers of this position are William James, twentieth-century cyberneticists like Norbert Weiner, and biologists like Henri Atlan. The idea that relations are continuous and indivisible is an extension of monism, but one whose specificity runs in close proximity to the quantum problem of nonlocality. Like Bohr's electron, which only exists in movement, Henri Bergson radicalizes Zeno's paradox to argue that all things, including time, are continuous rather than mechanical and discrete (Bergson and Hulme, 1912).[3] Bergson also adds to the claim of continuity a number of things that are real but do not take up space. Bergson calls these intensive rather than extensive things. The category of intensive changes describes forces whose intensity makes a difference, but that this intensity cannot be measured in space or discrete units. For instance, we can consider the intensity of rage or sadness. This allows Bergson to consider forces like meaning or affect, which change systems even if they are not mechanically describable. Put differently, the category of intensive things means we are not stuck with the barren world of physical causal closure. Yet we also do not have to invent a spiritual realm or second substance for those nonphysical things that are real, but only in their relation. Intensive differences are a kind of predecessor to what complexity theorists call emergent phenomena.

To avoid the problem of monism becoming a kind of reactionary determinism where everything is just the result of matter senselessly interacting, French sociologist Gabriel Tarde offers the ideas of a relationality and intention at the heart of all things. This is similar to the vitalist principle of *élan vital* put forward by Bergson but without the pesky parallelism. For Tarde, everything is a society from top to bottom, and humans in particular are an imitative and entangled species rather than individualistic and cut off from direct experience. However, humans only have this ability because all species, particles, and even stars are entangled, and transactional in imitative and innovative ways (Tarde and Lorenc, 2012). All things are innovating and synching swarms at multiple scales from crowds, to nations, to planetary scale assemblages. Tarde's relational properties also extend from the macro to the quantum and back again. This allows Tarde to replace causality and structure with what he calls polygenesis, where one investigates how each thing or process is made rather than beginning from presumptions about structures or ideal types as explanatory tools (Tonkonoff, 2013).

Fourth, alongside complementarity, we have Alfred North Whitehead's claim that we should abandon essence and identity in favor of process, relations, and rhythm (Whitehead, 1919). Following this line of reasoning requires that the limits of logic be defined by the world rather than by humans. Whitehead argues that any *rational* explanation of the cosmos and the event of humans within it requires abandoning the principle of noncontradiction much in the way that Bohr would articulate the abandoning of causality in his theory of complementarity. According to Whitehead, the terms "coherent and logical" need to be replaced by the terms "applicable and adequate" (Whitehead et al., 1985: 3). Lastly, for the process to be understood, empiricism could not subsist on the naive realism of observation.

Empiricism required an experimental and speculative metaphysics as much as it needed science and observation. For Whitehead, neither observation nor rationalism was a sufficient condition of knowledge; again, like Bohr, knowledge included the observer and the observed in its production and therefore the appearance of things was just that: an appearance that fell victim to what he called the fallacy of misplaced concreteness (Whitehead, 1997: 91).

Put side by side, it becomes apparent that physics in no way has a monopoly over the seemingly key concepts of complementarity, entanglement, or even the wave particle duality. In fact, as I will continue to argue, quantum physics is only a sliver of the quantum crisis, for which I think philosophy and social theory were undergoing similar crises, in many cases a full generation before Einstein, Bohr, Schrodinger, and Heisenberg. Furthermore, relational theories make a significant contribution beyond their apparent similarity to physics particularly for what the questions of causality, locality, process, scale, and the epistemological status of laws and change in the universe mean for us as humans coping with those crises.

I address in more detail in the subsequent sections how relational theories also conceptualize questions about the relationship between epistemology and ontology that quantum theorists were often either hesitant to offer or simply did not ask in the first place. To demonstrate this point, I draw attention to the explicit and implicit dialogue between philosophy and physics as it developed over the end of the nineteenth and beginning of the twentieth century.

Newtonian and Bergsonian Time

In 1948, mathematician and scientific polymath Norbert Wiener published *Cybernetics or Control and Communication in the Animal and the Machine.* The new science of cybernetics was meant to be a theory of everything. In part, the insights of quantum physics and their probabilistic character were supplemented by the stochastic character of larger scales of matter and further connected through a profound relationalism or transactionalism often characterized as information. Everything is chancy, everything is connected, and those connections—feedbacks and effectors—can be recorded as information. Matter, life, and everything are a signal-to-noise ratio, where order is a signal and noise is the chaos or potentiality it draws upon. Furthermore, following Heisenberg and Bohr's rejection of Kant's a priori schema, Wiener highlights that unlike Newtonian systems in which causality could be run forward and backward without changes in the casual relations, this new science of things relies on time independent of whether or not humans were watching. That is, order and change are time-dependent and irreversible evolutionary processes. Wiener describes this break with a timeless, mechanical world as a shift from Isaac Newton to Henri Bergson. The mention of Bergson might not be sufficient evidence to claim that philosophy played a defining role in a quantum shift of scientific cosmologies and the subsequent turn to probabilistic and stochastic approaches behind nearly every scientific breakthrough of the twentieth and twenty-first centuries. However, and more importantly, Wiener's attention to Bergson suggests that the *evolutionary* or temporal character, as well as other intensive differences not captured by the experimental findings of quantum physics, was essential to an understanding of systems as something other than giant Newtonian clocks. According to Wiener, even sciences like astronomy that think of themselves as cyclical, predictable, and mechanical find that their stability is the effect of the experience of time. On longer, nonhuman time scales, even the elegant movement of the planets acquires the contingent and fleeting character of meteorology (Wiener, 1948, 34–35). Alongside the disruptive theories of scientists like Ludwig Boltzman and James Clerk Maxwell, Weiner cites the ideas of Spinoza and Leibniz as essential to returning the mind and other complex phenomena back to the observable world (4). According to Wiener, Spinoza—with his view of the continuous nature of the will and the world as one substance, two modes—helped bring the contingent and creative character of the world back to reality. In Weiner's estimation, it was the dynamical vision of Leibniz's monads that made possible a vision of complexity in which things could be interinvolved and at the same time retain some distinctiveness. However, even these advances were insufficient. Leibniz's monads, according to Wiener, are "a Newtonian solar system writ small" as there is no alteration of each monad in their involvement, "no transfer…from one to the other" (41). What was missing was the evolutionary or creative character of time. Bergson's contribution was to present a series of real changes not in the substance or atoms of things but in the passage or evolution of relations in time. Like contemporaneous advances in thermodynamics, time matters. In Wiener's words, "Vitalism has won to the extent that even mechanisms correspond to the time-structure of vitalism" (40). More than Bergson's *elan vital* is implicit in the statement: the success that Weiner is describing is the evolutionary principle of relational thought developed significantly by others. Charles Peirce, a contemporary of Bergson, took up the evolutionary or temporal problem with a clarity eerily prescient of the insights of quantum experiments that would come decades later. Responding to research on light from the 1880s and incongruities between atomic theory and thermodynamic measurements during the same period, Peirce speculated that light is both a wave and a particle and that atoms may not be mechanically Newtonian. Seeking to understand the dual nature of light in the *Monist* journal in 1891, Pierce writes: "When we come to atoms, the presumption in favor of a simple law seems very slender. There is room for serious doubt whether the fundamental laws of mechanics hold good for single atoms and it seems quite likely that they are capable of motion in more than three dimensions" (Peirce and Wiener, 1966, 147).

Max Planck would explain that very complicated nature of light a decade later. Bohr would develop the Copenhagen interpretation three decades later to reconcile the nonmechanical character of the electron. Several decades after that, John Stewart Bell would provide experimental evidence in the debate over entanglement and nonlocality, that is, Peirce's atomic behavior outside the third dimension. What is most important about Peirce's ability to extrapolate many of the major problems of quantum theory from the simple observation of experimental data in the late nineteenth century is the philosophical position inspired by all that "spooky" data. Contrary to the constructivist position of philosophers of science like Thomas Kuhn, who see changes in laws as paradigm shifts, Peirce tried to account for the very nature of change in nature. According to Peirce, the indeterminacy of things, the weirdness at the margins of physics, was not just a problem of scientific progress. For Peirce, reality is not sitting around waiting for a better hypothesis to gain hegemony. Instead, Peirce argues, "the only possible way of accounting for the laws of nature and for uniformity in general is to suppose them results of evolution. This supposes them not to be absolute, not to be obeyed precisely. It makes an element of indeterminacy, spontaneity, or absolute chance in nature" (Peirce and Wiener, 1966: 148).

Like Bergson and soon after James's 1909 coining of the multiverse in his Pluralistic Universe lectures (Rubenstein, 2015: 3), Peirce was building a relational ontology of things, where the very *laws* of matter are themselves subject to change at the margins due to the interaction of things over time. James and Peirce were not alone. French sociologist Gabriel Tarde joins this crowd, writing in 1899:

> The mysterious basement of the phenomenal world may be quite as rich in differences, though differences of another sort, as the upper stories of visible,

superficial reality.... Something far more important than a mere increase of difference is constantly taking place, namely the differentiations of the differences
themselves. The process of change is itself undergoing a change. (Tarde, 2013)

The idea that change changes resonates with the later findings of quantum theory
of the more adventurous of physicists such as Bohr and Heisenberg. However,
it is the more radical ontological claim about the status of "laws," rather than
the more moderate claim of Bohr and Heisenberg about the epistemological
status of laws, that gives these thinkers the opening to productively question the
Newtonian universe decades before experiments could be designed to do so.
Insofar as a kind of intuition must always precede even the most experimental
of experiments, the intuition of Bohr and others thrived for decades in the pluralistic cosmologies of relational thinkers like Peirce, James, Bergson, and Tarde.
And, according to Weiner, these thinkers continued to exert an influence as the
disruptive waves of quantum physics found their way into other fields and areas
of application, such as biology and chemistry, and new integrative fields, such as
systems theory and ecology.

From Forerunners to Interlocutors

The insights of Peirce, James, Bergson, and Tarde were not lost on quantum
researchers. This is not a story where two ships pass in the night in pursuit of
the same destination, never to know the other is there. The next generation of
relational thinkers, as well as Bergson himself, continued to engage with science,
including many of the scientists involved in the break from classical to quantum
physics. Bergson debated Einstein publicly on relativity.[4] While many declared
Einstein the winner, the advances made following the Bergsonian line of thinking
in cybernetics and chemistry suggest otherwise. Chemist Ilya Prigogine in particular repeated a similar debate with Einstein, resulting in a Nobel Prize and
the outline of a time-dependent complexity theory that underwrites everything
from climate models to dynamical systems theory. Theorized and then demonstrated by Prigogine, contra Einstein, time is far from an illusion. The entirety of
chemistry and life depends on a real arrow of time rather than a "symmetrical"
and "reversible" view of time at the heart of both classical and much of quantum
physics (Prigogine and Stengers, 1997). From Prigogine's perspective, Bergson
was not too radical in his dualistic position of mechanical time and experienced
time—he was not radical enough. The real of time, an evolution in matter itself, is
at the heart of nature according to Prigogine.

Again, though, we did not have to wait for Prigogine to correct the dualism lingering in Bergson's theory of matter and memory. Whitehead, who also directly

engaged Einstein and quantum physics in his 1922 book *The Principle of Relativity*, took on a fully monist approach inspired by James, an approach very similar to that of Peirce and Tarde. Rather than a parallelist account of matter and experience, Whitehead described the dual nature of things as dipolar: two aspects of one substance. Much like a magnet can have two opposing forces, positive and negative, in one object, so can matter have conscious and nonconscious properties. Also, somewhat opposite of Bergson's more caustic challenge to quantum physics, Whitehead saw the quantum revolution as the agent provocateur that awoke him from the dogmatic slumber of rationalism.[5] According to Whitehead:

> When I went up to Cambridge early in the 1880s...nearly everything was supposed to be known about physics....By 1900 the Newtonian physics were demolished....I have been fooled once [by the claim of certainty] and I am damned if I will be fooled again....There is no more reason to think that Einstein's relativity is final than Newton's *Principia*. The danger is dogmatic thought.[6] (Whitehead and Price, 2001: 314)

Despite being inspired by relativity, Whitehead, like Bergson, found physics insufficient for the pursuit of larger existential and cosmological questions particularly related to how creativity, change, and complexity enter the world. In Whitehead's words:

> A way of life is something more than the shifting relations of bits of matter in space and in time. Life depends upon such external fact. The all-important aesthetic arises out of them, and is deflected by them. But, in abstraction from the atmosphere of feeling, one behavior pattern is as good as another; and they are all equally uninteresting. (Whitehead, 1947: 15)

Whitehead's version of relativity and subjectivism was not "pixilated," as some commentators have described Einstein's and Planck's quantum view of the world (Crease and Goldharber, 2014). For Whitehead there is no discreetness between objects, nor a smallest possible unit or instant, meaning no quanta. Whitehead emphasized the significance of wholes rather than parts all the way up and down. Change occurs not in the accumulation of bits. Rather, the world emerges as a process, or what philosophers beginning with Heraclitus call becoming. The emphasis on process and the rhythm rather than the physicalist composition of that process allows Whitehead to be a monist without falling into the strict contingency of a mechanical universe. This is to say that quantum physics may be able to account for the substance of life, but everything we call interesting about life is actually an aesthetic domain of intensity, movement, and rhythm, and not simple extension.

Heisenberg comes to a very similar conclusion about the limits of scientific thinking:

> The hope of understanding all aspects of intellectual life on the principles of physics is no more justified than the hope of the traveler who believes he will have obtained the answers to all problems once he has journeyed to the end of the world. (Heisenberg, 1979: 24)

According to Bergson, the false assumption identified by Heisenberg is not rare but instead a deeply ingrained habit of mind in the dominant strands of Western thought. These assumptions are baked into language and the common pursuit of scientific research. According to Bergson we often fall into the trap of presuming that every question can be attacked by breaking up things into the smallest component part:

> But it may be asked whether the insurmountable difficulties presented by certain philosophical problems do not arise from our placing side by side in space phenomena which do not occupy space, and whether, by merely getting rid of the clumsy symbols round which we are fighting, we might not bring the fight to an end. When an illegitimate translation of the unextended into the extended, of quality into quantity, has introduced contradiction into the very heart of the question, contradiction must, of course, recur in the answer. (Bergson, 2001: 3–4)

So, we can journey to the end of the material world, as Heisenberg says, meaning we can know the quantum characteristics of it, but the ontic enclosure, knowing every detail down to the smallest unit, does not get us any closer to any of the problems of meaning making that are emergent from it. Beyond calling into question the tendency of breaking things into pieces to make them simpler to understand, one that is as strong in the social sciences as it is in the natural sciences, we should also consider how this interchange between physics and philosophy demonstrates the movement of thought itself. Neither the physicists nor the philosophers moved in a straight line from questions to answer.

Therefore, the fear that physics could replace or colonize the social sciences seems unfounded. It is not like we can work out all of the quantum problems and then suddenly discover the secrets of the social order. If we follow the way questions migrated from philosophy to physics and back again, then we should allow things like the quantum crisis in physics, or the crisis of scale in Whitehead, or the crisis of extension and intension in Bergson to change our orientation without a fear of finality. And we should be particularly open to these external provocations when we encounter things like tsunamis, which we cannot predict, and world-changing events that we cannot make sense of, like Donald Trump or hurricanes that change the outcome of elections. After the provocation, we work our way back out through the problems raised rather than forward with a new theory to test.

Despite how much this description of thinking contradicts the hypothesis testing we presume is at the heart of science, I think this is also a more accurate picture of what inspired Bohr and Heisenberg. They did not start with a mountain of data and inductively come to the Copenhagen interpretation or the uncertainty principle. Like many other Europeans at the time, they were versed in the whole history of philosophy, from which they drew a rich mix of intuition, inspiration, and speculation to seek out new kinds of data. Schrödinger's book *Nature and the Greeks* (2014) is a prime example of this kind of "extracurricular" study. So are Bohr's and Heisenberg's frequent references to the inspiration of Democritus and Lucretius in their revisiting of the seemingly settled principles of classical physics (Bohr, 2010; Heisenberg, 1979).[7]

From Quantum Philosophy to Quantum Social Theory

John Dewey and Arthur Bentley came to quantum physics after they had developed their initial theory of transactionalism in their 1949 book *Knowing and the Known*. Their inspiration came mostly from Maxwell's *Matter and Motion* for developing a method of inquiry that could take into account the exchange between rather than the mutual absorption of "structure of knowings" and the "physical cosmos" (Dewey and Bentley, 1949: 310). For Dewey and Bentley, Maxwell and Faraday and their initial understandings of Einstein gave them the ability to make generalizations about how knowledge functioned without violating the principles of how we understand the physical world. However, Dewey and Bentley would go on to find that Einstein was insufficient to the epistemological and ontological challenges of establishing knowledge as something simultaneously irreducible to mechanics and yet not in violation of it.

This is a thoroughly monist position without, as Alexander Wendt often says, a world of zombies (Wendt, 2015: 153). In a letter to Bentley dated December 27, 1949, Dewey is critical of Einstein's seeming lack of attention to the transaction between the knower and the known. Concluding the letter, Dewey says of Einstein, with a marked sense of disappointment, "he is fundamentally a Kantian" (Dewey et al., 1964: 614–615). Dewey's reading of Einstein is confirmed in Einstein's later writings. Published a year after Dewey and Bentley's correspondence, Einstein says in one of his late essays titled "Time, Space, and Gravitation," that he believes Kant's greatest achievement is positing that there must be an a priori internal schema for ordering the sense data of the external world. Like Kant, Einstein writes, speaking about the external world, "The fact that it [the world] is comprehensible is a miracle" (Einstein, 1950: 61).

Several months later in another letter to Bentley dated May 22, 1950, Dewey makes a sharp contrast between Einstein's Kantianism and Bohr's understanding of the role of the investigator and the apparatus in the making of reality. According to Dewey, unlike Einstein, in Bohr, there is a "recognition of the transactional property of experiment" (Dewey et al, 1964: 631) The subsequent six letters over the next two months concern primarily what Bentley and Dewey can learn and contrast between Bohr and Heisenberg's understandings of uncertainty. What they arrive at is a kind of resonance but not precise overlap between what Bohr refers to as "the individual and his surroundings" and what Dewey and Bentley call the "transactional connection of organism-environing media" (Bentley, 1964: 633). Heisenberg's own philosophical writings confirm this kinship. For Heisenberg, the insights of quantum physics are so out of sync with previous understandings of reality that they invalidate the very idea that the limits of knowledge can in some sense be specified a priori before investigation, which is the entire project of Kant's *Critique of Pure Reason*. Using the example of Wilson's cloud chamber experiments, Heisenberg points out that scientists felt comfortable describing what they saw as the path of an electron. That description, according to Heisenberg, was not at all a problem until there was new seemingly contradictory experimental data. Heisenberg's point is that there is no "a priori criterion" for fixing the language of Wilson's experiment before the subsequent quantum data came in. Instead, the rules of what could be known and what was known changed because our experience of the world changed, and not simply our thinking (Heisenberg, 1979: 45–46). To put it differently, the world changed thought. This is an impossible event within the Kantian schema of human consciousness.

For Kant, and much of philosophy after *The Critique of Pure Reason*, the structure of understanding must already be contained within the two schemas of space and time for possible experience. According to Kant, "These rules for understanding are not only true a priori but are rather every source of all truth, i.e., of the agreement of our cognition with objects, in virtue of containing the ground of the possibility of experience, as the sum total of all cognition in which objects may be given to us" (Kant et al., 2009: 339–340). Therefore, for Kant, datum should not be able to alter the boundaries of the thinkable. Rather, the thinkable ought to be the boundaries of what datum can be experienced. Heisenberg posits that the findings of quantum theory suggest that we need now "a sufficiently thorough" philosophical investigation of Kant's premises given the "new outlook" (Heisenberg, 1979: 21). Unlike physicists such as Stephen Hawking or at times Einstein who declared that physics makes philosophy obsolete, Heisenberg sees quantum findings as a reason to start philosophical inquiry anew. However, like many of the other relational thinkers such as James, he cautions against assuming that any new philosophical positions will be anything other than provisional.

Conclusion

The position developed in this chapter, built on the insights of the relational revolutions in philosophy and the quantum revolutions in physics, contains claims to how the empiricism of the real world works. Therefore, the opposition to this position cannot be the complaint that it is inconvenient or that one *prefers* the other world any more than one can complain about gravity when designing an airplane. Unlike poststructuralism or other hermeneutic approaches, this is not an argument for how to interpret the world. It is a claim about the world as such, that is, conditions of possibility for interpreting. As for how we should approach such a world, a world made out of matters of concern lends itself quite well to the idea that theory is a task rather than a riddle to be solved. This is easier said than done, but what else is there to do but begin here where we are.

Bohr provides a good example of what such a research ethos could look like. As is evident by his extensive collections of talks and philosophical writings, Bohr was frequently asked to speak at gatherings of nonphysicists. Whether to biologists, to humanists, or to philosophers, Bohr began almost all of his talks with the words "It is only with great hesitation..." (Bohr, 2010: 23). The modesty of Bohr's beginning was joined by the strength of his conviction that his quantum findings suggested the necessity to reconsider the common sense of everything, from biology to philosophy. That conviction was earned through experimental research, but it was first and foremost what Bergson called an intuition.

This showing or presentation of philosophical problems rather than proofs of philosophical answers is much closer to the style of Bohr's philosophical writings as well as his speeches to nonphysicists. In one such moment in his 1937 essay, "Biology and Atomic Physics," Bohr celebrates the way Einstein's theory of relativity opened up thinking to consider the nature of reality in ways that were in Bohr's words "unprecedented" (Bohr, 2010: 18). However, Bohr, goes on to warn against accepting Einstein's confidence that we can distinguish easily between the observer and the observed, and warns further against trying to graft this confidence onto the biological and social world as Einstein's position rests on the assumption of the regularity of the behavior of the material world. Instead, Bohr suggests the way in which the crisis of quantum research itself is analogous to other kinds of crises of other fields. Bohr writes:

For a parallel to the lesson of atomic theory regarding the limited applicability of such customary idealisations, we must in fact turn to quite other branches of science such as psychology, or even to the kind of epistemological problems with which already thinkers like Buddha and Lao Tse have been confronted, when trying to harmonize our position as spectators and actors in the great dram of existence. Still, the recognition of an analogy in the purely logical character of the problems which present themselves in so widely separated fields of human interest does in no way imply acceptance in atomic physics of any mysticism foreign to the true spirit of science, but on the contrary it gives us an incitation to examine whether the straightforward solution of the unexpected paradoxes met with in the application of our simplest concepts to atomic phenomena might not help us to clarify conceptual difficulties in other domains of experience. (Bohr, 2010: 20)

Bohr is not using quantum theory here as a metaphor, nor is he trying to colonize the other fields with a kind of final scientific explanation. Instead, he is horizontalizing the endeavors of philosophy, the social sciences, and even religion as pursuits of a more general set of problems that are similarly inspiring to physics and may benefit from the ways physicists came to deal conceptually with problems at odds with accepted logic. In this way, for Bohr, the value of his research for nonphysicists was showing how quantum research questioned common-sense understandings of even the most basic assumption of reality rather than physics providing a new foundation on which other modes of inquiry could stand. What Bohr is referring to as "incitation" is in the same conceptual neighborhood as what Bergson called intuition or an "intellectual sympathy" by which one places oneself within an object in order to coincide with what is unique in it and consequently inexpressible.

Bergson, Tarde, Peirce, and James, later joined by Dewey, Whitehead, and Bentley, all saw intuition as a vital philosophical tool. Intuition is always employed whether we like it not. And yet intuition is often seen as a kind of methodological sin. We hide our intuitions rather than expose them to contestation and the pursuit of others. What I think Bohr, Heisenberg, and the relational philosophers who preceded and then joined them have to offer—rather than a quantum theory of International Relations—is an inclination for speculative thinking inspired by the world rather than limited by a desire for how we wished the world worked. If this is what the "Q effect" is on International Relations, then the fear of science envy, the colonization by science, and the risk of metaphoric appropriation seem unfounded, unlikely, and untimely.

Almost twenty years ago a number of critically inclined International Relations theorists published an article entitled "God Gave Physics the Easy Questions" (Bernstein et al., 2000). The article is meant to strike a blow against scientism by showing how distinct the social sciences are from the "hard" sciences. In some sense, the authors hoped to widen the disciplinary gap between the social and natural world. However, the long dialogue from Bergson to Bell suggests there are no easy problems, and that the territorial dispute between humanistic theory and scientific inquiry is a recent and far-from-inevitable problem of contemporary scholarship. The world in which scholars like Bergson and Einstein debated is only a few generations removed and certainly not impossible to reclaim. The only requirement is that we all agree that it is the whole world and everything in it that is up for debate. James called this radical empiricism. Contemporary thinkers like Brain Massumi have called it extreme realism. The name matters less than the insight James made more than one hundred years ago:

> It is difficult not to notice a curious unrest in the philosophical atmosphere of the time, a loosening of old landmarks, a softening of oppositions, a mutual borrowing from one another on the part of systems anciently closed, and an interest in new suggestions, however pale, as if the one thing sure were the inadequacy of the extant school-solutions. The dissatisfaction with these seems due for the most part to a feeling that they are too abstract and academic. Life is confused and superabundant, and what the younger generation appears to crave is more of the temperament of life in its philosophy, even though it were at some cost of logical rigor and of formal purity. (James, 2003)

Notes

1. This chapter is just one possible quantum story that I believe relaxes the deadlock of the debates enumerated earlier. Along the way I have repeatedly asked the question that Kathy Ferguson always reminds me to ask: "where are the women?" I have spent significant time trying to find them and my only conclusion is that they have been erased from the conversations of this generation. One notable exception is in the transcripts of Alfred North Whitehead where "Mrs. Whitehead" appears frequently as a philosophical interlocutor but not in any of the conversations about physics that I could find. I do not believe the search to be a lost cause, only my failure, for now.

2. I use the term "relational philosophies" because the thinkers outlined here do not lend themselves to a school. There was certainly a longstanding dialogue between all of them crossing oceans and generations. However, it would not be accurate to call them all pragmatists as that would really only cover James, Dewey, and maybe Peirce. Similarly, regional terms like "Continental" or "Anglo-American" also are simultaneously too big and too small. What unifies all of these thinkers is the effort to break out of what Tristan Garcia has called Kant's "metaphysics of access" where philosophy is circumscribed to the question of how we access the world rather than what is in the world—including ourselves (Garcia et al., 2014).

3. In strict philosophical terms Bergson is really a parallelist very close, I think, to Spinoza. However, given the anemic categories of materialism and idealism that dominate contemporary International Relations, Bergson gets to hang out with the Monists and is in many ways much closer to thinkers like James and Peirce than the neo-Kantian thought of International Relations constructivists.

4. For an extensive engagement with the terms and outcome of the debate see Canales (2015).

5. It is worth noting that Whitehead's thinking and its emphasis on process and the evolution of laws had a tremendous impact on many of the scientific theories of the twentieth century including Stephen Jay Gould's major renovations of Darwin and Gregory Bateson as well as scientists like Prigogine, Lynn Margulis, Stuart Kauffman, and Brian Goodwin (Prigogine and Stengers, 1997; Sagan and Margulis, 2003; Kauffman, 1993; Gould, 2002; Goodwin, 2001)

6. I discovered this quote in William Connolly's forthcoming essay "The Lure of Truth."

7. Rubenstein's history exhaustively substantiates the long conversation between philosophy and physics well beyond what can be addressed in this article (2014).

Bibliography

Alker, Hayward R. "The Powers and Pathologies of Networks: Insights from the Political Cybernetics of Karl W. Deutsch and Norbert Wiener 1." *European Journal of International Relations* 17, no. 2 (June 2011): 351–351.

Barad, Karen Michelle. *Meeting the Universe Halfway: Quantum Physics and the Entanglement of Matter and Meaning.* Durham, NC: Duke University Press, 2007.

Bashir, Samiya A. *Field Theories.* Brooklyn, NY: Nightboat Books, 2017.

Bennett, Jane. *Influx and Efflux: Writing Up with Walt Whitman.* Durham, NC: Duke University Press, 2020.

Bennett, Jane. *Vibrant Matter: A Political Ecology of Things.* Durham, NC: Duke University Press, 2010.

Bentley, A. F. *Inquiry into Inquiries: Essays in Social Theory.* Classic Reprint. Fb&c Limited, 2017. https://books.google.com/books?id=275KtAEACAAJ.

Bergson, H., and T. E. Hulme. *An Introduction to Metaphysics.* New York, New York: G. P. Putnam's Sons, 1912. https://books.google.com/books?id=D24YAAAAIAAJ.

Bergson, Henri. *Creative Evolution.* Mineola, NY: Dover, 1998.

Bergson, Henri. *Matter and Memory.* New York: Zone Books, 1988.

Bergson, Henri. *Time and Free Will: An Essay on the Immediate Data of Consciousness.* Mineola, NY: Dover Publications, 2001.

Bernstein, Steven, Richard Ned Lebow, Janice Gross Stein, and Steven Weber. "God Gave Physics the Easy Problems: Adapting Social Science to an Unpredictable World." *European Journal of International Relations* 6, no. 1 (March 2000): 43–76. https://doi.org/10.1177/1354066100006001003.

Bersani, Leo, and Ulysse Dutoit. *Forms of Being: Cinema, Aesthetics, Subjectivity.* London: BFI, 2010.

Bohm, David, and Basil J. Hiley. *The Undivided Universe: An Ontological Interpretation of Quantum Theory.* Reprint. London: Routledge, 1996.

Bohr, Niels. *Atomic Physics and Human Knowledge.* Dover Books on Physics. Mineola, NY: Dover Publications, 2010.

Bohr, Niels. *Atomic Theory and the Description of Nature.* The Philosophical Writings of Niels Bohr. Vol. 1. Woodbridge, CT: Ox Bow Press, 1987.

Bohr, Niels, Jan Faye, and Henry J. Folse. *Causality and Complementarity: Supplementary Papers.* The Philosophical Writings of Niels Bohr. Vol. 4. Woodbridge, CT: Ox Bow Press, 1998.

Bousquet, Antoine, Jairus Grove, and Nisha Shah. "Becoming War: Towards a Martial Empiricism." *Security Dialogue* 51, nos. 2–3 (April 2020): 99–118. https://doi.org/10.1177/0967010619895660.

Canales, Jimena. *The Physicist & the Philosopher: Einstein, Bergson, and the Debate That Changed Our Understanding of Time.* Princeton, NJ; Oxford: Princeton University Press, 2015.

Cavell, Stanley. *This New yet Unapproachable America: Lectures after Emerson after Wittgenstein.* University of Chicago Press ed. Frederick Ives Carpenter Lectures 1987. Chicago: University of Chicago Press, 2013.

Charbonnier, Pierre, ed. *Comparative Metaphysics: Ontology after Anthropology.* Reinventing Critical Theory. Lanham, MD: Rowman & Littlefield International, 2016.

Connolly, William E. *Facing the Planetary: Entangled Humanism and the Politics of Swarming.* Durham, NC: Duke University Press, 2017.

Connolly, William E. *Climate Machines, Fascist Drives, and Truth.* Durham, NC: Duke University Press, 2019.

Crease, Robert P., and Alfred S. Goldhaber. *The Quantum Moment: How Planck, Bohr, Einstein, and Heisenberg Taught Us to Love Uncertainty.* 1st ed. New York: W. W. Norton & Company, 2014.

De Castro, Eduardo Viveiros. *Cannibal Metaphysics.* Minneapolis: University of Minnesota Press, 2017.

Der Derian, James. "From War 2.0 to Quantum War: The Superpositionality of Global Violence." *Australian Journal of International Affairs* 67, no. 5 (November 2013): 570–585. https://doi.org/10.1080/10357718.2013.822465.

Deutsch, K. W. *The Nerves of Government: Models of Political Communication and Control.* New York: Free Press, 1974. https://books.google.com/books?id=_1e9tgEACAAJ.

Dewey, J., and A. F. Bentley. *Knowing and the Known.* Boston, MA: Beacon Press, 1960. https://books.google.com/books?id=nijXAAAAMAAJ.

Dewey, J., A. F. Bentley, S. Ratner, and J. Altman. *John Dewey and Arthur F. Bentley: A Philosophical Correspondence, 1932–1951.* Newark, NJ: Rutgers University Press, 1964. https://books.google.com/books?id=DVRAAAAIAAJ.

Easton, David. *A Systems Analysis of Political Life.* New York: Wiley, 1965.

Einstein, Albert. *Out of My Later Years: The Scientist, Philosopher, and Man Portrayed through His Own Words.* New York: Philosophical Library/Open Road, 2015.

Einstein, Albert, Hanoch Gutfreund, and Jürgen Renn. *Relativity: The Special & the General Theory.* 100th anniversary ed. Princeton, NJ: Princeton University Press, 2015.

Garcia, Tristan, Mark Allan Ohm, and Jon Cogburn. *Form and Object: A Treatise on Things.* Speculative Realism. Edinburgh: Edinburgh University Press, 2014.

Goodwin, Brian C. *How the Leopard Changed Its Spots: The Evolution of Complexity.* Princeton ed., with new preface. Princeton Science Library. Princeton, NJ: Princeton University Press, 2001.

Gould, Stephen Jay. *The Structure of Evolutionary Theory.* Cambridge, MA: Belknap Press of Harvard University Press, 2002.

Heisenberg, Werner. *Philosophical Problems of Quantum Physics.* Woodbridge, CT: Ox Bow Press, 1979.

Henning, Brian G., and Adam Christian Scarfe, eds. *Beyond Mechanism: Putting Life Back into Biology*. Lanham, MD: Lexington Books, 2013.

James, William. *Essays in Radical Empiricism*. Mineola, NY: Dover Publications, 2003.

James, William. *A Pluralistic Universe: Hibbert Lectures at Manchester College on the Present Situation in Philosophy*. Lincoln: University of Nebraska Press, 1996.

Jerome, Fred, and Rodger Taylor. *Einstein on Race and Racism*. New Brunswick, NJ: Rutgers University Press, 2006.

Kant, Immanuel, Paul Guyer, and Allen W. Wood. *Critique of Pure Reason*. 15. print. The Cambridge Edition of the Works of Immanuel Kant, general ed.: Paul Guyer and Allen W. Wood[...]. Cambridge: Cambridge University Press, 2009.

Kauffman, Stuart A. *The Origins of Order: Self-Organization and Selection in Evolution*. New York: Oxford University Press, 1993.

Margulis, Lynn, and Dorion Sagan. *Acquiring Genomes: A Theory of the Origin of Species*. London, England: Basic Books, 2003.

Maxwell, James. *The Scientific Papers of James Clerk Maxwell 2 Volume Paperback Set the Scientific Papers of James Clerk Maxwell: Volume 1*. Ed. W. D. Niven. Cambridge: Cambridge University Press, 2011.

Peirce, Charles S., and Philip P. Wiener. *Selected Writings: Values in a Universe of Chance*. New York: Dover, 1966.

Phillips, Rasheedah. *Black Quantum Futurism: Theory and Practice*. Vol. 1. Philadelphia, Pennsylvania: Afrofuturist Affair, 2015.

Prigogine, I., and Isabelle Stengers. *The End of Certainty: Time, Chaos, and the New Laws of Nature*. 1st Free Press ed. New York: Free Press, 1997.

Prigogine, Ilya, Isabelle Stengers, and Alvin Toffler. *Order out of Chaos: Man's New Dialogue with Nature*. New York, New York: Bantam Books, 1984.

Rubenstein, Mary-Jane. *Worlds without End: The Many Lives of the Multiverse...in Which Are Discussed Pre-, Early-, and Postmodern Multiple-Worlds Cosmologies: The Sundry Arguments for and against Them: The Striking Peculiarities of Their Adherents and Detractors: The Shifting Boundaries of Science, Philosophy, and Religion: And the Stubbornly Persistent Question of Whether Creation Has Been "Designed."* New York: Columbia University Press, 2014.

Schrödinger, Erwin. *Nature and the Greeks: And Science and Humanism*. Canto Classics ed. Cambridge: Cambridge University Press, 2014.

Shaviro, Steven. *The Universe of Things: On Speculative Realism*. Posthumanities 30. Minneapolis: University of Minnesota Press, 2014.

Sprout, Harold Hance. *Ecological Perspective on Human Affairs*. Princeton, NJ: Princeton University Press, 2015.

Sprout, Harold, and Margaret Sprout. *Toward a Politics of the Planet Earth*. Impression. New York: Van Nostrand Company, 1973.

Strawson, Galen, and Anthony Freeman, eds. *Consciousness and Its Place in Nature: Does Physicalism Entail Panpsychism?* Exeter, UK; Charlottesville, VA: Imprint Academic, 2006.

Tarde, G. *Social Laws—An Outline of Sociology*. Read Books, 2013. http://www.myilibrary.com?id=891665.

Tarde, Gabriel de, and Theo Lorenc. *Monadology and Sociology*. 2012.

Tonkonoff, Sergio. "A New Social Physic: The Sociology of Gabriel Tarde and Its Legacy." *Current Sociology* 61, no. 3 (May 2013): 267–282. https://doi.org/10.1177/001139211 3477578.

Wendt, Alexander. *Quantum Mind and Social Science: Unifying Physical and Social Ontology*. Cambridge; New York: Cambridge University Press, 2015.

Whitehead, A. N. *An Enquiry Concerning the Principles of Natural Knowledge*. Oxford, UK University Press, 1919. https://books.google.com/books?id=QBhWAAAAMAAJ.

Whitehead, A. N. *Essays in Science and Philosophy*. Vol. 72. Philosophical Library, 1947. https://books.google.com/books?id=5YXCtwEACAAJ.

Whitehead, A. N. *The Principle of Relativity with Applications to Physical Science*. Creative Media Partners, 2015. https://books.google.com/books?id=g5Y4AAAAIAAJ.

Whitehead, Alfred North. *Science and the Modern World: Lowell Lectures, 1925*. New York: Free Press, 1997.

Whitehead, Alfred North, David Ray Griffin, and Donald W. Sherburne. *Process and Reality: An Essay in Cosmology: Gifford Lectures Delivered in the University of Edinburgh during the Session 1927-28*. Corr. ed., 1st Free Press paperback ed. New York: Free Press, 1985.

Whitehead, Alfred North, and Lucien Price. *Dialogues of Alfred North Whitehead*. 1st ed. A Nonpareil Book. Boston: David R. Godine, 2001.

Wiener, Norbert. *Cybernetics or Control and Communication in the Animal and the Machine*. 2nd ed., 10. print. Cambridge, MA: MIT Press, 2000.

Wittgenstein, Ludwig, and G. E. M. Anscombe. *Philosophical Investigations: The German Text, with a Revised English Translation*. 3rd ed. Malden, MA: Blackwell Publishing, 2003.

Wittgenstein, Ludwig, and Georg Henrik von Wright. *Culture and Value*. Chicago: Chicago University Press, 2006.

5

A Conceptual Introduction
to Quantum Theory

Michael Schnabel

Introduction

Quantum mechanics, although mathematically very well understood, remains difficult to wrap one's mind around. Our common sense and intuition mainly apply to the way macroscopic objects behave on an everyday basis. This behavior is well captured and formalized by classical physics. Yet, experimental evidence leaves us no other choice but to accept that the "operating system" of the world ultimately is quantum, not classical [1, 2]. The quantum aspects of matter were first observed at the beginning of the twentieth century by examining the properties of matter on atomic and subatomic scales. These experiments revealed that matter at such small scales behaves very differently than in the macro-world: quantum particles only manifest their particle nature when explicitly "asked" to do so within an experimental setup. When not, that is, when not being watched too closely, they morph into an "imaginary probability-wave" that allows them to do strange things, such as seemingly passing through two separate slits at the same time, interfering with themselves, and recombining behind the slit when "asked," once again, to behave as a localized particle. Obviously, there is no classical analog for such a behavior, and it is difficult to come by with a proper description using words and language. However, mathematically, this is not a problem: the particle's state, when not observed, is described by a quantum superposition of states at multiple locations that can be geometrically represented as a point in an abstract vector space, just as its "reasonable" cousin manifesting as a localized particle. Hence, when it comes to quantum mechanics, the abstract mathematical description allows us to precisely state what we are talking about and to get a conceptual hold of the quantum objects, despite their apparent weirdness. The same applies to other features characteristic of the quantum world, such as Heisenberg uncertainty, incompatibility of measurements, and entanglement: mathematically relatively easy to conceptualize, but hard to do so in words. Other than sometimes conveyed, the mathematics of quantum mechanics isn't particularly difficult and mostly relies on concepts from linear algebra and group theory. However, the interpretation of the

conceptual framework of quantum mechanics and the implications for our understanding of reality still remain open questions. Here we will adopt the viewpoint of
the Copenhagen interpretation as the most common among the various interpretations that all yield to the same math and thus can be considered equivalent.[1] As
the great variety of interpretations suggests, and as the pioneers of quantum mechanics quickly realized, quantum mechanics has far-reaching implications, first
and foremost regarding the role of the observer, and thus of subjective experience
per se, in shaping reality by the mere act of observing, measuring, or, simply put,
questioning. Therefore, quantum mechanics, although it originated from a careful
analysis of the behavior of matter and particles at very short spatio-temporal scales,
continually returns the question back to us, asking about the role we play as observers, individually but also collectively, when observations are communicated
thereby establishing, confirming, or dismissing aspects of a shared, constructed
reality. This is where quantum theory touches on the cognitive and social domain.
Hence, what at first may look like a stretch, namely to ask for possible implications
of quantum theory on areas other than physics such as cognitive sciences [8–10],
social sciences and International Relations [11, 12], behavioral decision-making
and economics [13–15], finance [16, 17], game theory [18, 19], and even arts [20],
can be seen as a natural development and will be explored in subsequent chapters
of this volume. This chapter will provide an introduction to some key concepts of
quantum theory that will be contrasted with their classical counterparts to point
out where subtle yet pivotal differences arise. We will use basic probability theory
and linear algebra to describe the main concepts, which will be further elaborated
in examples and illustrated by figures, with the hope to help readers less familiar
with the mathematical language see for themselves that quantum theory is fairly
geometrical and mainly boils down to simple operations with vectors, rotations,
and projections. Given the limited space, we won't strive for mathematical rigor or
originality. Most of the material presented here can be found in the referenced literature that the reader is encouraged to consult in more depth on their own. Good
places to start would be [8–10].

Classical Setting

Classically, the world is perceived as made of **matter** and composed of physical
things (mountains and trees, **objects** such as a glass on a table) that can be named
and that may have certain attributes (such as shape, color, weight, temperature,
mass, etc.) by which they can be conceptualized and their properties quantified,
classified, and further analyzed. In such a classical, "naïve realist" setting there
also are **individual agents** with **subjective experience** that may act as **observers**,

move things around, and plan ahead what to have for dinner. Events occupy some region in space and time and occur even when nobody is watching [21]. The same applies to systems, that is, delimited parts of the world (e.g., a pot of water on the stove or the weather in Chicago), whose properties depend on their state, which may change over time. A system's state at time t may correspond to a distinct element in the set of all possibilities

$$x(t) \in \Omega = \{x_1, x_2, ...\}$$

called a sample space Ω. The sample space of a die, for instance, would be written as

$$\Omega = \{1, 2, 3, 4, 5, 6\}.$$

Let's put the die in a shaker and throw it. Classically, it will settle on a number, say $x = 5$. However, before lifting the cup and inspecting the die, the particular outcome is hidden. Our incertitude about the die's state prior to looking can be expressed in terms of a probability distribution, $P(x)$, that consists of real, positive numbers $P(x_i) \geq 0$ that represent the probability of a given outcome x_i. Probabilities of all possible, mutually exclusive outcomes have to add up to 1,

$$\sum_{i=1}^{6} P(x_i) = 1$$

The probability distribution $P(x_i)$ represents our current subjective knowledge (or incertitude) about the system's state and may change over time as new information is accumulated. Right after the throw, the die could be in each of the six possible states, and therefore,

$$P(x_i) = 1/6.$$

After revealing the die's actual state, $x = 5$, the probability distribution is updated to

$$P(x_i) = \begin{cases} 1 & x_i = 5 \\ 0 & x_i \neq 5 \end{cases}$$

and the incertitude is removed. This example can be extended to more complex scenarios such as weather forecasting, where the system's state may be characterized by a combination of multiple attribute dimensions, such as geographical location, temperature, sunniness, windiness, snow levels, etc., and the forecast would consist of a model that makes predictions about the **joint probability** *P(location, T, sun, wind, snow)* of all imaginable combinations. Thus, in a classical setting events are specified by **combinations** of different outcomes and their associated probabilities, where the combinations consist of **operations acting on sets** (as sometimes depicted by **Venn diagrams**), such as union and intersection, and their associated **Boolean logic**. This is the framework of classical probability theory axiomatized by **Kolmogorov** in the 1930s.

Quantum Setting

The mathematical and probabilistic framework of quantum theory is based on **geometrical projections,** which allows an extension of the rules of probability into the realm of negative and complex numbers[2] by means of **probability amplitudes** that are not restricted to positive numbers[3]. As we will see, this extended probabilistic framework comes with intriguing features, such as quantum superposition and quantum interference, that go beyond what would be possible in a classical setting.

To lay out the differences between the two probabilistic frameworks, let's start out classically by considering a very simple example: tossing a coin that can display either Heads (*H*) or Tails (*T*). Classically, the sample space is represented by a set consisting of two elements,

$$\Omega = \{H, T\}.$$

The player's knowledge about the coin's state is described by a probability distribution $P(x)$ that is updated after every toss just as for the die discussed earlier. Let's assume the coin is "unfair," that is, that Heads and Tails occur with probabilities $P(H) = 1/3$ and $P(T) = 2/3$, respectively, and that the player is aware of that. Hence, before revealing the coin's actual state, the player will conceive it as a **(classical) mixture,** analogous to the task of randomly picking a ball from a basket filled with 30 balls, out of which 10 are labeled *H* and 20 labeled *T*. The classical framework corresponds to the common way of thinking about probabilities, and it leads to a consistent formalism that has proven useful wherever statistical modeling is being applied. One may ask whether that is the only way of building a probability theory and it turns out that the answer is no.

The discovery of quantum mechanics at the beginning of the 20th century revealed that a scientific paradigm based on set theory and classical probabilities would only provide an incomplete and therefore unsatisfactory description of

physical phenomena and their states, and suggested to replace that classical picture by a new framework built on **linear algebra** and the **logics of projections
in vector spaces** [24]. The vector space at the core of the quantum probabilistic
framework is called the **Hilbert space**[4] and serves as a "container" that is sufficiently large to represent the various (conceptual) dimensions required to completely characterize a system's state within a given context. The dimensionality
of the Hilbert space can be arbitrary and will depend on the number of mutually exclusive outcomes. For the quantum version of our coin two dimensions
will be sufficient, as there are just two mutually exclusive outcomes. The coin's
(quantum) state is represented by a vector Ψ, whose length (or norm) is 1, that
is, $\|\Psi\| = 1$. In our two-dimensional example a state may be written as a vector

$$\Psi = \begin{pmatrix} x \\ y \end{pmatrix}$$

with numbers[5] $x, y \in \mathbb{R}$ that satisfy the constraint

$$\|\Psi\| = \sqrt{x^2 + y^2} = 1$$

imposed by the normalization. Therefore, in two dimensions, vectors that
qualify as states describe a unit circle with radius 1 (as shown in Figure 5.1a). As
we will see later, the normalization ensures that the probabilities for all possible
outcomes properly sum up to 1. What defines a state (and all its properties) is the
orientation of Ψ, but *not* its direction.[6]

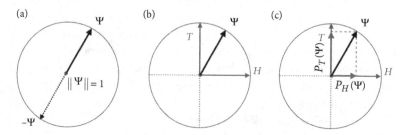

Figure 5.1 (a) A quantum state Ψ is represented by a vector of length 1 in the
Hilbert space. States that differ by a sign (or complex phase) such as Ψ and $-\Psi$
represent the same state. (b) The eigenstates of observables (here H and T) define an
orthogonal basis of the Hilbert space. (c) The probability of observing H depends
on the projection $P_H(\Psi)$ of the state Ψ onto the axis defined by H as described by
Born's rule.

Hence, Ψ and its antipode $-\Psi$ (dotted in Figure 5.1a) are considered equivalent representations of the *same* quantum state.

In quantum theory, inquiring about a system's state can only be achieved via **measurements**. Mathematically, measurements are represented by **observables** that serve as an "interface" to access and probe the quantum state Ψ. An observable can be compared to a multiple-choice test that comes with a complete list of possible answers to a specific question. The observable "Which side of the coin is facing up?" has two possible answers, H and T, that are mutually exclusive. Geometrically, **mutually exclusive outcomes** are represented by **orthogonal axes** in the Hilbert space. This is illustrated in Figure 5.1b. The axes are specified by the observable's **eigenstates**, which in our example are chosen as follows:

$$H = \begin{pmatrix} 1 \\ 0 \end{pmatrix} \text{ and } T = \begin{pmatrix} 0 \\ 1 \end{pmatrix}.$$

Here, H is represented by the horizontal axis and T by the vertical axis. Therefore, the distinct cases $\Psi = H$ and $\Psi = -H$ both represent a coin that displays "Heads," and $\Psi = T$ and $\Psi = -T$ a coin that displays "Tails."

Upon performing a measurement and determining its outcome, the state Ψ "collapses" onto either T or H.[7] Each of the possible outcomes has a certain probability of being observed that is specified by **Born's rule** described a bit further later. However, apart from these probabilities, it is not possible to tell in advance which one of the possible outcomes will manifest; the selection is essentially probabilistic.[8] The updated state (after the measurement) then consists of either

$$\Psi = T \quad \text{or} \quad \Psi = H;$$

that is, the new state *becomes* the observed result. In the absence of an intrinsic dynamics (which we will discuss later), subsequent measurements of the *same* observable will always return the *same* outcome; that is, remeasuring a state $\Psi = T$ will again yield T.

The observable's eigenstates, H and T, are orthogonal to each other and form a **basis** of the two-dimensional space, which means that any vector (and therefore also any state Ψ) can be written as a **linear superposition** of H and T,

$$\begin{pmatrix} x \\ y \end{pmatrix} = x \cdot \begin{pmatrix} 1 \\ 0 \end{pmatrix} + y \cdot \begin{pmatrix} 0 \\ 1 \end{pmatrix} = x \cdot H + y \cdot T$$

that we will also refer to as **quantum superposition**. A "quantum coin" described by a quantum superposition

$$\Psi = x \cdot H + y \cdot T \qquad (5.1)$$

expresses the **potentiality** of Ψ to manifest as either H or T in a subsequent measurement. According to the formalism of quantum theory, the possible outcomes, here H and T, will occur with probability $P(H|\Psi)$ and $P(T|\Psi)$, which can be calculated from Ψ via **Born's rule**. In short, Born's rule simply states that

$$P(H|\Psi) = |x|^2 \text{ and } P(T|\Psi) = |y|^2. \qquad (5.2)$$

Since the coefficients x and y can also be negative, they cannot possibly represent probabilities themselves. Born's rule prescribes how to turn them into probabilities by taking the absolute value and squaring. The coefficients x and y in a quantum superposition are also called **probability amplitudes**. The probabilities properly sum up to 1,

$$P(H|\Psi) + P(T|\Psi) = x^2 + y^2 = 1,$$

as a consequence of the normalization of quantum states.

Expressed geometrically, Born's rule is saying that the probability of observing a given outcome, such as H, when performing a measurement on a quantum state Ψ is obtained by **projecting** the vector Ψ onto the axis representing H,

$$P(H|\Psi) + P(T|\Psi) = x^2 + y^2 = 1,$$

which returns a vector pointing parallel to H as shown in Figure 5.1c and then calculating the squared length of that projection, $\|P_H(\Psi)\|^2 = |x|^2$, to arrive at the same result for the probability $P(H|\Psi) = |x|^2$, stated earlier.

A quantum version of the unfair coin in the example above would read

$$\Psi^{(1)} = \sqrt{1/3} \cdot H + \sqrt{2/3} \cdot T$$

or its antipode

$$\Psi^{(2)} = -\Psi^{(1)} = -\sqrt{1/3} \cdot H - \sqrt{2/3} \cdot T.$$

Besides these two possibilities there also is

$$\Psi^{(3)} = \sqrt{1/3} \cdot H - \sqrt{2/3} \cdot T$$

and its antipode

$$\Psi^{(4)} = -\Psi^{(3)} = -\sqrt{1/3} \cdot H + \sqrt{2/3} \cdot T$$

that all result in[9]

$$P(H \mid \Psi) = 1/3 \text{ and } P(T \mid \Psi) = 2/3.$$

At first glance it seems as if the quantum probabilistic framework is nothing more but a fancy revamp of the classical one. However, that is not the case and there are important, though subtle, differences worth pointing out:

1. The first pertains to the act of **observation**: classically, measurements simply reveal a system's (pre-)existing state and thereby merely lift the observer's ignorance, but observation itself doesn't affect the system. In the quantum framework the observation imposes a particular reference frame specified by the eigenstates of the observable, and the act of measurement "forces" the system to update its state via quantum collapse (projection) onto *one* of the possible outcomes. Registration of that outcome affects the quantum state in an *irreversible* manner; one may say that measurements *create* reality, not just reveal it (as would be the case in a classical setting). This refers to Wheeler's "**observer participancy**" [25].

2. Prior to an observation, the state Ψ may be in a quantum superposition with respect to various possible outcomes (such as in Equation 3.1), which expresses its **potentiality** to manifest as either state if measured. However, to say that the quantum superposition Ψ is simultaneously both[10] T and H would be misleading and incomplete. Prior to imposing any observable's reference frame, and even after, the state is simply Ψ. Quantum superpositions lack a classical analog. Figuratively speaking, a quantum superposition may be compared to a child as she relates to her parents. Can the child be reduced to a mixture of her parents? Not quite so! It is important to point out that a quantum superposition Ψ is not to be confused with a mixture that we discussed in the classical case, such as 50:50 H vs. T. Such **classical mixtures** can also be described within

the quantum framework by means of density matrices that lie beyond the scope of this chapter.

3. In general, it is not possible to read out or measure the quantum state Ψ in its entirety. For this, one would have to find a way to "peek into the Hilbert space" without applying any projection,[11] which is not possible. Hence, Ψ can only be probed via observables. But these will lead to a collapse of the wave function and thereby erase some information about the prior state Ψ. Classically, it is possible to measure a system's state to an arbitrary precision, theoretically at least, though in practice there will be limitations even here.

4. Probabilities are strictly positive, whereas probability amplitudes can be positive, negative, or even complex. The fact that the quantum probabilistic framework is based on probability amplitudes instead of probabilities provides an extra layer of flexibility that allows the possibility to observe effects such as quantum interference.

Classical Dynamics

Differences between the classical and quantum description of states also pertain to the dynamics that describes the way a system changes over time. Classically, at time t_0 the system's state $x(t_0)$ is described by some element in the sample space of all possible states. At a later time $t_1 > t_0$ the state $x(t_1)$ may be different, $x(t_1) \neq x(t_0)$. For multiple time points $t_0 < t_1 < t_2 < \cdots < t_m$ one obtains a **sequence**

$$x(t_0) \rightarrow x(t_1) \rightarrow x(t_2) \rightarrow \cdots \rightarrow x(t_m)$$

that represents the system's **history** between $t = t_0$ and $t = t_m$ and may be visualized as a **trajectory** in sample space (Figure 5.2a). The transition between two subsequent time points $x(t_i) \rightarrow x(t_i + 1)$ may be deterministic or probabilistic. In a **deterministic dynamical system** the future is determined by the **initial conditions**; that is, perfect knowledge about the state $x(t_0)$ at time t_0 would (in principle, at least) uniquely specify the trajectory $x(t)$ at all future times $t > t_0$. Mathematically, the dynamics of such systems can be written as a **differential equation** of the general form[12]

$$dx(t) = F[x(t)]dt \qquad (5.3)$$

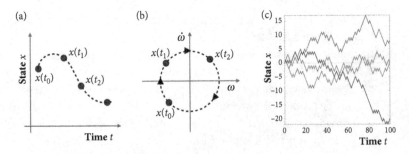

(a)   (b)   (c)

Figure 5.2 (a) Schematic representation of a trajectory in sample space. (b) Phase space representation of a pendulum. (c) Example trajectories of a random walk.

that constitutes a **predictive model**, which is based on the hypothesis that the change $dx(t)$ exhibited by a system in the next time step dt is precisely determined by the system's current state $x(t)$ by means of a specific model F chosen to accurately describe the dynamics of a given system. **Laws of classical physics** typically belong to that category. As a simple example one may consider a pendulum of length L that swings back and forth due to the gravitational acceleration g. Its state at any given moment is completely characterized by two quantities: its deflection relative to the vertical axis measured in terms of an angle ω, and its angular velocity $\dot{\omega} = d\omega/dt$. Hence, the pendulum's state $x(t) = (\omega(t), \dot{\omega}(t))$ can be represented as a point in a two-dimensional plane, called **phase space** (Figure 5.2b). Knowing $x(t_i)$ at any given time t_i, it is possible to calculate the pendulum's state at any time $t > t_i$ in the future.[13] The periodic back and forth of the pendulum translates into a circular motion along closed circles in state space. However, "perfect knowledge" of the initial conditions at time t_i, that is, the precise values of ω and $\dot{\omega}$, is a mathematical idealization that, in practice, can only be realized within some (possibly very small yet finite) error bounds. For so-called **integrable systems** (such as the pendulum) small uncertainty about the initial condition will result in small uncertainty in the prediction. However, for **nonintegrable systems** small uncertainties about the initial conditions are quickly amplified and will yield to **deterministic chaos** (e.g. "butterfly effect," weather forecasting, turbulent flows), which severely restricts any kind of long-term predictability[14] [26]. A third class of dynamical systems relevant here are **stochastic dynamical systems**, which also incorporate randomness, that may represent some fluctuating environment (such as chemical reactions, diffusion, spreading of diseases, etc.) or a source of uncertainty (stock market, noisy sensory signals, opinion dynamics, etc.). Mathematically, these systems can be written as **stochastic differential equations** that have a similar form as the model earlier,

$$dx(t) = F[x(t)]dt + dW(t),$$

but include a fluctuating **random noise** term, here represented by the Wiener increment $dW(t)$ [27]. A simple example of such an equation is a **random walk** (Figure 5.2c). Note that now two trajectories may turn out differently even if their initial state was the same. Hence, in stochastic systems predictions can only be made in a probabilistic way. Likewise, the reconstruction of the dynamics for earlier times here is not possible anymore, since the dynamics is no longer deterministic but **irreversible**. Stochastic systems tend to "forget" their initial condition after a while.

However, a probabilistic description can be applied to both deterministic and stochastic dynamical systems when the state is expressed in terms of a probability distribution $P(x)$ over the set of all possible states $x \in \Omega$ just as in the example of the die or coin discussed earlier. Because of the dynamics of $x(t)$, this probability will also depend on time t so that we write $P(x;t)$ and ask how $P(x;t)$ evolves in time. Assuming a discrete and finite sample space, one has N different states, $x_1, x_2, \ldots x_N$, and $P(x;t)$ can be written as a vector

$$\mathbf{P}(t) = (P(x_1;t), P(x_2;t), \ldots, P(x_N;t))$$

that satisfies the normalization condition

$$\sum_{i=1}^{N} P(x_i;t) = 1$$

at all times t. For discrete time steps of size Δt the dynamics can be written

$$P_i(t + \Delta t) = \sum_{j=1}^{N} A_{ij} P_j(t), \tag{5.4}$$

where the entries of the **transition matrix** A_{ij} specify the **transition probability** of the system to make a jump from a particular state x_j to state x_i within one time step. Accordingly, Equation 5.4 describes how the overall state at time t, represented by the probability distribution $\mathbf{P}_j(t)$, changes to $\mathbf{P}_j(t + \Delta t)$ one time step later. This type of model dynamics is called a **Markov chain**. As a simple example let us consider a hopscotch that has three tiles in a row that we may call *Left, Middle, Right*, that is,

$$\Omega = \{L, M, R\} = \{x_1, x_2, x_3\}.$$

Suppose that from tile M a player can only jump to tile R or L with equal probability,

$$P(M \to R) = 1/2 = P(M \to L),$$

whereas from tile R the player may either jump to L or M or simply remain at R with probability

$$P(R \to L) = 1/4 = P(R \to R) \text{ and } P(R \to M) = 1/2,$$

and, likewise, from tile L,

$$P(L \to L) = 1/4 = P(L \to R) \text{ and } P(L \to M) = 1/2.$$

These transition probabilities correspond to the following transition matrix:

$$A = \begin{pmatrix} A_{11} & A_{12} & A_{13} \\ A_{21} & A_{22} & A_{23} \\ A_{31} & A_{32} & A_{33} \end{pmatrix} = \begin{pmatrix} 1/4 & 1/2 & 1/4 \\ 1/2 & 0 & 1/2 \\ 1/4 & 1/2 & 1/4 \end{pmatrix}$$

Let's further assume that a player starts out at M at time $t = 0$, which corresponds to the probability distribution

$$\mathbf{P}(t = 0) = \begin{pmatrix} 0 \\ 1 \\ 0 \end{pmatrix}$$

depicted in the *leftmost column* of Figure 5.3. For simplicity in the following we set $\Delta t = 1$. After one time step (i.e., at time $t = 1$), the player will transition either to R (with probability $P(M \to R) = A_{32} = 1/2$) or to L (with probability $P(M \to L) = A_{12} = 1/2$), and indeed

$$\mathbf{P}(t = 1) = A \cdot \mathbf{P}(t = 0) = \begin{pmatrix} 1/2 \\ 0 \\ 1/2 \end{pmatrix},$$

which corresponds to a **mixture** of the two states, R and L. Hence, at $t = 1$ the player will be located at either R or L with equal probability (Figure 5.3, *middle column*).

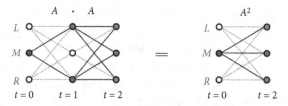

Figure 5.3 The classical dynamics of the initial state M at $t = 0$ after two time steps *(left)* corresponds to one step using the transition matrix $A^2 = A \cdot A$ *(right)*.

Such classical mixtures should *not* be confused with quantum superpositions mentioned earlier. Finally, letting the play advance for one further time step, one obtains

$$\mathbf{P}(t = 2) = A \cdot \mathbf{P}(t = 1) = \begin{pmatrix} 1/4 \\ 1/2 \\ 1/4 \end{pmatrix}$$

(Figure 5.3, *right column*) for the predicted histogram of player positions after two jumps. We will compare that result to a similar quantum model in the next section that will serve as a toy model for the double-slit experiment.

Quantum Dynamics and Interference

How is dynamics described within a quantum setting? As discussed previously, a system's state is represented by a normalized vector $\Psi(t)$ in the Hilbert space. For the examples in this section we will consider a three-dimensional Hilbert space, in which quantum states are represented by three-dimensional vectors

$$\Psi = \begin{pmatrix} x \\ y \\ z \end{pmatrix}$$

that satisfy the normalization condition

$$\|\Psi\| = \sqrt{|x|^2 + |y| + |z|^2} = 1.$$

As the system evolves, $\Psi(t)$ will change accordingly. Due to the normalization $\|\Psi(t)\| = 1$, the length (or norm) remains fixed, which means that the tip of the vector $\Psi(t)$ will trace a trajectory along the surface of a **unit sphere** as depicted in Figure 5.4a. As it turns out, the dynamics of a quantum state is also described by a linear differential equation, called the **Schrödinger equation**.

Without going into any more detail here it, suffices to say that the dynamics described by the Schrödinger equation geometrically corresponds to a **flow**, that is, a **continuous rotation** of the state vector that preserves its length (see Figure 5.4a). This dynamics differs from the relaxation and equilibration of the probability distribution that one observes in classical systems in many ways.[15] Furthermore, the quantum dynamics as described by the Schrödinger equation is deterministic. For finite time intervals the dynamics can be written as

$$\Psi(t + \Delta t) = U\Psi(t),$$

where U describes a so-called **unitary** transformation[16] that rotates the state vector $\Psi(t)$ by a certain amount without affecting its length. Only now the rotation is discrete and no longer continuous since we are considering snapshots separated by time intervals Δt. Again, in the following, we set $\Delta t = 1$.

As an example, let us once more consider three mutually exclusive outcomes, $\Omega = \{L, M, R\}$, which can be represented by vectors

$$L = \begin{pmatrix} 1 \\ 0 \\ 0 \end{pmatrix}, \ M = \begin{pmatrix} 0 \\ 1 \\ 0 \end{pmatrix}, \ R = \begin{pmatrix} 0 \\ 0 \\ 1 \end{pmatrix}$$

that also constitute an orthogonal basis of the three-dimensional Hilbert space (see Figure 5.4b). We will use that scenario as a toy model to develop some intuition about the **quantum interference** observed in the famous **double-slit**

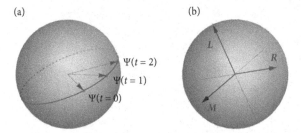

Figure 5.4 (a) The dynamics of a quantum state $\Psi(t)$ corresponds to a rotation on a unit sphere in the Hilbert space, which in this example is assumed to be three-dimensional. (b) The eigenstates of the position observable, R, M, and L, form an orthogonal basis of the three-dimensional Hilbert space.

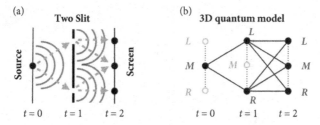

Figure 5.5 (a) Schematic of the double-slit setup. The quantum object leaves the source at $t = 0$, then passes the plane with two slits at $t = 1$, and is detected on the screen at $t = 2$. (b) Toy model representation of the dynamics by means of a three-dimensional model.

experiment.[17] The setup we have in mind is depicted in Figure 5.5a: At $t = 0$ a quantum object leaves the source at location M moving in a rightward direction. At $t = 1$ it arrives at a plane that has two slits, L and R. Classically, it would have to pass through one of the slits. As we will further explain below, quantum mechanically it can remain in a quantum superposition and behave *as if* it were passing *through both slits* at once. At $t = 2$ the object's location is detected on the screen at one of three possible locations, R, M, and L. A corresponding model representation is depicted in Figure 5.5b and will be developed next.

We consider a quantum object whose state at $t = 0$ is

$$\Psi(t = 0) = M;$$

that is, the object leaves the device through the middle aperture (Figure 5.6a). The state at $t = 1$, that is, one time step later, is obtained from

$$\Psi(t = 1) = UM,$$

where we consider a unitary matrix U of the following form:

$$U = \begin{pmatrix} 1/2 & \sqrt{1/2} & -1/2 \\ -\sqrt{1/2} & 0 & -\sqrt{1/2} \\ -1/2 & \sqrt{1/2} & 1/2 \end{pmatrix}.$$

At time $t = 1$ the object has reached the second plane. What will be its state? $\Psi(t = 1)$ is obtained from

$$\Psi(t=1) = UM = \begin{pmatrix} 1/2 & \sqrt{1/2} & -1/2 \\ -\sqrt{1/2} & 0 & -\sqrt{1/2} \\ -1/2 & \sqrt{1/2} & 1/2 \end{pmatrix} \cdot \begin{pmatrix} 0 \\ 1 \\ 0 \end{pmatrix} = \begin{pmatrix} \sqrt{1/2} \\ 0 \\ \sqrt{1/2} \end{pmatrix},$$

which can also be written as

$$\Psi(t=1) = \sqrt{1/2} \cdot L + \sqrt{1/2} \cdot R, \tag{5.5}$$

and corresponds to a quantum superposition of L and R (Figure 5.6b). Note that our "knowledge" about the state at $t = 1$ here is based on the prediction from the model dynamics but *not* on an actual observation.[18] Letting the system evolve for one additional time step, its state at time $t = 2$ will be

$$\Psi(t=2) = U\Psi(t=1) = UU\Psi(t=0) = U^2\Psi(t=0) = U^2M.$$

For the squared matrix $U^2 = U \cdot U$ one gets

$$U^2 = \begin{pmatrix} 0 & 0 & -1 \\ 0 & -1 & 0 \\ -1 & 0 & 0 \end{pmatrix}$$

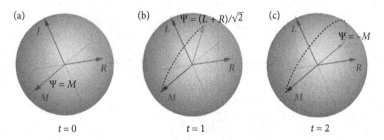

Figure 5.6 (a) Geometrical way of depicting the dynamics of a quantum object when its location is measured at $t = 2$ but not in between, thereby preserving the quantum superposition at $t = 1$: the object leaves the source at M at $t = 0$ and describes a trajectory as indicated by the dotted curve that yields to the final state $\Psi = -M$ at $t = 2$, which is equivalent to M.

such that

$$\Psi(t=2)=-M$$

which is equivalent to M since two states that just differ by a relative sign or a complex phase are considered to represent the same state (Figure 5.6c). Hence, when measuring its position at $t = 2$, the object will be found at M with probability 1 since, according to Born's rule (see Equation 5.2),

$$P(M;t=2)=P(M\,|\,\Psi(t=2))=P(M\,|-M)=|-1|^2=1$$

and nowhere else, since

$$P(L;t=2)=P(L\,|-M)=|0|^2=0,$$

and likewise $P(R;t=2)=0$ due to the mutual orthogonality of L, M, and R. This can be summarized by the probability distribution

$$\mathbf{P}(t=2)=\begin{pmatrix}0\\1\\0\end{pmatrix} \tag{5.6}$$

The result, however, will be different *if* one tries to pin down "how" the object travels from M at $t = 0$ to its final position at $t = 2$ by *also* observing (i.e., measuring) its position at $t = 1$. At $t = 1$ the state $\Psi(t = 1)$ is a quantum superposition of R and L as described in Equation 5.5) and depicted in Figure 5.7a. Therefore, measuring the object's location at $t = 1$ will result in a 50:50 chance of obtaining either R or L, since

$$P(L;t=1)=P(L\,|\,\Psi(t=1))=1/2$$

and

$$P(R;t=1)=P(R\,|\,\Psi(t=1))=1/2.$$

This can also be written as a probability distribution

$$\mathbf{P}(t=1)=\begin{pmatrix}1/2\\0\\1/2\end{pmatrix}.$$

Assuming the measurement at $t = 1$ yields L, the updated state becomes $\Psi(t = 1) = L$ (shown in Figure 5.7b) and at $t = 2$ on ends up with

$$\Psi'(t=2)=UL=1/2L-\sqrt{1/2}M-1/2R,$$

which is a quantum superposition of *all three* locations (Figure 5.7c). Likewise, if the measurement at $t = 1$ yields R, the updated state becomes $\Psi(t = 1) = R$, which, at $t = 2$, will again result in a quantum superposition

$$\Psi'(t=2)=UR=-1/2L-\sqrt{1/2}M+1/2R.$$

Applying Born's rule in both cases, one obtains the following probability distribution for $t = 2$:

$$\mathbf{P}(t=2)=\begin{pmatrix}P(L\,|\,\Psi'(t=2))\\P(M\,|\,\Psi'(t=2))\\P(R\,|\,\Psi'(t=2))\end{pmatrix}=\begin{pmatrix}1/4\\1/2\\1/4\end{pmatrix} \tag{5.7}$$

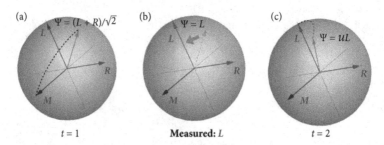

(a) $\Psi = (L + R)/\sqrt{2}$ (b) $\Psi = L$ (c) $\Psi = uL$

$t = 1$ Measured: L $t = 2$

Figure 5.7 (a) Geometrical way of depicting the dynamics of a quantum object when its location is also measured at $t = 1$, here with the outcome L as shown in (b). The state $\Psi(t = 1) = L$ then is allowed to evolve for one additional time step and at $t = 2$ becomes the quantum superposition $\Psi(t = 2) = UL = 1/2L - \sqrt{1/2}M - 1/2R$, shown in (c).

which clearly differs from the previous distribution in Equation 5.6. Hence, probing a quantum state at an intermediary step (here, $t = 1$) can affect the probabilities at a later time (here, $t = 2$). This effect is called **quantum interference** and can be **constructive** or **destructive** when it increases or decreases the probability in comparison to the classical scenario in which the state at every time step is measured. In our example, when only measuring the outcome at $t = 2$, the object will always be found at M. In contrast, if also checking the object's location at $t = 1$, the probability of finding the object at M at $t = 2$ is only $1/2$ (constructive interference), while the probability of finding it elsewhere (at R and L) now is $1/4$ compared to 0 before (destructive interference). Note that when the location of the quantum object is measured at all time steps, the probabilities correspond exactly to the classical example discussed in the previous section: it effectively turns into a classical object!

Incompatibility of Observables

Another important feature that has no classical analog is the **incompatibility** of observables. As explained earlier, the information encoded in a quantum state can only be accessed or queried indirectly via observables whose eigenstates represent all possible outcomes to a given question. These eigenstates are orthogonal to each other and form a basis of the Hilbert space. So far we only considered a single observable, which allowed asking one type of question, such as about a quantum object's position. What if one were to ask about the object's velocity instead? Since the state vector Ψ is supposed to carry *all* the relevant information available about the system, there should be a way to measure its velocity too. Indeed, there is, and it comes in the form of another observable, V, whose eigenstates represent the various velocities that can be realized by the object. However, the eigenstates of V point in different directions than the eigenstates of X (i.e., the observable for position). That means that it is *not* possible to measure the position and velocity of a quantum object *simultaneously*: the observables X and V are **incompatible**, and sharp measurements of an object's position will erase information about its velocity and vice versa. This incompatibility of complementary projections of a quantum state underlies the **wave-particle duality** as well as **Heisenberg's uncertainty principle**.

Here we briefly explain incompatible observables and the resulting uncertainty by means of a simple example that may be more accessible as it doesn't refer to concepts from classical mechanics.[19] Let's consider an athlete, Bob, and his trainer, Alice. Prior to a training session Bob faces a choice: *Running*, *Swimming*, or *Cycling*, Figure 5.8a. While exercising he cannot eat. After the training session his trainer will ask him to select some food: *Muesli*, *Fruits*, or *Noodles* (Figure 5.8b). The two sets of eigenstates that represent the two different

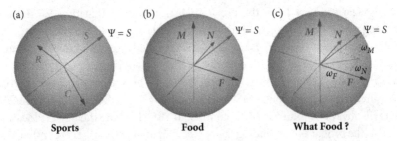

Figure 5.8 Different contexts (here: "Sports" and "Food") can be represented by different observables and their reference frames specified by their eigenstates (*Cycle, Run, Swim* and *Fruit, Noodles, Muesli*). The quantum state Ψ can be decomposed with respect to both reference frames: here $\Psi = S$ and $\Psi = w_M \cdot M + w_F \cdot F + w_N \cdot N$ both describe the same state. Note that Ψ is sharp in the sports context but a linear superposition in the food context.

contexts, sports and food, each form a complete basis of the Hilbert space, but they are rotated relative to each other, and therefore incompatible. At the very beginning of a session Bob is exclusively focused on his training, say swimming (Figure 5.8c). Bob's current **mental state** of *Swimming* may be represented as

$$\Psi = S,$$

which means that its coordinate representation in the sports frame (R, S, C) is **sharp** or **certain**:

$$\Psi = \begin{pmatrix} 0 \\ 1 \\ 0 \end{pmatrix}_{\text{Sports}}.$$

However, the *same* state when written in terms of the food eigenstates (M, F, N)

$$\Psi = S = w_M \cdot M + w_F \cdot F + w_N \cdot N$$

has the coordinate representation

$$\Psi = \begin{pmatrix} w_M \\ w_F \\ w_N \end{pmatrix}_{\text{Food}}$$

with coefficients that are obtained from a **coordinate rotation** and in general don't vanish,

$$w_M \neq 0, \ w_F \neq 0, \ w_N \neq 0$$

Hence, if Alice were to ask him about his food preference, Bob would be **undecided** or **uncertain** (Figure 5.8c). He may either answer that he doesn't know and continue swimming or randomly pick an answer with probabilities

$$P(M) = |w_M|^2, P(F) = |w_F|^2, P(N) = |w_N|^2$$

according to Born's rule. A bit later, as the hunger sets in, Bob's mind may gravitate toward a particular type of food, which would be reflected in changed weights and a different mental state

$$\Psi' = w'_M \cdot M + w'_F \cdot F + w'_N \cdot N$$

A predilection for a particular food, noodles say, may be represented by weights that satisfy

$$|w'_N| > |w'_F|, \text{ and } |w'_N| > |w'_M|.$$

When asked about his preference then, Bob's choice may be much clearer and result in a high probability of picking noodles and an updated state $\Psi = N$. However, if right as Bob is sitting down for lunch Alice asks him about which sport he'd like to embark on next, again he will feel conflicted since his mind is currently sharply set on noodles, $\Psi = N$, which corresponds to a (quantum) superposition in the sports context,

$$N = w_R \cdot R + w_S \cdot S + w_C \cdot C.$$

Here these examples are simply meant as metaphors to explain the concept of incompatible observables and the **(Heisenberg) uncertainty**, which arises whenever a state is sharp with respect to one observable (or context) and fuzzy with respect to another observable (or context). However, the idea of exploring that analogy between mental states and quantum states and checking its applicability beyond a metaphorical level lies at the heart of a fairly recent field, **quantum cognition**, that has produced very promising results. The interested reader is encouraged to explore the excellent literature on that topic (e.g., [8–10, 29] and references therein).

Outlook

In this brief introduction we encountered quantum theory as a different kind of probability theory in which states are geometrically represented by vectors instead of elements in a set as in a classical setting. This vector representation provides a more flexible framework for describing and handling the probabilities of possible outcomes as they may apply to a variety of different contexts, even incompatible and conflicting ones. We saw that the quantum framework is particularly well suited for expressing potentialities and ambiguities in terms of quantum superpositions, as well as contextual effects, which makes it very interesting for applications beyond physics, such as cognitive sciences and computational linguistics [9, 30]. A key feature of quantum theory that we haven't touched upon here at all, and which Schrödinger even called *the* characteristic trait of quantum mechanics, is **entanglement**. Also, we didn't talk about **order effects** and **cognitive puzzles**, which would naturally be discussed next. To learn more about order effects, cognitive puzzles, and entanglement, we refer the reader to [8–10, 14] and to [31], which provide a clear and nontechnical introduction.

Acknowledgments

The author thanks the organizers of the 2018 workshop "Quantum Theory and the International" at the Mershon Center for International Securities Studies, Ohio State University, for their invitation that initiated this work, and Seth Lichter and Daniel Diermeier, as well as an anonymous reviewer for helpful feedback on earlier drafts of the manuscript.

Notes

1. For an overview about the various interpretations, see [3–7].
2. For an introduction to complex numbers see Wikipedia: en.wikipedia.org/wiki/Complex_number.
3. An excellent description of this approach to quantum mechanics can be found in [2]; also see [22, 23].

4. A Hilbert space is a complex vector space equipped with an inner product that allows the projection of vectors onto each other and the measurement of lengths and angles.
5. The coefficients can also be complex, $x, y \in \mathbb{C}$, but for simplicity here we assume $x, y \in \mathbb{R}$.
6. More precisely, quantum states are represented by **equivalence classes** called **rays**; that is, two vectors Ψ and $e^{i\phi}\Psi$ that differ by an arbitrary **complex phase** $e^{i\phi}$, $\phi \in [0, 2\pi]$, are considered to represent the same state.
7. This is sometimes referred to as the "**collapse of the wave function.**"
8. The nature of that selection process in quantum physics is still an open question known as the "**measurement problem.**"
9. Note that, while the states $\Psi^{(1)}$ and $\Psi^{(2)}$ as well as $\Psi^{(3)}$ and $\Psi^{(4)}$ represent the same quantum state, this isn't the case for $\Psi^{(1)}$ and $\Psi^{(3)}$, $\Psi^{(2)}$ and $\Psi^{(3)}$, etc., that are considered different quantum states.
10. That is, dead *and* alive as in **Schrödinger's cat.**
11. One may project onto the full Hilbert space, but this would simply be the identity operator, which is a trivial observable that doesn't tell us anything tangible about Ψ. Such an operation would yield "Ψ is Ψ" and be as useful as not looking at all.
12. Depending on whether the functional $F[x]$ is linear or a higher-order polynomial in x, the dynamics is called **linear** or **non-linear**.
13. For deterministic systems it is even possible to reconstruct the state at earlier time points in the past.
14. A simple example of a nonintegrable dynamical system exhibiting chaos would be the motion of a ball on a two-dimensional billiard table with rounded reflecting edges instead of strictly rectangular ones (e.g., a Bunimovich stadium billiard).
15. Quantum dynamics typically leads to **oscillations** as the state keeps rotating around the sphere.
16. More precisely, U is a **unitary operator** that preserves the norm and is invertible. Application of U allows going back and forth in time between measurements. But one can't go beyond measurements, as these lead to a collapse of the state vector, which is an irreversible event.
17. A proper quantum mechanical analysis of the double-slit experiment can be found in textbooks on quantum mechanics such as [28], Chapter 37, also accessible online here: www.feynmanlectures.caltech.edu/I_37.html.
18. An observation of the object's position at this stage would destroy the quantum superposition, as we will see further later.
19. Our custom example has the advantage that we can just use real numbers. The proper description of the velocity observable and its eigenstates, even for a simple toy model, would require us to use complex numbers.

References

[1] Wojciech Hubert Zurek. Quantum Darwinism. *Nature Physics*, 5(3):181–188, 2009.
[2] Scott Aaronson. *Quantum Computing since Democritus*. Cambridge University Press, 2013.

[3] Bryce S. Dewitt. Quantum mechanics and reality. *Physics Today*, 23N9:30–35, 1970.

[4] Christopher A. Fuchs and Asher Peres. Quantum theory needs no "interpretation." *Physics Today*, 53:70–71, 2000.

[5] Jeffrey A. Barrett. *The Quantum Mechanics of Minds and Worlds*. Oxford University Press, 2001.

[6] Christopher A. Fuchs. Qbism, The Perimeter of quantum Bayesianism. *arXiv:1003.5209*, 2010.

[7] Philip Ball. *Beyond Weird*. University of Chicago Press, 2018.

[8] Jerome R. Busemeyer and Peter D. Bruza. *Quantum Models of Cognition and Decision*. Cambridge University Press, 2012.

[9] Peter D. Bruza, Zheng Wang, and Jerome R. Busemeyer. Quantum cognition: A new theoretical approach to psychology. *Trends in Cognitive Sciences*, 19(7):383–393, 2015.

[10] Andrei Khrennikov. Quantum-like modeling of cognition. *Frontiers in Physics*, 3:77, 2015.

[11] Karen Barad. *Meeting the Universe Halfway*. Duke University Press, 2007.

[12] Alexander Wendt. *Quantum Mind and Social Science*. Cambridge University Press, 2015.

[13] Vyacheslav I. Yukalov and Didier Sornette. Processing information in quantum decision theory. *Entropy*, 11(4):1073–1120, 2009.

[14] Reinhard Blutner and Peter beim Graben. Quantum cognition and bounded rationality. *Synthese*, 193(10):3239–3291, 2016.

[15] E. Haven and A. Khrennikov. *Quantum Social Science*. Cambridge University Press, 2013.

[16] Martin Schaden. Quantum finance. *Physica A: Statistical Mechanics and Its Applications*, 316(1–4):511–538, 2002.

[17] David Orrell. *Quantum Economics and Finance: An Applied Mathematics Introduction*, Panda Ohana Publishing, 2020.

[18] David A Meyer. Quantum strategies. *Physical Review Letters*, 82(5):1052, 1999.

[19] Jens Eisert, Martin Wilkens, and Maciej Lewenstein. Quantum games and quantum strategies. *Physical Review Letters*, 83(15):3077, 1999.

[20] Kathryn Schaffer and Gabriela Barreto Lemos. Obliterating thingness: An introduction to the "what" and the "so what" of quantum physics. *Foundations of Science*, 2019.

[21] N. David Mermin. Is the moon there when nobody looks? Reality and the quantum theory. *Physics Today*, 38:38–47, 1985.

[22] Lucien Hardy. Quantum theory from five reasonable axioms. *arXiv preprint quant-ph/0101012*, 2001.

[23] Lucien Hardy. Why quantum theory? In: *Non-locality and Modality*, 61–73. Placek, T. & Butterfield, J. (Eds.). Springer, 2002.

[24] Garrett Birkhoff and John Von Neumann. The logic of quantum mechanics. *Annals of Mathematics*, 37(4):823–843, 1936.

[25] J. A. Wheeler. Law without law. In: *Quantum Theory and Measurement*, 182–213. Wheeler, J. A., & Zurek, W. H. (Eds.). Princeton University Press, 1983.

[26] Michael Tabor. *Chaos and Integrability in Nonlinear Dynamics: An Introduction*. Wiley, 1989.

[27] N. G. Van Kampen. *Stochastic Processes in Physics and Chemistry, Third Edition* (North-Holland Personal Library). North Holland, April 2007.

[28] Richard P. Feynman, Robert B. Leighton, Matthew Sands, and R. Bruce Lindsay. *The Feynman Lectures on Physics, Vol. 3: Quantum Mechanics*, volume 19. Addison-Wesley, 1966.

[29] Zheng Joyce Wang and Jerome R. Busemeyer. *Cognitive Choice Modeling*. MIT Press, 2021.

[30] Dominic Widdows. *Geometry and Meaning*. No. 172 in CSLI lecture notes. CSLI Publications, 2004.

[31] Thomas Filk. *"Quantum" and "Quantum-Like": An Introduction to Quantum Theory and Its Applications in Cognitive and Social Sciences*. iASK, Institute of Advanced Studies, November 2020.

PART 2.
SCIENCE AND TECHNOLOGY

6

The Quantum Moonshot

Shohini Ghose

The first journey ever taken by humans in a vehicle guided by a computer was perhaps one of the most important journeys in history. This small step in the development of computers enabled a giant leap for humanity—the landing on the moon by Armstrong and Aldrin on July 20, 1969. History marks the moment as an unqualified success, but this otherworldly achievement almost never happened. Moments before touchdown on the moon's surface, the computer guiding the lunar lander crashed and rebooted five times in less than five minutes. At the time, it was the smallest and most powerful solid-state computer ever designed, a thirty-kilo marvel of engineering with a processor consisting of the latest silicon-based integrated circuits rather than old vacuum tube technology. Nonetheless, with a processing power millions of times less than today's smartphones, the guidance computer was overloaded by an unexpected input in the crucial moments before the landing. It was human judgment and skilled manual piloting by Neil Armstrong that saved the day. The enormous subsequent impact of the Apollo moon program on science, politics, and society is well documented. The legacy of the seemingly faulty guidance computer is equally noteworthy. The guidance software was later adapted for use in military jet piloting systems. Furthermore, the success of California-based Fairchild Instruments, the maker of the computer's silicon chips, spawned a host of other companies and the birth of Silicon Valley. The head of research and development at Fairchild, Gordon Moore, left the company and went on to cofound Intel. Moore famously predicted a trend that is popularly known as "Moore's law": the number of transistors on a computer chip doubles roughly every two years. While the law has held for half a century, the development of quantum computers could finally prove Moore wrong. The reason his law will be violated is because the framework of computing itself is changing. Adopting this new quantum framework requires a significant shift in thinking and an examination of its potential impact on science and society.

A Classical versus Quantum Computing Framework

Five decades of ever-increasing miniaturization as predicted by Moore has resulted in spectacular increases in computing power compared to the Apollo guidance computer. Today a single handheld iPhone (weighing a lot less than thirty kilograms) has enough processing power to simultaneously land a hundred million lunar modules safely on the moon. And yet, the rules of computing used by the Apollo computer remain identical to the ones implemented by the iPhone. Both are devices that perform calculations by using binary logic. In this binary-based classical computing framework, all information can be expressed as a combination of 0s and 1s—binary digits or bits. All computations therefore can be performed by implementing a series of operations to flip the values of the bits or not, based on the task at hand. This wonderfully simple framework is astonishingly powerful, taking us all the way from the Apollo computer to modern phones, laptops, and supercomputers. It is also a universal framework, allowing the flexibility of programmable devices that can send email as well as solve differential equations. The main difference between the iPhone and the Apollo computer is thus not in the underlying classical computing framework, but in the number, speed, and efficiency of the binary logic operations being performed.

A shift to a quantum computing framework entails a move away from precise binary logic. Quantum mechanics has always challenged binary models and interpretations. In 1905, when Einstein suggested an elegant particle theory of light to explain the photoelectric effect, it clashed with Maxwell's beautiful wave equations for light. Similarly, when De Broglie offered a wave model for electrons, atoms, and other matter, it contradicted their evident particle nature. His theory was nevertheless eventually confirmed in the lab. Such experimental evidence of both particle and wave behavior could not be ignored. The binary division of matter and light in the universe as particle versus wave had to be abandoned, and the theory had to be unified. Schrödinger came up with a mathematical solution in the form of a quantum wave equation; wave and particle combined in one description. Born offered a radical probabilistic interpretation of the wave function solutions of Schrödinger's equation as probability amplitudes whose magnitudes predicted the likelihoods of measurement outcomes rather than the precise outcome of a measurement.

An inescapable consequence of the quantum theory is the uncertainty principle that bears its discoverer Heisenberg's name. The quantum uncertainty principle, a result derived from the mathematical foundations of quantum theory, places strict limits on the amount of information that can be known about a quantum particle. It states that every property of an individual quantum particle like an electron or a photon cannot be simultaneously known with perfect precision. For example, precisely knowing the location of an electron makes it impossible to simultaneously know where it's going or how fast it's moving—its momentum. Conversely, knowing its momentum precisely precludes simultaneous knowledge about its position. It is important to note that this is not due to faulty measurements or errors. This balancing act is built into the theory itself, making it impossible to avoid quantum uncertainty.

In the language of computing, uncertainty means that a quantum bit (qubit) need not be precisely 0 or 1 but could be in a superposition of wave functions such that there is some probability that quantum bit is 0 and some probability that it is 1. Such unpredictability may seem problematic in the context of computing given that the goal of computations is to find a precise answer. However, the new quantum computing framework is built on the revolutionary idea proposed in the 1980s that embracing uncertainty can lead to more powerful paradigms for information processing.

Quantum Security

An early example of the power of quantum uncertainty came from the field of secure communications, whose importance has become abundantly clear in the world of Zoom meetings during COVID-19. Thanks to uncertainty and the probabilistic nature of quantum theory, information encoded in qubits cannot be perfectly copied—a law known as the no-cloning theorem. Thus, hackers attempting to secretly copy and read keys used for encryption will be thwarted by the no-cloning theorem. This allows the development and deployment of quantum key distribution (QKD) protocols that are the only unconditionally secure encryption schemes known today. QKD can outperform current encryption approaches based on computational algorithms because it relies on the laws of physics rather than on computational or mathematical complexity for security. No current or future classical computer would pose a threat to quantum encryption standards unless hackers could violate the laws of quantum mechanics. Even future quantum computers would not enable hackers to get around the fundamental laws of the universe.

Quantum encryption is beginning to move out of research labs into real-world settings in government, industry, and society. The European Commission's patent analysis of selected quantum technologies shows a steep increase in corporate patent applications for QKD over the most recent period where data are available, from 2012 to 2016, predominantly in China. The US National Institute of Standards and Technology (NIST) is working on standardizing quantum-proof encryption standards. And QKD research and development is underway in many parts of the world including Canada, the European Union, South Korea, Japan, Russia, Egypt, and the United Kingdom. While current classical information security standards remain robust for the near future, they will inevitably become vulnerable to improved classical computers and perhaps eventually to quantum computers. Changing over current worldwide infrastructure and standards to quantum-secure encryption protocols could take decades.[1] A well-structured and responsible rollout of the technology will require immediate action and planning on a global scale.

Information security is just one of many potential applications of the new framework of quantum computing that goes beyond deterministic binary computing and incorporates quantum probabilistic phenomena. A pair of quantum bits can interact with each other and get entangled in such a way that individually each qubit remains in a fluid unknown state of 0 or 1, but because they are entangled they are locked together. So, if one of them is measured to be 0, the other one is definitely a 0, no matter how far away it is in the universe. Similarly, if one of them is measured to be 1, the other will definitely be 1, even though they may not communicate during that time. Entanglement is a strange quantum balancing act of connection combined with uncertainty that provides another powerful knob in the toolbox of quantum computing. Perhaps one of the most mindboggling applications of entanglement is teleporting of quantum information from one location to another in such a way that the information disappears at one location and is perfectly (but not instantly) reconstructed at another location far away. Entanglement, teleportation, and other related communication protocols are already moving away from research settings. While we won't be able to teleport macro-scale human forms to the moon, these advances could form the basis for a future quantum-enhanced internet and enable secure network communications.[2]

Beyond Classical Computing

The quantum computing toolbox not only enables novel communication schemes but also vastly expands the landscape for computing. Classical deterministic binary logic is but a tiny part of this much broader computing framework that allows qubits to be infinitely fluid in value between 0 and 1, and thus an infinitely fluid set of logic operations to be performed. From this perspective, given its restricted set of operations, the success of classical computing is certainly impressive. Furthermore, thanks to the vision of Moore and others, current classical computers are stunningly fast, efficient, and small, and are more than sufficient for most of our everyday needs. The question, therefore, is what additional benefits quantum computing can offer. Answering this requires identifying current limitations of classical computing when it comes to addressing the most pressing global issues we face today.

In the age of pandemics, one of the most critical areas of need for research and development to overcome existing limitations is in health care. Quantum science and technology has long played a role in the health care industry—from the development of better sensing and diagnostics technologies to the analysis of the quantum chemistry of molecules for drugs and vaccine development. Calculations to simulate the behavior and quantum properties of impor-tant molecules such as penicillin are routinely performed on ever more pow-erful classical computers. Nevertheless, simulations of molecules consisting of a few hundred atoms or more remain out of reach of even the most powerful supercomputers today, thanks to the exponential scaling of the classical simula-tion complexity with the number of atoms. Quantum computers offer a way past this limitation. A fully quantum simulation of molecules on a quantum com-puter could avoid the exponential scaling problem via calculations that operate using the same quantum properties of the molecules being simulated. Even a small-scale quantum computer in the near future may be sufficient to perform simulations impossible on any current classical system. Quantum simulations have the potential to impact not just health care but also materials design for a multitude of applications, including building better batteries, solar cells, protec-tive clothing, and construction materials, to name a few.

The challenges posed by global issues such as climate change and pandemics go beyond health care and information security to supply chain logistics, food security, diagnostics, travel, and energy use. A quantum framework can po-tentially help to address limitations in these areas as well. For example, recent research has also shown that entanglement-based sensors can beat the resolu-tion of the best existing microscopes. Future applications of this advancement may help to improve medical imaging and navigation systems. Additionally, quantum algorithms for optimization of multiparameter problems (such as, for example, delivery logistics) could tackle tasks too difficult for current computers. Searching through unsorted big data sets such as climate or energy data is an-other significant area where quantum search algorithms may have an impact.

Quantum Challenges

Over the past few years, governments around the world have poured billions of dollars into quantum research and development. Industry has paid attention too, and prototype quantum computers have already been built by companies such as IBM and Google. Despite the microscopic sizes of the qubits powering these devices, Moore's law certainly does not apply to these first-generation quantum computers. They bear little resemblance to laptops or smartphones. One of the earliest quantum processors existed in liquid form. IBM's computer, strangely reminiscent of pre-Apollo classical computers, takes up an entire room for operations. Despite their early-stage nonoptimal design, simple tasks implemented on these computers have already demonstrated a quantum advantage. Further testing will help identify performance benchmarks and guide design and hardware improvements.

The single biggest challenge in scaling up the technology is the issue of errors. While interaction between qubits can lead to entanglement that powers quantum speedup for computations, interaction of the qubits with other particles in the environment can cause unwanted entanglement and errors in the computation. Errors, however, are common in current computers as well. In fact, the seeming "failure" of the Apollo guidance computer was actually a successful implementation of error detection and error correction in the most extreme of situations.

For years before the launch of the Apollo 11 mission, programmers and engineers on Earth worked on building a computer that could avoid or recover from every possible error they could think of. In designing the system, the highest priority was given to protecting navigation data that was critical to final landing of the astronauts on the lunar surface. This was so important that it was hardwired into the operating system. If the processor got overwhelmed with too many tasks, then it would shut down and reboot, thus deleting all but the mission-critical data and allowing it to continue with high-priority tasks. Thus, during the landing, when data from a misaligned antenna kept overloading the processor, it did exactly what it was wired to do. It corrected the error by rebooting while never losing the mission-critical data for navigation.

Current classical computers have sophisticated error diagnostics and error correction techniques built in. However, detecting and correcting quantum errors is significantly more challenging due to the nondeterministic nature of quantum information. How does one correct a qubit if one does not know what value, 0 or 1, it is? One approach is to isolate all the qubits completely and try to control their environment so well that there is almost no possibility of an error caused by interactions with unwanted particles. This is the approach currently used by IBM, Google, and other teams building qubits using the superconducting approach. The cost is high: qubits must be kept at temperatures colder than outer space, which requires a room full of cooling and control equipment. Environmental interactions with the quantum system can produce decoherence—loss of information—as qubits collapse or fall out of a state of superposition. These interactions can be due to the slightest variances in vibration, stray radiation, or magnetic fields. Environments built to house quantum processors are extraordinarily precarious and expensive, as any interaction from even a stray electron could cause the entire system to decohere. In spite of Herculean efforts to build isolated quantum systems, the quantum processors have a fairly high rate of error and would require additional quantum error correction in the future for robust long-time operation. Quantum error correction codes have been developed, that can be used across diverse quantum systems.

Classical error correction techniques have inspired the formulation of elegant quantum error correction algorithms that can diagnose and correct all types of qubit errors while preserving the fluid quantum state of the qubit. The trick is to entangle the qubits with additional helper qubits that can be measured to diagnose the errors. The overhead in terms of helper qubits to correct all errors scales linearly with the number of qubits, but it sets the goal for large-scale quantum computers at a few thousand qubits (including helpers) in order to perform a significant error-free calculation that is beyond the reach of current classical computers. This is unrealistic in the near term and thus highlights the need for further exploration of hybrid quantum-classical approaches and the identification of problems that are not as sensitive to quantum errors, so that an approximate solution is sufficient.

A Global Quantum Future?

Given the challenges outlined here, it is difficult to predict where the field of quantum computing will go in the next few years. But although the future of the technology is not clear, the power of quantum theory and the eye-opening, paradigm-shifting nature of quantum information processing is undeniably exciting. Probing and pushing the boundaries of computing with this new framework offers the potential of gaining fundamental insights into the nature of information, computational complexity, the boundaries between quantum and classical, and causal structures in spacetime. Furthermore, large-scale quantum computers, if developed in the future, together with machine learning could open new frontiers of exploration in physics, chemistry, and biology.

Fifty-two years ago, in the wake of the Apollo 11 mission's success, the classical computing landscape dramatically increased. The resulting application of computing in every part of society was entirely unpredictable at that point. Examining the evolution of classical computing over the past fifty years can help to understand the benefits and drawbacks of the classical information age and thereby build the quantum information age more intentionally and responsibly.

The field of quantum information processing has rapidly grown at the confluence of research in physics, computer science, mathematics, chemistry, and engineering. The meeting of so many disciplines provides exciting possibilities but also raises questions about the nature of collaboration versus competition in research and development across academia, government, and industry, and across international borders. Given the potential impact on many aspects of society including health care, security, energy, and finance, it is worth asking which disciplines are not part of the quantum confluence described earlier. Notably, quantum computing research teams in both academia and industry currently do not include experts in law, ethics, politics, psychology, equity, or inclusion. This perhaps explains why Google and other companies can glibly make claims about achieving "quantum supremacy" without any understanding or unpacking of the appropriateness of this term. It in fact follows from a history of questionable terminology in quantum theory, such as "master" equation and "ancilla/slave" particles, that remains unquestioned. Furthermore, the field must tackle additional questions about the responsible rollout of the technology: Who will control the knowledge and technology and how will it be regulated? How will access be granted and for what purposes? How can technology be developed in a way that is sustainable and inclusive? In a quantum world, how will social, political, and financial structures evolve and adapt?

The unfettered development of artificial intelligence and Blockchain in recent years has underlined the necessity of understanding the social, legal, and environmental repercussions of developing technologies. Additional lessons can be learned from history. For example, the Industrial Revolution led to clear benefits for society but also triggered environmental consequences that contributed to the existential crisis facing humanity today. Despite this, there is currently no clear plan or worldwide discussion to address the potential societal, environmental, and ethical ramifications of quantum science and technology.

It is notable that the Massachusetts Institute of Technology (MIT) team who designed the flight software for the Apollo mission was led by computer scientist Margaret Hamilton. It was her team's ingenuity in programming and ability to account for the unknown that helped to make Apollo's first and subsequent landings a success. Despite her critical contributions, her role and the role of other women who worked at the National Aeronautics and Space Administration (NASA) since the early days of the space program are not widely known. The consequences of erasing women and minorities from the history of science are still being felt today—science, and physics in particular, remains overwhelmingly the domain of white men. It does not require much analysis or scientific brilliance to realize that ignoring half the talent pool in the world is hugely detrimental to scientific progress, and particularly to progress in cutting-edge areas like quantum computing, where creativity, imagination, and new approaches to problem-solving from many different perspectives are especially valuable.

Quantum theory itself perhaps provides hints about a framework for building a just, sustainable, and egalitarian quantum future. At the heart of the theory lie uncertainty and indeterminism, written into the fundamental postulates of the theory. The key insight from quantum computing is that this is not a hindrance but a superpower. A global initiative to plan for a socially responsible quantum information age could be guided by a set of quantum-inspired postulates that center quantum thinking and focus on embracing and adapting to uncertainty and creating powerful connections.

The old Apollo guidance computer was a machine expressly designed to function in uncontrolled circumstances without risking its central mission. It did so by allowing for the unknown. The quantum moonshot will require a similar plan.

Notes

1. Historically, it has taken nearly two decades to fully deploy today's modern public key cryptography infrastructure. Recognizing the urgency of the current situation, the NIST is paving the way in its support for the transition to postquantum or quantum-resistant cryptography across national systems in the United States.
2. In 2017 China established the first commercial private quantum communication network in its northern province of Shandong (Reuters, "China Sets Up First 'Commercial' Quantum Network for Secure Communications," 2017).

Bibliography

Bennett, C., & Brassard, G. (1984). Quantum cryptography: Public key distribution and coin tossing. *Proceedings of IEEE International Conference on Computers, Systems and Signal Processing, 175*, 8.

Bird, J. (2007). *Engineering Mathematics*. Newnes.

Bohr, N. (1949). Discussions with Einstein on Epistemological Problems in Atomic Physics. In Paul Arthur Schilpp (ed.), *The Library of Living Philosophers*, Volume 7. Albert Einstein: Philosopher-Scientist. Open Court, 199–241. Cambridge University Press.

Boole, G. (1847). *The Mathematical Analysis of Logic Being an Essay Towards a Calculus of Deductive Reasoning*. London: Macmillan.

Born, M. (1926). Zur Quantenmechanik der Stoßvorgänge. *Zeitschrift für Physik, 37*, 863.

Chen, Y. A., et al. (2021). An integrated space-to-ground quantum communication network over 4,600 kilometres. *Nature, 589*, 214.

Davisson, C., & Germer, L. (1928). Reflection of Electrons by a Crystal of Nickel. *Proceedings of the National Academy of Sciences of the United States of America, 14*, 317.

de Broglie, L. (1925). Recherches sur la théorie des quanta (Researches on the quantum theory), Thesis. *Annales de Physique, 3*, 22.

Einstein, A. (1905). On a heuristic point of view about the creation and conversion of light. *Annalen der Physik, 17*, 132.

Einstein, A., Podolsky, B., & Rosen, N. (1935). Can quantum-mechanical description of physical reality be considered complete? *Physical Review, 47*, 77.

Finilla, A., Gomez, M., Sebenik, C., & Doll, D. (19944). Quantum annealing: A new method for minimizing multidimensional functions. *Chemical Physics Letters, 219*, 343.

Goodkind, A., Jones, B., & Berrens, R. (2020). Cryptodamages: Monetary value estimates of the air pollution and human health impacts of cryptocurrency mining. *Energy Research & Social Science, 59*, 101289.

Grover, L. (1996). A fast quantum mechanical algorithm for database search. In *Proceedings of the Twenty-eighth Annual ACM Symposium on Theory of Computing*, 212.

Heisenberg, W. (1927). Über den anschaulichen Inhalt der quantentheoretischen Kinematik und Mechanik. *Zeitschrift für Physik, 43*, 172.

Mantelero, A. (2018). AI and Big Data: A blueprint for a human rights, social and ethical impact assessment. *Computer Law & Security Review, 34*, 754.

Maxwell, J. C. (1865). A dynamical theory of the electromagnetic field. *Philosophical Transactions of the Royal Society of London, 155*, 459.

Moss, S. (2021). Cooling quantum computers. *Cooling Supplement.* https://www.datacenterdynamics.com/en/analysis/cooling-quantum-computers/

Nielsen, M., & Chuang, I. (2010). *Quantum Computation and Quantum Information.* Cambridge: Cambridge University Press.

Planck, M. (1900). Über eine Verbesserung der Wienschen Spektralgleichung. *Verhandlungen der Deutschen Physikalischen Gesellschaft, 2*, 237.

Porter, A., & Ivie, R. (2019). Women in physics and astronomy, 2019. *AIP Report.* https://www.aip.org/sites/default/files/statistics/women/Women%20in%20Physics%20and%20Astronomy%202019.1.pdf

Rivest, R., Shamir, A., & Adleman, L. (1978). A method for obtaining digital signatures and public-key cryptosystems. *Communications of the ACM*, 120. https://dl.acm.org/doi/10.1145/359340.359342

Schrödinger, E. (1926). An undulatory theory of the mechanics of atoms and molecules. *Physical Review, 28*, 1049.

Schrödinger, E. (1935). Die gegenwärtige Situation in der Quantenmechanik. *Naturwissenschaften, 23*, 807.

Shor, P. (1994). Algorithms for Quantum Computation: Discrete Logarithms and Factoring. In *Proceedings 35th Annual Symposium on Foundations of Computer Science*, 124. IEEE Computer Society. Press.

Shor, P. (1995). Scheme for reducing decoherence in quantum computer memory. *Physical Review A, 52*, R2493.

Yin, J., et al. (2020). Entanglement-based secure quantum cryptography over 1120 kilometres. *Nature, 582*, 501.

7

Climate Politics and Social Change

What Can Cognitive and Quantum Approaches Offer?

Karen O'Brien and Manjana Milkoreit

Introduction

The 2015 Paris Agreement on climate change was widely heralded as a political breakthrough; its ambitious temperature targets immediately generated optimism and hope. At last, the international community was taking climate change seriously. Meeting these ambitious objectives, however, is another story. Many experts are skeptical, noting that especially the aspirational temperature goal of 1.5°C is unrealistic, and that without carbon capture and storage technologies, the agreement is destined to fail (Anderson 2015). Others point to the limited number of realistic scenarios that are compatible with the goal (Warszawski et al. 2021). Yet some remain hopeful, emphasizing that the future is a choice, and that it is up to every individual to make a difference (Figueres and Rivett-Carnac 2020). Success depends on many factors, including political will and timely action. How do we activate this will and action? What might it take to align decisions and actions with outcomes at all levels of society, such that they contribute to meeting the Paris Agreement's goal to remain "well below 2°C," and ideally below 1.5°C?

Meeting climate goals requires both social change and systems change. Social change involves transforming relationships and interactions to influence norms and institutions (Moore et al. 2014), while systems change refers more broadly to the processes and patterns that result from such relationships and interactions (for example, economic systems, political systems, and food systems). In terms of climate change, it is unclear how social change and systems change will come about across multiple scales, particularly within a very short time frame. Although there have been endless appeals for individuals to change their behaviors, political will and timely action are generally considered the domain of national politics and International Relations (IR).

Classical or conventional perspectives on international politics focus on collective actors, especially states, as the key agents generating or preventing systems change. Their ability to control material resources—to wield structural power—in their collective interest is thought to determine outcomes. It is rare that individuals are seen as contributing to the types of transformations needed to limit projected increases in average global temperatures. In fact, individuals generally do not matter in this account of social change and systems change; they merely represent (i.e., act on behalf of) governments, corporations, labor unions, or civil society organizations, verbalizing and pursuing the usually short-term interests of these organizations. National leaders are the exception since they are considered to wield structural and institutional power though their formal position of authority (e.g., their ability to direct militaries or spend public funds).

A quantum paradigm, as interpreted through quantum social science, offers a different perspective. It posits that social structures, including norms, rules, regulations, and institutions, are not real, but specific outcomes of the collapse of "superpositions of shared mental states—social wave functions" (Wendt 2015, 258). Together with its view of individuals as nonlocally entangled through language and meaning making, it presents a different way of understanding the dynamics of social change, introducing a much larger role for individuals in scaling transformative change (O'Brien 2021). Recognizing phenomena such as nonlocal entanglement, superpositions, complementarity, and potentiality, a quantum social paradigm also highlights consciousness, intentionality, and meaning. Quantum social change can be described as "a conscious, nonlinear, and non-local approach to transformations that is grounded in our inherent oneness. It recognizes that we are entangled through language, meaning, and shared contexts, and that our deepest values and intentions are potential sources of individual change, collective change, and systems change. This recognition, when expressed through a particular quality of agency, can shift systems and cultures in a manner that is both equitable and sustainable" (O'Brien 2021, 4). From this perspective, individual change, collective change, and systems change occur not only through classical relationships of causality but also through nonlocal entanglement, which provides each individual with wider spheres of influence.

The difference between classical and quantum approaches to social change matters when it comes to climate governance. A quantum perspective shifts our attention beyond material power structures to highlight the role of individuals in perpetuating these structures through the process of meaning making and the use of language, as well as "intra-actions" within one entangled system (Wendt 2015; Barad 2007). It sensitizes us to the interdependence of mind, matter, and physical reality. As opposed to a more deterministic classical account, a quantum view presents social reality, including physical-material reality, as highly dynamic, constantly in the making, and open to change through changes in meaning. New (shared) understandings of reality create new (collective) behaviors, which in turn affect social and material realities. For example, in describing changes in marriage equality laws (i.e., same-sex marriage) in the

United States, Waddock et al. (2020) discuss how changing cultural memes led to social changes by shaping attitudes, behaviors, and social norms. They emphasize that these changes highlight the importance of both language and fundamental values. This dynamism and the corresponding potential for systems change are rooted in the human mind and its ability to generate and change systems of meaning.

Using this insight as a starting point, in this chapter we explore the potential for linking both cognitive and quantum approaches to climate change governance, highlighting the role of individuals in generating social change and systems change. We start with a recognition that even within the same material-structural landscape, the language of climate change can have a strong influence on climate politics at all levels. Approaching climate change politics as a multiscale process of meaning making (Hulme 2009), we consider the role of individual cognitive processes in generating, sharing, and intra-acting upon new meanings. We start with a discussion of quantum social change and the importance of language and meaning, then build on Milkoreit's (2017) account of cognition in international climate change governance and the concept of belief systems to illuminate the nature of individual political cognition and its role in changing collective meanings. We use three brief examples to illuminate the importance of climate language and its use by individuals in very different positions of (non) material power: US presidents, diplomats negotiating international climate change agreements, and climate activists. We conclude by reflecting on the ways that both cognitive and quantum approaches might expand our political imagination and contribute to much-needed changes in actual practices that can lead not only to stronger climate governance but also to quantum social change.

Social Change and Systems Change: A Quantum Perspective

Sociologists and political scientists have long theorized social relations and social systems, and it is beyond the scope of this chapter to summarize these ideas. However, Wendt (2015, 12) argues that most of these theories have been by default built on the "causal closure of classical physics," in that "materialism, determinism, locality, and so on—were deeply ingrained in the minds of social scientists. These assumptions were taken to be true of reality as a whole, and thus fundamental constraints on social scientific inquiry." Classical understandings of social change and systems change have been adopted within global change research and extended to include insights on emergence from complexity science and chaos theory (Urry 2005). Research on climate change politics and governance has drawn attention to social constructions, social dynamics, and relations of power (Ciplet et al. 2015), bringing in concepts such as governmentality and assemblages (Müller 2015; Lövbrand et al. 2009). There has also been increasing attention to (transnational) networks of actors (Bulkeley et al. 2014) and the processes of orchestration (Hale and Roger 2014).

Generally speaking, however, research on social change and systems change is based on the understanding that classical physics governs the macro level. The relationship between individuals and collectives from a classical perspective is a vertical one that is based on shared identities and aggregations of common interests. Systems change is a struggle for power among competing interests, influenced largely by those who control material resources and shape and influence the social discourse through various media. From a classical perspective, apart from leaders and charismatic individuals, most people do not play a significant role in social change. This is possibly one reason that political analyses of Greta Thunberg's role in climate governance have so far remained limited (Sabherwal et al. 2021; Zulianello and Ceccobelli 2020).

From a quantum perspective, the relationship between individuals and collectives is horizontal, in that people are connected through shared mental states and meanings that collapse a social wave function into a particular actuality (Wendt 2015). Wendt's quantum social theory introduces a flat ontology that recognizes that social structures are "distributed across many different individuals, each of whose free decisions to collapse the structure's social wave function make it a material reality in that moment" (Wendt 2015, 264). Consistent with a process ontology, one can think of social structures as continuously popping in and out of existence through practices. However, because humans are entangled in social structures that are held together by social and cultural norms, some practices are more likely or probable than others (Watts and Stenner 2003). This suggests a mutual co-constitution of mind and matter and hence material reality: matter affects thought, thought imposes meaning on matter, and meaning affects practices and can remake matter.

A quantum lens on social change provides both a perspective and a vocabulary to communicate that "social reality is not what it seems" (O'Brien 2021). In particular, the concepts of entanglement, nonlocality, and potentiality reinforce the notions of holism that are eminent in many other worldviews, including in indigenous knowledge and wisdom traditions. Researchers in the environmental humanities have explored a relational perspective that is linked to process philosophy and relational worldviews (Roberts 2014; Walsh et al. 2020; Mancilla Garcia et al. 2020). This includes Karen Barad's agential realism, which is based on quantum physics and the idea that meaning and matter are generated through intra-actions (Barad 2007). According to agential realism, which includes more-than-human intra-actions, our participation within nature is constitutive of reality: "matter is not a thing but a doing, a congealing of agency" through which phenomena "come to matter" (Barad 2007, 394). This opens up for an understanding of agency not just as action, but as responsibility, or response-ability (Barad 2007). Applying this to structures, including norms, rules, policies, and agreements that influence greenhouse gas emissions, the role of agency in transforming social systems really does matter (O'Brien 2021).

From the perspective of quantum social science, language plays an important role in IR, in that meaning is enacted through speech acts (Fierke and Antonio-Alfonso 2018; Wendt 2015). Physicist David Bohm (Bohm 1996, 6) considers shared meaning as "the 'glue' or 'cement' that holds people and societies together." Speech acts play an important role in establishing shared meaning and shaping the material world, and they affect both the speaker and the listener. As Wendt puts it (2015, 234), "In the quantum view the language in each of our heads is a superposition of potential meanings that are actualized only by its collapse in speech acts." Sociologist John Shotter (2014, 307) argues that words serve to direct people's attention, especially toward anticipating what will happen next: "It is only too easy to take our words as being representative of already existing differences on the objective side, rather than as doings in the situation of their utterance."

Context is important here, not merely as cognitive input for the decision maker, but as a condition for the mutual constitution of mind and matter, and a source of meaning making. Speech acts turn language as a potentiality into a reality—they collapse a range of possible meanings into an actual understanding and generate actions, but this requires a shared context. As an example of how speech acts create nonlocal intra-actions, Wendt (2015, 194) refers to the death of Socrates, which left his wife Xantippe a "widow" not by direct causality, but by virtue of the culturally shared meaning associated with marriage. She is then treated as a widow through specific actions that materialize her new identity. According to Wendt's quantum social theory, "by participating in a shared language, the content of individuals' thoughts is entangled with other minds and thus irreducibly contextual" (Wendt 2015, 255).

Speech acts are thus both relational and contextual, and they can be used both to inspire actions by others and to dismiss and disempower others from taking action. Language influences (and is influenced by) continuous intra-actions that have consequences for structures and systems. It "measures" cognitive processes, revealing thoughts of the individual but also something about all the related phenomena that have shaped thinking (Milkoreit 2017). Language and speech acts are important from a quantum perspective precisely because of the potential for nonlocal correlations of shared meaning to contribute to practices that shape a material reality that supports all life. These correlations are based on the concept of quantum coherence, which refers to a nonlocal, correlated situation where the wave functions of two or more particles are entangled, such that when measuring one, information is instantly gained about the others. Based on quantum consciousness theory, Wendt (2015, 3) speculates that subjectivity can be considered a macroscopic quantum mechanical phenomenon, and as such, "human beings and therefore social life exhibit quantum coherence—in effect, that we are walking wave functions." Wendt (2015, 32) points out that this coherence is nonmaterial and "can only be known from the inside, through experience."

When language and intra-actions are based on a classical view of the world—one that is fragmented, disconnected, and deterministic—climate governance reflects this and contributes to a material reality that is unsustainable. When language and intra-actions recognize entanglement, nonlocality, and potentiality, as well as values that are aligned with the well-being of all, climate governance is more likely to support sustainability. If the co-constitution of mind and matter is an entangled phenomenon associated with an inherent wholeness, then each person matters (O'Brien 2021). This is as true for climate politics as it is for the social change and systems change needed to achieve climate goals.

Given the centrality of shared meaning making to a quantum account of systems change, we now explore the process of generating and changing shared meanings. To deepen our understanding of the nature of meaning making, beliefs, and speech acts, especially when and how meaning systems can change, we turn to a social-cognitive account that is not quantum-theoretical. This perspective shares important ontological commitments with quantum social theory, most importantly, the notion of relationality and the importance of context, which allows for an instructive conversation about agency and theories of social change. Cognition facilitates relationality in the sense that it connects the individual mind and body with everything else in the world. Indeed, the perception and mental representation of material, social, and ideational realities and the corresponding process of meaning making provide the foundation of relations, including a recognition of entanglement. In other words, the mind is needed for a relational ontology.

Cognition in Relation to a Quantum Approach to Systems Change

Meaning making is a dynamic process between individual minds, collectives, and physical realities, such as weather patterns or a walk in the woods, in which communication through language and story plays an outsized role. To follow, we address first the nature and functioning of individual minds, and second the processes for changing or creating new kinds of shared meanings within individual minds and social groups.

Individual Minds

A simplified but useful way to conceptualize cognition is to conceive of minds as complex systems or networks of interdependent concepts ("mental representations"). In this model of cognition as belief systems, meaning is not inherent in a particular concept but emerges from the relationships between them and the way information flows (i.e., "is processed") within this specific network structure. The relationships and interdependencies between concepts give rise to beliefs, identities, worldviews, and ideologies (Homer-Dixon et al. 2013); they are at the root of collective action as well as conflict (Homer-Dixon et al. 2014). Different aspects of a person's belief system (e.g., their identity as a parent or their beliefs about renewable energy or the resilience of nature) can be thought of as subnetworks or subsets of a larger network of ideas.

The connections between ideas are not random; neither are the mental processes (e.g., reasoning, decisions) they generate. A fundamental ordering principle for the mind is coherence within a system of related beliefs (Thagard 2000). In a classical sense, the concept of coherence refers to the quality of being logical and consistent, but it is generally not relevant for processes of meaning making and disconnected from emotions. For example, policy scholars have long been interested in policy coherence—the alignment of goals and actions within a particular policy domain (May et al. 2006), but also across different scales and sites of governance (e.g., Fertel et al. 2013). This type of coherence is particularly important for international climate governance, which relies heavily on widely distributed emission reduction efforts across multiple scales and sites. It has been a major point of contention in recent discussions about the role of national net-zero emission targets and their timing to contribute to the achievement of the Paris Agreement's temperature goal (e.g., Soest et al. 2021).

From a cognitive perspective, the need for coherence implies that ideas have to make sense as they relate to each other and to the material-social world; that is, they need to follow the rules of logic, be consistent with each other and with observations about the world ("evidence"), and, more generally, mutually reinforce each other. Coherence in this sense cannot be reduced to rationality or rational choice as it is used in much of classical social science (i.e., reasoning as a form of calculation). Instead, it is a system-level property that emerges from "a largely unconscious process in which many pieces of information are combined in parallel into a coherent whole... the result of mentally balancing many complementary and conflicting pieces of information until they all fit together in a satisfying way" (Thagard 2000, 3). Coherence is context dependent and complex, meaning that the network components activated in a particular situation give rise to coherent thoughts given the contextual setting and stimuli (e.g., a family dinner table or a pipeline protest) and the associated meanings as well as material realities. This enables the existence of contradictory or inconsistent beliefs within a person's mind over time and across different contexts.

Importantly, coherence is also emotional ("hot"), where the emotional valences of concepts, ideas, and propositions influence meaning and decision-making, e.g., leading to the embrace or rejection of a new idea, argument, or theory (Thagard 2006). Concepts that form belief systems have positive or negative emotional valences. For example, for most people the concept of climate change has a negative valence, either because of its expected impacts on all life on the planet or because of the potential effects of policies that seek to limit climate change. The emotional valence of a specific concept affects all other concepts it is related to. In our climate change example, a person who is concerned about negative climate impacts on his or her community would likely also have a concept of "climate action" or "climate policy" that has a positive valence, while a person worried about the "costs of climate action" would attach a negative valence to this concept.

Given this understanding of cognition as hot coherence, it is possible to investigate and visually represent, for example, the belief systems of negotiators and nongovernmental organization (NGO) representatives regarding climate change and multilateral cooperation. Figure 7.1 provides an example of such a visualization using cognitive-affective mapping (Findlay and Thagard 2014; Homer-Dixon et al. 2013, 2014). The network graph (cognitive-affective map, CAM) depicts a small section of the belief system of an NGO (youth) representative regarding solutions for the climate problem at the 2012 climate negotiations.

We can think of the mind as the gate between material and discursive realities on the one hand, which serve as inputs into cognitive processes, and the political decisions made and behaviors performed on the other. Information, e.g., regarding the beliefs of other actors or the dominant norms related to a given political domain, has to pass through that gate, where it "gets processed" by the actor's mind and leads to cognitive outputs in the form of decisions and actions. Further, cognition involves a large number of scale-crossing processes, connecting molecular and neural activity within a single person's brain and body with the person's social and institutional interactions, as well as with his or her material-environmental experiences (Thagard 2014). This multilevel perspective re-emphasizes the relational nature of cognition: the mind is "embedded in a multilevel system, connected to other minds as to the material world of objects and beings" (Milkoreit 2017, 68), where the individual and the social system scales are interdependent and mutually affect each other. Importantly, "neither the individual nor the social deserves to be prioritized.... [T]he interaction and mutual interdependence between the individual mind and the social environment are key to understanding existing beliefs and belief dynamics" (Milkoreit 2017, 11).

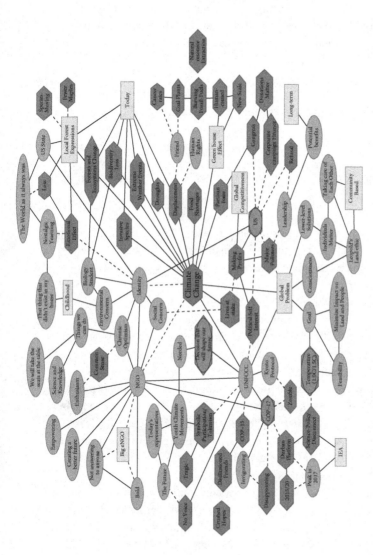

Figure 7.1 Cognitive-affective map: Beliefs of a youth activist regarding climate change and international cooperation, 2012.

The network graph is based on interview data from 2012 and visualizes the belief system of a youth climate activist with a focus on the emotional content of beliefs. Each network node represents a concept or belief mentioned during the interview, which is linked to multiple other concepts or beliefs. Each concept has a specific emotional valence: (green) ovals represent positive concepts (e.g., "youth climate movements"); (red) hexagons represent negative concepts (e.g., "climate change"). Neutral concepts are represented with (yellow) rectangles. Superimposed (purple) ovals and hexagons indicate ambivalence—the emotional valence can change depending on context. Two different kinds of links exist: solid lines represent emotionally coherent or mutually supportive relations between concepts; dashed lines represent relations between concepts that are incoherent or (emotionally) opposed. Meaning emerges from these elements: concepts, their emotional (affective) valence, and the relationships between them.

Source: Milkoreit (2017). An introduction to cognitive-affective mapping with further references can be found here: https://cascadeinstitute.org/resources/cognitive-affective-mapping/.

This perspective on cognition is aligned with a quantum perspective, which does not see individuals as discrete entities, but rather as an [I/we] that is entangled through language, shared meaning, shared contexts, and innate values (O'Brien 2021). The idea that individuals are separate and distinct is associated with a shared belief system that is firmly grounded in a Western worldview and its classical assumptions about subject-object and human-nature dualities. To follow, we consider how cognitive approaches can contribute insights on shifting shared meanings about the nature of reality.

Remaking Shared Meaning and Reality

While belief system stability over time is an important feature of our mental experience, the mind is an open system with great potential for change and novelty. This can take many different forms, including (1) learning (Chi and Roscoe 2002) e.g., based on new observations and experiences, (2) imagination (Kind and Kung 2016) e.g., based on reading fiction, (3) creativity (Sawyer et al. 2003) e.g., based on interactions with colleagues, and (4) belief change (Thagard 1992). Given the nature of the mind—including its complex, dynamic systems of beliefs—and the need for coherence, belief revisions are in fact *processes* of system/network reorganization. For a new belief, value, or norm to be adopted, it is necessary to integrate this new idea into an existing system of beliefs.

To the extent that a new idea conflicts with or challenges existing beliefs (i.e., creates incoherence), it will either be rejected or require changes at a larger system scale—the adjustment, replacement, or reorganization of (connections between) a number of related ideas to create a new set of coherent beliefs, i.e., a different network structure. This has important implications for climate politics. As Milkoreit states (2017, 222), "Because our minds have a tendency to maintain the coherence of a belief system, a [climate] negotiator will most likely reject proposals that disturb the negotiator's cognitive-emotional balance without creating a new one." Hence, coherence acts both as a constraint and a facilitator of change at different scales of a belief system.

Given that cognitive change is a form of system change, it is useful to draw on the idea of multiple stable states—different cognitive "basins of attraction" (Beer 2000; Wang et al. 2016)—and the notion of regime shifts during which the system moves from one basin to another (Scheffer 2009; Mathias et al. 2020; Leeuw and Folke 2021). Depending on the kind and scale of change required, the "pathway" between the existing ("old") and new system of beliefs, i.e., the steps required to move from one set of coherent ideas to another, might not be easily identifiable, and multiple pathways might be available. A series of bridging concepts between two coherent belief systems might be needed.

The process of changing one's mind can take time, starting with the accumulation of evidence that contradicts a current belief, e.g., that climate change will not affect one's hometown. Often other people or groups and their role in one's life, e.g., authorities, in-group members, and trusted media channels vs. perceived others, play an important role in disrupting a stable belief system and weakening certain components, e.g., by arguing that a certain event was linked to climate change. If and when other people's arguments, words, expressions, and behaviors change, these changes can affect the way the mind interprets reality, including the kinds of interpretations (meanings) that are possible at any point in time.

While components of an existing belief system become unstable, e.g., by breaking certain connections between ideas or encouraging the removal of a set of concepts, an alternative network structure has to be created, consisting of new concepts and beliefs that can be adopted to achieve coherence. These new ideas can come from our social and environmental context or be generated in the mind through creative and imaginative processes.

Individual-cognitive and collective-communicative processes of meaning making are closely connected. Members of social groups tend to have very similar belief and meaning systems; that is, they share mental representations of their group, e.g., Canadians, Buddhists, free climbers, and their social and environmental reality, and they are keenly aware of how their shared beliefs differ from those of other groups, e.g., how conservative views on gun control differ from progressive ones. If one would compare their cognitive-affective maps, one would find a significant amount of overlap between their networks of concepts and associated emotional valances. Through group members' behavior and their communication with each other, especially their language, they constantly reinforce—stabilize—their shared beliefs and understandings of the world. At the same time, each group member has the power to undermine this stability by behaving or using language in a new way. The extent of this power might depend on the person's position in the group (e.g., his or her seniority or expertise-based authority). But every group member has some ability to shape the meanings that are shared by the group and to challenge and change them over time.

This is where quantum approaches to social change come into play, in that the metaphors, methods, and meanings of quantum physics intra-act with the cognitive processes described above. Whereas metaphors such as quantum leaps and entanglement can serve as bridging concepts toward another way of relating to social change, and methods such as Q Methodology can provide ways of studying the dynamic and entangled nature of beliefs, quantum social theory reminds us that the concept of entanglement is not only a metaphor, but also a reality and it is increasingly seen as relevant to macro-scale processes (Wendt 2015; Lehtonen 2019; O'Brien 2021). Such a perspective recognizes the power and potential of individuals to contribute to social change and systems change, not as "classic individuals" but as "quantum individuals", i.e., both individuals and collectives entangled through language and shared meaning. In the next section, we explore what all of this might mean for climate politics.

Speech Acts in Climate Politics

Climate change is a collective action problem that calls for both individual and societal responses at an unprecedented rate and scale to decrease the likelihood of severe, widespread, and irreversible impacts on people and ecosystems (IPCC 2014, 2018). IR scholarship has focused on diverse approaches to climate politics to explore cooperation and conflict among rational actors. This includes game theoretical (Jervis 1988; Barrett 2016) and neoliberal-structural approaches (Keohane and Victor 2016), and social constructivist accounts of norms (Ciplet et al. 2015; Mitchell and Carpenter 2019) and identities (Hochstetler and Milkoreit 2014). While the role of states is important, the mindsets and cognitive patterns of leaders, negotiators, representatives of NGOs, and climate activists have received less attention (e.g., George 1969; Bonham 1993; Astorino-Courtois 1995). Most IR theories do, however, assume that collective political actors like states or companies have mental states (e.g., interests, goals) and emotions (e.g., fear, pride), and that they perform complicated cognitive tasks, such as cost-benefit calculations or moral reasoning. But so far, the discipline has rarely investigated, either theoretically or empirically, "the mental and communicative processes that create these shared beliefs" (Milkoreit 2017, 4). Yet, as we argue in this chapter, through entanglement, leaders, negotiators, activists, *and* others play a key role in climate politics.

National Leaders: The Case of the United States

National leaders play an important role in climate politics. Following Leibniz, Wendt (2015, 270) considers leaders to be "dominant" monads when it comes to collapsing a state's "wave function" of potential into actual outcomes, in that others momentarily give up their potential to respond. Because these choices have nonlocal consequences, Wendt (2015, 270) emphasizes that "the intentions and character of leaders are crucial in determining which policies are realized. Even in highly constrained situations, small differences in leaders can make big differences in what actually happens." As dominant leaders in the international system, US presidents have considerable structural-material power to influence climate policy, but also individual linguistic potential to create social and systemic change. For example, we can contrast the language of two US presidents regarding climate change, based on a comparative analysis of speeches given by Presidents Donald Trump in 2017 and Joseph Biden in 2021. A conventional IR perspective would recognize that President Biden faces a largely unchanged material-structural landscape compared to that of the Trump presidency, yet these two leaders' beliefs and actions related to climate change are dramatically different. We can explore the meanings they each articulated, their own perceptions of agency, and the kinds of agency enabled by the stories they tell.

In his first year in office, and just months after the United States had formally joined the Paris Agreement, President Trump announced his intention to withdraw from the treaty, while hinting at his intention to "renegotiate" a better deal for the United States in a speech in the White House Rose Garden (White House 2017). In the following years, his administration largely ignored the international climate negotiations, stopped all related international funding contributions, and went hard to work at dismantling climate and environmental policies domestically. President Biden, who took office in 2021, rejoined the Paris Agreement as soon as he was inaugurated and issued an executive order on climate change that introduced an "all-of-government approach" (Executive Office of the President of the United States 2021). He also published a new and arguably ambitious Nationally Determined Contribution, discussed climate change in his first address to Congress (White House 2021), and hosted a Virtual Leaders' Summit on Climate Change to reinvigorate the international political process in April 2021. Each man used very different language to talk about climate change—each developed their own meaning system of interdependent beliefs about the Paris Agreement.

Let's first consider the language of President Trump. The story he told in his Rose Garden speech on June 1, 2017, is one of economic relations among independent states that are in competition with each other, where the United States is part of a "rigged" global trade and financial system. Trump's story portrays the Paris Agreement as an unfair constraint on the American economy, burdening its workers, industries, and taxpayers while allowing others, especially China, to do as they wish (i.e., grow), while not promising any significant effect on the climate. In Trump's version of reality, the agreement disadvantages and even "punishes" the United States to the "exclusive benefit of other countries," threatening to lead to "lost jobs, lowered wages, shuttered factories, and vastly diminished economic production." In this belief system, America is being taken advantage of by others, and President Trump would rectify this unfair situation by withdrawing from the Paris Agreement. The president was the hero protecting the United States, especially American workers and businesses, from the exploitative efforts of other nations—and thus the main political agent wielding power. There was no belief in an entity called the international community and no shared or collective interest in addressing a global problem; the term "climate change" did not appear once in the speech and the term "climate" only showed up as the "climate accord" or the "climate fund." In his belief system, there were only states competing for economic success—very much a reflection of conventional IR scholarship.

While this announcement and the later withdrawal letter had formal legal consequences—removing the United States from the Paris Agreement—it also had immediate effects on the existing landscape of meaning in which all political actors related to climate change are entangled. For example, Trump's exclusive focus on competitive relations with China affected both the way China's representatives perceived of themselves and their relationship to the United States, and influenced the kinds of language they would likely use in future conversations with American diplomats. Trump's 2017 speech had immediate nonlocal effects on the future perception of American diplomats involved in United Nations Framework Convention on Climate Change (UNFCCC) processes (e.g., during the Conference of Parties (COP23) in Germany). Other delegates would approach American negotiators with significantly lowered expectations, considering them as unhelpful or possibly even obstructive in the ongoing effort to implement the Paris Agreement.

The speech also affected identities of various American economic actors as beneficiaries of the president's protection, especially coal workers and energy company executives, likely deepening loyalty and support for the president. At the same time, the new stance of the White House toward international climate governance also rallied subnational governments in the United States, cities, businesses, and civil society actors to step into the federal void. This led to the emergence of new actors (e.g., the We Are Still in Coalition), their identities as international representatives of the United States, and their practices, such as running the Climate Action Center and sending a "US Delegation of Climate Leaders" to COP23. Trump's speech also had important effects on the beliefs of NGO representatives and the strategies they would pursue in the coming years to wield influence against rather than with the US federal government. It likely also affected the thoughts of young people involved in the Sunrise Movement and globally, including Greta Thunberg.

Now we turn to President Biden's language during his first six months in office, which produced a very different story. As revealed on several occasions, including remarks delivered on January 27, 2021 (White House 2021a), remarks during the Virtual Leaders Summit on Climate on April 23rd, 2021 (White House 2021b), and remarks during his first address to Congress on April 28, 2021 (White House 2021c), he also emphasized the importance of the American economy, especially American jobs, but framed in a completely different way. For Biden, the climate crisis presents an opportunity to "rebuild the nation" and its infrastructure, to revitalize its economy, and to address existing inequalities and injustices. He repeatedly labeled climate change as an existential threat that requires urgent and ambitious action, acknowledging the reality of past and present climate impacts on various regions of the United States. We also see that Biden's vision for America is focused on the potential benefits of climate policies. He points to millions of "good-paying jobs" that will be created as the result of responding to the existential threat of climate change, such as electricians installing energy-efficient technologies and electric-vehicle charging stations. In Biden's mind, climate action will drive economic and social success and inclusion, bettering society in multiple ways.

President Biden's international narrative strongly corresponds with this domestic story. While perceiving a competitive economic landscape (especially with a view to China) is a continuation of the Trump narrative, he talks about the climate crisis as one of several global problems that the United States cannot solve alone—collective action is necessary. Biden recognizes a community of states that experiences shared threats and advances shared solutions. The "common purpose" of international cooperation should be to support the most vulnerable and to "increase our collective resilience." Global climate change not only presents clear and present dangers but also offers economic and developmental opportunities. Collective international action will generate jobs and wealth all around the world.

Like Trump's story, Biden's system of ideas affects and enables different actors, identities, and agents. Oil and gas executives were not offered the identity of being under special presidential protection but instead were given warnings regarding the planned elimination of fossil fuel subsidies and the end of leases on public lands ("no more 'handouts'"). At the same time, young people and climate advocates were invited and encouraged to cooperate with the federal government: "Your government is going to work with you." Biden also addressed workers in the fossil fuel industry, including coal miners, who had played prominent roles in Trump's speeches. Describing them as those who "helped build this country," he talked about revitalizing "the economies of coal, oil, and gas, and power plant communities" with "new good-paying jobs."

The continuities between Trump's and Biden's stories can indicate two very different things. First, both men might perceive some dimensions of reality in some similar ways; for example, they share a reality and its meaning regarding competitive relations between the United States and China. Second, these continuities could also indicate a form of path dependency in the meaning landscape and the related physical and social realities that force President Biden to speak to some of the realities emphasized or even created by President Trump. For example, Biden had to address the role of coal workers (and more generally fossil fuel industry workers), who featured often in Trump's speeches and policymaking as the heroes at the center of American energy production and "dominance." He had to both acknowledge the importance of these workers and impose a new set of meanings regarding the role of coal and fossil fuel in the future US economy, as well as the hero identity of these professionals. Biden's language shifted the focus from individual workers to the communities where they lived and created a future vision in which they would be employed in "good-paying" but different jobs, e.g., capping oil wells and reclaiming mines. Their communities would turn into "hubs of economic growth." The continuities and differences between these leaders have ripple effects across the globe, influencing other actors in international politics. To follow, we examine the role of diplomats in climate politics.

Diplomats: The Role of Climate Change Negotiators

A quantum perspective draws attention to the role of individual diplomats in creating shared meaning through their use of language, both in the specific context of the climate negotiations and at any particular points in time. Negotiators are entangled in a context linked to the historically-developed meanings of words (e.g., responsibility, equity, ambition) and identities (e.g., the most vulnerable countries) and their relationship to material-environmental conditions associated with climate change. Most IR scholars still tend to conceive of this context in more simple and mechanistic ways, i.e., as material structures. Yet, through their specific, individual use of language, negotiators have the potential in any given moment of the political process to create new realities and meanings that are entangled with others, especially those who share similar values or relate to similar contexts. Importantly, the relationships they find themselves in are constantly open to being remade through speech acts.

Negotiators representing state governments in the UNFCCC exercise political agency through their use of language and speech acts that influence the negotiation process and its textual and institutional outcomes, e.g., in plenary statements, bilateral conversations, or alliance meetings. The negotiator's agency-through-speech is linked in multiple ways to domestic or intraorganizational conditions in a multiscale system (DeSombre 2000; Milkoreit 2019; Putnam 1988), which contribute to the belief and meaning system of each negotiator. These influences include prior speech acts by leaders and the ideas, identities, and meanings enabled by these leaders, as discussed earlier. They are also influenced by other changes in the world, such as national-scale leadership changes or climate-related extreme weather events (Milkoreit 2017).

Shaped by these influences, individual diplomats hold beliefs regarding their own government's negotiation goals and domestic conditions for implementing international obligations, the country's historical role and influence in the negotiation process, i.e., its identity in the negotiations, e.g., as an obstructionist, and the main norms that should guide the process. At the same time, each negotiator holds beliefs regarding the shared goals of the international community and their implications for national action, and the interests and normative orientations of other negotiation parties. The negotiator's interdependent beliefs regarding these two scales—the national-domestic and the international-collective—form a coherent belief system, which informs the language used during the negotiations. For example, individual American diplomats attending earlier climate negotiation sessions of the UNFCCC had specific mental representations of the United States as a political actor and its negotiation goals (e.g., "an agreement with similar obligations for China and India"), which they shared with other members of their delegation, with non-American negotiators, with people in the US State Department, and with then-president Obama.

For example, Todd Stern, the US special envoy for climate change under the Obama administration, and head of the US delegation to the UNFCCC between 2011 and 2016, is attributed with saying, "If equity is in, we are out" during an informal but intense "huddle" of negotiators in Durban in 2011, when the negotiation community attempted to give the process a new direction after the failed Copenhagen summit. Stern's comments referred to the role of equity in a new negotiation mandate, indicating strong resistance of the United States to this particular word, its associated meanings, and negotiation dynamics. As Pickering et al. (2012, 423) explain, "Wealthy countries resisted the inclusion of equity on the ground that the term had become too closely yoked to developing countries' favored conception of equity." Different conceptions or meanings would lead to different negotiation dynamics and outcomes (realities). Todd Stern's focus on language sought to limit the kinds of future realities the negotiations would create.

A large number of mental representations like Todd Stern's conceptions of the role of equity can form different constellations of coherent belief systems in the mind of American negotiators. For example, the concept of equity—labeled CBDR for the principle of "common but differentiated responsibilities"—was embedded in the mind of a US negotiator interviewed by Milkoreit in 2012 and depicted in the cognitive-affective map shown in Figure 7.2.

Multiple factors influence the formation of these beliefs at the individual and group levels and how they change over time. These include observations of the behavior of other actors (e.g., US presidential elections and domestic policy debates), economic and technological changes, such as the declining costs of solar power generation, and the availability of new scientific information, such as research on biophysical feedbacks and potential tipping points. The ongoing interaction between cognitive states and social-material system dynamics generates a constantly changing set of potential beliefs for any individual

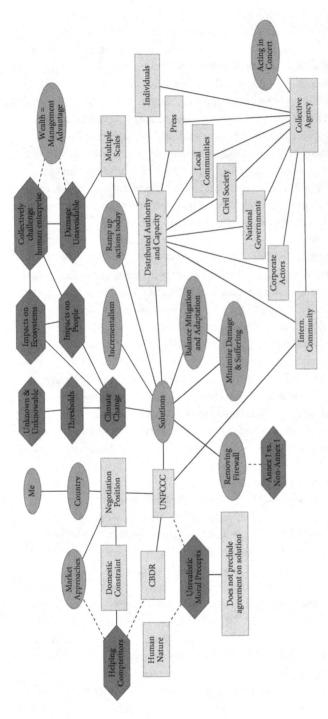

Figure 7.2 Cognitive-affective map (CAM) of US delegate to the United Nations Framework Convention on Climate Change (UNFCCC), 2012. This CAM is based on interview data and visualizes a subset of beliefs held by a member of the US delegation to the international climate negotiations in 2012. All beliefs relate to climate change (an emotionally negative concept represented as a hexagon) and the role of the UNFCCC in addressing climate change ("Solutions"). The concept node "CBDR" (common but differentiated responsibilities) is used to refer to conceptions of equity in the climate negotiations. For this negotiator, the principle had a neutral valence (rectangle), but the person identified "Unrealistic Moral Precepts" as a negative dimension of the negotiations (hexagon). Different parties to the negotiations had developed very different understandings of equity and CBDR, which this delegate considered unhelpful when trying to reach an international agreement.
Source: Milkoreit (2017).

and group, which can be actualized at any given moment through speech acts. For example, in the case of the US delegation at COP21 in Paris, presidential speeches, White House briefings, and delegation meetings enabled the creation and change of collective beliefs over time, e.g., regarding the willingness of China to accept transparency measures, the costs of achieving 1.5°C, or, importantly, the unwillingness of the US Congress to ratify a new international climate agreement (Milkoreit 2019). These shared beliefs formed the foundation of and also constrained the diplomats' (and delegation's) speech acts in various negotiation settings and the corresponding perceptions of and interactions with the United States by other negotiators.

Climate Change Activists: The Case of Grete Thunberg

Leaders and diplomats have received considerable attention among IR scholars for their role in climate policy, but activists are playing an increasingly visible role in shaping meanings about climate change. Climate change activism takes many forms, but the role of young people in expressing their dissent against the status quo has been particularly prominent in recent years (O'Brien et al. 2018). Over the past two years, the "Greta Thunberg effect" and the Fridays for Future movement have entered climate politics in surprising ways, challenging leaders to take climate change more seriously. In Twitter interactions between Greta Thunberg and several world leaders, the leaders typically use speech acts to reduce her credibility, often labeling her as immature and irrelevant. However, in the exchanges that follow, Thunberg does not "follow the script" defined by those with power, and instead she writes her own story, taking ownership of the narrative. Such a display of irreverence toward world leaders has drawn positive attention to Thunberg's cause, particularly among her followers:

I

Thunberg tweeted: "Indigenous people are being literally murdered for trying to protect the forest from illegal deforestation. Over and over again. It is shameful that the world remains silent about this."

Bolsonaro in a media interview: "Greta said that the Indians died because they were defending the Amazon. It's impressive that the press is giving space to a brat ["pirralha"] like that."

Thunberg changed her Twitter bio to "Pirralha."

II

Trump tweets in response to a video of Thunberg discussing suffering people, dying ecosystems, and looming mass extinction: "She seems like a very happy young girl looking forward to a bright and wonderful future. So nice to see!"

Thunberg changed her Twitter bio to "A very happy young girl looking forward to a bright and wonderful future."

While social media can be seen through a classical lens as a way of connecting to opinion leaders (by "following" them), in the case of Thunberg, "adults in power witnessed a teenager using social media as a direct communication channel" (Jung et al. 2020, 14). Through a quantum lens, Thunberg's speech acts can be seen as a nonlocal expression of agency that both empowers and provokes others. Her tweets reached many different actors, e.g., other heads of state, youth activists, news media, and were interpreted differently, according to the ways that they make sense of the world and their social context. In particular, the cynicism expressed by leaders may have strengthened a sense of dissent and resistance among youth activists. As Jung et al. (2020, 5) note, the social interactions related to her tweets can be considered representative of current forms of social conflict: "Twitter has been a political battlefield for both sides. Climate change issues are increasingly related to policy and political context." By not responding to the diminishing comments of global leaders in the expected manner, Thunberg both influences shared meaning and increases her agency in international climate politics.

Thunberg also opens the way for others to express their agency by challenging the status quo. When young people's values and worldviews diverge from those holding power, they can express their dissent in a variety of ways, beyond protests and social movements, to reclaim, reframe, and transform their future (O'Brien et al. 2018). From a quantum perspective, every individual can "collapse" a social wave function in ways that benefit both people and the planet and, through nonlocal entanglement, contribute to both social change and systems change.

Implications for Agency and Theories of Social Change

In this chapter, we have explored how a combination of cognitive and quantum approaches can provide new insights into meaning making, agency, and the potential to act in time to make a difference in responding to climate change. Both approaches recognize the importance of the availability of ideas and processes of collective meaning making in politics and social change. Both also acknowledge that cognition does not function like a machine, but rather is open to novelty and surprise. A cognitive approach to climate politics suggests that "People can change their minds over time, and the cognitive interactions of multiple individuals can produce different and sometimes unexpected results" (Milkoreit 2017,

6). A quantum approach emphasizes that these unexpected results influence our intra-actions and have nonlocal consequences that extend our sphere of influence (Wendt 2015). From a quantum perspective, individual agency and collective agency are entangled, and both play a vital role in social change and systems change (O'Brien 2021).

A quantum lens extends this idea of relationality to a holistic conception of the world, where *everything* is inherently entangled, such that it no longer makes sense to think of actors or organizations as clearly bounded and independent. From this perspective, one could argue for a shift from IR to intraglobal relations, and from causal agency to intra-active agency. Combining a cognitive and quantum approach reveals the many ways in which the context for climate policy is shaped by leaders, negotiators, and activists through speech acts in every moment; each of them emphasizes different relationships and intra-actions, reinforcing or redefining meaning with real-world, material consequences.

What does all of this mean in practice for climate politics? First, it points to the importance of being able to imagine and enact alternatives. Given the potential for changes in collective meaning through intra-actions between individual minds, collectives, and their material environment, anybody and everybody can be a source of, or contributor to, social change. Imagination, storytelling, and narrative provide important tools for generating and communicating these alternative meanings within groups of people (Milkoreit 2016). Stories generally play an important role in human cognition, especially in the development of normative and moral thinking (Gottschall 2013; Churchland 2011). The nature of stories allows a person to adopt a different perspective for a little while, seeing the world through somebody else's eyes, and "testing" an alternative meaning system.

Second, it points to the power of individuals to influence the social wave function, "pulling" new structures into existence through practices that are aligned with shared meanings and values that support all life. While traditional IR looks to leaders of states as the dominant forces in society through their control of material power, more and more people are becoming aware of their own power and agency through language—both as individuals and as collectives. Agency is, by nature, a collective process that gives humans the power to continuously and intentionally enact alternative futures through a dynamic process of intra-activity and materialization. For example, young people in Germany appealed to the highest court to expand a 2019 law to reduce carbon emissions to almost zero by 2050, and in 2021 the court ruled in their favor. The idea that each individual matters and can generate quantum social change both within and beyond their spheres of influence through speech acts and practices holds the potential to transform climate politics from a rational endeavor based on calculated interests to a passionate movement to secure a thriving world for all (O'Brien 2021).

In concluding, we recognize that quantum social theory is only one part of a larger movement to replace classical social theory, and it has been challenged on a number of grounds, not the least because it is associated with the constraints of the natural sciences and mathematics (Allan 2018). Yet a "quantum turn" is emergent in the social sciences and humanities, and it shows promise as an alternative way of thinking about society's potential for radical change (Barad 2007; Haven and Khrennikov 2013; Wendt 2015; El Khoury 2015; Zanotti 2019; Der Derian and Wendt 2020). It can be considered significant to sustainability transformations from multiple perspectives, including in relation to the metaphors, methods, or meanings associated with climate change response (O'Brien 2016). A quantum social paradigm reveals the relatedness and interdependence of individual and collective agency, which can generate change at all scales. Yet drawing attention to quantum perspectives does not repudiate or deny the importance of other approaches. As we have shown, a cognitive approach provides both theories and methods for understanding the dynamics of meaning making in climate politics, and a quantum perspective reveals the power of language and meaning making in social change.

References

Allan, Bentley B. 2018. "Social Action in Quantum Social Science." *Millennium* 47 (1): 87–98. https://doi.org/10.1177/0305829818781690.

Anderson, Kevin. 2015. "Duality in Climate Science." *Nature Geoscience* 8 (12): 898–900. https://doi.org/10.1038/ngeo2559.

Astorino-Courtois, Allison. 1995. "The Cognitive Structure of Decision Making and the Course of Arab-Israeli Relations, 1970–1978." *Journal of Conflict Resolution* 39 (3): 419–438.

Barad, Karen. 2007. *Meeting the Universe Halfway: Quantum Physics and the Entanglement of Matter and Meaning*. 2nd printing ed. Durham, NC: Duke University Press Books.

Barrett, Scott. 2016. "Collective Action to Avoid Catastrophe: When Countries Succeed, When They Fail, and Why." *Global Policy* 7 (May): 45–55. https://doi.org/10.1111/1758-5899.12324.

Beer, Randall D. 2000. "Dynamical Approaches to Cognitive Science." *Trends in Cognitive Sciences* 4 (3): 91–99. https://doi.org/10.1016/S1364-6613(99)01440-0.

Bohm, David. 1996. *On Dialogue*. London and New York: Routledge.

Bonham, G. 1993. "Cognitive Mapping as a Technique for Supporting International Negotiation." *Theory and Decision* 34 (3): 255–273.

Bulkeley, Harriet, Liliana Andonova, Michele M. Betsill, Daniel Compagnon, Thomas Hale, Matthew J. Hoffmann, Peter Newell, Matthew Paterson, Charles Roger, and Stacy D. VanDeveer. 2014. *Transnational Climate Change Governance*. Cambridge: Cambridge University Press.

Chi, Michelene T. H., and Rod D. Roscoe. 2002. "The Processes and Challenges of Conceptual Change." In *Reconsidering Conceptual Change: Issues in Theory and Practice*, edited by Margarita Limón and Lucia Mason, 3–27. Kluwer Academic Publishers: Dordrecht, Netherlands. http://link.springer.com/chapter/10.1007/0-306-47637-1_1.

Churchland, Patricia Smith. 2011. *Braintrust: What Neuroscience Tells Us about Morality.* Princeton, NJ: Princeton University Press.

Ciplet, David, J. Timmons Roberts, and Mizan R. Khan. 2015. *Power in a Warming World: The New Global Politics of Climate Change and the Remaking of Environmental Inequality.* Cambridge, MA; London: MIT Press.

DeSombre, Elizabeth. *Domestic Sources of International Environmental Policy: Industry, Environmentalists, and U.S. Power.* Cambridge, MA: The MIT Press.

Der Derian, James, and Alexander Wendt. 2020. "'Quantizing International Relations': The Case for Quantum Approaches to International Theory and Security Practice." *Security Dialogue* 51 (5): 399–413. https://doi.org/10.1177/0967010620901905.

El Khoury, Ann. 2015. *Globalization Development and Social Justice: A Propositional Political Approach.* 1st ed. London; New York: Routledge.

Executive Office of the President of the United States. 2021. "Executive Order 14008 of January 27, 2021: Tackling the Climate Crisis at Home and Abroad." https://www.fede ralregister.gov/documents/2021/02/01/2021-02177/tackling-the-climate-crisis-at-home-and-abroad.

Fertel, Camille, Olivier Bahn, Kathleen Vaillancourt, and Jean-Philippe Waaub. 2013. "Canadian Energy and Climate Policies: A SWOT Analysis in Search of Federal/Provincial Coherence." *Energy Policy* 63: 1139–50. https://doi.org/10.1016/j.enpol.2013.09.057.

Fierke, K. M., and Francisco Antonio-Alfonso. 2018. "Language, Entanglement and the New Silk Roads." *Asian Journal of Comparative Politics* 3(3): 194–206 . https://doi.org/10.1177/2057891118762521.

Figueres, Christiana, and Tom Rivett-Carnac. 2020. *The Future We Choose: Surviving the Climate Crisis.* New York: Alfred A. Knopf.

Findlay, Scott D., and Paul Thagard. 2014. "Emotional Change in International Negotiation: Analyzing the Camp David Accords Using Cognitive-Affective Maps." *Group Decision and Negotiation* 23 (6): 1281–1300. https://doi.org/10.1007/s10726-011-9242-x.

George, Alexander L. 1969. "The 'Operational Code': A Neglected Approach to the Study of Political Leaders and Decision-Making." *International Studies Quarterly* 13 (2): 190–222.

Gottschall, Jonathan. 2013. *The Storytelling Animal: How Stories Make Us Human.* 1st ed. Boston: Mariner Books.

Hale, Thomas, and Charles Roger. 2014. "Orchestration and Transnational Climate Governance." *Review of International Organizations* 9 (1): 59–82. https://doi.org/10.1007/s11558-013-9174-0.

Haven, Emmanuel, and Andrei Khrennikov. 2013. *Quantum Social Science.* 1st ed. Cambridge; New York: Cambridge University Press.

Hochstetler, Kathryn, and Mahjana Milkoreit. 2014. "Emerging Powers in the Climate Negotiations Shifting Identity Conceptions." *Political Research Quarterly* 67 (1): 224–235. https://doi.org/10.1177/1065912913510609.

Homer-Dixon, Thomas, Jonathan Leader Maynard, Matto Mildenberger, Manjana Milkoreit, Steven J. Mock, Stephen Quilley, Tobias Schröder, and Paul Thagard. 2013. "A Complex Systems Approach to the Study of Ideology: Cognitive-Affective Structures and the Dynamics of Belief Systems." *Journal of Social and Political Psychology* 1 (1): 337–363. https://doi.org/10.5964/jspp.v1i1.36.

Homer-Dixon, Thomas, Manjana Milkoreit, Steven J. Mock, Tobias Schröder, and Paul Thagard. 2014. "The Conceptual Structure of Social Disputes: Cognitive-Affective Maps as a Tool for Conflict Analysis and Resolution." *SAGE Open* 4 (1): 215824401452621. https://doi.org/10.1177/2158244014526210.

Hulme, Mike. 2009. *Why We Disagree about Climate Change: Understanding Controversy, Inaction and Opportunity*. 4th edition. Cambridge: Cambridge University Press.

IPCC. 2014. "Climate Change 2014: Impacts, Adaptation and Vulnerability. Part A: Global and Sectoral Aspects." Contribution of Working Group II to the Fifth Assessment Report of the Intergovernmental Panel on Climate Change. Cambridge; New York: Cambridge University Press.

IPCC. 2018. "Global Warming of 1.5 °C." An IPCC Special Report on the impacts of global warming of 1.5°C above pre-industrial levels and related global greenhouse gas emission pathways, in the context of strengthening the global response to the threat of climate change, sustainable development, and efforts to eradicate poverty, V. Masson-Delmotte, P. Zhai, H. O. Pörtner, D. Roberts, J. Skea, P.R. Shukla, A. Pirani, W. Moufouma-Okia, C. Péan, R. Pidcock, S. Connors, J. B. R. Matthews, Y. Chen, X. Zhou, M. I. Gomis, E. Lonnoy, T. Maycock, M. Tignor, T. Waterfield (eds.).

Jervis, Robert. 1988. "Realism, Game Theory, and Cooperation." *World Politics* 40 (3): 317–349.

Jung, Jieun, Peter Petkanic, Dongyan Nan, and Jang Hyun Kim. 2020. "When a Girl Awakened the World: A User and Social Message Analysis of Greta Thunberg." *Sustainability* 12 (7): 2707. https://doi.org/10.3390/su12072707.

Keohane, Robert O., and David G. Victor. 2016. "Cooperation and Discord in Global Climate Policy." *Nature Climate Change* 6 (6): 570–575. https://doi.org/10.1038/nclimate2937.

Kind, Amy, and Peter Kung. 2016. *Knowledge through Imagination*. Oxford: Oxford University Press.

Leeuw, Sander van der, and Carl Folke. 2021. "The Social Dynamics of Basins of Attraction." *Ecology and Society* 26 (1). https://doi.org/10.5751/ES-12289-260133.

Lehtonen, Pinja. 2019. "Q Methodology Can Revitalise Agency in IR." *New Perspectives* 27 (3): 27.

Lövbrand, Eva, Johannes Stripple, and Bo Wiman. 2009. "Earth System Governmentality: Reflections on Science in the Anthropocene." *Global Environmental Change* 19 (1): 7–13. https://doi.org/10.1016/j.gloenvcha.2008.10.002.

Mancilla Garcia, Maria, Tilman Hertz, and Maja Schlüter. 2020. "Towards a Process Epistemology for the Analysis of Social-Ecological System." *Environmental Values* 29 (2): 221–239. https://doi.org/10.3197/096327119X15579936382608.

Mathias, Jean-Denis, John M. Anderies, Jacopo Baggio, Jennifer Hodbod, Sylvie Huet, Marco A. Janssen, Manjana Milkoreit, and Michael Schoon. 2020. "Exploring Non-Linear Transition Pathways in Social-Ecological Systems." *Scientific Reports* 10 (1): 1–12. https://doi.org/10.1038/s41598-020-59713-w.

Milkoreit, Manjana. 2016. "The Promise of Climate Fiction: Imagination, Storytelling and the Politics of the Future." In *Reimagining Climate Change*, edited by Paul Wapner and Hilal Elver, 171–191. Routledge Advances in Climate Change Research. New York: Routledge.

Milkoreit, Manjana. 2017. *Mindmade Politics: The Cognitive Roots of International Climate Governance*. Cambridge, MA: MIT Press.

Milkoreit, Manjana. 2019. "The Paris Agreement on Climate Change—Made in USA?" *Perspectives on Politics* 17 (4): 1019–1037. https://doi.org/10.1017/S1537592719000951.

Mitchell, Ronald B, and Charli Carpenter. 2019. "Norms for the Earth: Changing the Climate on 'Climate Change.'" *Journal of Global Security Studies* 4 (4): 413–429. https://doi.org/10.1093/jogss/ogz006.

Moore, Michele-Lee, Ola Tjornbo, Elin Enfors, Corrie Knapp, Jennifer Hodbod, Jacopo A. Baggio, Albert Norström, Per Olsson, and Duan Biggs. 2014. "Studying the Complexity of Change: Toward an Analytical Framework for Understanding Deliberate Social-Ecological Transformations." *Ecology & Society* 19 (4): 54.

Müller, Martin. 2015. "Assemblages and Actor-networks: Rethinking Socio-material Power, Politics and Space." *Geography Compass* 9 (1): 27–41. https://doi.org/10.1111/gec3.12192.

O'Brien, Karen. 2021. *You Matter More Than You Think: Quantum Social Change for a Thriving World*. Oslo: cCHANGE Press.

O'Brien, Karen L. 2016. "Climate Change and Social Transformations: Is It Time for a Quantum Leap?" *Wiley Interdisciplinary Reviews: Climate Change* 7 (5): 618–626. https://doi.org/10.1002/wcc.413.

O'Brien, Karen, Elin Selboe, and Bronwyn M. Hayward. 2018. "Exploring Youth Activism on Climate Change: Dutiful, Disruptive, and Dangerous Dissent." *Ecology and Society* 23 (3). http://www.jstor.org/stable/26799169.

Pickering, Jonathan, Steve Vanderheiden, and Seumas Miller. 2012. "'If Equity's In, We're Out': Scope for Fairness in the Next Global Climate Agreement." *Ethics & International Affairs* 26 (04): 423–443. https://doi.org/10.1017/S0892679412000603.

Putnam, Robert. 1988. "Diplomacy and Domestic Politics: The Logic of Two-Level Games." *International Organization* 42 (3): 427–460.

Roberts, Tom. 2014. "From Things to Events: Whitehead and the Materiality of Process." *Environment and Planning D: Society and Space* 32 (6): 968–983. https://doi.org/10.1068/d13195p.

Sabherwal, Anandita, Matthew T. Ballew, Sander van der Linden, Abel Gustafson, Matthew H. Goldberg, Edward W. Maibach, John E. Kotcher, Janet K. Swim, Seth A. Rosenthal, and Anthony Leiserowitz. 2021. "The Greta Thunberg Effect: Familiarity with Greta Thunberg Predicts Intentions to Engage in Climate Activism in the United States." *Journal of Applied Social Psychology* 51 (4): 321–333. https://doi.org/10.1111/jasp.12737.

Sawyer, Robert Keith, Vera John-Steiner, Seana Moran, Robert J. Sternberg, Mihaly Csikszentmihalyi, David Henry Feldman, Howard Gardner, and Jeanne Nakamura. 2003. *Creativity and Development*. Oxford: Oxford University Press.

Scheffer, Marten. 2009. *Critical Transitions in Nature and Society*. Princeton, NJ: Princeton University Press.

Shotter, John. 2014. "Agential Realism, Social Constructionism, and Our Living Relations to Our Surroundings: Sensing Similarities Rather Than Seeing Patterns." *Theory & Psychology* 24 (3): 305–325. https://doi.org/10.1177/0959354313514144.

Soest, Heleen L. van, Michel G. J. den Elzen, and Detlef P. van Vuuren. 2021. "Net-Zero Emission Targets for Major Emitting Countries Consistent with the Paris Agreement." *Nature Communications* 12 (1): 2140. https://doi.org/10.1038/s41467-021-22294-x.

Thagard, Paul. 1992. *Conceptual Revolutions*. Princeton, NJ: Princeton University Press.

Thagard, Paul. 2000. *Coherence in Thought and Action*. Life and Mind. Cambridge, MA: MIT Press.

Thagard, Paul. 2006. *Hot Thought: Mechanisms and Applications of Emotional Cognition*. Cambridge, MA: MIT Press.

Thagard, Paul. 2014. "The Self as a System of Multilevel Interacting Mechanisms." *Philosophical Psychology* 27 (2): 145–163. https://doi.org/10.1080/09515089.2012.725715.

Urry, John. 2005. "The Complexities of the Global." *Theory, Culture & Society* 22 (5): 235–254. https://doi.org/10.1177/0263276405057201.

Waddock, Sandra, Steve Waddell, and Paul S. Gray. 2020. "The Transformational Change Challenge of Memes: The Case of Marriage Equality in the United States." *Business & Society* 59 (8): 1667–1697. https://doi.org/10.1177/0007650318816440.

Walsh, Zack, Jessica Böhme, and Christine Wamsler. 2020. "Towards a Relational Paradigm in Sustainability Research, Practice, and Education." *Ambio* 50: 74–84. https://doi.org/10.1007/s13280-020-01322-y.

Wang, Shaoli, Libin Rong, and Jianhong Wu. 2016. "Bistability and Multistability in Opinion Dynamics Models." *Applied Mathematics and Computation* 289 (October): 388–395. https://doi.org/10.1016/j.amc.2016.05.030.

Warszawski, Lila, Elmar Kriegler, Timothy M. Lenton, Owen Gaffney, Daniela Jacob, Daniel Klingenfeld, Ryu Koide, et al. 2021. "All Options, Not Silver Bullets, Needed to Limit Global Warming to 1.5 °C: A Scenario Appraisal." *Environmental Research Letters* 16 (6): 064037. https://doi.org/10.1088/1748-9326/abfeec.

Watts, S., and P. Stenner. 2003. "Q Methodology, Quantum Theory and Psychology." *Operant Subjectivity* 26 (3): 155–173.

Wendt, Alexander. 2015. *Quantum Mind and Social Science: Unifying Physical and Social Ontology*. Cambridge; New York: Cambridge University Press.

White House, United States. 2017. "President Trump Announces U.S. Withdrawal from the Paris Climate Accord." June 1, 2017. https://trumpwhitehouse.archives.gov/artic les/president-trump-announces-u-s-withdrawal-paris-climate-accord/.

White House, United States. 2021a. Remarks by President Biden Before Signing Executive Actions on Tackling Climate Change, Creating Jobs, and Restoring Scientific Integrity, January 27, 2021. https://www.whitehouse.gov/briefing-room/speeches-remarks/2021/01/27/remarks-by-president-biden-before-signing-executive-actions-on-tackling-climate-change-creating-jobs-and-restoring-scientific-integrity/.

White House, United States. 2021b. Remarks by President Biden at the Virtual Leaders Summit on Climate Session 5: The Economic Opportunities of Climate Action. April 23, 2021. https://www.whitehouse.gov/briefing-room/speeches-remarks/2021/04/23/remarks-by-president-biden-at-the-virtual-leaders-summit-on-climate-session-5-the-economic-opportunities-of-climate-action/.

White House, United States. 2021c. "Remarks by President Biden in Address to a Joint Session of Congress." White House. April 29, 2021. https://www.whitehouse.gov/briefing-room/speeches-remarks/2021/04/29/remarks-by-president-biden-in-address-to-a-joint-session-of-congress/.

Zanotti, Laura. 2019. *Ontological Entanglements, Agency and Ethics in International Relations: Exploring the Crossroads*. London: Routledge.

Zulianello, Mattia, and Diego Ceccobelli. 2020. "Don't Call It Climate Populism: On Greta Thunberg's Technocratic Ecocentrism." *Political Quarterly* 91 (3): 623–631. https://doi.org/10.1111/1467-923X.12858.

8

These Are Not the Droids You're Looking For

Offense, Defense, and the Social Context of Quantum Cryptology

Jon R. Lindsay

Introduction

Quantum mechanics is often described as a mysterious force. It surrounds us and penetrates us; it binds the galaxy together. Eccentric wizards defy common sense by manipulating superposition and entanglement. Yet a dark side there is! The security of public key infrastructure (PKI) depends on the computational difficulty of factoring and related mathematical problems. PKI, in turn, is vital for military and civil cybersecurity and personal privacy. In theory, a quantum computer can solve the factoring problem exponentially faster than classical supercomputers. The prospect of a fully armed and operational quantum computer thus threatens the integrity of cyberspace itself.

Many experts have a very bad feeling about this. According to one prominent physicist, "If a quantum computer is ever built, much of conventional cryptography will fall apart."[1] Some even refer to a coming "cryptocalypse."[2] As a congressman from Texas writes, "The impact of quantum on our national defense will be tremendous.... The consequences of mastering quantum computing, while not as visual or visceral as a mushroom cloud, are no less significant than those faced by the scientists who lit up the New Mexico sky with the detonation at the Trinity test site 72 years ago."[3]

Quantum computing may be a technological terror, but the ability to destroy a protocol is insignificant next to the power of social context. There are at least two reasons to be skeptical of quantum threat narratives. First, persuasive prophesies of technological disruption are self-defeating if they encourage the development of actionable countermeasures. New post-quantum or quantum-safe protocols are already maturing. Meanwhile, many engineering problems must be solved before we witness the firepower of a fully operational quantum computer. Effective cryptographic offsets will likely be available and implemented well before a quantum cryptanalytic offense becomes feasible. Second, even if there is a technical breakthrough, intelligence practice depends as much on political and organizational implementation as scientific potential. An advantage in espionage or counterintelligence ultimately depends more on administrative and strategic factors than technological sophistication. There is every reason to believe that the practical reality of classical politics will swamp the scientific potential of quantum computing.

This chapter explores the gap between science fiction and social practice in quantum cryptology. It begins with a brief introduction to the quantum threat to PKI and the quantum-safe offsets that have developed to offset it. It then describes how institutional complements to technological capability shape intelligence advantage. As a result, the advent of quantum information technology is likely to make intelligence contests more complicated but not more decisive.[4] Social context will be with you, always.

The Phantom Menace—Quantum Offense

With the blast shield down, eavesdroppers can't see anything. Cryptography uses mathematical protocols to disguise meaningful data as meaningless noise. Symmetric encryption uses the same key for encryption and decryption. Examples include the famous Enigma machine and modern block ciphers like Advanced Encryption Standard (AES). Asymmetric encryption, by contrast, uses different keys for encryption and decryption. The public key can be openly revealed to allow anyone to send encrypted messages that only the recipient can decrypt with the private key. Reversing the process, the private key can also be used to create digital signatures that anyone can verify with the public key. Alice can thus send secure messages that only Bob can read, even though Eve has access to the public key; and Alice can verify that the responses come from Bob, which Eve cannot forge without the private key.[5]

Asymmetric encryption was invented a long time ago in a galaxy far, far away—that is, by British intelligence officers and American academics in the 1970s.[6] Their protocols rely on so-called one-way functions that are easy to compute in one direction but hard to reverse. For example, it is easy to multiply prime numbers together but harder to factor the product. Factoring may be easy for small numbers (e.g., $15 = 3 \ast 5$), but it becomes much harder for large numbers. The computational intractability of factoring (and related problems) is what guarantees the security of asymmetric protocols like Rivest-Shamir-Adleman (RSA) that are widely used in PKI.[7] Using the fastest classical algorithm discovered to date, a common desktop computer would still need more than six quadrillion years to crack a 2,048-bit RSA key.[8]

In 1994, however, Peter Shor demonstrated that the factoring problem can be solved in a clever way with the mathematics of quantum mechanics.[9] Shor's algorithm runs in polynomial rather than exponential time. Because the difference between n^2 and 2^n is significant when n is very large, exponential improvements in running time and resource consumption are very important. In principle, Shor's algorithm could enable a large-scale quantum computer with twenty million functional quantum bits (qubits) to successfully attack 2,048-bit RSA keys in a matter of hours.[10] The fastest classical supercomputers today, by contrast, would require many galactic lifetimes to compute the same result. A quantum computer might even make the Kessel Run in less than twelve parsecs.

For many years, however, experts were not frightened by the sorcerer's ways. For all practical purposes, it seemed infeasible to build an actual machine that could run Shor's algorithm at scale with reliable error correction. To crack RSA with the most efficient method devised to date, a quantum computer would have to keep twenty million qubits in coherence (i.e., maintaining superposition and entanglement without losing quantum information) for several hours.[11] This has always appeared to be a daunting task. Besides, the task of updating cryptographic protocols for PKI everywhere would be a long and costly slog that was hard to justify without a more tangible cryptographic threat. Over a decade after Shor's landmark result, the quantum threat seemed little more than a theoretical curiosity.

Yet by the early 2010s, academic and corporate labs began demonstrating working prototypes that could factor small numbers.[12] In September 2019, a team of scientists from Google and the University of California, Santa Barbara, achieved a major experimental milestone known as "quantum supremacy." Using a quantum computer known as "Sycamore," they maintained fifty-three qubits in coherence for three minutes and ran a quantum algorithm faster than could be simulated by the world's fastest classical supercomputer.[13] This dramatic improvement was still a long way from implementing the twenty million coherent qubits needed to crack RSA. Yet it suggests that further progress is possible, not only to crack RSA but also (and perhaps more realistically) to optimize database searches. Sycamore might be likened to the Wright Flyer, a harbinger of technological revolution.[14]

The emerging quantum threat to PKI is a striking instance of what cybersecurity professionals call a "class break," a vulnerability that categorically affects an entire class of technology versus just particular targets.[15] Shor's algorithm, given the availability of a working quantum computer, would be about the biggest class break imaginable. There is no simple patch available because entirely new cryptosystems, operating on entirely new principles, will have to be developed and implemented throughout digital society. The systematic compromise of cybersecurity would thus be a strategic problem of the first order.

This is because PKI underwrites the security of military communications, financial transactions, and intellectual property and the privacy of civil society around the world. Digital signatures produced with RSA certify the authenticity of digital messages and facilitate the installation of software from trusted vendors. Breaking RSA would make it possible to decrypt secure data and install arbitrary code on protected networks.[16] All networks and applications on those networks, public or private, that relied on vulnerable cryptography would be put at risk. Confidential data could be collected, altered, or deleted. Personal, financial, legal, logistic, and operational data could be manipulated to influence tactical and strategic operations. Malware could be installed at will to enable espionage or disrupt critical infrastructure. Disinformation could be disseminated from the secure accounts of senior officials, heightening the credibility of foreign deception efforts. The authentication codes protecting sensitive equipment and weapons stockpiles could be falsified, facilitating illicit proliferation.

The National Security Agency (NSA) General Counsel explains the intelligence implications thusly: "The strategic advantage here would be for one country to surreptitiously acquire such a capability and maintain it for perhaps several years or more. Other countries would not realize that everything from their weapons systems to financial transactions would be vulnerable during that period; and that would include not only current activity but also the historic, encrypted communications collected and retained by the winner in anticipation of this very capability."[17] The former president of a major research university argues that Chinese progress in quantum technology, to include the first quantum science satellite and large-scale quantum network connecting Beijing and Shanghai, "presents the United States with its new 'Sputnik moment.'... Whoever gets this technology first will also be able to cripple traditional defenses and power grids and manipulate the global economy."[18]

Indeed, China named quantum informatics a key plank in its "Thirteenth Five-Year Plan" for technology and innovation, and it is building the world's largest quantum laboratory.[19] China hopes not only to improve its general economic competitiveness by investing in quantum technology but also to shore up its perceived vulnerability to US cyber operations—highlighted by the Snowden leaks—by developing more secure quantum networks. Chinese strategists have even started writing about "quantum hegemony," the notion that control of the economically and militarily vital information domain will go to the side that is the first to master quantum information science.[20]

It is far from clear how well either China or the United States will be able to operationalize quantum technology, even as there are reasons to suspect that the US military and intelligence community may have important relative advantages in this respect. The state of the art in Chinese quantum computing is still a little short for a stormtrooper. What is clear, however, is that geopolitical competition has become a major catalyst for both countries to invest in quantum information science. Active political rivalry on the scientific frontier makes the cyber offense-defense balance more important, even as it tends to make it more ambiguous.

A New Hope—Quantum Defense

Analysis of the plans provided by Peter Shor has demonstrated a weakness in the battle station. The threat of quantum cryptanalysis (code breaking) has thus inspired the development of various forms of quantum-safe cryptography (code making). These include classical postquantum cryptography (PQC) and quantum key distribution (QKD).[21] Table 8.1 summarizes these different technologies. Defensive innovation in quantum-safe cryptography (PQC and QKD) is inspired, in part, by the threat posed by Shor's algorithm and experimental progress in quantum computers. If workable offsets can be fielded soon, the quantum threat window may not ever open in the first place. Then you can go about your business—move along.

PQC works by using mathematical problems difficult for both classical and quantum computers to solve (i.e., PQC is not vulnerable to Shor's algorithm). Candidate problems include finding the shortest vector in a lattice, decoding error correction codes, and solving systems of multivariate equations over finite fields.[22] PQC runs on classical computers, providing security against

Table 8.1 Classical and quantum information technologies compared

Application	Classical information technology	Quantum information technology
General applications that rely on cryptography for security	Intelligence, communication, administration, command and control, automation, governance, diplomacy, law enforcement, science, engineering, manufacturing, finance, commerce, advertising, entertainment	Scientific modeling and simulation, quantum sensing and measurement, data storage and search, machine learning and artificial intelligence
Classical cryptography vulnerable to quantum cryptanalysis	Rivest–Shamir–Adleman (RSA) Diffie-Helman (DH) Elliptic curve cryptography (ECC) Advanced Encryption Standard (AES) Secure Hash Algorithm (SHA)	Shor's algorithm provides an exponential speedup vs. RSA, DH, and ECC. Grover's algorithm provides a polynomial speedup vs. AES and SHA.
Quantum-safe cryptography	Postquantum cryptography (PQC)	Quantum key distribution (QKD)

classical and quantum attacks. Because quantum computers have very specialized applications, classical computers will almost certainly remain the best choice for many applications. Even quantum systems will still incorporate some classical components. Therefore, PQC will be needed to ensure the security of classical computers in the future.

The US National Institute of Standards and Technology (NIST) is currently evaluating, and will soon certify, new standards that can be incorporated into cyber systems. NIST "has initiated a process to develop and standardize one or more additional public-key cryptographic algorithms...that are capable of protecting sensitive government information well into the foreseeable future, including after the advent of quantum computers."[23] The NIST has received, and is evaluating, nearly seventy submissions from two dozen countries.[24] The NSA, meanwhile, has signaled that it "will initiate a transition to quantum resistant algorithms in the not too distant future," cautioning against adopting strong protocols like elliptic curve cryptography and instead waiting for PQC.[25]

While the NIST should approve PQC alternatives within the next few years, the full transition could still take a decade more. Previous transitions (e.g., to AES) took much longer than anticipated due to economic and organizational constraints. In the ideal case, new PQC protocols would simply be swapped in for current cryptographic primitives to minimize the need to re-engineer all the other systems that depend on them. More likely, however, "PQC standardization...will need a new wineskin to hold the new wine."[26] So long as classical computing power continues to increase, the additional computational overhead of PQC will probably not pose a general barrier to implementation. However, the greater resource intensiveness of PQC could pose a problem for more constrained and bandwidth-limited military applications (such as ship-to-shore networks). This problem might be mitigated by judiciously limiting the use of computationally intensive primitives within the overall cryptographic system, just as slower RSA is used to open a session conducted with faster AES today.

A more esoteric alternative to PQC is QKD. Quantum mechanics can be leveraged to create new kinds of communication networks that use a totally different approach to cryptography. QKD exploits the Heisenberg uncertainty principle to detect the presence of an eavesdropper. Since the act of measuring quantum data can change them, an eavesdropper in the channel would increase detectable error rates. QKD thus makes it possible to securely distribute unique keys between geographically separated parties (which was the original justification for inventing asymmetric encryption like RSA). The practical feasibility of QKD over large distances, including between satellites in orbit and ground stations, has been demonstrated in numerous experiments.[27] Research is underway to develop quantum routers and networks that can preserve entangled states while scaling up to greater numbers of users, higher bandwidths, and longer distances, along with reliable quantum repeater and memory devices that do not destroy quantum state.[28]

QKD challenges may be less formidable than those associated with general-purpose quantum computing, but they are still difficult. The same mechanism that prevents the eavesdropper from copying the data (i.e., the act of tapping the quantum circuit causes an increase in random errors) also enables the adversary to impose a service denial attack on the quantum channel. An attempt to copy data every time it is transmitted has the potential to force every connection to reset. QKD also does not protect data integrity against side channel attacks on the engineering implementation of the system or social engineering attacks on the gullibility of human operators. Elaborations such as "measurement-device-independent QKD" can close some loopholes, but they still assume that the preparation of photons for transmission will be unobserved and that communicators will also have an authenticated classical channel.[29] This does not preclude some types of man-in-the-middle attacks. Any transition to quantum communication infrastructure (using QKD) will also be fraught with difficulty. Quantum networks rely on very different principles than does the installed base of classical digital networks around the world. If switching to PQC will be hard, QKD could be even harder. Adoption of PQC, insofar as security motivates consideration of quantum networking, will probably be more feasible for most organizations and states. As cryptographer Tom Berson wryly notes, QKD is a "new, difficult, expensive way to achieve an outcome which we have, for decades, been achieving easily and cheaply."[30]

For most practical network applications, PQC to shore up classical networks will be available more quickly, feasibly, and reliably without attempting to transition to a wholly new quantum network architecture protected by QKD. Quantum networking may yet become attractive for novel applications other than cryptography that have no classical equivalent, such as certifying deletion or sharing out quantum computational resources.[31] Nevertheless, it will likely be PQC rather than QKD—classical rather than quantum protocols—that will provide widespread protection against the threat of quantum cryptanalysis. The widespread implementation of PQC is going to be especially difficult for enterprise systems with widespread dependencies on legacy cryptosystems (and RSA). This transition is sure to be long and complicated.

The technological window of vulnerability to the quantum threat depends on relative estimates about the maturation of offensive and defensive innovation. Nontechnical considerations also affect the size of the window. Foremost among these is the length of time that secrets need to be kept.[32] The latent value of secrecy will vary depending on the encrypted data's content and policy priorities. Some secrets are extremely perishable, such as the current location of mobile military assets in war or a negotiating position in a deal that will be concluded in the next few days. By contrast, weapon designs and other capabilities that require significant investment may need longer protection if revelation would enable an adversary to develop countermeasures. Intelligence sources and methods are particularly sensitive. Historical data can enable the adversary to better understand an adversary's doctrine or even identify long-running operations. For example, the ongoing decryption and analysis of the KGB "Venona files" by Western counterintelligence continued to illuminate KGB methods throughout the Cold War.[33]

Predicting the interaction of scientific progress, international politics, and secret intelligence is always difficult. Resolution of the many uncertainties and empirical speculations mentioned previously will take further assessment of technical progress and, indeed, further technical progress. How much confidence can we have that the quantum threat window will not open? While current trends suggest that defense is maturing faster than offense, a future breakthrough is always possible. A well-resourced intelligence agency like the NSA might develop a working quantum computer in secret before the completion of PQC implementation. Yet as quantum computing expert Scott Aaronson points out, "It seems improbable that the NSA could be that far ahead of the open world without anybody knowing it."[34] Scientists and intelligence agencies would most likely detect a great disturbance in the Force before being totally surprised. The PQC transition, by contrast, is already underway and should be well advanced within the next decade.

The Force Awakens—Classical Intelligence

Advances in PQC or QKD should not be taken to mean, however, that everything's perfectly all right now, or that we're all fine here, thank you. Assume for the sake of argument that all the practical obstacles to fielding a working quantum computer can be overcome. Assume that an intelligence adversary successfully tests Shor's destructive power on our home PKI. Any intelligence advantage realized from this feat of decryption will still depend on many further choices, by many actors, with many transaction costs and frictions along the way.[35] A common refrain of the military innovation literature is that technological possibilities do not determine strategic outcomes.[36] Social practices coordinate the invention and operation of material systems while organizational behavior is constrained and enabled by technological structures.[37] This is doubly true for agencies that traffic in secrecy and duplicity. Subterranean statecraft complicates the purity of scientific possibility. Indeed, intelligence is a wretched hive of scum and villainy.

Quantum threat narratives tend to ignore the social context of intelligence practice and extrapolate directly to radical intelligence advantage. If, for instance, a quantum computer could break public encryption protocols, this could provide a major collection advantage. If, conversely, quantum communications could provide unbreakable security, this could provide a major protection advantage. Yet cryptographic protocols are just mathematical functions. Organizations must implement them in software, hardware, and bureaucratic routine to reliably encrypt and decrypt data. An organization's flawed implementation of strong protocols creates self-inflicted vulnerabilities that skilled attackers can and do exploit. Operational security (OPSEC) thus depends not only on strong cryptographic technology but also on bureaucratic security policy and the conscientiousness of personnel. Organizational institutions may either compensate for technological vulnerabilities or undermine technological strengths.

On the other side of the intelligence contest, likewise, a signals intelligence (SIGINT) organization must be able to recognize and exploit the target's technological and organizational weaknesses. Sophisticated cryptanalytic technology will provide little advantage if the attacker lacks the technical and organizational skill to engineer an intrusion, protect its security, and deliver its products to intelligence consumers.

To steal valuable secrets, the target must possess some valuable secrets in the first place. The target must be reliant on secrecy to protect a bargaining advantage, an operational capability, or intellectual property, or there will be nothing of value to discover in all the data collected. Relevant secrets, furthermore, must be encoded in a medium that is exposed to collection and vulnerable in principle to decryption, not committed to memory or recorded on paper that does not circulate. Put simply, the target must make some OPSEC mistakes. A formidable target might also run counterintelligence operations to deceive the SIGINT collector by planting fake data. While quantum computing might support bulk decryption of intercepted data, it does little to improve the agency's access and placement for intercepting valuable data in the first place, especially if the target has a relatively strong OPSEC and counterintelligence posture.

Then the intelligence agency must be able to identify and make sense of the secrets it has collected. After cryptanalysts break the target's cryptosystem, they must process and decrypt the relevant secrets out of a huge volume of traffic they have collected. Advanced SIGINT agencies like the NSA already can only process a small percentage of what they collect. Quantum decryption would result in bigger haystacks to sift without necessarily revealing more needles. To the degree that quantum methods like Grover's algorithm provide a modest (polynomial) speedup for searches, quantum computers can marginally improve artificial intelligence (AI). Yet more information and improved computation also have the potential to create new analytical burdens and confusions.[38] Quantum optimization of machine learning will do little to fix, and may even exacerbate, the longstanding challenges of AI, which have more to do with the complexity of human intentionality and situated interaction than technical implementation.[39] Making sense of secrets will still depend on human analysts who are intuitively familiar with the subject matter and able to discriminate wheat from chaff, detect enemy deception, corroborate SIGINT with other sources of intelligence, and assess the veracity and relevance of the overall intelligence picture.[40] Intelligence success is rarely the result of a single great operation or a lucrative single source. It is almost always the result of a lot of hard work, prior investment, and mundane organizational processes.

Once a SIGINT organization has produced valuable and vetted intelligence, the product must be delivered to a cleared, interested, and available customer. Intelligence consumers—military commanders or civilian policymakers—must be open to receiving new information that can inform a decision, and they have to trust the intelligence professionals providing the data. Bias or disinterest will reduce the policy relevance of the intelligence signal. Politicization may suppress or redirect it altogether.[41] Myriad intelligence-policy pathologies arise from bureaucratic and political incentives to undermine or distort a SIGINT coup. Even in the best of circumstances, customers face cognitive challenges of their own in making sense of intelligence amid all the other forms of information flooding in.

The political impact of intelligence ultimately depends on strategic interaction between organizations. If action based on sensitive sources creates suspicion for the target that its communications have been compromised, then it is likely to alter OPSEC behavior to preclude future exploitation. Fearing the loss of future information, intelligence producers and consumers might decide that the operational gains from acting on intelligence do not outweigh the potential losses to future intelligence. An intelligence advantage then remains unrealized or latent. If intelligence does influence a decision, the determination of whether it actually makes a difference will be difficult to make in any given case. Complexity and nonlinear feedback, moreover, can foil the most reasonable decisions.[42] While there are important applications of quantum computing in the early stages of the intelligence cycle—technical decryption prior to all-source analysis—it offers little additional advantage for the dissemination and application of intelligence.

Similar considerations apply to the cryptographic defense. We do not have to wait for QKD or PQC to probe the impact of perfect cryptography on International Relations. It is an unappreciated irony of history that strong classical cryptography has helped unleash an epidemic of cyber insecurity. Partly this is because attackers can use encryption to hide, but even more this is because defenders often fail to use encryption properly. As NSA contractor Edward Snowden observed in 2013, the NSA could not break PKI directly and thus had to resort to more indirect attacks: "Encryption works. Properly implemented strong crypto systems are one of the few things that you can rely on. Unfortunately, endpoint security is so terrifically weak that NSA can frequently find ways around it."[43]

Perfect cryptography does not translate into perfect security so long as SIGINT agencies can find a way to copy data before it gets encrypted, steal cryptographic keys that are stored insecurely, exploit hardware characteristics that betray software operations, or trick gullible users into providing credentials. Implementation matters. The power to destroy a planet can be compromised by a thermal exhaust port that leads directly to the reactor system. Likewise with cybersecurity. The mathematical strength of an encryption protocol effectively shifts the incentives for exploitation to other vulnerabilities in the software, hardware, and organizational implementation of a cryptosystem. Even in a world of strong quantum-safe cryptography, therefore, SIGINT can still thrive if the target's organizational OPSEC policy and practices are weak.

The net result for the intelligence balance is ambiguous. On one hand, QKD and PQC will cancel out whatever security problems quantum computing creates. On the other hand, quantum and classical systems will still depend on complex implementations by, with, and for human users, who will generally tend to be ignorant, complacent, or unconcerned about cybersecurity. Sociotechnical complexity and gullible humans will undermine the theoretical security of QKD and PQC, just as it does for strong cryptography and PKI today. More perversely, large-scale quantum networks might even improve public trust in cryptosystems, which would then simply become more attractive targets for SIGINT agencies with the means and moxie to exploit side channels and human weaknesses. Cyber espionage today flourishes despite strong cryptosystems. Indeed, intelligence is experiencing something of a new gilded age. Future defenses provided by quantum-safe cryptosystems will, likewise, be only as good as the people who maintain and employ them.

As summarized in Table 8.2, intelligence advantage is a function of not only cryptographic technology but also organizational institutions.[44] Strong cryptosystems (robust protocol and implementation) and a coordinated security posture (defense is relatively more capable than offense) result in an OPSEC advantage. At the extreme, this corresponds to the quantum threat narrative about

Table 8.2 Intelligence advantage as a function of cryptographic infrastructure and the relative capacity of organizational institutions

Defense vs. offense	Strong cryptosystem	Weak cryptosystem
Coordinated organization	OPSEC advantage	SIGINT failure
Uncoordinated organization	OPSEC failure	SIGINT advantage

the end of intelligence or "cryptocalypse." Weak systems (poor implementations of insecure protocols) and an uncoordinated posture (offense is relatively more capable than defense) are a boon for SIGINT, which at the extreme corresponds to the end-of-secrecy narrative or "going dark."

The quantum threat debate tends to focus on technological possibilities and offsets, as described in the preceding sections. Yet the mixed categories in Table 8.2 include organizational mistakes made by the competitors. An OPSEC failure occurs when strong cryptography is available but lax security policy or complacent behavior undermines it. In this case, the relatively more capable SIGINT attacker can exploit the sociotechnical implementation of the defender's cryptosystem. A SIGINT failure occurs when exploitable technical vulnerabilities and potent cryptanalytic methods exist but the target organization compensates with protective countermeasures or the attacker is overwhelmed by the complexity of the intelligence process. Actual cryptosystems often fall somewhere between the strong and weak extremes. Relative organizational capacity, likewise, is usually somewhere between coordinated and uncoordinated. The dynamic interaction of technologies and organizations continues haltingly and indefinitely. This interaction tends to increase the complexity of the intelligence problem without, however, delivering either side a lasting intelligence advantage.

In evaluating the technical factors that create, and limit, the quantum window of vulnerability, therefore, it is imperative to bear in mind that many different social and political factors shape intelligence advantage in any given situation. Organizational institutions, human behavior, industrial policy, and strategic interaction can squander technological advantages. They can also compensate for technological weaknesses. Even if quantum-safe networks are not available before quantum computers, protecting some secrets will still be possible. Target organizations will still find ways to hide their most valuable secrets by using physically isolated networks or abstaining from digital encoding altogether. Conversely, even in a world of secure quantum-safe networks, it still will be possible to collect secrets by attacking the insecure human endpoints of the network. Strong cryptography, classical or quantum, does not automatically translate into strong information security. Gullible humans, flawed security policy, and sociotechnical complexity can inadvertently expose data protected by quantum-safe systems.

Endemic friction in the sociotechnical implementation of cryptology is something of an insurance policy for *both* offense and defense in any of these scenarios. The actual performance of either quantum decryption or quantum-safe encryption is unlikely to live up to its full potential. Even if I am too pessimistic about the scientific prospects of quantum computing relative to quantum-safe alternatives, quantum computers will still have to operate in human organizations that offer little reason for optimism. Information assurance begins and ends with a workforce that understands and cares about the confidentiality, integrity, and availability of relevant data. More complex information technologies require an even higher level of technical acumen and awareness from personnel, and an even stronger commitment on the part of leadership to maintaining a robust cybersecurity posture. Offensive cyber advantage, conversely, depends on knowing how to exploit the behavior of organizations that fail to maintain their guard.

Hokey Religions and Ancient Weapons

Quantum computing is not as clumsy or random as classical methods. It is an elegant weapon for a more civilized age. Quantum computing may improve scientific research, drug discovery, and practical communication. Yet some actors will be seduced by the dark side. Quantum computing thus seems like a great disturbance in cryptology, as if millions of datagrams suddenly cried out in terror and were suddenly decrypted.

Even so, the quantum sorcerer will meet her match in competitive politics and bureaucratic culture. If the engineering hurdles to an operational large-scale quantum computer can be cleared, which is by no means assured, strategic counteraction and organizational friction remain. No technical advantage can be sustained forever, if indeed it can even be realized in the first place. Classical societies implement quantum computers. The practice of politics at the macroscale will tend to overwhelm the potential of quantum science at the microscale.

The reader may find my lack of faith in quantum computing disturbing. Yet I am not suggesting that there is any room for complacency about the quantum threat. Indeed, part of my argument relies on practitioners *not* being complacent about it. The very plausibility and danger of a technological threat is what mobilizes scientific and institutional action. The more inevitable the doomsayer's prophesy appears, the harder its potential victims work to postpone catastrophe.[45] In forecasting technological futures, therefore, epistemology becomes entangled with ontology. For example, British fears that "the bomber will always get through" catalyzed innovation in air defense, which won the Battle of Britain. This counteraction does not happen by itself, of course. To realize an effective scientific capability or countermeasure, actors must invest resources and political will.[46] Actors may show little interest in preventative action when a threat is diffuse, far away, or hard to understand. Yet as time horizons shorten and threats begin to seem more palpable, the imperative for preventative action becomes more urgent.[47] The incentives to invest in applied scientific research will also tend to increase when a geopolitical rival invests in the same threatening technology. Balancing in politics and balancing in science can become one and the same.

Quantum computing may seem like the ultimate cyberweapon, likewise, with enough power to destroy an entire planet's cryptography. Yet the magnitude and credibility of the quantum threat is already inspiring the search for countermeasures to mitigate the threat. Cryptographers have identified alternatives to RSA that rely on different mathematical problems believed to be intractable for both classical and quantum computers. The US government, moreover, is taking the quantum threat particularly seriously because China is betting big on quantum technology. As the undersecretary for science at the US Department of Energy pointed out in 2020, "The dollars we have put into quantum information science have increased by about fivefold over the last three years."[48] The quantum threat long seemed diffuse and uncertain, but real experimental progress and surprising achievements by geopolitical competitors underscore the urgency of the threat. The prospect of quantum decryption sometime in the next few decades is sufficiently likely, and the risks of relying on vulnerable protocols sufficiently great, that many states have already placed a high priority on quantum-safe alternatives. Ultimately, however, offensive or defensive advantage depends on social context.

Social scientists have flown from one side of the galaxy to the other, and they have studied a lot of strange stuff, but they've never seen anything to make them believe there's one all-powerful technological force controlling everything. The offense-defense balance in any era, and in any situation, depends on specific organizational and geostrategic context, not simply general technical characteristics.[49] Technical trends can establish the boundary conditions for any potential window in which offense has the advantage, but the construction and exploitation of this window depends on contingent historical choices. The window of technological opportunity can and does change as actors take the initiative to build new weapons and find new ways to use them. A fleeting offensive advantage can still be consequential within the window of time before defensive innovation prevails. The question is how long it takes for any given threat, or countermeasures to it, to become practically feasible.

The transition to a post-quantum world will be long and hard. While quantum computers will fall short of their offensive promise, so will quantum-safe offsets. Serious concerns thus remain in the gray zone between absolute offensive or defensive advantage. Some valuable data encrypted with vulnerable protocols may remain valuable for many years. Some intelligence agencies will be determined and skillful enough to collect this data now and in the future. Some of their targets are vulnerable today, and will remain so in the future, because they have weak classical OPSEC today, and they will have weak quantum OPSEC in the future. The classical rebellion against the quantum revolution is sure to inspire many sequels and spinoffs.

Notes

1. Gilles Brassard quoted in Lo and Lütkenhaus 2007. See also Mulholland, Mosca, and Braun 2017.
2. Craw 2018.
3. Hurd 2017.
4. A more detailed presentation of these arguments can be found in Lindsay 2020a, 2020c.
5. These characters are typically used to illustrate interactions across the two endpoints of a communication (Alice and Bob) and the adversary in the midpoint (Eve).
6. Singh 1999, 243–292.
7. Rivest, Shamir, and Adleman 1978.
8. DigiCert 2018.
9. Shor 1994. For an accessible summary see Aaronson 2007. See also National Academies of Sciences, Engineering, and Medicine 2019, 3-3—3-5.
10. Gidney and Ekera 2021.
11. Ibid.
12. A solid-state machine in 2012 was able to "run a three-qubit compiled version of Shor's algorithm to factor the number 15, and successfully find the prime factors 48% of the time." See Lucero et al. 2012.
13. Arute et al. 2019.
14. Aaronson 2019.
15. Schneier 2017.
16. Mulholland, Mosca, and Braun 2017.
17. Gerstell 2019.
18. Nikias 2018.
19. Central Committee of the Communist Party of China 2016; Barrett 2019.
20. Kania and Costello 2018; Owen and Gorwa 2016.
21. Other interesting applications are beyond the scope of this chapter. For a survey of potential applications, see Biercuk and Fontaine 2017; National Academies of Sciences, Engineering, and Medicine 2019.
22. Chen et al. 2016; Lauter 2017; Bernstein et al. 2017.
23. Computer Security Resource Center 2016.
24. Moody 2018.
25. The NSA notes that "for those partners and vendors that have not yet made the transition to Suite B elliptic curve algorithms, we recommend not making a significant expenditure to do so at this point but instead to prepare for the upcoming quantum resistant algorithm transition." Quoted in Schneier 2015.
26. Chen 2017.
27. Townsend 1994.
28. Diamanti et al. 2016; Simon 2017; Wehner, Elkouss, and Hanson 2018; Acín et al. 2018.
29. Diamanti et al. 2016, 1–2.
30. Berson 2019.
31. Simon 2017; Wehner, Elkouss, and Hanson 2018.
32. See Mosca 2015.

33. Warner 2014, 153.
34. Rich and Gellman 2014.
35. Lindsay and Cheung 2015; Gilli and Gilli 2018.
36. Reviews include Grissom 2006; Griffin 2017.
37. See, inter alia, Bijker et al. 1987; Bowker and Star 1999; Orlikowski 2000.
38. Lord 2007; Mandel 2019.
39. Broussard 2018; Smith 2019.
40. Jervis 2011.
41. Rovner 2011.
42. Jervis 1998; Betts 2000.
43. Snowden 2013.
44. This argument, developed in depth in Lindsay 2020a, is an application of the general information practice framework in Lindsay 2020b, chap. 2.
45. Dupuy 2015.
46. Paarlberg 2004.
47. Edelstein 2017.
48. Metz 2020.
49. See, inter alia, Glaser and Kaufmann 1998; Biddle 2001; Slayton 2017.

References

Aaronson, Scott. 2007. Shor, I'll Do It. *Shtetl-Optimized*. https://www.scottaaronson.com/blog/?p=208. Accessed November 22, 2021.

Aaronson, Scott. 2019. Why Google's Quantum Supremacy Milestone Matters. *New York Times*. https://www.nytimes.com/2019/10/30/opinion/google-quantum-computer-sycamore.html. Accessed November 22, 2021

Acín, Antonio, Immanuel Bloch, Harry Buhrman, Tommaso Calarco, Christopher Eichler, Jens Eisert, Daniel Esteve, et al. 2018. The Quantum Technologies Roadmap: A European Community View. *New Journal of Physics* 20 (8): 080201.

Arute, Frank, Kunal Arya, Ryan Babbush, Dave Bacon, Joseph C. Bardin, Rami Barends, Rupak Biswas, et al. 2019. Quantum Supremacy Using a Programmable Superconducting Processor. *Nature* 574 (7779): 505–510.

Barrett, Eamon. 2019. Google and NASA Have Claimed Quantum Supremacy, but China Is Not Far Behind the U.S. *Fortune*, October 30. https://fortune.com/2019/10/30/quantum-supremacy-china-us-google/. Accessed November 22, 2021.

Bernstein, Daniel J., Nadia Heninger, Paul Lou, and Luke Valenta. 2017. Post-Quantum RSA. *Cryptology ePrint Archive*. https://eprint.iacr.org/2017/351.pdf.

Berson, Tom [@nd2t]. 2019. Tweet Message. Twitter, July 23, 4:30 p.m. https://twitter.com/nd2t/status/1153779489639239681. Accessed November 22, 2021.

Betts, Richard K. 2000. Is Strategy an Illusion? *International Security* 25 (2): 5–50.

Biddle, Stephen. 2001. Rebuilding the Foundations of Offense-Defense Theory. *Journal of Politics* 63 (3): 741–774.

Biercuk, Michael J., and Richard Fontaine. 2017. The Leap into Quantum Technology: A Primer for National Security Professionals. *War on the Rocks*. https://warontherocks.

com/2017/11/leap-quantum-technology-primer-national-security-professionals/. Accessed April 7, 2018.

Bijker, Wiebe E., Thomas P. Hughes, Trevor Pinch, and Deborah G. Douglas, eds. 1987. *The Social Construction of Technological Systems: New Directions in the Sociology and History of Technology.* Cambridge, MA: MIT Press.

Bowker, Geoffrey C., and Susan Leigh Star. 1999. *Sorting Things Out: Classification and Its Consequences.* Cambridge, MA: MIT Press.

Broussard, Meredith. 2018. *Artificial Unintelligence: How Computers Misunderstand the World.* Cambridge, MA: MIT Press.

Central Committee of the Communist Party of China. 2016. The 13th Five-Year Plan for Economic and Social Development of the People's Republic of China (2016–2020). Beijing: Central Compilation & Translation Press. https://en.ndrc.gov.cn/policies/202105/P020210527785800103339.pdf. Accessed November 22, 2021.

Chen, L. 2017. Cryptography Standards in Quantum Time: New Wine in an Old Wineskin? *IEEE Security Privacy* 15 (4): 51–57.

Chen, Lily, Stephen Jordan, Yi-Kai Liu, Dustin Moody, Rene Peralta, Ray Perlner, and Daniel Smith-Tone. 2016. *Report on Post-Quantum Cryptography.* Gaithersburg, MD: National Institute of Standards and Technology.

Computer Security Resource Center. 2016. Announcing Request for Nominations for Public-Key Post-Quantum Cryptographic Algorithms. *National Institute of Standards and Technology.* https://csrc.nist.gov/news/2016/public-key-post-quantum-cryptographic-algorithms. Accessed February 14, 2018.

Craw, Victoria. 2018. Quantum Computing set to Revolutionise Everything from National Security to Drug Design and Financial Investments. *News.com.au.* http://www.news.com.au/technology/innovation/inventions/quantum-computing-set-to-revolutionise-everything-from-national-security-to-drug-design-and-financial-investments/news-story/2b495e494f47ee43b3975f5e884f11af. Accessed February 14, 2018.

Diamanti, Eleni, Hoi-Kwong Lo, Bing Qi, and Zhiliang Yuan. 2016. Practical Challenges in Quantum Key Distribution. *npj | Quantum Information* 2: 16025.

DigiCert. 2018. Check Our Numbers: The Math Behind Estimations to Break a 2048-bit Certificate. Archived on October 4, 2018 at https://web.archive.org/web/20181004033325/https://www.digicert.com/TimeTravel/math.htm.

Dupuy, Jean-Pierre. 2015. *A Short Treatise on the Metaphysics of Tsunamis.* Translated by M. B. DeBevoise. East Lansing: Michigan State University Press.

Edelstein, David M. 2017. *Over the Horizon: Time, Uncertainty, and the Rise of Great Powers.* Ithaca, NY: Cornell University Press.

Gerstell, Glenn S. 2019. I Work for N.S.A. We Cannot Afford to Lose the Digital Revolution. *New York Times*, sec. Opinion. https://www.nytimes.com/2019/09/10/opinion/nsa-privacy.html. Accessed September 10, 2019.

Gidney, Craig, and Martin Ekera. 2021. How to Factor 2048 Bit RSA Integers in 8 Hours Using 20 Million Noisy Qubits. *Quantum* 5: 433. https://doi.org/10.22331/q-2021-04-15-433.

Gilli, Andrea, and Mauro Gilli. 2018. Why China Hasn't Caught Up Yet: Military-Technological Superiority and The Limits of Imitation, Reverse Engineering, and Cyber-Espionage. *International Security* 43 (3): 141–189.

Glaser, Charles L., and Chaim Kaufmann. 1998. What Is the Offense-Defense Balance and Can We Measure it? *International Security* 22 (4): 44–82.

Griffin, Stuart. 2017. Military Innovation Studies: Multidisciplinary or Lacking Discipline? *Journal of Strategic Studies* 40 (1–2): 196–224.

Grissom, Adam. 2006. The Future of Military Innovation Studies. *Journal of Strategic Studies* 29 (5): 905–934.

Hurd, Will. 2017. Quantum Computing Is the Next Big Security Risk. *Wired*. https://www.wired.com/story/quantum-computing-is-the-next-big-security-risk/. Accessed November 22, 2021.

Jervis, Robert. 1998. *System Effects: Complexity in Political and Social Life*. Princeton, NJ: Princeton University Press.

Jervis, Robert. 2011. *Why Intelligence Fails: Lessons from the Iranian Revolution and the Iraq War*. Ithaca, NY: Cornell University Press.

Kania, Elsa B., and John Costello. 2018. *Quantum Hegemony? China's Ambitions and the Challenge to U.S. Innovation Leadership*. Washington, DC: Center for a New American Security.

Lauter, K. 2017. Postquantum Opportunities: Lattices, Homomorphic Encryption, and Supersingular Isogeny Graphs. *IEEE Security Privacy* 15 (4): 22–27.

Lindsay, Jon R. 2020a. Demystifying the Quantum Threat: Infrastructure, Implementation, and Intelligence Advantage. *Security Studies* 29 (2): 335–361.

Lindsay, Jon R. 2020b. *Information Technology and Military Power*. Ithaca, NY: Cornell University Press.

Lindsay, Jon R. 2020c. Surviving the Quantum Cryptocalypse. *Strategic Studies Quarterly* 14 (2): 49–73.

Lindsay, Jon R., and Tai Ming Cheung. 2015. From Exploitation to Innovation: Acquisition, Absorption, and Application. In *China and Cybersecurity: Espionage, Strategy, and Politics in the Digital Domain*, edited by Jon R. Lindsay, Tai Ming Cheung, and Derek S Reveron, 51–86. New York: Oxford University Press.

Lo, Hoi-Kwong, and Norbert Lütkenhaus. 2007. Quantum Cryptography: From Theory to Practice. *Physics in Canada* 63 (4): 191–196.

Lord, Kristin M. 2007. *The Perils and Promise of Global Transparency: Why the Information Revolution May Not Lead to Security, Democracy, or Peace*. Albany: State University of New York Press.

Lucero, Erik, R. Barends, Y. Chen, J. Kelly, M. Mariantoni, A. Megrant, P. O'Malley, et al. 2012. Computing Prime Factors with a Josephson Phase Qubit Quantum Processor. *Nature Physics* 8 (10): 719–723.

Mandel, Robert. 2019. *Global Data Shock: Strategic Ambiguity, Deception, and Surprise in an Age of Information Overload*. Stanford, CA: Stanford University Press.

Metz, Cade. 2020. White House Earmarks New Money for A.I. and Quantum Computing. *New York Times*. https://www.nytimes.com/2020/02/10/technology/white-house-earmarks-new-money-for-ai-and-quantum-computing.html. Accessed November 22, 2021.

Moody, Dustin. 2018. Let's Get Ready to Rumble: The NIST PQC "Competition," presented at the PQCrypto 2018, Fort Lauderdale, FL. https://csrc.nist.gov/Presentations/2018/Let-s-Get-Ready-to-Rumble-The-NIST-PQC-Competiti.

Mosca, Michele. 2015. *Cybersecurity in an Era with Quantum Computers: Will We Be Ready?* Tokyo. 5th International Conference on Quantum Cryptography (QCrypt).

Mulholland, J., M. Mosca, and J. Braun. 2017. The Day the Cryptography Dies. *IEEE Security Privacy* 15 (4): 14–21.

National Academies of Sciences, Engineering, and Medicine. 2019. *Quantum Computing: Progress and Prospects*. Washington, DC: National Academies Press.

Nikias, C. L. Max. 2018. This Is the Most Important Tech Contest since the Space Race, and America Is Losing. *Washington Post*. https://www.washingtonpost.com/opinions/this-is-the-most-important-tech-contest-since-the-space-race-and-america-is-losing/2018/05/11/7a4a4772-4e21-11e8-b725-92c89fe3ca4c_story.html%20. Accessed November 22, 2021.

Orlikowski, Wanda J. 2000. Using Technology and Constituting Structures: A Practice Lens for Studying Technology in Organizations. *Organization Science* 11 (4): 404–428.

Owen, Taylor, and Robert Gorwa. 2016. Quantum Leap: China's Satellite and the New Arms Race. *Foreign Affairs*. https://www.foreignaffairs.com/articles/2016-09-07/quantum-leap. Accessed November 22, 2021.

Paarlberg, Robert L. 2004. Knowledge as Power: Science, Military Dominance, and U.S. Security. *International Security* 29 (1): 122–151.

Rich, Steven, and Barton Gellman. 2014. NSA Seeks to Build Quantum Computer That Could Crack Most Types of Encryption. *Washington Post*. https://www.washingtonpost.com/world/national-security/nsa-seeks-to-build-quantum-computer-that-could-crack-most-types-of-encryption/2014/01/02/8fff297e-7195-11e3-8def-a33011492df2_story.html. Accessed November 22, 2021.

Rivest, R. L., A. Shamir, and L. Adleman. 1978. A Method for Obtaining Digital Signatures and Public-Key Cryptosystems. *Communications of the ACM* 21 (2): 120–126.

Rovner, Joshua. 2011. *Fixing the Facts: National Security and the Politics of Intelligence*. Ithaca, NY: Cornell University Press.

Schneier, Bruce. 2015. NSA Plans for a Post-Quantum World. *Lawfare*, August 21. https://www.lawfareblog.com/nsa-plans-post-quantum-world. Accessed November 22, 2021.

Schneier, Bruce. 2017. Class Breaks. *Schneier on Security*. https://www.schneier.com/blog/archives/2017/01/class_breaks.html. Accessed September 8, 2019.

Shor, Peter W. 1994. Algorithms for Quantum Computation: Discrete Logarithms and Factoring. In *Proceedings of the 35th Annual Symposium on Foundations of Computer Science*, 124–134. Los Alamitos, CA: IEEE Computer Society.

Simon, Christoph. 2017. Towards a Global Quantum Network. *Nature Photonics* 11 (11): 678–680.

Singh, Simon. 1999. *The Code Book: The Science of Secrecy from Ancient Egypt to Quantum Cryptography*. New York: Random House.

Slayton, Rebecca. 2017. What Is the Cyber Offense-Defense Balance? Conceptions, Causes, and Assessment. *International Security* 41 (3): 72–109.

Smith, Brian Cantwell. 2019. *The Promise of Artificial Intelligence: Reckoning and Judgment*. Cambridge, MA: MIT Press.

Snowden, Edward. 2013. NSA Whistleblower Answers Reader Questions. *The Guardian*. https://www.theguardian.com/world/2013/jun/17/edward-snowden-nsa-files-whistleblower. Accessed November 22, 2021.

Townsend, P. D. 1994. Secure Key Distribution System Based on Quantum Cryptography. *Electronics Letters* 30 (10): 809–811.

Warner, Michael. 2014. *The Rise and Fall of Intelligence: An International Security History*. Washington, DC: Georgetown University Press.

Wehner, Stephanie, David Elkouss, and Ronald Hanson. 2018. Quantum Internet: A Vision for the Road Ahead. *Science* 362 (6412): eaam9288.

9

Quantum Technology Hype
and National Security

Frank L. Smith III

Quantum theory has practical applications to security practice. The special properties of quantum mechanics can be used as tools, including new kinds of computers, secret codes, and sensors. These technologies are now fashionable for their revolutionary potential. "The impact of quantum on our national defense will be tremendous," according to US Representative Will Hurd. "The 20th century gave birth to the Nuclear Age," and "today, we are on the cusp of an equally momentous and irrevocable breakthrough: the advent of computers that draw their computational capability from quantum mechanics" (Hurd, 2017). Similarly, according to Pan Jianwei, China's lead scientist on the world's first quantum communication satellite, "a key period for the development of quantum computing is coming, which is like the bamboo shoots popping out after the rain" (Yi, 2017). Google, IBM, and Microsoft seem to agree (Hackett, 2019; Castelvecchi, 2017). Google is the first to claim "quantum supremacy," namely, "going beyond what can be achieved with ordinary digital computers" (Preskill, 2012: 2), and its researchers argue that "we are only one creative algorithm away from valuable near-term applications" (Arute et al., 2019: 510).

It is uncertain whether quantum technologies will live up to these high expectations. If they fall short, they will not be alone. We interpret new and emerging technologies based on collective expectations about imagined futures: including our dreams and nightmares. These expectations are often unmet following hyperbole or hype. Technology hype is considered in the literature on business and marketing, as well as in science and technology studies (STS). The implications for national security, however, are overlooked and understudied.

What is technology hype? How does it relate to national security? And to what effect? In this chapter, I introduce the concept of technology hype into security studies. Quantum technologies provide an initial proof of this concept, which applies to other new and emerging technologies as well--ranging from artificial intelligence (AI) and autonomy to biotechnology and hypersonic weapons. Technology hype also has normative implications for how social scientists talk about these tools in the context of International Relations.

I argue that technology hype is intimately related to national security. A rational perspective on hype as an exaggeration relates to the literature on threat inflation. A performative perspective on hype as expectant discourse relates to securitization theory. Given gaps in existing theory, I sketch new propositions about hype as common in the national security community with variable acceptance, familiar content, and significant consequences for technology and politics. I find supporting evidence in hype over quantum technologies. Audience acceptance in the US national security community varies, in part with familiarity, and consequential decisions follow in the form of extraordinary measures. Since hype can be cyclical, my analysis implies that humility is warranted when citing these technologies as support for quantum approaches to International Relations. As a further counterpoint, it also illustrates the utility of remaining agnostic about technological futures and ontological foundations.

This chapter therefore draws inspiration from attempts to "quantize international relations," but it does not embrace a quantum approach. I proceed as follows. First, I review arguments about technology hype, particularly the Gartner Hype Cycle. Next, I compare and contrast technology hype with security studies on threat inflation and securitization theory. Finding room for improvement, I briefly outline my own theory of hype and security. I then turn to a case study of quantum technology, which supports my propositions. Finally, after calling for more empirical research, I conclude by arguing for more middle-range theory to help understand the latest quantum "revolution."

Technology Hype: From Business and Marketing to STS

The novelty of new and emerging technologies means that our expectations about them are constructed around considerable uncertainty and indeterminacy. What they will be, how they will be used, who will use them, and why are all open questions, often with significant implications for security. Answers are contingent on choices yet to come, leaving us with no more or less than our expectations. Uncertainty and indeterminacy are inherent here, as they are in International Relations and quantum social theory (Wendt, 2015). In the case of quantum technologies, like other technologies, our expectations are "real-time representations of future technological situations and capabilities" (Borup et al., 2006: 286). What do we expect from future technology? Quite a lot, according to the literature on business and marketing.

Gartner Hype Cycle

The concept of technology hype was advanced by Jackie Fenn and Mark Raskino at the business consulting firm Gartner (Fenn and Raskino, 2008: xiii). Branded the Gartner Hype Cycle, this model describes collective expectations about technology. It combines two different curves into one, as shown in Figure 9.1. On the left is a bell curve, which depicts a sharp rise in early expectations that then fall due to disappointment. Falling expectations dovetail with an S-curve on the right. This curve rises gradually before flattening out, mirroring a pattern cited in other literature to describe the diffusion of innovation over time (e.g., Rogers, 1962).

The Gartner model is divided into several stages of causes and consequences. An initial breakthrough or demonstration provides an *innovation trigger,* which builds buzz and captures the imagination. Gartner currently places quantum computing in this initial phase; perhaps the same can be said about quantum approaches to International Relations. The swell of attention builds into a *peak of inflated expectations,* as publicity and investment fuel a bubble of overenthusiasm.

According to Fenn and Raskino, these initial stages of technology hype are caused by "human nature," particularly our attraction to novelty, social contagion, and decision heuristics. Other authors stress the pressure to publish and commercialize research, as well as biases against reporting negative results in academic publications and the popular press (e.g., Caulfield and Condit, 2012). Another potential cause is that modern societies expect technological change. It happened in the past (e.g., industrialization), and, through science fiction, we tell stories about change in the future (Elhefnawy, 2018; Furman and Musgrave, 2017).

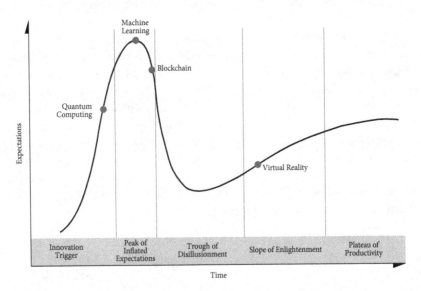

Figure 9.1 The Gartner Hype Cycle (adapted from Panetta, 2017).

Impatience builds when results fail to meet initial expectations, however. "The same psychological and social factors that drove the excitement upward now begin to drive it right back down again" (Fenn and Raskino, 2008: 34). Waning interest creates a *trough of disillusionment*. Ongoing learning then builds a *slope of enlightenment*, whereby increasing knowledge supposedly informs more realistic expectations. Last is the *plateau of productivity*, when the technology is realistically valued and widely adopted. Overall, the Gartner Hype Cycle depicts a version of "Amara's law," namely, that "we tend to overestimate the effect of a technology in the short run and underestimate the effect in the long run" (Fenn and Raskino, 2008: 84).

Critical Review

The Gartner Hype Cycle is more of a business product than scholarly exercise. It is vulnerable to substantial criticism. Despite looking like a wave, for instance, there is no underlying wave equation as in quantum theory (Steinert and Leifer, 2010: 258). The dependent variable is questionable as well. Expectations and visibility (the bell curve) are not the same kind of phenomena as diffusion and adoption (the S-curve), so combining them confuses what is being described (Dedehayir and Steinert, 2016: 33). Nor does the empirical evidence conform to this bimodal curve. Hype patterns vary for technologies ranging from hybrid cars to gene therapy and superconductivity, with multiple peaks and troughs (Jun, 2012; Lente et al., 2013). Technology assessments by Gartner aren't consistent either, all of which suggests that "individual technologies do not necessarily behave according to the model's assumptions" (Dedehayir and Steinert, 2016: 34).

Maybe "superposition" could reconcile the Gartner model with the empirical evidence, namely, by treating the bimodal curve as a general description that combines many different hype patterns. However, a more fundamental critique applies to the analytical perspective on hype in this model. Hype describes particular kinds of expectations or real-time representations of the future. These representations can be analyzed from either a rational or performative perspective.

The Gartner model is a rational perspective. It portrays hype as an exaggeration. Whether sincere or dishonest, positive or negative, hype is inaccurate and accepting it is irrational. "The sudden, illogical acceleration of expectations around an innovation is a form of 'irrational exuberance'" (Fenn and Raskino, 2008: 26). As a result, this sort of "realist position assumes that there is a calculable difference in the present between expectations and the real worth of something such that expectations can be adjusted 'rationally' according to fluctuations in value" (Borup et al., 2006: 288). In other words, hype is not only inaccurate but also knowable as such at the time.

The problem with this perspective is that new and emerging technologies are inherently uncertain and indeterminate. So is the future. It is problematic to presume that differences between expectations and real worth or future value can be measured, especially early on. This is not to say that technology assessment is useless. But technological uncertainty and indeterminacy mean that measurements and forecasts are imperfect at best and open to multiple interpretations. Given "interpretive flexibility" (Pinch and Bijker, 1987: 40), it is difficult to authoritatively operationalize this definition of hype as exaggeration.

An alternative approach is a performative perspective, favored by STS literature on the sociology of expectations (Lente and Rip, 1998; Brown et al., 2000; Brown and Michael, 2003; Borup et al., 2006; Lente et al., 2013). Here hype is not an inaccurate forecast but rather an expectant kind of language, rhetoric, or discourse. Positive hype refers to "revolution" or "breakthrough" (Brown and Michael, 2003; Saffo, 1991) and, similarly, "exponential" growth or "disruption." Negative hype may refer to failure, impossibility, or irrelevance.

The content of this discourse can be identified as grandiose, extravagant, or extreme, and its consequences can be studied, all while remaining agnostic about whether the expectations involved will ever prove correct. "A perceived gap between early expectations and eventual technological development is thus not an accurate indicator of a hype" (Lente et al., 2013: 1616). Nor is it necessary to resolve technological uncertainty or indeterminacy to analyze hype. By way of analogy to quantum theory, we don't need to "collapse" the wave function of potential futures. Instead, we can remain ambivalent about new technologies.

Technology Hype and Security Studies

The concept of technology hype is rarely related to security studies. References to threat inflation and securitization are far more common. While these arguments are similar, they also differ in several respects.

Threat Inflation

When imported into security studies, a rational perspective on technology hype appears similar to threat inflation. Threat inflation can be defined as "claims that go beyond the range of ambiguity that disinterested experts would credit as plausible" via worst-case assertions, double standards, and circular logic (Kaufmann, 2004: 8). Causes include elite manipulation, bureaucratic incentives, special interests, public ignorance, and uncritical coverage in the press (e.g., Lowi, 1969; Cavanaugh, 2007; Thrall and Cramer, 2009). Examples range from the Soviet threat during the Cold War to terrorism and "weapons of mass destruction" as justifications for the 2003 Iraq War (e.g., Mearsheimer and Walt, 2003; Mueller, 2005).

Arguments about threat inflation acknowledge uncertainty. Yet they still assume that disinterested analysis is possible and recognizable as such. Expert assessments and a healthy marketplace of ideas supposedly weed out inaccuracies in real time. Therefore, threat inflation is knowable as exaggeration, like a rational perspective on hype. Similar critiques apply as well. "The concept of threat inflation is deeply utopian" (Van Rythoven, 2016: 491), as is the heroic assumption of a rational baseline for forecasting future technology. Uncertainty and indeterminacy leave threat intelligence open to debate. New and emerging technologies are no less ambiguous.

Heroic assumptions about rational, disinterested, or independent analysis can also overlook contingent or "entangled" outcomes such as self-fulfilling prophecies. Shared expectations help construct the very facts and artifacts in question, from conflict spirals to new and emerging technologies. For instance, Moore's law—the expectation that transistor density doubles every two years—helped drive the development of digital computers since the 1960s (Moore, 1996; Lente and Rip, 1998: 206). Expectant language is distinct but not fully separable from the technology that it describes. With quantum technologies, physics constrains but does not uniquely determine the knowledge pursued or the tools developed and used. Hype can influence these choices, regardless of whether it is accurate or informed by seemingly disinterested analysis.

There are other important differences between threat inflation and technology hype, even from a rational perspective. Hype can be optimistic. It's not just about the worst case but the best as well. In addition to techno-optimism, hype is also cyclical. Expectations about future technology can rise and fall repeatedly. They may not simply inflate and then deflate, stabilize, or normalize over time. Something else is going on.

Securitization Theory

A performative perspective on technology hype is likewise similar and yet not the same as securitization theory. Both address the roles and identities of elite actors and target audiences that articulate and interpret speech. Both hype and securitization link specific rhetorical structures—be they about revolution and breakthrough or threat and survival—to extraordinary measures (Buzan et al., 1998: 26).

Both hype and securitization can fail (Ruzicka, 2019; Åtland and Ven Bruusgaard, 2009). When accepted as legitimate, however, both call for extraordinary measures. Like securitization, technology hype can enable some outcomes and constrain others by setting the agenda and mobilizing resources (Bakker and Budde, 2012; Lente et al., 2013). Implicitly or explicitly, positive hype calls for extraordinary measures, particularly urgent investments—money, time, attention—into research and development. Again, these investments affect the facts and artifacts involved. They also benefit associated coalitions or networks of identities, interests, and "relevant social groups" (Pinch and Bijker, 1987: 30), such as scientists, engineers, and other stakeholders. If we set aside the human/nonhuman divide, then the performative work of hype can be said to enact some of the heterogeneous assemblages of social agents and material objects described by actor-network theory (e.g., Latour, 2005). Like any network, sociotechnical expectations are relational.

Methodologically, both hype and securitization can be studied via discourse analysis, content analysis, ethnographic research, and process tracing, as well as experiments. Visual images likewise present both with related challenges and opportunities. Distinctions between the Copenhagen School and Paris School of security studies are debatable, but both hype and securitization can be theorized as being either so exceptional as to fall outside normal politics or so common as to remain political and routine. Either way, the concepts of time and the future are integral to both.

Despite these similarities, there are important differences between securitization theory and technology hype. First, securitization emphasizes existential threat and fear for the survival of a referent object. However, as noted earlier, hype can be optimistic and hopeful. Granted, fear is an emotion, hope is more of a feeling, and the connotations of hype are not always positive. For example, Congressman Hurd describes quantum computing as a "momentous and irrevocable breakthrough" that "presents both an unprecedented opportunity and a serious threat." Yet the extraordinary measures he calls for are not to stop, slow, or safeguard this dual-use technology but rather that "the United States must lead" (Hurd, 2017). Self and Other identities are evident in Hurd's longer statement (e.g., the China threat). But so are attraction and aversion, and the actors he emphasizes are not limited to military and intelligence agencies. Instead of the danger and fear that characterize securitization, hype includes the promise of positive potential, along with a larger cast of characters.

Second, as with threat inflation, cyclical expectations about technology are difficult to square with securitization theory. There is considerable normative, theoretical, and empirical debate around desecuritization (Hansen, 2012), including its timing and sequence. Yet if desecuritization is rare, slow, or unidirectional, then it doesn't align well with the oscillating expectations associated with hype cycles.

Third, interpretations of performativity differ. While most literature from STS privileges a performative perspective, it also interprets performativity as allowing for external and material realities. Technology hype is "grounded in the material," and so "the performativity . . . is conducted in material settings, where bodies and texts, for example, come into contact or close proximity" (Michael, 2000: 33). In contrast, "as a performative and intersubjective practice, securitization has largely ignored the role of 'things' in the articulation of insecurities" (Aradau, 2010: 493). A performative perspective on technology hype aligns with sociological, contextual, and externalist approaches to securitization theory, but it breaks from more philosophical, poststructural, and internalist variants (Balzacq, 2015).

Theoretical Propositions: Technology Hype and National Security

The similarities between technology hype, threat inflation, and securitization theory indicate that hype is applicable to security studies. Their differences hint at how a theory of hype could predict or explain novel facts about security. I therefore sketch several propositions for what this might look like as a new "middle-range theory" (e.g., Geels, 2007). In doing so, I focus on the national security community (i.e., the military sector), and I define hype as a kind of performative discourse that invokes exceptional expectations about future technologies.

Technology Hype Is Common

Is technology hype normal? I hypothesize that it is common, even within the national security community. This proposition is somewhat counterintuitive. After all, military and intelligence agencies invest in seemingly rational technology assessment. The armed forces are also portrayed as conservative, bureaucratic, and risk-averse organizations. As a result, they may be less likely to engage in hyperbole, buy snake oil, or suffer disillusion.

That said, there is reason to suspect that "hype is everywhere" (Fenn and Raskino, 2008: 10), including the national security community. Uncertainty is not only a defining feature of new technologies and quantum mechanics but also the security dilemma (Jervis, 1978). Moreover, many military and intelligence agencies are forward-looking and technologically intensive organizations. They are sensitive to surprise and first-mover advantages. They buy equipment from industry and are thus bombarded with marketing. Some armed services are even predisposed to love new technology (Builder, 1989).

The US national security community has, at times, accepted exceptional expectations about new technology and appeared prescient in hindsight. Consider Albert Einstein's letter to President Roosevelt about the atomic bomb in 1939. Einstein did not use the words "revolution" or "breakthrough," but his expectant discourse stressed novelty and the need for extraordinary measures. "Recent work," he wrote, "leads me to expect that the element of uranium may be turned into a new and important source of energy in the immediate future.... Extremely powerful bombs of a new type may thus be constructed" (Einstein-Szilard Letter, 1939). Einstein also cited the German threat in his call for "quick action." The Manhattan Project and subsequent bombings of Hiroshima and Nagasaki turned these exceptional expectations into terrifying new realities.

Other cases contrast early enthusiasm with subsequent disappointment. For instance, exceptional expectations are explicit in the phrase "revolution in military affairs" (RMA). Buoyed by victory in the 1991 Gulf War, advocates of the RMA argued that new information technologies could transform armed conflict. By investing in them and related concepts such as "network-centric warfare," the United States could supposedly enjoy "information dominance" and "lock in" decisive victories quickly and cheaply (e.g., Cebrowski and Garstka, 1998). This idea influenced decision-making about the wars in Afghanistan and Iraq. It then fell out of favor. Some commentators came to criticize the RMA as fundamentally misguided (McMaster, 2008), while others pointed to robots as the "real" revolution (Singer, 2009). It is reasonable to hypothesize that such discourse is common. The national security community is not immune.

Not All Hype Is Accepted

Just because technology hype is normal does not mean it is successful. As with attempted securitization, hype can fail to be accepted or acted upon by the national security community. For better or worse, this audience accepts some hype: just not all of it, and not in equal measure.

Some technologies are discounted or dismissed. For example, the US military slashed research and development for defense against biological weapons in the 1970s (Smith, 2014). At the same time, the Soviet Union was building the largest biological weapons program in the world, and the invention of genetic engineering had triggered what came to be called the biotechnology revolution. Whether such instances are coded as the rejection of positive hype or acceptance of negative hype, variation in what discourse is accepted needs to be explained.

Acceptable Hype Is Familiar

What technology hype is accepted? Ironically, despite references to revolution, I hypothesize that what the hype audiences accept depends on ordinary or established identities and interests. We accept the hype we want, embracing exceptional expectations so long as they are still familiar. We may expect quantum computers to be revolutionary, for instance, while still imagining them to be computers that will be used as such.

Said another way, acceptable hype is an extension of what Thomas Kuhn described as "normal science" (Kuhn, 1962). Acceptable hype involves novelty, but novelty entertained inside an established paradigm or framework. "Innovations that fit within that framework are more likely to attract attention and generate excitement" (Fenn and Raskino, 2008: 33). In contrast, anomalies that fall outside an audience's framework are dismissed (Smith, 2014). If expectant discourse about new technology is compatible with established identities and interests inside the national security community, then military and intelligence agencies will be more likely to entertain expectations beyond the current state of the art.

Of course, we don't always get what we want, say, or expect. Material constraints and opportunities influence outcomes, consistent with a modest interpretation of performativity. Interactions between material and ideational factors explain why hype is cyclical. Think of technology like fashion (even in the context of security). Styles of clothing repeatedly come and go. On one hand, status signaling and other deeply social relationships drive change. On the other hand, wear and tear—entropy and friction—contribute to turnover; the visible spectrum limits our color options; and the clothes we construct are constrained by their physical properties and the environment. These material factors limit the range of creative expression, within which trends in fashion tend to oscillate over time.

Like clothing, vogue technology is what states and other actors make of it (Wendt, 1992). But only to a point. Material things can be disconfirming. For hype over these things to cycle, there must be an impulse to entertain exceptional expectations about similar technologies again and again. As with questions about what hype is accepted in the first place, repetition suggests that some audiences repeatedly give some representations of the future the benefit of the doubt, even after having been disappointed in the past. Correspondence with established identities and interests may explain why. Here again, we accept hype that we want, or at least recognize, time after time.

Accepted Hype Is Consequential

So what? Even when material constraints and opportunities influence outcomes, they don't fully determine them. Since expectations influence choice, hype is consequential for how we construct technology and politics.

There are winners and losers. The resources mobilized for some objects and actors come at the expense of others. Accepted hype provides power relative to alternative options. Disappointment complicates the distribution of limited resources. For instance, in artificial intelligence, the phrase "AI winter" describes "a period of retrenchment during which funding decreased and skepticism increased" (Bostrom, 2014: 8). It has happened more than once. The chill in investment may overcorrect earlier overshoot when viewed from a rational perspective. From a performative perspective, discourse about revolution and breakthrough can be reinterpreted as misguided or premature (Brown and Michael, 2003). But reinterpretation does not negate the effect of previously accepted hype. When research and development are path dependent and history is inefficient (David, 1985; March and Olsen, 1998), cyclical expectations can have a lasting impact on technology.

Hype is also consequential for International Relations. When accepted by the national security community, technology hype stands to influence the security dilemma, arms races, and threat perceptions. The intensity of the security dilemma is a function of technology expressed through the "offense-defense balance" and "offense-defense differentiation" (Jervis, 1978). Offensive and defensive applications of new technologies could both be hyped, all else being equal. However, if acceptable hype depends on established identities and interests, and militaries are biased toward offense (Snyder, 1984), then the hype they accept may make the security dilemma more intense.

Similarly, the extraordinary measures legitimized by hype may be indistinguishable from the abnormal and intensive investments associated with arms races. Expectations about the future can fuel an "anticipation-reaction process" in the development of new weapons (Brown, 1992: 5). Hype can also interact with interpretations of the "technological imperative" (Buzan, 1987), which motivates militaries to acquire new technologies from commercial markets for fear of falling behind adversaries armed with access to those same markets.

Since military and intelligence agencies are actors as well as audiences, they both consume hype and contribute to it. The mystique of lethal applications, military specifications, and secret or classified information can engage other audiences. If intelligence agencies invest in quantum technologies, for instance, this association inspires others' imagination. If accepted abroad, then hype over the technologies pursued by one country can signal capabilities and intentions, as well as identity, status, and prestige.

More theory is needed. The relationships I propose between technology hype and national security are plausible and consequential enough to warrant further examination. Quantum technologies provide an instructive case study.

Quantum Hype and Security

Whatever else they may be, quantum technologies are uncertain and new. Quantum technologies use the special properties of atomic and subatomic systems—electrons, photons, ions—to do work. These physical objects are represented by mathematical abstraction as quantum bits (i.e., qubits). Qubits can be used to acquire, process, and transmit information in new ways. These functions correspond to three related but distinct kinds of quantum technologies: sensors, computers, and communications.

For quantum computers, the idea of using the special properties of atomic and subatomic systems to process information was first proposed by Richard Feynman in 1981. By leveraging quantum superposition and entanglement via qubits, quantum computers may be able to solve some difficult or intractable math problems faster than digital computers. Quantum communications use similar properties to create secret codes, particularly for symmetric cryptography via quantum key distribution (QKD). Charles Bennett and Gilles Brassard invented the first protocol that applied quantum mechanics to this kind of cryptographic communication in 1984. Quantum sensors are probably the oldest technology to leverage quantum information, with plans for the first atomic clock published in 1949.

Are these technologies hyped? The association between "quantum" and "revolution" predates the facts and artifacts just described. By most accounts, the theory of quantum mechanics revolutionized the study of physics in the early twentieth century. This association with revolution is often coupled with reference to weirdness and thus novelty (even today, after a century of study). For example, Schrodinger's cat is a thought experiment about quantum superposition involving a "diabolical device," containing an unobserved feline that is simultaneously dead and alive. Einstein famously criticized quantum entanglement as "spooky action at a distance." Niels Bohr and Feynman are also quoted as having said that "if you think you understand quantum theory," or if you "are not shocked" by it, "then you don't understand." This discourse provides fertile ground for imagination.

Do You Guys Just Put the Word "Quantum" in Front
of Everything? (*Ant-Man and the Wasp*, Marvel Studios, 2018)

Exceptional expectations are now evident in discourse about quantum technologies. "There is a second quantum revolution coming," according to
physicists Jonathan Dowling and Gerard Milburn, "which will be responsible for most of the key physical technological advances in the 21st century" (Dowling and Milburn, 2003: 1655). Similar references to revolution
and breakthrough feature in the popular press. "A quantum revolution is
coming" (Pandya, 2019), as reported in *Forbes*, and "quantum computers will
revolutionize artificial intelligence, machine learning and big data" (Marr,
2017). Elsewhere, a "quantum computing breakthrough could help 'change
life completely.' ... [I]t is the Holy Grail of science" (Johnston, 2017). These
tropes aren't limited to English. For example, "China has made important
breakthroughs in the development of miniaturized quantum communication
systems" (Haitao, 2017), according to a translation from the Xinhua News
Agency. Interest fluctuates over time, however. As illustrated with Google
Trends data in Figure 9.2, there are multiple peaks and troughs in internet
search traffic for quantum computing.

Another indicator is recognition of hype by scientists and engineers, even
as these same groups contribute to exceptional expectations. "It used to be

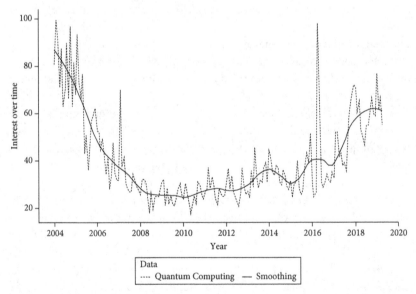

Figure 9.2 Google Trends data. Normalized volume of search queries for "quantum
computing" around the world (proportionate to time and location).

that if you were working in this area, you were the optimist telling everyone how great it's going to be," according to Graeme Smith, a theoretical physicist. "But then things shifted, and now researchers like me can't believe the things we're hearing.... There's almost a race to the bottom in making claims about what a quantum computer can do" (quoted in Gomes, 2018). According to Scott Aaronson, a computer scientist, "The hype that drives me nuts comes from rounding this fascinating reality down to the sorts of thing a science-fiction writer would invent," as well as "conventional" hype about "commercial breakthrough[s]" that don't stand up to scrutiny (quoted in Horgan, 2016). What scientists and engineers count as a quantum computer is controversial (Reimer, 2007; Aaronson, 2008). If or when these machines will ever be built is contested as well (Moskvitch, 2018). Even in business, Gartner argues that "quantum computing is heavily hyped" (Panetta, 2017).

Quantum hype is often related to security. As reported by Vice Media, "Quantum computing poses a mortal threat to computer security as we know it" (Oberhaus, 2017). A breakthrough or—wordplay in the *Sunday Times*—a "quantum leap for computers will put every secret at risk" (Whipple, 2018). Similarly, "you cannot think about the future of cyber war without understanding the momentous changes that are about to happen," according to Richard Clarke and Robert Knake, "with the advent of quantum computing" (Clarke and Knake, 2019: 254).

This rhetoric is not baseless, even from a rational perspective. Cyber security on the internet depends on encryption and authentication using public key cryptography, which in turn depends on a mathematical trick that exploits the difficulty of dividing large numbers into prime factors. In 1994, Peter Shor published a quantum algorithm for fast factoring. It is possible that Shor's algorithm could break public key cryptography if run on a powerful quantum computer. Such a machine was not believed to exist in 1994. By most accounts, it does not exist today. Yet the possibility that it might in the future is described as a looming cause of "the crypto-apocalypse" (Oberhaus, 2017).

"Fortunately, however, what quantum mechanics takes away with one hand, it gives back with the other" (Nielsen and Chuang, 2011: 582), at least according to expectant discourse about quantum communications. An "unhackable quantum internet" using QKD is portrayed as the technical fix to the security problems created by quantum computers. "In order to defend against quantum hacking, we need quantum security," namely, "a quantum network," as described by *Newsweek* in reporting on how a "new breakthrough heightens [the] 'technology arms race'" (Medrano, 2018). This reporting followed previous press on how yet another "quantum breakthrough heralds [a] new generation of perfectly secure messaging" (*MIT Technology Review*, 2017). This discourse appears exaggerated from a rational perspective: theoretically perfect secrecy differs from practical implementation, and quantum computers have other applications to security beyond cryptography. Nevertheless, it is not necessary to adjudicate the technical details in order to analyze the discourse at work.

In addition, "there's a lot of hype around quantum sensing" (Davies and Kennedy, 2017: 17). One article about a "breakthrough" that relies on "spooky" quantum entanglement is titled "The End of Stealth? New Chinese Radar Capable of Detecting 'Invisible' Targets 100km Away" (Chen, 2016). Others argue that "this one new piece of technology might make submarines completely obsolete" (Roblin, 2019). Or it might expose stealth aircraft, leaving the F-35 strike fighter and B-2 bomber "naked in the sky" (Mannix, 2019).

Security is therefore a prominent theme in expectant discourse about quantum technologies. Using Factiva data in Figure 9.3, I chart the amount of news about quantum computers, communications, and sensors that cites both security ("military" or "threat") and hype ("revolution" or "breakthrough"). On the one hand, frequencies vary across these technologies. Hype and security are currently most frequent in stories about quantum computers. On the other hand, they all trend upward. Regardless of whether these trends ultimately map onto the bimodal Gartner model, hype relating quantum technologies to security is increasingly common.

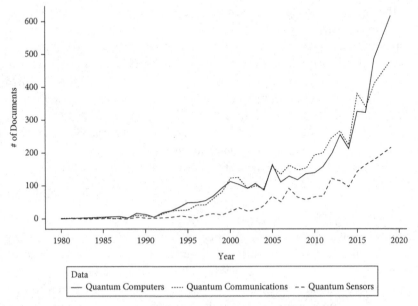

Figure 9.3 Factiva global news data. Frequency of documents that cite specific kinds of quantum technologies along with discourse about security and hype.

Variable Acceptance and Security Practice

Is quantum technology hype accepted and acted upon by the national security community? Prima facie evidence indicates that acceptance varies across military and intelligence agencies. For instance, seemingly unimpressed in 2015, the US Air Force Scientific Advisory Board concluded that:

> Quantum key distribution significantly increases system complexity but is unlikely to provide an overall improvement in communication security. . . . Despite claims heralding imminent breakthroughs, as of now no compelling evidence exists that quantum computers can be usefully applied to computing problems of interest to the Air Force. (USAF Scientific Advisory Board, 2015)

As a result, this report recommended that the Air Force invest in quantum sensors for navigation and other well-established missions.

At nearly the same time, however, the US National Security Agency (NSA) reported that "there is growing research in the area of quantum computing, and enough progress is being made that NSA must act now." Specifically, its Information Assurance Directorate "will initiate a transition to quantum resistant algorithms in the not too distant future" (NSA, 2015). These algorithms need not be quantum, and funding data is incomplete. Still, while acting on quantum-resistant algorithms, the NSA also sought to build "a cryptologically useful quantum computer" as "part of a $79.7 million research program titled 'Penetrating Hard Targets'" (Rich and Gellman, 2014).

Interpretive flexibility over what to expect from quantum technology dates back decades. Today, "a global race is developing," according to the US National Science and Technology Council, "in recognition of the potential implications of a [quantum]-based technological revolution" (US NSTC, 2016: 3). The US National Quantum Initiative Act of 2018 provides $1.2 billion for research and development because, according to the White House, "this next great technological revolution has far-reaching implications for job creation, economic growth and national security" (Cordell, 2018). Meanwhile, the European Union launched its own €1 billion Quantum Flagship initiative in 2018. Russia hopes to catch up with a 50 billion rouble investment. Although reliable information on Chinese investment in quantum technology is limited, "it appears that the recent and current levels of funding will amount to billions of dollars, likely at least tens of billions of RMB" (Kania and Costello, 2018: 9). Beijing launched its quantum "megaproject" in 2016. In order "to develop a quantum computer and other 'revolutionary' forms of technology that can be used by the military," China is also building the largest quantum research facility in the world (Chen, 2017).

These are extraordinary measures. Granted, what goes up may come down. Positive hype may fall out of favor, along with investment, in which case a "quantum winter" may follow. Either way, the extraordinary measures underway are impactful. Process tracing is beyond the scope of this chapter; more research is needed on the relationship between technology hype and the security dilemma. Yet quantum technologies provide an initial proof of concept. They are often hyped, and security is a prominent theme therein. The national security community doesn't always accept this discourse. But military and intelligence agencies appear to entertain exceptional expectations that are compatible with their established identities and interests, regardless of references to revolution. Finally, substantial resources have been mobilized. These resources shape not only facts and artifacts on the ground but also perceptions of great power competition and a "race" that, at least rhetorically, is not far removed from an arms race.

Particle or Wave? Implications for Theory

While reflexive enough not to call it a revolutionary breakthrough, I argue that a theory of technology hype holds considerable promise for security studies and how social scientists understand quantum technologies. Knowing what hype is and how it works can inform better theory and policy. Regardless of whether or not we accept expectant discourse about quantum technologies, the evidence of hype should give us pause. Will the appeal of quantum social science collapse if quantum computers fall out of fashion, for instance? Are we referring to this technological "revolution" to reinforce rather than overturn our established lines of argument about International Relations theory? Does the way we talk about quantum technologies hinge on heroic assumptions about the future? If so, then analytic humility may be a useful tonic for hype in the social and natural sciences alike.

Our choices are rarely neutral. The approach I choose in this chapter is a middle-range theory. It is eclectic. A middle-range theory can combine and extend concepts from business and marketing, STS and sociology, threat inflation and securitization, and, as I have shown, even quantum social theory.

A middle-range theory of hype and security is also agnostic in several respects. It does not require predicting the future of technology in order to analyze the content and consequences of imagined futures. The technical details are relevant, and ignoring them is dangerous. But wagering on their ultimate resolution isn't strictly necessary. "Statements about future technological performance are not received as factual descriptions to be verified or falsified in due course." Instead, "technological futures are forceful" in their own right (Lente, 2000: 43). That force shapes security.

As with predicting the future, a middle-range theory is "agnostic about what society is 'really' made of" (Fearon and Wendt, 2002: 53). Just as I do not wager on the future of quantum technologies, I do not "place bets on what are deeply contested philosophical issues" (Wendt, 2006: 182). Inspiration is drawn from quantum approaches, including analogies and metaphors about uncertainty and indeterminacy. My choice to investigate quantum technologies and national security isn't coincidental in this regard. Unlike quantum social theory, however, a middle-range theory does not attempt to unify physical and social ontology. I don't doubt the need for ontological investigations (Wight, 2006: 13), and I concede that my agnostic stance sidesteps philosophical questions about "materialism" versus "physicalism" (Wendt, 2015: 9), among others. It's a pragmatic tradeoff. It's also a worthy option moving forward, as illustrated by my analysis of quantum technology hype.

References

Aaronson, S (2008) Desultory D-Wave. *MIT Technology Review*. https://www.technolog yreview.com/s/409952/desultory-d-wave/.

Aradau, C (2010) Security That Matters: Critical Infrastructure and Objects of Protection. *Security Dialogue* 41(5): 491–514.

Arute, F, Arya, K, Babbush, R, Bacon, D, Bardin, JC, Barends, R, Biswas, R, et al. (2019) Quantum Supremacy Using a Programmable Superconducting Processor. *Nature* 574(7779): 505–510.

Åtland, K, & Bruusgaard KV (2009) When Security Speech Acts Misfire: Russia and the Elektron Incident. *Security Dialogue* 40(3): 333–353.

Bakker, S, & Budde, B (2012) Technological Hype and Disappointment: Lessons from the Hydrogen and Fuel Cell Case. *Technology Analysis & Strategic Management* 24(6): 549–563.

Balzacq, T (2015) The "Essence" of Securitization: Theory, Ideal Type, and a Sociological Science of Security. *International Relations* 29(1): 103–113.

Borup, M, Brown, N, Konrad, K, & Lente, V (2006) The Sociology of Expectations in Science and Technology. *Technology Analysis & Strategic Management* 18(1): 285–298.

Bostrom, N (2014) *Superintelligence: Paths, Dangers, Strategies*, Oxford, Oxford University Press.

Brown, E (1992) *Flying Blind: The Politics of the U.S. Strategic Bomber Program*, Ithaca, NY, Cornell University Press.

Brown, N, & Michael, M (2003) A Sociology of Expectations: Retrospecting Prospects and Prospecting Retrospects. *Technology Analysis & Strategic Management* 15(1): 3–18.

Brown, N, Rappert, B, & Webster, A (2000). *Contested Futures: A Sociology of Prospective Techno-science*, New York, Ashgate.

Builder, C (1989) *The Masks of War: American Military Styles in Strategy and Analysis*, Baltimore, Johns Hopkins University Press.

Buzan, B (1987) *An Introduction to Strategic Studies: Military Technology and International Relations*, New York, St. Martin's Press.

Buzan, B, Waever, O, & Wilde, J (1998) *Security: A New Framework for Analysis*, London, Lynne Rienner.

Castelvecchi, D (2017) Quantum Computers Ready to Leap Out of the Lab. *Nature* 541(7635): 9–10.

Caulfield, T, & Condit, C (2012) Science and the Sources of Hype. *Public Health Genomics* 15(3–4): 209–217.

Cavanaugh, J (2007) From the "Red Juggernaut" to Iraqi WMD: Threat Inflation and How It Succeeds in the United States. *Political Science Quarterly* 122(4): 555–584.

Cebrowski, A, & Garstka, J (1998) Network-centric Warfare: Its Origin and Future. *Proceedings of the Naval Institute* 124(1): 28–35.

Chen, S (2016) The End of Stealth? New Chinese Radar Capable of Detecting "Invisible" Targets 100km Away. *South China Morning Post*, September 21.

Chen, S (2017) China Building World's Biggest Quantum Research Facility. *South China Morning Post*, September 11.

Clarke, R, & Knake, R (2019) *The Fifth Domain: Defending our Country, Our Companies, and Ourselves in the Age of Cyber Threats*, New York, Penguin Press.

Cordell, C (2018) Trump Signs National Quantum Initiative into Law. *Fedscoop*, December 26.

David, P (1985) Clio and the Economics of QWERTY. *American Economic Review* 75(2): 332–337.

Davies, A, & Kennedy, P (2017) *From Little Things: Quantum Technologies and Their Application to Defence*. https://www.aspi.org.au/report/little-things-quantum-techn ologies-and-their-application-defence.

Dedehayir, O, & Steinert, M (2016) The Hype Cycle Model: A Review and Future Directions. *Technological Forecasting and Social Change* 108: 28–41.

Dowling, J, & Milburn, G (2003) Quantum Technology: The Second Quantum Revolution. *Philosophical Transactions of the Royal Society of London* 361(1809): 1655–1674.

Elhefnawy, N (2018) *Technological Hype and the Military Balance*. https://papers.ssrn.com/sol3/papers.cfm?abstract_id=3182383.

Einstein-Szilard Letter (2019). Wikipedia, August 2019. https://en.wikipedia.org/wiki/Einstein%E2%80%93Szil%C3%A1rd_letter.

Fearon, J, & Wendt, A (2002) Rationalism v. Constructivism: A Skeptical View. In: Carlsnaes, W, Risse, T, & Simmons, BA (eds.), *Handbook of International Relations*, Thousand Oaks, Sage: 52–72.

Fenn, J, & Raskino, M (2008) *Mastering the Hype Cycle: How to Choose the Right Innovation at the Right Time*, Boston, Harvard Business Press.

Furman, D, & Musgrave, P (2017) Synthetic Experiences: How Popular Culture Matters for Images of International Relations. *International Studies Quarterly* 61(3): 503–516.

Geels, F (2007) Feelings of Discontent and the Promise of Middle Range Theory for STS: Examples from Technology Dynamics. *Science, Technology, & Human Values* 32(6): 627–651.

Gomes, L (2018) Quantum Computers Strive to Break Out of the Lab. *IEEE Spectrum*, March 22.

Hackett, R (2019) Business Bets on a Quantum Leap. *Fortune*, May 21.

Haitao, X (2017) China Has Made Important Breakthroughs in the Development of Miniaturized Quantum Communication Systems. *Xinhua News Agency*, December 12.

Hansen, L (2012) Reconstructing Desecuritisation: The Normative-Political in the Copenhagen School and Directions for How to Apply It. *Review of International Studies* 38(3): 525–546.

Horgan, J (2016) Scott Aaronson Answers Every Ridiculously Big Question I Throw at Him. *Scientific American,* April 21.

Hurd, W (2017) Quantum Computing Is the Next Big Security Risk. *Wired,* December 7.

Jervis, R (1978) Cooperation under the Security Dilemma. *World Politics* 30(2): 167–214.

Johnston, I (2017) Quantum Computing Breakthrough Could Help "Change Life Completely," Say Scientists. *Independent,* February 1.

Jun, S-P (2012) A Comparative Study of Hype Cycles among Actors within the Socio-technical System: With a Focus on the Case Study of Hybrid Cars. *Technological Forecasting and Social Change* 79(8): 1413–1430.

Kania, E, & Costello, J (2018) Quantum Hegemony? China's Ambitions and the Challenge to U.S. Innovation Leadership. September. https://www.cnas.org/publications/reports/quantum-hegemony.

Kaufmann, C (2004) Threat Inflation and the Failure of the Marketplace of Ideas: The Selling of the Iraq War. *International Security* 29(1): 5–48.

Kuhn, T (1962) *The Structure of Scientific Revolutions,* Chicago, University of Chicago Press.

Latour, B (2005). *Reassembling the Social,* Oxford, Oxford University Press.

Lente, H. (2000) Forceful Futures: From Promise to Requirement. In: Brown, N, Rappert, B, & Webster, A (eds.), *Contested Futures: A Sociology of Prospective Techno-science,* New York, Ashgate: 43–64.

Lente, H, & Rip, A (1998) Expectations in Technological Developments: An Example of Prospective Structures to Be Filled in by Agency. In: Disco, C, & Meulen, B (eds.) *Getting New Technologies Together, Studies in Making Sociotechnical Order,* Berlin, De Grutyer: 209–229.

Lente, H, Spitters, C, & Peine, A (2013) Comparing Technological Hype Cycles: Towards a Theory. *Technological Forecasting and Social Change* 80(8): 1615–1628.

Lowi, T (1969) *The End of Liberalism: Ideology, Policy, and the Crisis of Public Authority,* New York, W.W. Norton.

Mannix, L (2019) China Is Building a Radar That Can See Stealth Bombers. Should We Be Worried? *Sydney Morning Herald,* April 13.

March, J, & Olsen, J (1998) The Institutional Dynamics of International Political Orders. *International Organization* 52(4): 943–969.

Marr, B (2017) How Quantum Computers Will Revolutionize Artificial Intelligence, Machine Learning and Big Data. *Forbes,* September 5.

McMaster, HR (2008) On War: Lessons to Be Learned. *Survival* 50(1): 19–30.

Mearsheimer, J, & Walt, S (2003). An Unnecessary War. *Foreign Policy,* November 3.

Medrano, K (2018). Can We Build a Hack-proof Internet Using Quantum Physics? New Breakthrough Heightens "Technology Arms Race." *Newsweek,* January 12.

Michael, M (2000) Futures of the Present: From Performativity to Prehension. In: Brown, N, Rappert, B, & Webster, A (eds.), *Contested Futures: A Sociology of Prospective Techno-science,* New York, Routledge: 21–42.

MIT Technology Review (2017) Quantum Breakthrough Heralds New Generation of Perfectly Secure Messaging. https://www.technologyreview.com/s/609294/quantum-breakthrough-heralds-new-generation-of-perfectly-secure-messaging/.

Moore, G (1996) Can Moore's Law Continue Indefinitely? *Computerworld,* July 15.

Moskvitch, K (2018) The Argument against Quantum Computers. *Quantamagazine,* February 7.

Mueller, J (2005) Simplicity and Spook: Terrorism and the Dynamics of Threat Exaggeration. *International Studies Perspectives* 6(2): 208–234.

Nielsen, M, & Chuang, L (2011) *Quantum Computing and Quantum Information*, Cambridge, Cambridge University Press.

NSA (2015) *Cryptography Today: NSA Suite B Cryptography*. August 19. https://web.archive.org/web/20151123081120/https://www.nsa.gov/ia/programs/suiteb_cryptography.

Oberhaus, D (2017) How Encryption Will Survive the Crypto-apocalypse. *Motherboard*, September 19.

Pandya, J (2019). A Quantum Revolution Is Coming. *Forbes*, May 25.

Panetta, K (2017) The CIO's Guide to Quantum Computing. *Smarter with Gartner*. https://www.gartner.com/smarterwithgartner/the-cios-guide-to-quantum-computing/.

Pinch, T, & Bijker, W (1987). The Social Construction of Facts and Artifacts: Or How the Sociology of Science and the Sociology of Technology Might Benefit Each Other. In: Bijker, WE, Hughes, TP, & Pinch, TJ (eds.), *The Social Construction of Technological Systems*, Cambridge, MIT Press: 17–50.

Preskill, J (2012) Quantum Computing and the Entanglement Frontier. https://arxiv.org/abs/1203.5813.

Reimer, J (2007) D-Wave Demonstrates Quantum Computer . . . or a Black Box in a Fridge. *ars technica*, February 18.

Rich, S, & Gellman, B (2014) NSA Seeks to Build Quantum Computer That Could Crack Most Types of Encryption. *Washington Post*, January 2.

Roblin, S (2019) This One New Piece of Technology Might Make Submarines Completely Obsolete. *The Buzz*, May 18.

Rogers, E (1962) *Diffusion of Innovations*, New York, Free Press.

Ruzicka, J (2019) Failed Securitization: Why It Matters. *Polity* 51(2): 365–377.

Saffo, P (1991) "Revolution" the Hype Word of Computer Industry Advances. *InfoWorld*, February 4.

Singer, P (2009) *Wired for War: The Robotics Revolution and Conflict in the 21st Century*, New York, Penguin Press.

Smith III, F (2014) *American Biodefense: How Dangerous Ideas about Biological Weapons Shape National Security*, Ithaca, NY, Cornell University Press.

Snyder, J (1984) Civil-Military Relations and the Cult of the Offensive, 1914 and 1984. *International Security* 9(1): 108–146.

Steinert, M, & Leifer, L (2010). Scrutinizing Gartner's Hype Cycle Approach. Conference paper, PICMET 2010 Proceedings: 254–266.

Thrall, T, & Cramer, J (2009). *American Foreign Policy and the Politics of Fear: Threat Inflation since 9/11*, London, Routledge.

US NSTC (2016) Advancing Quantum Information Science: National Challenges and Opportunities. https://www.whitehouse.gov/sites/whitehouse.gov/files/images/Quantum_Info_Sci_Report_2016_07_22%20final.pdf.

USAF Scientific Advisory Board (2015) Utility of Quantum Systems for the Air Force: Study Abstract. http://www.scientificadvisoryboard.af.mil/Portals/73/documents/AFD-151214-041.pdf?ver=2016-08-19-101445-230.

Van Rythoven, E (2016) The Perils of Realist Advocacy and the Promise of Securitization Theory: Revisiting the Tragedy of the Iraq War Debate. *European Journal of International Relations* 22(3): 487–511.

Wendt, A (1992) Anarchy Is What States Make of It. *International Organization* 46(2): 391–425.

Wendt, A (2006) Social Theory as Cartesian Science: An Auto-critique from a Quantum Perspective. In: Guzzini, S, & Leander, A (eds.), *Constructivism and International Relations: Alexander Wendt and His Critics*, New York, Routledge: 181–219.

Wendt, A (2015) *Quantum Mind and Social Science: Unifying Physical and Social Ontology*, Cambridge, Cambridge University Press.

Whipple, T (2018) Quantum Leap for Computers Will Put Every Secret at Risk. *Sunday Times*, February 3.

Wight, C (2006) *Agents, Structures and International Relations: Politics as Ontology*, Cambridge, Cambridge University Press.

Yi, Y (2017) China's Quantum Leap. *XinhuaNet*, October 17.

PART 3.
QUANTIZING IR

10

Quantum Pedagogy

Teaching *Copenhagen* and Discovering Affinities with Dialectical Thinking in International Relations

Thomas Biersteker

Introduction

Quantum pedagogy? What could that possibly mean? Ordinarily, I would encourage some cautious self-reflection when scholars trained in Political Science start borrowing ideas and metaphors from Physics to describe their ideals for research approaches to the study of International Relations. This is, after all, what behavioral scientists did in the 1960s and 1970s, something for which they were sharply criticized by some (Bull, 1966; Krippendorff, 1982; Alker & Biersteker, 1984; Ashley, 1984). Classic textbooks like Russett and Starr's *World Politics: The Menu for Choice* explicitly described Physics as the ideal role model for their scientific research enterprise (Russett & Starr, 1981). The second chapter of their widely used US International Relations textbook explicitly articulated this view when they discussed methods and approaches appropriate for the study of International Relations.

While I believe it is imperative to engage in scientific research and analysis of the social world—indeed, now more than ever—we need to be clear about what we mean when we invoke science. Scientific research entails both uncertainty about the outcomes of research and systematic analysis of phenomena under study, and there are many ways and methods appropriate for the conduct of scientific research. More relevant to the present volume, we also need to be clear about the kind of ideas we invoke from Physics. There is certainly nothing wrong with drawing upon ideas and metaphors from other disciplines. Indeed, that is what typically drives conceptual knowledge forward in International Relations and Political Science, from rational choice theory to poststructuralism. It turns out, however, that most of the scholars associated with the "Behavioral Revolution in the Social Sciences" in the 1960s and 1970s who were deliberately pursuing a scientific approach to International Relations were implicitly modeling their research and analyses on ideas of Physics that were closer to Newtonian understandings of the subject (i.e., classical Physics) than they were to quantum theoretical approaches that emerged in the 1920s. While Physics had been the role model for some IR scholars over the past half century, they seem to have missed the revolutionary developments in theoretical Physics that emerged in the form of quantum theory. I did not fully appreciate this until I began to co-teach a university-level course in Physics myself.

Teaching Copenhagen

I taught International Relations in the Political Science Department and International Relations Program at Brown University in Providence, Rhode Island, for fifteen years. One of the distinctive characteristics of the Brown University undergraduate curriculum at the time was that it had no general, liberal arts requirements. Students were free to choose from a rich variety of courses in a competitive and widely varied free market of departmental course offerings. Smart, self-confident eighteen-year-olds do not like to be told what courses to take. This made Brown an extremely popular undergraduate institution, and one of the most difficult four-year colleges in the United States into which students sought admission. Brown became popularly known as the "hip Ivy," securing a position where it was able to attract 50 percent of the students who were jointly admitted to Brown as well as to Harvard, Yale, or Princeton. In the rarified and exceedingly competitive market of elite educational institutions globally, Brown was able to attract an extremely bright and creative group of undergraduate students. They tended to be quirky, independent, and sometimes brilliant. It was a delight to teach them, as it is always refreshing to be challenged by, and to learn from, one's students. Brown's dirty secret, however, was that a student could graduate from the university without obtaining a broad, liberal arts education. It was possible to be narrowly specialized and take virtually all of your courses in one department. Of course, most students did not do this, as a former provost educated at the nearly polar opposite of the Brown curricular approach, the University of Chicago, once indicated. He said that in studies the university had conducted of its graduating students, most decided to give themselves a liberal education. The difference was that they chose to do this themselves, facilitated by an academic advisor who helped them design their own curriculum during their second year of college, not because they were forced into it by general education requirements.

While Brown students might have ventured across disciplines in pursuit of a liberal arts education, few braved the more formidable berm between the natural and the social sciences. Given Brown's lack of distribution requirements, most students not majoring in mathematics or the hard sciences simply avoided courses in those departments to pursue their primary interests and maintain their grade point averages. This proved to be a great frustration for Brown's only Nobel laureate, Leon Cooper, who taught its Introduction to Physics course. Cooper received the Nobel Prize in Physics in 1972 for his pioneering research on superconductivity and the properties of materials at extremely low temperatures approaching absolute zero.[1] Cooper was concerned that the liberal, market-oriented nature of the Brown curriculum was such that many students would never be exposed at the college level to what he enthused was "the beauty of Physics." Thus, he took it upon himself to develop creative and novel ways to attract students to his survey course, Physics 10, Introduction to Physics. It was one of his creative ideas that led him to approach me to co-teach the course with him, something I did for two consecutive years in 2001 and 2002.

One day in late May, at a reception following Brown's annual commencement ceremonies, Cooper approached me and asked whether I was familiar with Michael Frayn's play *Copenhagen* (1998). I said I was not, and he said I must read it. He said he was thinking of using it as a vehicle to attract students to his Introduction to Physics course the following academic year, and since the play involved issues associated with the early development of nuclear weapons, and because I directed the university's Watson Institute for International Studies, he proposed that I coteach it with him. He also recruited a colleague from the History Department, Abbott Gleason, a specialist on twentieth-century Russian history, along with the head of the university's Theater Arts Department, Oscar Eustis, who was also then head of the leading theater company in Providence, the Trinity Reparatory Theater.[2]

Michael Frayn's play *Copenhagen* concerns the visit of German physicist Werner Heisenberg to the home of his Danish mentor, Niels Bohr, in German-occupied Denmark in September of 1941, arguably at the height of Nazi Germany's control of Europe. No one knows exactly what they spoke about during their walk around Bohr's neighborhood, but given their role in the development of quantum theory and the theory's potential application for the development of nuclear weapons, there is much speculation about their conversation. We know the conversation ended abruptly and that they were subsequently estranged, but there is a great deal of uncertainty about their meeting (appropriate, given Heisenberg's close association with the uncertainty principle). Indeed, the character of Bohr's wife, Margarethe, asserts the centrality of uncertainty by posing the question, "Why did he [Heisenberg] come to Copenhagen?" at the very beginning of the play.

Was Heisenberg on an intelligence mission, trying to find out how far along the allies were in the development of a nuclear weapon? Was he trying to secure Bohr's assistance in solving a technical problem associated with the German program? Or was he seeking moral advice from his mentor about his own involvement with the German program? Frayn structures his play around these different

questions, without ever fully resolving them. He does so by using three coun-
terfactual scenarios, different premises from which the same dialogue begins.
Because of the different starting assumptions, however, the conversation unfolds
in different directions, with different outcomes in each scenario (uncertainty
again). There are only three characters in the play—Bohr, Heisenberg, and Bohr's
wife, Margarethe. In most productions, they are staged to circle one another like
electrons around a nucleus throughout the performance. The play takes its name,
Copenhagen, both from the physical setting of the play (and their meeting) and
from the school of physicists associated with Niels Bohr, the Copenhagen school
of theoretical physics, that developed quantum theory in the 1920s.

Cooper thought that the course should begin with a reading of the play and
asked Eustis to select three actors from his reparatory company to read the play
in the first few sessions of the course during Brown's shopping period, before
students had fixed their course schedule for the term. Having three talented actors reading the script of a brilliant and riveting play for the first few sessions
was a good strategy for attracting potential students who otherwise might be
hesitant about taking Physics courses at the college level. It was not just a gim-
mick, however. Cooper and Eustis encouraged the class to read Plato's dialogue
Ion (1937) as an accompanying reading to familiarize them with the basic question that motivated the highly interdisciplinary course. In the dialogue, Socrates
interrogates Ion, who had just won a festival competition in a neighboring town
reciting the work of Homer. Ion specialized in the recitation of Homer, and the
dialogue explores whether the words of the muse alone conveyed sufficient
meaning for an inspired performance or whether the deeper knowledge of the
author and his works that Ion possessed made a critical difference in his understanding and presentation of the material. By analogy, the question posed for
the Introduction to Physics course was: would you understand and appreciate
Michael Frayn's play Copenhagen more (or differently) if you had a deeper understanding of the concepts from Physics that motivate its characters and its plot?

In both of the years we taught the course, we began with a reading of the
play with the same three actors each year.[3] The course then proceeded in a
nonlinear manner both years, with students encouraged to interrupt faculty
lectures on different topics we chose related to the play, its historical setting,
physics, or the consequences of quantum theory with any questions they might
have. Depending on the nature of the question, one, or sometimes several, of
the instructors would provide a response (or engage in a discussion prompted
by the question, as the case may be). Most of the dialogues were between myself and the historian, Abbott Gleason, since we covered similar topics drawn
broadly from the social sciences. We did not venture to provide answers about
the physics, though we did venture opinions about the staging of the play or the
German pronunciation of the actors. The only differences in the two years we

offered the course were that in the second year, the reading and rehearsal of the play dominated the structure of the course, as each session was devoted to the reading and rereading of short sections of the play, as we learned was the norm when actors were rehearsing a play with a director. The other difference was that the actors themselves audited the course the second year, staying on after their initial performance to attend the entire course with the students (to determine, in a sense, whether their performance would be enhanced by their knowledge of the Physics). Each of the four instructors gave individual lectures on topics of our choice. Cooper introduced us into the historical development of classical physics and core content of quantum physics (Cooper, 1992), Eustis described the staging of the play and the devices he used to direct actors, and Gleason provided the historical context of twentieth-century European History. For my part, I offered three stand-alone lectures: one on the use of historical counterfactuals in causal analysis of unique, nonrecurring events like the end of the Cold War that was inspired by Frayn's three scenarios; one on the multiple dimensions of the identity of Werner Heisenberg as characterized by Frayn in the play; and a third on the nature of different approaches to the social sciences.

After the students had been introduced to the revolution in theoretical physics, the differences between wave versus particle theory, experimental illustrations of quantum leaps, Schrödinger's cat experiment, and concepts like superposition and entanglement, I gave a lecture on the different conceptions of "science" in the social sciences. In particular, I focused on their implications for different approaches to analysis and interpretation in International Relations. I drew extensively from the second chapter of an unpublished book manuscript that I had coauthored with my PhD thesis supervisor from the Massachusetts Institute of Technology (MIT), the late Hayward R. Alker Jr.[4] Along with colleagues from east and south Asia, we criticized prevailing approaches to the teaching and analysis of the subject of International Relations and argued for taking a dialectical approach to the subject. Chapter two of the manuscript is devoted to a discussion of our approach and described what we meant when we called for a more dialectical approach to our field. It would be rather undialectical to attempt to define dialectics, forcing it into a fixed, unchanging position, so the chapter is divided into a discussion of elements that we associate with a historical, hermeneutic, open-ended dialectical approach. In a dialectical fashion, we contrasted what we characterized as modern, synthetic, open-ended (nondeterministic) dialectics with what we termed an analytical-empirical scientific approach to world affairs that we associated with the mainstream of our field, at least as it is taught in the United States and much of Europe.

Alker and I coauthored the chapter when we were together for a month in Tokyo in 1999, interacting with Takashi Inoguchi, one of Alker's other former PhD advisees and a coauthor of the book project. In the chapter, we described non-Western forms of dialectical thinking, differentiated our approach from the teleological determinism of Marxist-Leninist ideas, and elaborated on six aspects of our approach. We argued that it (1) entailed a social process that proceeds from contradiction; (2) was composed of multiple, often contradictory, coexisting conceptions of world order; (3) was pervaded by changing and identity-modifying interrelationships; (4) fused theory and practice in doctrines; (5) proposed an ontology of change; and (6) illustrated how theory develops dialectically through critique and contradiction.

I summarized our approach in matrix form (with references to Heisenberg's matrix mathematics as discussed in the play and the course) by sketching separate columns for the dialectical approach we were proposing and contrasting it (dialectically) with the analytical scientific approaches that dominate much of the scholarship and teaching of International Relations. The dialectical and analytical scientific as we labeled them were the columns, while they were contrasted with rows describing their different understandings of perspectivism and interconnectedness, their different understandings of theory and practice (and their relationships), their different conceptions of change, their ideas about theory development, and, finally, their different scientific role models and concepts of rationality and inference. A shortened version of the table is reproduced in Table 10.1. Please note that this table is only a summary of the argument contained in the *Dialectics of World Orders* book chapter, and its full content is not further elaborated upon in this chapter. It is also important to note that we are not suggesting that the analytical-empirical scientific approach is illegitimate or should not be utilized in social research. Within contextually acknowledged and recognized boundaries, many patterns in the social world can be analyzed with utility using these methods and this approach. What is illegitimate, however, is the claim that the analytical-empirical approach is the *only* legitimate way to pursue scientific research, a practice that can sometimes be observed in some highly critical, anonymous reviews submitted to scholarly journals in International Relations.[5]

At the conclusion of my presentation, Cooper offered the first comment and asked how anyone could call what I had described as the "behavioral analytical scientific approach" scientific. He said, it is positively Newtonian! He argued that the alternative approach I had outlined, the dialectical, was much closer to the conception of science associated with quantum theory and contemporary physics. He was particularly taken by the idea that some conventional International Relations scholars consciously took Physics as their scientific role model, and he challenged their understanding of Physics.

Just what were the elements within the matrix that made Cooper think the open-ended, synthetic dialectical approach was more analogous to quantum theory and contemporary physics? Several elements apparently stood out to him,

Table 10.1 Contrasting a modern, open-ended dialectical approach with a conventional, analytical-empirical scientific approach to International Relations

Modern, open dialectical approach	Analytical-empirical scientific approach
Dialectical inquiry is a social process and proceeds by the making, developing, criticizing, and reformulation of claims, theses, or arguments. It is grounded in open-ended knowledge cumulation and stresses context-sensitive innovation, distrust, and skepticism.	Scientific inquiry is conducted by scholars in the pursuit of enlightenment and truth. The purpose of social scientific inquiry is to analyze, explain, and predict, grounded in the search for emerging trends, recurring patterns, and their consequences.
Perspectivism	
The world is composed of and by multiple, often contradictory world-ordering theories and practices, none of which, taken alone, captures reality. Taken together, they compose reality.	There is a single world order at any given time, governed by timeless, universal "truths" verifiable by objective empirical tests, using procedures modeled on the natural sciences.
Interconnectedness	
Interrelationships are pervasive, constantly changing, and often identity modifying. Parts and wholes are often intrinsically interrelated and can mutually constitute each other.	Analytical distinctions between subjects and objects, cause and effect, the material and the ideal, dependent and independent variables, and theory and practice are important in social research.
Theory and practice	
Theories and practices are closely interrelated through policy doctrines, and the knowledge interests of major actors are often reflected in scholars' theoretical assessments.	Theory and practice are analytically separable into distinct categories of activity, though some attempt to "bridge the gap."
Change	
Change and situations of nonequilibrium are the norm, and as events change, so too do the concepts used to comprehend them. Qualitative, transformational change is incorporated along with quantitative change. The principal sources of change are often internal.	Periods of equilibrium and stability are the central focus of analysis, and incremental or quantitatively measurable change is of central concern. The principal sources of change are external, from independent variables.
Theory development	
Every theoretical account provides the premise for its successor, which may transcend it. Be wary of universal claims and axiomatic, deductive arguments. Theoretical constructs need to be understood within the contexts from which they emerge.	Theory develops through gradual cumulation and discovery and is the product of axiomatic, deductive reasoning subjected to empirical testing. The best scientific theories offer the most parsimonious explanations and transcend their contexts across time and space.
Scientific role models and concepts of rationality and inference	
Traditional dialectical philosophy, history, and the life sciences are role models. Dialogical reasoning, abductive inference, and emergence are concepts of reasoning and inference.	Physics and the life sciences are role models. Instrumental rationality with inductive and deductive inference are concepts of reasoning and inference.

and focusing on them from the standpoint of a theoretical physicist might give us some insights into what quantum pedagogy might look like. We were both outlining a critique of prevailing approaches in the field of International Relations and at the same time sketching out an alternative approach. It was just that, an alternative approach to the field, a detailed set of ideas about how to think about our subject. As such, it was profoundly pedagogical—perhaps even the basis for a quantum pedagogy.

Elements of Quantum Pedagogy

Much of the Introduction to Physics course had considered the duality of wave and particle theories of atomic particles, so the idea of superposition and the fundamental indeterminacy of the location of individual particles occupied much of our attention. At a deeper, ontological level, ideas about entanglement were also pervasive, as were ideas from Werner Heisenberg about uncertainty and Niels Bohr about complementarity. I will take up each in term, beginning with entanglement, to illustrate how elements of the approach we had developed for thinking dialectically about International Relations apparently resonated with ideas from quantum theory.

Entanglement

One of the headings in our matrix contrasting dialectical and conventional, analytical-empirical approaches was "Interconnectedness." We argued that interrelationships are pervasive, constantly changing, and often identity modifying. We also made the case for a holistic approach to the study of International Relations and asserted that parts and wholes are often intrinsically interrelated and can both mutually constitute and influence each other. Although we did not make any specific references to quantum theory, quantum entanglement suggests that the quantum state of any particle or group of particles cannot be described independently of the state of the others, even if they are widely separated.

The conception of world orders that we defined in the first chapter of our manuscript argued that different, sometimes incommensurable, conceptions of world order not only coexisted with one another but also were often interpenetrated by one another. One example of this was that the US-led conception of capitalist power balancing that prevailed in the West in the late twentieth century was intrinsically defined in its opposition to the alternative of socialist internationalism that prevailed in the East. While the two coexisted, both the capitalist West and socialist East were interpenetrated with small populations that shared some core elements of the "other's" world order views, at least to a certain extent. At times, this fueled both Cold War hysteria in the West (like McCarthyism in the United States) and brutal repressions in the East (from Soviet gulags to the Chinese cultural revolution). Yet each world order interpenetrated the other, and they also engaged in imitative behavior to justify taking extreme measures in the name of state preservation, from interventions in the developing world like Vietnam or Afghanistan, to suspensions of civil liberties at home that each defined as "exceptional." Their imitative behavior also extended to arms development, intelligence gathering, and covert activities. Their actions could not be described or defended independently of each other.

We also argued that our subject, International Relations, should incorporate ideas of constitutive relationships, that parts and wholes were intrinsically interrelated, and that they could be mutually constitutive. Like the Master/Slave relationship, Center/Periphery relationships in the world system should be viewed as co-constitutive and parts of a larger whole. We argued for the creation of genuinely international or global histories, rather than parochial national ones, and endorsed an approach that contended that every account or interpretation of an event or situation is embedded (entangled) in a prior historical understanding. Thus, there is a need for an exploration of the historicity and dialectical development of our subject (in stark contrast to conventional approaches that tended to view history as a vast database from which to draw cases for systematic analysis). In contrast to conventional approaches to International Relations that attempted to make analytical distinctions between subject and object, cause and effect, material and ideal, dependent and independent variables, and theory and practice, we deliberately articulated an alternative approach that emphasized their deep and complex interrelationships. Everything is related to everything else. There is no single entry point for analysis and observations, but one can enter the analysis of a subject from any position (from which one should reflect upon their standpoint), and the whole is reproduced in each element of complex, interrelated systems.[6]

With specific reference to the relationships between theory and practice, we argued that theorists drew on examples from policy practice and historical experience prior to their initial theoretical formulations, while at the same time, even if they did not self-consciously reflect upon theory, policy practitioners routinely relied upon unarticulated theoretical concepts and constructs as they engaged in practice. We described the fusion of theory and practice in terms of doctrines, which we defined as legitimated rules of conduct that codified lessons learned from previous practices. Finally, we argued that theory is itself an important form of practice, an insight that subsequently informed our interest in approaches to pedagogy in different parts of the world (Alker & Biersteker, 1984; Biersteker, 2009; Hagmann & Biersteker, 2014).

Uncertainty

Uncertainty is related to entanglement by indeterminacy, in the sense that attempts to identify the precise location and velocity of quantum particles is contingent upon acts of observation or measurement. Werner Heisenberg's fundamental insight about the influence of measurement on objects—namely that in the process of observation of the world, we inevitably disturb or change it—can be seen in elements of the case we articulated for a dialectical approach for the analysis of International Relations.[7] It is not difficult to make the claim that certainty is difficult in the analysis of the social world. E. H. Carr made a similar claim for International Relations when he distinguished the social world from the physical world (Carr, 1939). Carr contended that analysis in the social world was fundamentally different from that in the physical, because the articulation and publication of ideas about policy often had influences on policy practitioners themselves. Critical analysts thus became part of the phenomena they studied. Although Carr's understanding of the physical world was closer to that of classical physicists than it was to quantum theory, he was acutely aware of the potential impacts of ideas on policy practices.

As already articulated earlier, we were challenging the dichotomous distinction between theory and policy. Beyond arguing that scholars needed to be consciously self-aware and recognize their involvement in the practices of International Relations, we also argued that the knowledge interests of major actors are often reflected in scholars' theoretical assessments of them. Hence, it was important to contextualize the teaching of International Relations. Theoretical constructions need to be understood within the contexts from which they emerge, taking into consideration globally shared events; the geographical, racial, gendered, and class-based vantage points from which those events are observed; the knowledge interests served by different theoretical questions and formulations (invariably influenced by sources of funding for research); personal experiences of the theorists themselves; and the intertextual disciplinary context within which they are situated. We also argued for sensitivity to the different ways that elements of social and personal context can be reflected in the construction of theory itself. We are not outside the object of our subject of study. As Carr argued in *The Twenty Years Crisis: 1919–1939*, our analysis and the actions we take to disseminate knowledge about International Relations are entangled with and influence the very object of our analysis.

Superposition

Probably the greatest similarity between quantum theory and a modern, synthetic, open-ended dialectical approach to International Relations is associated with the quantum idea of superposition. The principle of quantum superposition asserts that an individual particle could be in one of several different correlated configurations at any given moment and that the most general state of existence is a combination of these different possibilities. We spent a long time in the Introduction to Physics course discussing concepts and theoretical formulations associated with both wave and particle theory. The idea that one of these theoretical approaches had to be correct and the other wrong forced an unnecessary choice. They could both be right at the same time and interpreted as different ways to conceptualize the same phenomenon.

One does not need to choose between different theoretical formulations or world order understandings to determine which is superior or "correct." It might be that there could simultaneously be equally valid formulations, depending on one's vantage point. When I was first introduced to International Relations in a course taught by Hans Morgenthau at the University of Chicago, I was struck by the extent to which he went to dismiss classic theories of economic imperialism as ideology, arguing instead that international politics was best understood in terms of the pursuit of power by different states. He compared the foreign polices of different states with a typology he developed describing policies of the status quo, of imperialism, or of prestige (Morgenthau, 1971). It was a conception of imperialism that was entirely divorced from classical Marxist and non-Marxist theories of imperialism. For Morgenthau, imperialism was an ideological accusation cynically applied to others by imperialistic states to disguise their own intentions. Kenneth Waltz similarly dismissed theories of imperialism as "reductionist" in his classic *Theory of International Politics* (1979), but as Alker and I pointed out in a critique of Waltz's treatment of Lenin's theory of imperialism, Waltz made no effort to understand Lenin's work on its own terms and contextual vantage point (Alker & Biersteker, 1984). Waltz therefore failed to recognize that Lenin's work was potentially an alternative framework for understanding the world of International Relations, even if it failed on its own terms in its effort to mobilize the working classes to rebel against their mobilization for nationalistic purposes. Like Morgenthau, Waltz was intent on dismissing economic theories of imperialism in order to establish the superiority of his own theoretical framework. As Alker often commented in PhD seminars and informal conversations, however, "balance of power turned upside down was imperialism; turned inside out, it was coercive national integration." This suggests that the very practices that appeared central to maintaining the balance of power from the vantage point of someone located in the centers of power could simultaneously and legitimately be perceived as extensions of imperialism by those subject to those same practices. One did not have to choose between competing explanations (based on objective evidence), but a deeper understanding would comprehend that while neither alone captured reality, taken together they composed it. It was possible that both balance-of-power theory and imperialism theory (arguably both A and not-A) could potentially be equally valid. Thus, we should resist the temptation to reduce explanation to unitary theoretical frameworks or as unitary phenomena. This is both a subversive idea and simultaneously a substantive point for pedagogy.

A modern, open-ended dialectical approach to research and pedagogy does not dismiss alternative theoretical formulations but attempts to comprehend them from different perspectives and, to the extent possible, on their own terms. Simplistic or sham putdowns, or dismissive treatments of alternative frameworks, are not consistent with good scholarship. This does not mean that all theories and perspectives should be treated as equally valid or useful. They need to be interrogated critically, both dialogically and dialectically. The most devastating theoretical challenges are not necessarily constructed from outside the tradition, however, but are often contained in critiques that evaluate works from within their own theoretical tradition, or on their own terms as well. The pedagogical point here is that we have to learn to live with the fundamental undecidability that exists among competing theoretical frameworks rather than attempt to choose among them or force one upon or over another.

One of the first elements for comparison in the summary matrix I presented in the Introduction to Physics course contrasting modern, open dialectics with analytical-empirical approaches was "Perspectivism." We argued that the world is composed of (and by) multiple, often contradictory, world-ordering theories and practices. Just as in the case of the theoretical formulations just discussed, none of these conceptions of world order, taken alone, captures reality. Taken together, however, they compose reality. We argue not only that different world orders are interpenetrated by and influence one another but also that they coexist, sometimes in contradiction with and mutual incomprehension of one another. Indeed, world orders, rather than states, systems, or civilizations, are our core units of analysis. We argue that at any given point in time, more than one world order conception coexists with other world order conceptions, not only in competition, but also at times with completely incommensurable understandings of other world orders. During the Cold War, the fundamental divide was between capitalist West and socialist East, but there were also peripheral alternatives to both in the forms of authoritarian corporatism and collective self-reliance emanating from the developing world (Alker, 1981). Today, conceptions of a rules-based, liberal international order coexist and contend with a variety of different forms of corporatist authoritarianism (whether it has Chinese, Russian, Turkish, or Brazilian autocratic characteristics), as well as with extremist forms of Islamist transnationalism (whether in the form of Al-Qaida or ISIS). Adherents of extremist forms of Islamist transnationalism may be small in number, but not in their global impact. The continuing contestation between their world order views and those of the other two are evidenced by the commitment of acts of terrorism globally and the perception of the continuing threat they pose. They constitute the one threat to international peace and security that the UN Security Council continues to agree upon.

The concept of world orders implies that at any given moment, there are multiple, competing, and often incommensurable conceptions of world order that not only coexist but also simultaneously interpenetrate. World order in the singular is therefore composed of a multiplicity of coexisting world orders. There is no unitary world order, just as there is no unitary form or arrangement for global governance. The challenge for pedagogy is not to choose which among them is dominant or emergent at any given moment in time, but to comprehend their contradictions and to explore their identify-modifying interrelationships, including how a recessive or nascent form can emerge in a qualitative transformation from one world order form into another.

Complementarity

Niels Bohr introduced the concept of complementarity to describe the coexistence and duality of wave and particle theories. He contended that a complete knowledge of phenomena at a subatomic level required a description of the properties of both waves and particles. His resolution of difference is similar to the resolutions discussed in the previous section that described superposition. Not only can incommensurable world orders or mutually exclusive theoretical constructs coexist, but we also need not be forced to choose between or among them. A higher-level, more synthetic understanding would view these alternatives as complementary.

To suggest that practices of power balancing can be illustrations of imperialism is not a paradox. Taken together, they constitute reality. Similarly, despite the fact that difference lies at the heart of International Relations and that different world orders are often mutually incommensurable, empathetic understanding reduces tendencies to project meaning derived from one world order view onto another. We therefore need an inclusive (complementary) approach to accommodate the many contending perspectives that constitute our subject—the international, the global, the world. Internationally shared histories are difficult to write and full of tensions, disputes, and contradictions, but it is important to make the effort. Taken together, different, seemingly incommensurable understandings compose our world. World order (in the singular) is composed of the competition and interpenetration of different world orders (in the plural). In this sense, the principle of complementarity resolves the tensions of superpositionality. The idea of superposition allows for the possibility of the coexistence of simultaneously existing, legitimately informative, but contending theoretical perspectives, as well as for mutually incomprehensible world order conceptions. Complementarity enables a higher-order synthesis of theoretical perspectives and world order views.

Other Elements of a Dialectical Approach

While our alternative approach to pedagogy in International Relations contains a number of affinities with concepts derived from quantum theory—entanglement, uncertainty, superposition, and complementarity among them—the approach to research and teaching we articulated in the class at Brown as well as in our forthcoming book contains other important elements. Many of them were included in the matrix I presented in the Introduction to Physics course and are important to highlight here, even if they do not appear analogous to core elements of quantum theory. They are a central part of the alternative approach we were articulating and deserve mention.

First, change is a central concern in our approach, rather than a focus on equilibrium or periods of stability that appear to be challenged by change and whose transformation has to be explained (such as the Cold War order, American unipolarity, or the liberal world order). Change is assumed to be constant with a dialectical approach, and different types of change need to be distinguished in the analysis of International Relations. Quantitative, incremental changes sometimes lead to qualitative, transformational changes. Just as events change, so too do the concepts we use to comprehend them. It is for this reason that our work has long been associated with social constructivism, even though it predates the constructivist turn in International Relations theory (Checkel, 1998). State sovereignty is a social construct (Biersteker & Weber, 1996), and the meanings of core concepts of International Relations theory like state, sovereignty, and territory change qualitatively over time (Biersteker, 2012). In addition, within a dialectical framework, the principal sources of change are often (though not always) found to be internal, or intrinsic to an interconnected system of existing relationships itself. It is for this reason that systematic attention to, and incorporation of, history is so central to our analysis. Historical inheritances and historical constraints shape possibilities in a constantly changing environment independently of external influences or variables. History contains the basis of and for the future. Dialectical change is therefore directional, synthetic, and, at the same time, emergent.

Second, theory development is dialectical, rather than developing through gradual cumulation and discovery through axiomatic, deductive reasoning subjected to empirical testing. Every theoretical account provides the premise for its successor, which may (or may not) transcend it. Students and scholars of International Relations should therefore search for theoretical syntheses and look for order out of disorder, as well as disorder within apparent orders. One should be suspicious of universal claims and axiomatic-deductive requirements. Theoretical constructions need to be understood within the contexts from which they emerge. No analytical construct is ever "complete" or entirely adequate for all situations and will inevitably encounter anomalies (due to the ubiquitous nature of change just described) due to both internal developments and their shaping by external dynamics.

Third, synthesis of ideas, perspectives, and approaches is a central goal of our open-ended dialectical approach to teaching and research. Difference is at the heart of International Relations, both in its practices and in the analysis of those practices by scholars. The first step is to recognize those differences; the second is to attempt to understand them empathetically, on their own terms; while the third is to attempt to synthesize them into more inclusive understandings. It is for this reason that we challenge parochialism in pedagogy globally and encourage efforts to write internationally shared histories, rather than partisan and often parochial national ones.

Finally, the scientific role models for most conventional approaches to International Relations are classical physics and elements of the life sciences. Instrumental rationality, with inductive and deductive inference, drives their analysis. In an open-ended dialectical approach, traditional dialectical philosophy, history, and the life sciences are scientific role models. Dialogical reasoning, abductive inference, and the idea of emergence of nascent, recessive tendencies from within a dominant system are emphasized and encouraged.

Our original goal in proposing an open-ended, nondeterministic dialectical approach to International Relations was not to replay or reproduce the interparadigm struggles of the 1980s and 1990s, which regrettably are still underway in some departments today. Rather, it was to articulate a more inclusive approach, one that could accommodate many core elements of the conventional analytical-empirical approaches that still predominate in our field globally. Our effort to re-examine the scientific basis of mainstream International Relations seems all the more urgent today.

Conclusion

By illustrating elements of quantum physics that were evident in the project on the dialectics of world orders from its inception, I am not making the argument that we were already doing quantum International Relations before the editors of this volume, Alexander Wendt and James Der Derian, advanced the idea about taking quantum theory seriously over the course of the past two decades. Rather, we were developing an alternative approach to the subject—with implications for theorizing, conducting research, and pedagogy—that has resonances with or similarities to some core concepts from quantum physics. It shares with current quantum approaches a critique of prevailing scientific approaches and provides new insights for global International Relations.

We do not need the approval of physicists for our theoretical models and frameworks. Physics envy motivated some of the leading scholars associated with the behavioral revolution in the social sciences in the 1960s, as I indicated in the introduction. While there is much to be gained by drawing on the insights and ideas from other disciplines, if one is going to import them into the study of International Relations, one should at least make an effort to take into account their most recent theoretical ideas and developments.

Although the alternative approach presented in this chapter cannot be equated with quantum pedagogy, lecturing about dialectical approaches while teaching *Copenhagen* was an opportunity to discover some conceptual affinities with core elements of quantum theory. Like quantum, the dialectical approach is situated in sharp contrast to conventional methods and approaches taught as the core of International Relations theory. Introducing key quantum elements to that pedagogy is not only timely but also necessary if both the study and practice of International Relations is to be advanced.

Acknowledgments

I would like to thank James Der Derian, John A. Smetanka, and Ijaz S. Gilani for their comments on a previous version of this chapter.

Notes

1. The character Sheldon Cooper, featured in the American TV comedy *The Big Bang Theory*, was apparently modeled on, and partially named after, Leon Cooper.
2. Eustis is currently the artistic director of the Public Theater in New York.
3. The Trinity Reparatory Theater produced a production of the play the year following the second version of the course, with the same three actors in the leading roles. They invited the four professors who taught Introduction to Physics to join them on the stage, following the opening-night performance of the play.
4. The manuscript is currently under preliminary review for publication.
5. A recent example of this practice was the proposed rejection of an article by a reviewer because its authors failed to make clear distinctions between dependent and

independent variables and because they used qualitative comparative analysis, rather than regression models.

6. Hayward Alker made frequent reference to a seminar at MIT given by a leading dependency theorist from Brazil who argued that the entire history of imperialism and colonialism could be told from the contents of the coffee cup he was holding in his hand. The whole was reproduced in its parts or elements of its products.

7. The analogy I am making here is to Heisenberg's original formulation of the principle, not the more recent formulation (Erhart et al., 2012) about the quantum fluctuations that exist independently of measurement effects.

References

Alker, Hayward R., Jr., 1981. "Dialectical Foundations of Global Disparity" *International Studies Quarterly* 25 (1): 69–98.

Alker, Hayward R., Jr. and Thomas J. Biersteker, 1984. "The Dialectics of World Order: Notes for a Future Archeologist of International Savoir Faire" *International Studies Quarterly* 28 (2): 121–142.

Ashley, Richard, 1984. "The Poverty of Neo-realism" *International Organization* 38 (2): 225–286.

Biersteker, Thomas J., 2009. "The Parochialism of Hegemony" in *IR Scholarship around the World*, edited by Arlene Tickner and Ole Waever (London: Routledge Publishers): 322–341.

Biersteker, Thomas J., 2012. "State, Sovereignty, and Territory" in *The Handbook of International Relations*, 2nd edition, edited by Walter Carlsnaes, Thomas Risse, and Beth A. Simmons (London: SAGE Publications, Ltd): 157–176.

Biersteker, Thomas J. and Cynthia Weber, 1996. *State Sovereignty as Social Construct* (Cambridge: Cambridge University Press).

Bull, Hedley, 1966. "International Theory: The Case for a Classical Approach" *World Politics* 18 (3): 361–377.

Carr, Edward Hallett, 1939. *The Twenty Years Crisis, 1919–1939: An Introduction to the Study of International Relations* (London: Macmillan and Company, Ltd.).

Checkel, Jeffrey T., 1998. "The Constructivist Turn in International Relations Theory" *World Politics* 50 (2): 324–348.

Cooper, Leon N., 1992. *Physics: Structure and Meaning*. 1992 edition. (Hanover, NH: University Press of New England).

Erhart, J., S. Sponar, G. Sulyok, G. Badurek, M. Ozawa, and Y. Hasegawa, 2012. "Experimental Demonstration of a Universally Valid Error-Disturbance Uncertainty Relation in Spin Measurements" *Nature Physics* 8 (3): 185–189.

Frayn, Michael, 1998. *Copenhagen* (New York: Bantam Doubleday Dell Publishing Group).

Hagmann, Jonas and Thomas Biersteker, 2014. "Beyond the Published Discipline: Toward a Critical Pedagogy of International Studies" *European Journal of International Relations* 20 (2): 291–315.

Krippendorff, Ekkehart, 1982. "Review Essay: Bruce Russett, Harvey Starr: World Politics. The Menu for Choice" *Journal of Peace Research*, 19 (2): 197–202.

Morgenthau, Hans J., 1971. *Politics among Nations: The Struggle for Power and Peace* (New York: Alfred A. Knopf Publishers).

Plato, 1937. "Ion" in *The Dialogues of Plato*, Volume One, translated by B. Jowett (New York: Random House): 285–297.

Russett, Bruce M. and Harvey Starr, 1981. *World Politics: The Menu for Choice* (San Francisco: W.H. Freeman and Company).

Waltz, Kenneth N., 1979. *Theory of International Politics* (New York: McGraw Hill Publishers).

11

The Problématique of Quantization in Social Theory

A Category-Theoretic Way Forward

Badredine Arfi

The Quantum?

This book is an examination and elaboration of the claim and hope that, vaguely put, adopting a "quantum" approach (or approaches) to social/International Relations (IR) theory might provide much purchase in the task of advancing beyond existing shortcomings and shortfalls of IR theory. This chapter is about one issue that is foundational to the whole perspective, that is, the meaning and possibility of "quantization" of social/IR theory. The current "quantum fever" in social theory and IR is inescapably premised on the problématique of quantization in quantum mechanics. This is a serious issue since most social theorists who are exploring the "quantum" possibilities are not aware that they are engaged in a process of "quantization" and that the process of quantization (in physics) is a huge area of research and thinking. Understanding the importance of the problématique of quantization is a necessary preamble to the debate on whether one can develop a quantum social theory. By "understanding" I do not mean the philosophical and epistemological aspects of the issue. These are, of course, important, but this is not the task of this chapter. Rather, I focus on what physicists actually do, that is, how they develop "quantization" itself.

An inescapable starting point is the important question of what constitutes the "quantum" as such. In this regard the following is a list of positions that physicists will not disagree with:

1. Quantum theory is a variety of mathematical theories. When physicists speak of interpretations of quantum mechanics, they mean to say different mathematical theories as representations of quantum physics.
2. There is no quantum as such if it is not expressed in a mathematical formulation. He who says quantum says mathematical.

3. Not recognizing this means throwing away the "quantum" as such because
   when we express the quantum in a nonmathematical formalism we fall
   into the trap of making analogies and using metaphors. This is a problem
   because such analogies and metaphors are anchored in the conceptual languages of the classical world. This means that we use classical objects to express nonclassical features of the quantum. It is no wonder that we end up
   using terms like "weird" and "spooky" to speak of the quantum.

Based on these premises, I agree with Barad's [10] goal of seeking to recast
both quantum theory and social theory. However, I do not engage in interpretative translations of the quantum into (pre-selected) social-theoretic terms as
she does. Rather, I keep the quantum *qua* mathematically expressed, and I turn
social theory into its own mathematical conceptual framework—all of this with
a foundational caveat. I do not try to mold social theory into mathematical
frameworks, which from the start would undermine the whole process by falling
into the trap of some sort of a new exotic physics of society.

To this end, I learn from the history of quantum theory itself as shown in one
of the latest revolutionary developments in mathematical physics anchored in
new far-reaching developments in mathematics itself, that is, the formulation of
category theory as a foundation of *constructive* mathematics and its deployment
in mathematical physics, specifically quantum theory, to develop a *constructive-*
mathematical social theory. We need to keep in mind that the adjective "constructive" refers to a very specific type of mathematics and does not have the
same meaning as in IR social constructivism (although there undoubtedly is
some underlying philosophical and epistemological overlap).

To illustrate the importance of these, let me briefly consider two challenges
that we face when seeking to go beyond binarism in IR, a question that has of late
become a source of much scholarly writing and debate. Why binarism? Because
it is an excellent example of the pitfalls that social theory has built for itself by
anchoring itself in a classical worldview.[1]

In discussing binarism I specifically focus on two issues—"scale" and "logic"—
because they illustrate well the problem of binarism and are important to both
quantum physics and IR theory.[2] Quantum theory is known to question the classical understanding of "scale" and "logic," and so does a fast-growing trend of
theorizing in IR and social theory.

The binary logic of "either/or" is what often anchors our approach to IR
theory and empirical analyses (as well as practice), including so-called logics of
action such as the logic of consequences, the logic of appropriation, the logic of
argument, the logic of habit, the logic of practice, etc. A number of IR scholars,
including Katzenstein, are now advocating a logic of "both/and" and obviously
in doing so are joining ranks with many twentieth-century theorists, especially

those who are referred to as "continental" thinkers and social theorists (Jacques Derrida, Gilles Deleuze, and Jacques Lacan come to mind). On another front, sociologists (most prominently, Charles Ragin) and other social scientists have also advocated a "fuzzy-sets" approach, which is anchored in "fuzzy logic" instead of "crisp" logic, following the pioneering work by Lotfi Zadeh and subsequent generations of followers in a large number of disciplines, including artificial intelligence, computer sciences, and information science. There is even a strong body of literature on fuzzy physics, including fuzzy quantum theory.

Crisp logic stands essentially for Aristotelian logic, which is a binary logic of "either/or" possibilities. Social scientists/theorists who are interested in a "quantum" optics on the "social" should realize that they cannot do so adequately, coherently, and consistently without seriously rethinking the issue of logic, a position that almost a century ago von Neumann and Birkhoff took when they attempted (if ultimately unsuccessfully though) to formulate a "quantum logic." von Neumann and Birkhoff clearly and rightly understood "quantum logic" to be very different from the then-taken-for-granted classical logic underpinning classical physics.[3]

The issue of "quantum logics" as theoretical physicists and students of logic understand it today is a vast area of research in various disciplines (e.g., theoretical physics, quantum information, computer science, artificial intelligence, logic, philosophy, etc.), each based on its own merits. Let me mention here that whereas we have a tendency to think of logic as something universal (give and take, of course, critiques leveled by thinkers belonging to certain quarters of critical theory and the like), much research about logic nowadays starts with a conceptualization of logic as something that is "local" and "contextual" rather than "global" and "universal."

Let's consider now the issue of "scale." We know today from physics that the issue of scale is a defining feature of the delineation of quantum and classical regimes. The quantum regime is of a "microscopic" scale, which, in physics, is defined in terms of distance, temperature, time, energy, etc. Suffice it to remember the key role of the Planck constant —an extremely small number equal to $6.62607004 \times 10^{-34} \, m^2 kg \, / \, s$—in setting the scale for a quantum regime. Whereas there are many interesting theoretical discussions and experiments probing the possibility of a macro-quantum regime (see, e.g., [19]), it is widely believed that atomic and subatomic scales are the realms for quantum effects.

On the other hand, we know that the issue of scale is a determining feature of the "international" in IR. More broadly, in social theory and IR the issue of "global" vs. "local" has been studied in various ways such as micro vs. macro, structure vs. agency, etc. The "local" and "global" are nowadays so strongly mutually constitutive that scholars are now talking of *glocalization*.

We must, however, keep in mind that the notions of "micro" and "local" do not have the same meaning in quantum theory and IR. If we were to define scale literally in terms of spatial or temporal measures, the "local" in IR is indeed a "macro" when compared to the quantum regime—give and take, of course, efforts by IR scholars who believe that we can explain human life from micro to macro levels using quantum theory (e.g., Alexander Wendt's book [84]).

How can we make sense of these seeming similarities between IR and quantum theory? Does it mean that we can apply a quantum approach to the problems of scale and logic in IR just as quantum mechanics provided a solution to many lingering challenges in classical physics?

For example, one might argue that we can use quantum theory in an instrumental way, that is, by deploying its mathematics such as quantum probabilities (by which one usually means the Copenhagen version of quantum mechanics) as a computational framework used to explain what cannot be otherwise explained using classical ways of thinking, such as in the field of quantum decision theory (see, e.g., [15, 59]). Alternatively, one might assume like Wendt and a few others that we should "go quantum all the way down" and explain social life broadly speaking using a quantum theoretical framework (read this most of the time to mean the Copenhagen version of it and the notion of wave function). Alternatively, one might take inspiration from Karen Barad [10], who tries to reinterpret both quantum theory (more specifically, Niels Bohr's version of it) and social theory simultaneously in an effort to construct a perspective that brings together conceptual insights from both so as to forge a sort of hybrid theory of life.

I suggest that there is another way through which we can rethink both social theory (and IR) and quantum theory, and hence therewith examine possible formal affinities between the two. This third way is built on *category-theoretic approach* that provides a *constructivist* approach to mathematical thinking. This chapter provides a few pointers in this direction.

The rest of the chapter is divided into several sections. After introducing next the problématique of quantization, subsequent sections briefly present four different schemes of quantization. This list is far from exhaustive; the study of quantization schemes is indeed a flourishing subdiscipline of quantum theory with much diversity and richness. This discussion paves the way for considering the question of a social-theoretic quantization. I end the chapter with some thoughts on how a *category-theoretic approach* is best suited to theorize a defining feature of IR and social theory, that is, relationality, which to me is at the root cause of the issues of "logic" and "scale" mentioned earlier.

Caveat lector: That the chapter contains several mathematical expressions is part and parcel of the message that we cannot concisely and consistently think and write about quantization and the quantum outside a mathematical framework. However, this should not be understood as my calling for a quantification or, to coin it in a weird way, a "numericalization" of IR theory. While I am not against works of that nature, I seek something else! Indeed, category theory is a new brand of mathematics both philosophically and conceptually (*qua* constructivist mathematics) and practically as a sort of quasi-qualitative relational framework that allows us to theorize about social reality without metaphors, analogies, or translations of quantum theory, or anything else. And this, in itself, is a source of new inspirations that are revolutionizing quantum theory.

The Problématique of Quantization in Physics

For many scholars outside physics, the transition from the "classical" formulation of physics to the "quantum" version is either a mystery or not a question at all. However, for quantum physicists it has remained a challenge to theorize (and if possible build coherently and systematically from a set of first principles) the quantization process beyond the original very insightful and yet more or less ad hoc operationalization of quantization, as proposed by Dirac [22] and other physicists in the first decades of quantum mechanics.

Many physicists argue that the "classical" should come as a sort of "limit" to the "quantum," never mind the historical unfolding of the theory in the reverse order. That is, nature is foundationally quantum mechanical and it is only under certain conditions of decoherence that the "classical regime" emerges from the "quantum regime." As put by Dirac [22: 84–85], one of the pioneers in this respect:

> The value of classical analogy in the development of quantum mechanics depends on the fact that classical mechanics provides a valid description of dynamical systems under certain conditions, when the particles and bodies composing the systems are sufficiently massive for the disturbance accompanying an observation to be negligible. Classical mechanics must therefore be a limiting case of quantum mechanics. We should thus expect to find that important concepts in classical mechanics correspond to important concepts in quantum mechanics, and, from an understanding of the general nature of the analogy between classical and quantum mechanics, we may hope to get laws and theorems in quantum mechanics appearing as simple generalizations of well-known results in classical mechanics; in particular we may hope to get the quantum conditions appearing as a simple generalization of the classical law that all dynamical variables commute.

Dirac built the algebra[4] of the quantum dynamical variables based on the assumption that he could draw analogies between classical mechanics and quantum mechanics. This is his famous construction that the two sets of $\langle\cdot|$ and $|\cdot\rangle$ vectors when combined as $\langle\cdot|\cdot\rangle$ produce a (real or complex) number such as, for example, in getting the probability as $|\langle\psi|\psi\rangle|^2$, where ψ is the wave function or state. However, in pushing the analogy further, he reached a point at which he discovered that in going from the classical dynamics of variables to their quantum counterparts, there is the striking difference that they are now subject to an algebra in which the commutative axiom of multiplication does not hold, that is, the order of multiplying two quantities matters in that, for example, for two quantities A and B, AB is different from BA [22, 26].

Continuing with his reliance on drawing analogies from classical physics, Dirac considered the so-called Poisson bracket of two classical dynamical variables u and v in terms of position and momentum variables q and p. Dirac sought to derive analogous relations in the quantum case using quantum variables (or operators) instead of classical variables and a quantum Poisson bracket or commutator as it came to be known. Dirac then replaced the classical canonical coordinates q and momenta p (of the phase space) with their quantum equivalents; these are the famous quantum commutation relations, which Dirac calls "quantum conditions":

$$\left[Q_r, Q_s\right] = 0; \left[P_r, P_s\right] = 0; \left[Q_r, P_s\right] = \imath\hbar\delta_{rs} \tag{11.1}$$

with $\delta = 1$ for $r = s$ and $\delta = 0$ for $r \neq s$. Eq. (11.1) provides the foundations for the analogies that Dirac draws between classical and quantum mechanics. Dirac concludes that the classical Poisson brackets can be thought of as obtained from the quantum counterparts by taking the limit $\hbar \to 0$, which means that we reach the well-known result that in the classical case the position q_r and momentum p_s in the phase space always commute even when $r = s$, that is, for the same "particle." This is the *ad hoc* analogy that Dirac made. Taking the limit $\hbar \to 0$ is only meant symbolically since $\hbar$ is by definition a universal constant.

This very short historical brief on the commutators and their algebra is important to include in the discussion since what I am aiming at is to precisely examine whether and, if yes, how and to what extent we can relate quantum theory and social theory not in an *ad hoc* way built through analogies and metaphorical translations. Let me therefore examine further how physicists are nowadays trying to go beyond the more or less ad hoc procedure of canonical quantization of the early decades of the twentieth century to a more systematic theory of how classical physics theory and quantum theory can be related to one another.

In the following discussion I focus on three main approaches to mathematically theorizing systematically the transition from "classical" to "quantum" regime—that is, the process of theorizing quantization. The three approaches are known as *canonical quantization, deformation quantization,* and *noncommutative geometry quantization.*[5] We need to keep in mind two issues as we proceed:

First is the question of whether we can, or whether it makes sense to, "quantize" from a social theory as we know it, which has been developed by presupposing a classical worldview, to a more "quantized" or "quantized-like" worldview.

Second is the issue of whether we can do this without working within a mathematical framework and without resorting to deploying the latter in a metaphorical way (an issue that will be addressed in the last section of the chapter).

Canonical Quantization

The first approach to quantization agrees with Dirac's insights summarized earlier. The notion of canonical quantization, elaborated by Weyl, von Neumann, and Dirac [3], was to formulate self-adjoint operators Q_f on a Hilbert space[6] $L^2(\mathbb{R})$ as the quantum-counterpart real-valued functions $f(p,q)$ of the classical n-dimensional phase-space coordinates, a.k.a. canonical position and momentum observables

$$(p_1, p_2, \ldots, p_n, q_1, q_2, \ldots, q_n) \in \mathbb{R}^n \times \mathbb{R}^n,$$

where $\mathbb{R}$ is the line of real numbers. The quantization is represented as a linear mapping

$$Q : f \mapsto Q_f \tag{11.2}$$

from the space of quantizable observables to the Hilbert space of self-adjoint operators with the usual commutation relations

$$\left[Q_{p_j}, Q_{p_k}\right] = \left[Q_{q_j}, Q_{q_k}\right] = 0 ; \left[Q_{q_j}, Q_{p_k}\right] = \frac{1}{\hbar} 2\pi\delta_{jk} I \tag{11.3}$$

where I is the identity operator in the Hilbert space. The last nonvanishing commutator in Eq. (11.3) is the so-called noncommutativity of position and momentum operators, which means that these observables cannot possibly be measured simultaneously. This is known as the *Heisenberg uncertainty principle.*

The linear mapping $f \mapsto Q_f$ runs into serious difficulties when one tries to apply it to functions as simple as $p^2 q^2$ (and even more so for higher powers of the two variables q, p) as it leads to nonuniquely quantized expressions for the position and momentum observables. The problem has to do with the assumption of linearity of the mapping, whereas, as put by Ali and Engliš [3: 397], the matter of positing a linear function of momentum and position is just one of *computational convenience* as there is no physical motivation for it.

Eventually, this led to a rich and still growing research program about quantization known as *algebraic quantization*. This is based on the idea that the multiplicative structure of an algebra termed as *-algebra of quantum observables is a family of algebras parametrized in such a way so as to "converge" to classical physics based on the notion of phase space.

Very briefly put, quantum observables form a noncommutative algebra, call it A, which is part of a family of algebras A_h that are all defined with a multiplication $*_h$, and the latter is dependent on $\hbar$. The classical phase space is a limit reached as $\hbar \to 0$, with an algebra A_0. The $*_h$-multiplication defines an $*_h$-commutator that approaches the Poisson bracket as $\hbar \to 0$, that is,

$$\lim_{h \to 0} (f *_h g - g *_h f) / i\hbar = \{f, g\} \qquad (11.4)$$

Algebraic quantization thus seeks to construct a family A_h of noncommutative algebras starting from a Poisson bracket. There are different approaches for doing this. To illustrate this I consider in the following *deformation quantization* and *noncommutative geometry* approaches.

Deformation Quantization

The *deformation quantization* approach gives a precise and rigorous mathematical formulation to the correspondence principle through which quantum mechanics is said to be obtained from classical mechanics. The approach is formulated exclusively using functions of phase space variables. This creates, relatively speaking, a much less abrupt conceptual transition from classical mechanics to quantum mechanics when compared to other approaches.

The approach consists in starting with a given algebraic structure and then inquiring whether there exists a parametrized set of structures that are similar to this algebraic structure such that at a certain value of the parameter we recover the algebraic structure that we started with. The existence of such a family of structures is a field called a *deformation* of the initial structure. The general idea is to examine how one goes from one theory to a "nearby" theory in the field of theories as defined by the chosen parameter. We therefore go from classical algebras of functions (of canonical coordinates and conjugate momenta in the phase space) representing classical observables to quantum algebras of operators representing quantum observables through continuous transformations. When the transformations change the structure of the algebras in a continuous way, we speak of deformations.[7]

Starting from a Poisson manifold, that is, a smooth manifold of classical phase space equipped with Poisson bracket, one considers two smooth complex-valued functions to define a so-called $*$-product of two functions f and g to form a new smooth function defined as a power series using the deformation parameter $i\hbar$ (thought of as varying continuously) as follows:

$$f * g = fg + (i\hbar) C_1(f, g) + \cdots = \sum_{n=0}^{\infty} (i\hbar)^n C_n(f, g) \qquad (11.5)$$

The classical limit is obtained when $\hbar \to 0$ and then the $*$-product becomes the usual product in the classical phase space. The quantities $C_n(f, g)$ are functions of the derivatives of f and g and for any such three functions f, g, h we have the following set of equations:

$$C_0(f, g) = fg$$
$$C_1(f, g) - C_1(g, f) = \{f, g\} \qquad (11.6)$$
$$\sum_{j+k=n} C_j\big(C_k(f, g), h\big) = \sum_{j+k=n} C_j\big(f, C_k(g, h)\big)$$

Given these conditions, the coefficients $C_n(f, g)$ are such that the $f * g$ product is noncommutative. This means that we obtain a noncommutative algebra where the $*$-multiplication law is a deformation of the original (classical) commutative algebra. As defined, the coefficients $C_n(f,g)$ are arbitrary. However, imposing a requirement of associativity on the $*$-product radically restricts the choice of the coefficients and then reproduces a needed correspondence with the usual quantum commutator defined in terms of the $*$-product. That is, requiring that for any f, g, h functions we have $(f * g) * h = f * (g * h)$ leads to the usual quantum commutator $[f, g]^* = f * g - g * f$ of quantum mechanics. It also shows that

$$\lim_{\hbar \to 0} \left(\frac{1}{i\hbar} [f, g]_* \right) = \{f, g\} \qquad (11.7)$$

This is a precise formal representation of the so-called correspondence principle (in the theory of deformation quantization) that Dirac, Weyl, and Neuman postulated in an almost *ad hoc* way.

One should keep in mind that although $\hbar$ is used as a symbolic parameter formally accounting for the "deformation," it is not meant to be the so-called Planck constant of quantum physics; it becomes the latter only in the actual quantum case [44: 539]. The key challenge in all of this is to construct a *-product that is meaningful enough in the transition from the classical smooth manifold of the phase space to the quantum field; that is, it should satisfy the requirements stipulated in Eq. (11.7). Mathematicians have been able to construct such products (see [44] for examples). Different quantization schemes correspond to different equivalent classes of *-products [44: 540].

One of the most important lessons learned from deformation quantization is that there is no quantization scheme for systems with observables that depend on the coordinates or the momenta to a higher power than quadratic, which leads to a correspondence between the quantum mechanical and the classical equations of motion, and which simultaneously strictly maintains the Dirac–von Neumann requirement. The power of the framework of deformation quantization is that it gives to the correspondence principle a precise mathematical meaning that allows a construction of the *-product that is essential for transitioning from the classical Poisson bracket {,} to the quantum commutator [,] and associating operators in the quantum Hilbert space with their classical counterpart functions in the phase space.

Another lesson that we have learned from deformation quantization is that Dirac's and others' insights back in the early history of quantum mechanics on how to carry out the quantization using commutators in analogy with the Poisson brackets were ingenuous but an accident of history (so to speak)—even if it turned out to be more or less correct due to the very specific kinds of relationships that exist between position and momentum variables in the classical worldview. Had these been different, the lucky accident of history may not have happened.

This bring me to the important point that to follow through a process of making an analogy with quantum physics from what proved to be good for physics and take it into the realm of the "social" is, to say the least, a very wild guess. Hence, for those who are eager to quantize in social theory by drawing on a certain version of quantum mechanics (which in most cases is so-called Copenhagen interpretation) without much thought about the process of quantization itself, I strongly recommend taking a deep breath and thinking thoroughly about the whole process first.

The brief discussion in this section is precisely meant to clearly indicate that there is a lot more to the quantization process that physicists have of late been concerned with and that there is a diversity of quantization schemes. The obvious question, then, is why assume one (such as the Copenhagen scheme) and not another one? What makes this issue crucial is that we are not dealing with physics anymore, and hence to choose this or that quantization scheme needs to be in itself theorized in a coherent way (assuming, of course, for the sake of argument that it makes sense to speak of quantization in the case of the "social" in the first place, an assumption that is far from being clearly defensible). And by "theorized" I mean one should be able to show from first principles why and how such and such a quantization scheme does indeed apply to social theory by "endogenously" delineating a set of criteria from within the quantization scheme. The challenge is not just philosophical; quantum theory is a mathematical theory and hence the challenge of the possibility of a quantization as well as developing an actual scheme of quantization for the "social" must be addressed mathematically (assuming, of course, it can be satisfactorily addressed philosophically, which is far from being obvious).

Noncommutative Geometric Quantization

Not all theoretical physicists who are working on the foundations of quantum physics agree with deformation quantization, though. Shahn Majid [65: 3898], for example, argues that

> Clearly all of these problems are putting the cart before the horse: the real world is, to our best knowledge, quantum, so that should come first. We should build models guided by the intrinsic noncommutative geometry at the level of noncommutative algebras and only at the end consider classical limits and classical geometry (and Poisson brackets) as emerging from a choice, where possible, of "classical handles" in the quantum system. *In more physical terms, classical observables should come out of quantum theory as some kind of limit and not really be the starting point.* (emphasis added)

Majid belongs to the school that advances so-called quantum groups (and noncommutative geometry) as an approach to quantization. Geometric quantization is based on the age-old idea of a correspondence or duality between geometry and algebra (since Descartes formulated his analytic geometry). The idea is that "there is a duality between certain categories of geometric spaces and the corresponding categories of algebras representing those spaces" [58: xi]. The main idea of a noncommutative geometry approach is therefore that we need to fully exploit the fact that in going from classical mechanics to quantum mechanics, we go from a commutative algebra of classical observables to noncommutative algebra of quantum mechanical observables. As explained by Majid [64: 3898]:

> If the real world is quantum, then phase space and hence probably space-time it-self should be "fuzzy" and only approximately modeled by classical geometrical concepts. Why then should one take classical geometrical concepts...except other than as an effective theory or approximate model tailored to the desired classical geometry that we hope to come out. This can be useful but it cannot possibly be the fundamental "theory of everything" if it is built in such an il-logical manner. There is simply no evidence for the assumption of nice smooth manifolds other than now-discredited classical mechanics. And in certain domains such as, but not only, in Planck scale physics or quantum gravity, it will certainly be unjustified even as an approximation.

Noncommutative geometry is a powerful area of mathematics that has had much impact on theoretical physics in subfields of physics such as the Standard Model of elementary particles, the quantum Hall effect, renormal-ization in quantum field theory, and string theory. In fact, classical geometry (i.e., Euclidean geometry) is a special case of noncommutative geometry when expressed in algebraic terms. The equivalence between certain geometric spaces and certain algebras is key to the development of noncommutative geometry.

Going back to social theory, the issue is, then, what if instead of searching for a "quantum social theory" we would look for a noncommutative social theory? The situation can be summarized as follows. Most of our social theories are anchored in the theory of sets or at least presuppose some set-theoretic notions and principles or results. Moreover, they also assume that commutativity of sets/ within sets is a given, based on commutative topologies that are defined with sets of opens (or open sets). What if we were to consider situations where, as put by Oystaeyen [83: xiii–xiv],

> the problem...arises whether a noncommutative topology, defined on a non-commutative space in terms of a noncommutative type of lattice that replaces the set of opens, is to some extent characterized by sets (!) of noncommutative points.

Noncommutativity is especially interesting when considering quantum prob-ability. In other words, should we fully consider the noncommutative aspects of quantum mechanics? If so, then quantum probability, which plays an essential role in conceptualizing and interpreting all quantum measurements, should also be retheorized as being noncommutative. As proposed by Franz and Skalski [37], this can be done, in a first step, by reformulating the theory in terms of algebras of functions on a probability space, but why? Because as discussed earlier, using an algebraic framework allows us to clearly isolate where in the theory the assumption of commutativity occurs; this is clearly transparent in the commutative algebras that one ends up with. Then, in a second step, the commutativity condition is dropped so that we reformulate the theory in a noncommutative algebraic framework.

Category-Theoretic Quantization

Whereas the preceding quantization schemes are anchored in set theory and sets, there is a nascent approach that is not based on set theory, that is, a category-theoretic approach to quantization. This is a revolutionary approach in that it has gone beyond set theory as a framework and language of modern mathematics and formal logic. Before the advent of category theory, set theory, since it was formalized by Georg Cantor, had become a necessary tool for constructing consistent mathematical results (83; 66: 176). Many fields of knowledge, outside of mathematics proper, have nowadays adopted category theory as a mathematical approach, including quantum theory. Three simultaneous features of category theory make it quite powerful and very fungible:

1. It is relational in a very intuitive way. Category theory is primordially about relations in a primordial sense—relations between objects, and relations between relations. Category theory is as such the sine qua non relationalist framework for theorizing in all fields of knowledge, including social and IR theory, par excellence!
2. It has a very high level of abstractness, which makes it transportable across, and applicable to, any field of knowledge that values relations and relationality, without resorting to conceptual translating, transplanting, metaphorizing, or analogizing.
3. Category theory dislodges some of the most taken-for-granted notions of our theorizing about life as they have evolved for centuries, that is, set theory, Boolean logic, and Boolean algebra—taken-for-granted notions that have hampered further advances in theorizing beyond continuous and beleaguered wars between ontological and epistemological silos.

To illustrate, let's consider three (Aristotelian) principles of classical logic that anchor our knowledge endeavors—the principle of identity (i.e., for a thing *that is*, it has to be identical to itself), the principle of noncontradiction (i.e., a thing is OR is not, something cannot both be AND not be), and the principle of excluded middle (i.e., something can only either be OR not be). One can add to this list the classical rule of negation, that is, the negation of negation of a thing takes us back to the original thing.

Set theory and hence its corresponding algebra are both Boolean, and both abide by these principles (and a few others). Category theory generalizes this in that we end up having a Heyting algebra (and logic) within which in general the law of excluded middle is violated. This makes Boolean algebra a limiting case of Heyting algebra. This generalization gives category theory a much wider scope of validity and applicability as compared to set theory.[8] In category theory the notion of identity or equality was also found to be too restrictive and was replaced by the notion of "isomorphism" (or "equivalency"). This means that category-theoretic logic (so to speak) violates both the law of excluded middle and the law of identity, or at least weakens the law of identity into a law of isomorphism.

In theoretical physics, category theory is slowly but steadily creating a revolution in formulating solutions to key challenges that have puzzled physicists for decades. One such challenge is the formulation of a theory that would unify the three fundamental interactions of nature—electromagnetic, strong, and weak interactions—with gravity. Quantum field theory has led to a unification of the first three. Gravity has remained the exception. Formulating a quantum theory of gravity is one of the most challenging tasks that face the world of physicists. One very difficult hurdle in this regard is the assumed metrical nature of the spacetime manifold or continuum. One revolutionary offspring of Riemann's theory of manifolds in differential geometry occurred when Einstein deployed it in his theory of general relativity where he introduced the idea of a curved spacetime manifold. However, this ground-breaking proposal of topologically varying spacetime was anchored in a notion of spacetime that remained metrical. That the theory of general relativity has been experimentally validated beyond any doubts does not lessen the important challenge ahead, which is to unify the theory of general relativity and quantum mechanics.

To address such difficulties, physicists (see, e.g., John Baez [9: 240]) have deployed category theory as a means for probing possible connections between quantum theory and general relativity theory. Instead of working with Einstein's equations of general relativity, Baez explicates the algebraic topology (using category theory) underpinning these equations, a topology that is precisely the landmark innovation of Einstein when he moved beyond a flat Euclidean space to a curved pseudo-Riemannian space in expressing the field equations of general relativity. Baez takes into account the variability of space curvature via topological transformations. This means that space is described with a changing topology and hence we have "spaces" as objects in a category (called *nCob*) defined through topological variations in time. The dimension of time is included as the morphisms (relations called *cobordisms*) between topological spaces; the *cobordisms* represent the spacetime of general relativity.

Likewise, Baez expresses quantum theory using category theory by using a category *Hilb*, the objects of which are Hilbert spaces used to describe "states," and the morphisms of which are bounded linear operators used to describe "processes" [9: 240]. From a category-theoretic perspective the Hilbert spaces (of the states of a quantum system) become topologically variable and hence form a category (*Hilb*), the objects of which are Hilbert spaces that differ in terms of their topologies. The relations (morphisms) between these objects (Hilbert spaces) correspond to the usual linear operators of quantum mechanics. Therefore, when formulated using category theory, general relativity and quantum mechanics clearly show a strong structural similarity and even correspondence.

More directly relevant to the problématique of "global vs. local" mentioned earlier is how Zafiris and coworkers are deploying category theory to theorize the global-local connection in quantum theory. The question that Epperson and Zafiris [32] and others [25–27, 29, 35, 36, 47–49] are concerned with consists in reformulating quantum theory in a category-theoretic way to avoid all the limitations that set theory leads to, such as, for example, making a quantum representation universally or globally applicable. This is established by the famous 1967 Kochen-Specker theorem [60], which expresses the impossibility of probing the entire manifestation of a global system quantum-mechanically with the use of a single system of representation. It is impossible to recover the global information content of a global quantum observable using a single type of measurement device globally.[9] Doing it, according to Epperson and Zafiris [32], necessitates the introduction of continuously variable local standard algebras being capable of covering the global information completely. This constitutes a defining difference between classical and quantum physics since in classical physics it is possible to construct a global algebraic representation of the global information—which is nothing but a global Boolean algebra. Therefore, in quantum theory it is not possible to construct a global Boolean algebra [42, 66].[10]

Put in terms of formal logic (or, more precisely, propositional calculus), any theory of physics is constituted with propositions that are organized into a structure of meaningful statements using a certain propositional calculus and/or algebra. For theories of the classical world, Boolean algebra is the appropriate approach. However, for quantum theories, a non-Boolean logical structure is required as shown a long time ago by Birkhoff and von Neumann [11]. The Kochen-Specker theorem leads to the conclusion that a quantum logical algebra cannot be, or be embedded within, a Boolean algebra. What we need is so-called partial Boolean algebras. Zafiris et al. [88–100] tackle this difficulty by proposing to construct a global algebra of quantum information by *gluing* together local Boolean algebras of the observed information—with the constraint that the global algebra cannot be Boolean. For Epperson and Zafiris [32], this is a *relational representation* of quantum information with a possibility of multiplicities in the space of logic, not in some actual space where there are physical objects. This argument is anchored in an approach using category theory, which takes as "primitives" the relations (morphisms) between objects, and relations between relations. The process of selecting a scheme of how to handle the "local" information as experienced by the observer (and observing or measuring apparatuses) is called *localization*, with the important proviso that the localization scheme is topological, not metrical, in nature, and the connection of the local to the global is also topological, not metrical, in nature (i.e., using Whitehead's [85: 283–301] jargon: it is one of extension). The localization scheme is theorized through what is known as the *sheaf-theoretic* approach. The idea consists in constructing a coordinate frame of sorts much like the idea of Riemannian manifold theory where a global Euclidean space is replaced with, say, a manifold, with the latter being locally isomorphic (in one-to-one correspondence) with local Euclidean neighborhoods, keeping in mind that sheaf theory is relational all the way down (i.e., taking "relations" as "primitives" and not *relata*).

Having briefly discussed a number of quantization schemes, let us move on now to the key question of whether we can formulate a social-theoretic quantization. This is the question that is not asked by social scientists who seek to quantize social theory. In most cases, these scholars end up either simply borrowing concepts and notions from one quantization scheme (which in most cases is the so-called Copenhagen approach) or using metaphors and/or making analogical reasoning. I therefore think it is essential to raise this question on first-principle grounds.

Social-Theoretic Quantization?

Does it make sense to speak of a social-theoretic quantization? Or, more aptly, does it make sense to speak of a quantization of social theory so as to formulate a quantum social theory? This would mean that we have a classical social theory that we would like to quantize in some ways, if one were to follow the footsteps of canonical quantization (discussed earlier). If one believed that the "social" ensues from the "physical" all the way down, the question then would revolve around the issue of whether one can speak of quantization at the level of the "macro" human world instead of the usual "micro" world of physics where quantum effects are measured. This is not a new issue in physics as physicists have been considering quantum effects at the macro level as opposed to the micro level for quite some time now.

Subsuming the "social" under the "physical" in this way is the route that Alexander Wendt [84] takes. However, many social theorists would disagree with this position.[11] There is, however, another way of phrasing this discussion. Instead of seeking to build a quantum social theory, one can formulate an approach that would go beyond a social theory dominated or undergirded by a "classical worldview" to a postclassical worldview. To do this, we need to ask: What is it in the classical worldview that needs to be abandoned or at least corrected? And what do we replace it with?

The argument roughly goes as follows: IR and social theory in general have been basically anchored in a "classical worldview," which for the most part corresponds to classical physics, with the latter strongly determined by a Newtonian worldview. As physicists have quantized physics to produce quantum mechanics so, the argument goes, we need to follow suit and produce a quantized social theory.

This is more or less the route that Wendt takes in his book. Specifically, in anchoring his proposal, Wendt delineates six defining characteristics of what he terms as a classical worldview and which a quantum social theory should go beyond:

> materialism, atomism, determinism, mechanism, absolute space and time, and the subject-object distinction [84: 59].

He explicitly defines these characteristics as follows:

C.1. Atomism makes three claims: 1) large objects are reducible to the properties and interactions of smaller ones; 2) objects have definite properties; and 3) objects are fully "separable," meaning that their identity is constituted solely by their internal structure and spatio-temporal location rather than by relationships to other objects. [84: 61]

C.2. Determinism is the view that there is no inherent randomness in nature, that what happens in the present and future is completely fixed by the laws governing the motion of matter in the past. [84: 62]

C.3. All causation is mechanical and local....Mechanism and locality presuppose materialism, atomism, and determinism, and especially atomism or separability. To a significant extent, therefore, the fate of mechanical and local causation is bound up with the fate of those assumptions. [84: 63–64]

C.4. Space and time are defined in absolute terms, as objective realities independent of other phenomena in the universe. [84: 65][12]

C.5. A categorical distinction[13] exists between subjects and objects.... Maintaining this separation is considered essential to science, since otherwise there is the danger that knowledge will be contaminated by our choices and subjective beliefs. [84: 66][14]

I argue that all of these issues are more specifically anchored in set-theoretic perspectives (or parts thereof) and that it is only by going beyond set theory that we can reformulate social theory in ways that address these challenges. My proposal is: Going from set-theoretic theorization to *category-theoretic* theorization is a way out. The end product is a *non-Boolean relational* approach that offers a very different picture from what a classical worldview offers, and how we can go beyond it.

A careful reading shows that points C.2 through C.5 are in fact anchored in C.1, and that the latter is clearly formulated in a set-theoretic framework. Let me elaborate:

The first claim of atomism

is that large objects are reducible to the properties and interactions of smaller ones. This claim speaks of properties of objects and of the operation of inclusion of smaller objects into larger objects. We know from set theory that to speak of a property of an object is to mean that this object belongs to a subset of objects that share this property; that is, to have a property is nothing but the operation of membership (ϵ) in a subset that is included in a larger set. And subset inclusion is also a key operation of sets. Therefore, the first claim is nothing but a description of the two operations of "membership" and "inclusion" that define the elements of a set and subsets of a set.

The second claim that objects have definite properties

means an object has a property OR does not have it; that is, this object belongs qua member to a subset OR does not. The notion of having a property is a set-theoretic notion. That an object has a property or does not is dealt with in a set-theoretic framework through the notion of a characteristic function of a subset, which is defined as follows:

A characteristic function χ^K of a subset K of a set X, that is, $K \subseteq X$, is a set function from X to $\{0, 1\}$, that is,

$$\chi^K : X \to \{0,1\} \quad \text{such at} \quad \chi^K(x) = \begin{cases} 1 & \text{if } x \in K \\ 0 & \text{otherwise} \end{cases} \qquad (11.8)$$

The third claim is likewise a set-theoretic notion

in the sense that sets are defined as collections of elements and that an element is defined by its membership in the set, and its properties are defined by its memberships in various subsets of the larger set. That is, an element a of a set A that has properties P1,P2,P3 is an element of the various corresponding subsets A1,A2,A3 in A, respectively defined as follows:

- $a \in A_1 = \{x \in X \mid P_1(x)\} \subseteq A$

- $a \in A_2 = \{x \in X \mid P_2(x)\} \subseteq A$

- $a \in A_3 = \{x \in X \mid P_3(x)\} \subseteq A$

The challenge is to go beyond these aspects of atomism in a systematic and rigorous way in a way that does not simply rely on drawing analogies or deploying metaphors.

A reader could at this point inquire: why is relying on set-theoretic notions a challenge that needs to be addressed in seeking to go beyond the "classical worldview"? The answer is: the "classical worldview" is anchored in set theory and this makes the "classical worldview" built on the basis of classical logic, which does not fit, for instance, quantum theory. This implies that *for advocates of quantum social theory to remain consistent, they should abandon classical logic, which means going beyond set-theoretic logic too, and hence set theory.* Some social theorists have tentatively advocated deploying "quantum logic" in social theory. Although this is an ambitious goal, it would lead nowhere if only because there isn't ONE quantum logic but rather many, which implies that one has to make a choice and, if that indeed is the case, then one must provide a set of criteria for making a choice of ONE quantum logic among many alternative ones. When you add to this that most physicists do not take quantum logic to be a logic in the usual sense of the term and that quantum logics are not distributive, the deployment of such logics in theorizing social theory leads to a dead end, or, at best, it is done in an ad hoc way with no good justification for it.

In any case, there is another way for going beyond the "classical worldview" without seeking to quantize social theory. Instead of "quantizing," we would be better off by categorifying—moving from a set-theoretic to a category-theoretic approach, and the latter takes us *from atomism to relationalism.* This has already been done in theoretical physics by a number of researchers. For example, Isham et al. [23–27, 29] have developed a category-theoretic topological approach to theorizing in both classical and quantum physics.

Caveat lector: This does not mean projecting concepts and results from theoretical physics into social theory. No! The idea is that category-theoretic frameworks provide the necessary theoretical tools for applying *category-theoretic methodologies and results* under well-specified and rigorous conditions from one field of knowledge to another. Category-theoretic methodologies and results can be developed in any field of knowledge, and because these methodologies and results are universally applicable in category theory, they can be used in different fields of knowledge, with the crucial proviso that one is required to explicate unambiguously the criteria and conditions of these methodologies and results.

We can illustrate this by considering how conceptualizing the "global/local" is done in theoretical physics within a category-theoretic framework to theorize the global heterogeneity that Katzenstein [53] discussed. This means that the issue of scale as usually discussed in IR needs to be recast in topological terms where metric notions (whether spatial or temporal) become less conceptually determining than topological relations. Why? Because we got used to conceptualizing in social theory while presupposing (if in most cases implicitly) a classical worldview that is undergirded by Newtonian notions of continuous time and continuous, isotropic space as necessary backgrounds, where *continuity and isotropy are defined using metrical notions.* Therefore, when thinking about scale, we usually think of it in a metrical way.

In short, we need a conceptual shift by thinking of scale topologically and not metrically. Within category theory we can conceptualize "scale," and thus, the connections between "global" and "local," in purely relational terms using relational topology, that is, using morphisms (directed relations between objects of a category), functors (relations between categories), and (Gröthendieck) relational topology with its notion of site, which is the relational concept for the notion of "contextual." For example, conceptually relating the "global" and the "local" in such a relational framework means *topologically* gluing together local and global information together in a category-theoretic relational framework. Vice versa: going from the global to the local means topologically coarse-gaining the information contained in a global context into local information terms. It is not an accident that I am mentioning relationality in this discussion. In fact, relationality is at the heart of category theory.

Relationality in Category Theory

Whereas much has been written about relational social theory (and IR theory), not much, if any, has been written on the presupposed set-theoretic conceptual thinking that underpins the concepts of relationality that have been put forward, going as far as back Alfred N. Whitehead, who was among the first writers to call, for example, for process-based philosophy.[15]

A key characteristic of category theory, which makes it better suited than set theory as far as relationality is concerned, is that all we need to define a category are the objects and morphisms of the category. Moreover, it is even possible to forego the use of objects and work only with morphisms and functors (a special kind of morphisms), that is, pure relations. This has led to a body of literature that deals with so-called object-free categories. This makes morphisms—a.k.a. relations—the primitives of the theory. As such, we can speak of pure relationality in category theory.

The question of whether one can begin with relations without relata (or objects) has been an ongoing debate in the philosophy of mathematics and has been invigorated after category theory gained prominence in mathematical theory, whereas prior to that the debates were largely carried out using set-theoretic frameworks. Indeed, in a set-theoretic framework it is incoherent to claim relations without relata. As long as structures are defined through set-theoretic concepts and sets are defined with the operation of $\in$ (membership), we cannot escape relying from the very beginning, so to speak, on the members of the set, that is, the relata that are in relation. This is a very relevant discussion to the effort of recasting social theory in a category-theoretic framework. Why? Because not only has social theory been and continue to be the theater for debates on how to conceptualize structures, either in the form of structuralism or in the form of so-called agency-structure problématique, but also social theorists are (much like mathematicians and physicists [7, 8]) very divided on what structuralism is (and, of course, on whether it is a valid perspective). What is less discussed, however, is the fact that by and large the literature in social theory dealing with structures and structuralism is anchored in, and strongly shaped by, a set-theoretic conceptual framework.

Moreover, even the latest so-called turn to "relationality" in social theory [2, 12, 13, 21, 30, 39, 52, 55, 56, 61, 63, 64, 67, 69, 70, 71, 73–80, 82] is predominantly anchored in set-theoretic conceptualizations. This is definitely true for social network approaches to rationality as the notions of sets and memberships determine the notion of a network as sets of nodes and sets of links between these nodes, with sometimes the links hierarchically organized through subset relations and so on. And even when relationality is defined as a process (by following the legacy left by Alfred North Whitehead in his "Process and Reality" [85]), the notions of set theory and its Boolean algebra and logic are determinative of the thinking and discussions of processes and relations.

In Lieu of Conclusion

Social theory (and with it IR theory) is undoubtedly thriving. Yet it remains marred with many difficulties and shortcomings, many of which are anchored in a presupposed "classical worldview" that provides the theoretical background for many of the concepts and, more generally, frameworks in social theory. For many decades students of social theory have probed its ontological, epistemological, and methodological presuppositions, thereby seeking to formulate theories that might resolve lingering questions such as the notions of structures, agency, practice, logic, etc. Seeking to draw insights from and analogies with quantum theory, which has provided many solutions to difficult empirical and theoretical questions ensuing from espousing a classical worldview in physics, a number of IR and social theorists are examining the possibility of so-called quantum social science/theory.

Yet most of these works do not raise (or at least not deeply enough) the foundational question of what it means to "quantize" a theory or worldview in the social realm as opposed to the world of physics. This is a crucial issue that cannot be ignored. To put it simply: there are many different ways to quantize in physics, and the theory of quantization has developed in many different directions. Social/IR theorists who use quantum formalism in an instrumental way, such as, for example, the deployment of quantum probability theory in so-called quantum decision theory, are more or less agnostic about this issue. However, those interested in formulating a new noninstrumental approach to theorizing about the social cannot do so.

A second issue that is also ignored in the emerging literature is the nature of "concepts" in quantum theory and the "hidden" trap that comes with them if one is not careful enough. Specifically, quantum theory is mathematically formulated at the level of the concept; that is, whoever says "quantum" says a certain type of mathematical framework. Short of realizing this, one might fall into the trap of thinking, for example, of, say, Copenhagen "interpretation" of quantum mechanics as we usually deploy the term "interpretation" in the realm of social theory. This is a very unfortunate misunderstanding in that what physicists mean by "interpretation" is a chosen mathematical formulation with well-stipulated propositions, theorems, etc. This makes the task of formulating a "quantum" social theory a mathematical problem, and cannot be otherwise.

As a way of avoiding these problems, I suggest that we should not simply copy the footsteps of quantum physics by projecting what is essentially a physics formulation onto the social realm. Of course, one could do that, but that is precisely what led to much of extant social theory being built on a classical worldview, by which, as explained earlier in the chapter, one means adhering to many of the principles and propositions of classical logic and set theory. Moreover, theoretical physics has been challenged for decades with a number of lingering problems, such as the nature of spacetime and the formulation of a theory of quantum gravity, which of late has led many theoretical physicists to raise serious questions about the mathematical foundations of quantum theory. That is, the impasses that theoretical physics has been bumping into call for a new breed of mathematics called *constructive mathematics* within a framework of category theory, instead of set theory, which has provided the foundations of theoretical physics so far. This has led to a new conceptualization of quantum theory itself, including the problématique of quantization. And similar reconceptualizations have been taking place in other fields of knowledge, from computer science, to information theory, to music theory, and so on.

In a similar vein I am thus advocating a category-theoretic approach in social theory. That is, I am deploying category theory qua constructive mathematics to formulate a social theory that is essentially relationalist, and as such goes beyond the confines of the classical worldview; that it is relationalist comes from the fact that category theory is relational all the way down.

Notes

1. In a recent article Peter J. Katzenstein [54: 374], a decades-long observer of and practitioner in the IR discipline, succinctly writes:

   > I wish to make my case against the reliance on binaries that is pervading our analytical and political conceptual universe under a variety of labels—Western vs Non-Western, West vs Rest, and Occident vs. Orient.... [T]hese categories are pervasive in public and scholarly discourse. Advocates of a Chinese School of IR, for example, often rely on binary distinctions to establish the grounds that there is an inherent contradiction between American and Chinese theoretical approaches. Similarly, many Chinese and American scholars focus on common knowledge and theory without theorizing the relationship between them and tacit knowledge and worldviews. Both mistakes, this article argues, can be traced to a Newtonian view of the world that denies a central category of quantum physics, the entanglement of objects and processes.

   Katzenstein [53: 379] explains that "world politics is defined by persistent heterogeneity and diversity rather than homogeneity and convergence on American, European, or Western institutions, traditions, and theories.... [H]eterogeneity and diversity cannot be captured by binary distinction between Western and non-Western." And [54: 389] "the diversity and heterogeneity of world politics requires us to shed our habitual preference for arguing in terms of binary distinctions. 'Either/or' is often less helpful in our analysis of world politics than 'both/and.'"

2. Rigorously speaking, a logic is constituted of a language that is determined by a *syntax*, specifying its *formulas*, and by a *semantics*, specifying its meaning.

3. Quantum logic as constructed by von Neumann and Brikhoff was "(1) too radical in giving up distributivity (rendering it problematic to interpret the logical operations ∧ and ∨ as conjunction and disjunction, respectively); (2) not radical enough in keeping the law of excluded middle, which is precisely what intuition pumps like Schrödinger's cat and the like challenge. Thus it would be preferable to have a quantum logic with exactly the opposite features, i.e., one that is distributive but drops the law of excluded middle: this suggest the use of intuitionistic logic" [62: 459].

4. An algebra is a set of operations and relations, their respective properties, and the structures that these operations and relations operate on.

5. A few other quantization schemes that will not be discussed in here are Borel quantization, Berezin–Toeplitz quantization, Berezin quantization, and coherent state quantization [58: xi].

6. The Hilbert space of pure states takes the role of the phase space of classical mechanics. A Hilbert space is a vector space with complex inner product and is a complete metric space with distance defined using the inner product.

7. One such example is the passage from classical mechanics defined by its invariance group called the Galilei group denoted by $(SO(3) \otimes \mathbb{R}^3) \otimes \mathbb{R}^4$. A study of the deformations of its Lie algebra would lead to the Poincaré Lie algebra and its Euclidean version $SO(4) \otimes \mathbb{R}^4$.

8. Every Boolean algebra is a Heyting algebra, while the converse does not hold.

9. For some illustrative literature, see [16, 17, 28, 34, 35, 40, 50, 51, 53, 87, 100]

10. For illustrative literature on this, see [1, 18, 20, 31, 33, 36, 38, 41, 43, 45, 72, 81]. For a less technical discussion, see [46]

11. For a recent forum engaging Wendt's book on this and other issues, see [4, 5, 6, 14, 57, 68]. Let me remind the reader that Wendt relies on two key working assumptions in developing his approach: (1) a quantum-theoretic framework supplemented with (2) a panpsychist hypothesis about a proto-consciousness at every level of the universe. He argues that both are essential to his argument. I would, however, argue that (2) is more foundational than (1), especially to his claim about "quantum consciousness."

12. This statement is not a very accurate representation of a classical worldview if by which it is meant a classical worldview of classical physics since the advent of Einstein's theory of general relativity, as the latter relativizes both space and time. Wendt would most likely argue that what he terms as "classical worldview" is prior to the theory of general relativity, and that social theorists are not drawing from general relativity theory anyway. However, the issue is deeper than that since space and time are still a problem in the quantum worldview; this transpires in the fact that we do not have yet a widely accepted theory of quantum gravity that is supposed to unify quantum mechanics and gravity and, by the same token, address the problems of spacetime quantization. There is a number of works in progress that seek to do that. In fact, "space" has more or less been "quantized" (such as in the loop quantum gravity approach). However, the problem of time remains wide open (in loop quantum gravity, there is no notion of time at all at the quantum level!). As to social theorists, there is a large literature on temporality, its conceptualization, and its role in social theory, and these

temporalities are not taken as absolute. Having said this, I do not mean to imply that social theory has been able to completely escape the trap of a Newtonian conception of time, since even when it does, it has yet to formulate adequate notions of time and temporality.

13. The term "categorical" here is used not in the category-theoretic sense but rather in the usual way.

14. This is the problem of "measurement" that quantum physicists have been dealing with for a long time and have been able to formulate various approaches to it.

15. As put by Epperson and Zafiris, "Whitehead attempted to construct a rudimentary, quasi-set-theoretic framework of extensive connection in part IV of *Process and Reality*.... [O]ne finds in category theory, and in particular as pertaining to sheaf theory…, a rigorous formalism that would seem to satisfy all the demands Whitehead made of his 'theory of extensive connection' in part IV of *Process and Reality*, but was not able to fully satisfy via the set-theoretic conceptual framework he had earlier developed with Russell.... [U]nlike the quasi-set-theoretic framework of extensive connection given in part IV, category-sheaf theoretic regional contexts are fundamentally topological" [32: 182–183].

References

[1] Abramsky, Samson, & Duncan, Ross. 2006. A Categorical Quantum Logic. *Mathematical Structures in Computer Science*, 16(3), 469–489.

[2] Acharya, Amitav. 2016. Advancing Global IR: Challenges, Contentions, and Contributions. *International Studies Review*, 18(1), 4–15.

[3] Ali, S. Twareque, & Engliš, Miroslav. 2005. Quantization Methods: A Guide for Physicists and Analysts. *Reviews in Mathematical Physics*, 17(4), 391–490.

[4] Allan, Bentley B. 2018. Social Action in Quantum Social Science. *Millennium*, 47(1), 87–98.

[5] Arfi, Badredine. 2018. Challenges to a Quantum-Theoretic Social Theory. *Millennium*, 47(1), 99–113.

[6] Arfi, Badredine, & Kessler, Oliver. 2018. Forum Introduction: Social Theory Going Quantum-Theoretic? Questions, Alternatives and Challenges. *Millennium*, 47(1), 67–73.

[7] Awodey, Steve. 2004. An Answer to Hellman's Question: "Does Category Theory Provide a Framework for Mathematical Structuralism?" *Philosophia Mathematica*, 12(1), 54–64.

[8] Awodey, Steve. 2017. Structuralism, invariance, and univalence. *Chap. 4, pages 58–68 of*: Landry, Elaine (ed), *Categories for the Working Philosopher*. Oxford: Oxford University Press.

[9] Baez, John. 2006. Quantum Quandaries: A Category-Theoretic Perspective. *Chap. 8, pages 240–265 of*: Rickles, Dean, French, Steven, & Saatsi, Juha T. (eds), *The Structural Foundations of Quantum Gravity*. Oxford: Oxford University Press.

[10] Barad, Karen. 2006. *Meeting the Universe Halfway: Quantum Physics and the Entanglement of Matter and Meaning*. Durham, North Carolina: Duke University Press.

[11] Birkhoff, Garrett, & Neumann, John Von. 1936. The Logic of Quantum Mechanics. *Annals of Mathematics*, 37(4), 823.

[12] Brincat, Shannon. 2011. Towards a Social-Relational Dialectic for World Politics. *European Journal of International Relations*, 17(4), 679–703.

[13]Bucher, Bernd, & Jasper, Ursula. 2017. Revisiting "Identity" in International Relations: From Identity as Substance to Identifications in Action. *European Journal of International Relations*, 23(2), 391–415.

[14]Burgess, J. Peter. 2018. Science Blurring Its Edges into Spirit: The Quantum Path to Ātma. *Millennium*, 47(1), 128–141.

[15]Busemeyer, Jerome R., & Bruza, Peter David. 2012. *Quantum Models of Cognition and Decision*. Cambridge: Cambridge University Press.

[16]Butterfield, J., & Isham, C. J. 1999. A Topos Perspective on the Kochen-Specker Theorem II. Conceptual Aspects and Classical Analogues. *International Journal of Theoretical Physics*, 38(3), 827–859.

[17]Butterfield, J., & Isham, C. J. 2002. Topos Perspective on the Kochen-Specker Theorem. IV. Interval Valuations. *International Journal of Theoretical Physics*, 41(4), 613.

[18]Caspers, Martijn, Heunen, Chris, Landsman, Nicolaas, & Spitters, Bas. 2009. Intuitionistic Quantum Logic of an n-Level System. *Foundations of Physics*, 39(7), 731+759.

[19]Chen, Yanbei. 2013. Macroscopic Quantum Mechanics: Theory and Experimental Concepts of Optomechanics. *Journal of Physics B: Atomic, Molecular and Optical Physics*, 46(10), 104001.

[20]Dalla Chiara, Maria Luisa, Giuntini, Roberto, & Greechie, Richard. 2004. *Reasoning in Quantum Theory: Sharp and Unsharp Quantum Logics*. Dordrecht; Boston: Kluwer Academic Publishers.

[21]Dépelteau, François. 2008. Relational Thinking: A Critique of Co-Deterministic Theories of Structure and Agency. *Sociological Theory*, 26(1), 51–73.

[22]Dirac, P. A. M. 1967. *The Principles of Quantum Mechanics*. 4th edn. Oxford: Oxford Clarendon Press.

[23]Döring, A., & Isham, C. 2011. "What Is a Thing?": Topos Theory in the Foundations of Physics. *Pages 753–937 of*: Coecke, Bob (ed), *New Structures for Physics*. Berlin, Heidelberg: Springer Berlin Heidelberg.

[24]Döring, A., & Isham, C. J. 2008a. A Topos Foundation for Theories of Physics: I. Formal Languages for Physics. *Journal of Mathematical Physics*, 49(5), 053515.

[25]Döring, A., & Isham, C. J. 2008b. A Topos Foundation for Theories of Physics: II. Daseinisation and the Liberation of Quantum Theory. *Journal of Mathematical Physics*, 49(5), 053516.

[26]Döring, A., & Isham, C. J. 2008c. A Topos Foundation for Theories of Physics: III. The Representation of Physical Quantities with Arrows. *Journal of Mathematical Physics*, 49(5), 053517.

[27]Döring, A., & Isham, C. J. 2008d. A Topos Foundation for Theories of Physics: IV. Categories of Systems. *Journal of Mathematical Physics*, 49(5), 053518.

[28]Döring, Andreas. 2005. Kochen-Specker Theorem for von Neumann Algebras. *International Journal of Theoretical Physics*, 44(2), 139–160.

[29]Döring, Andreas, & Isham, Chris J. 2012. Classical and Quantum Probabilities as Truth Values. *Journal of Mathematical Physics*, 53(3), 032101.

[30]Emirbayer, Mustafa. 1997. Manifesto for a Relational Sociology. *American Journal of Sociology*, 103(2), 281–317.

[31]Engesser, Kurt, Gabbay, Dov M., & Lehmann, Daniel. 2007. *Handbook of Quantum Logic and Quantum Structures: Quantum Structures*. London: Elsevier.

[32]Epperson, Michael, & Zafiris, Elias. 2013. *Foundations of Relational Realism: A Topological Approach to Quantum Mechanics and the Philosophy of Nature*. Lanham, MD: Lexington Books.

[33] Eva, Benjamin. 2015. Towards a Paraconsistent Quantum Set Theory. *arXiv preprint arXiv:1511.01571*.

[34] Eva, Benjamin. 2016. Modality and Contextuality in Topos Quantum Theory. *Studia Logica*, **104**(6), 1099.

[35] Flori, Cecilia. 2013. *A First Course in Topos Quantum Theory*. Heidelberg: Springer.

[36] Flori, Cecilia. 2018. *A Second Course in Topos Quantum Theory*. Cham: Springer.

[37] Franz, Uwe, & Skalski, Adam. 2016. *Noncommutative Mathematics for Quantum Systems*. Cambridge IISc Series. Cambridge, UK: Cambridge University Press.

[38] Gibbins, Peter. 1987. *Particles and Paradoxes: The Limits of Quantum Logic*. Cambridge; New York: Cambridge University Press.

[39] Glick Schiller, Nina. 2012. Situating Identities: Towards an Identities Studies without Binaries of Difference. *Identities*, **19**(4), 520–532.

[40] Hamilton, J., Isham, C. J., & Butterfield, J. 2000. Topos Perspective on the Kochen-Specker Theorem. III. Von Neumann Algebras as the Base Category. *International Journal of Theoretical Physics*, **39**(6), 1413.

[41] Harding, John. 2009. A Link between Quantum Logic and Categorical Quantum Mechanics. *International Journal of Theoretical Physics*, **48**(3), 769.

[42] Heunen, Chris, Landsman, Nicolaas P., & Spitters, Bas. 2009. A Topos for Algebraic Quantum Theory. *Communications in Mathematical Physics*, **291**(1), 63–110.

[43] Heunen, Chris, Landsman, Nicolaas P., & Spitters, Bas. 2012. Bohrification of Operator Algebras and Quantum Logic. *Synthese*, **186**(3), 719.

[44] Hirshfeld, Allen C., & Henselder, Peter. 2002. Deformation Quantization in the Teaching of Quantum Mechanics. *American Journal of Physics*, **70**(5), 537–547.

[45] Isham, C. J. 1997. Topos Theory and Consistent Histories: The Internal Logic of the Set of All Consistent Sets. *International Journal of Theoretical Physics*, **36**(4), 785.

[46] Isham, C. J. 2005a. Is It True; or Is It False; or Somewhere in Between? The Logic of Quantum Theory. *Contemporary Physics*, **46**(3), 207–219.

[47] Isham, C. J. 2005b. Quantising on a Category. *Foundations of Physics*, **35**(2), 271.

[48] Isham, C. J. 2006a. A Topos Perspective on State-Vector Reduction. *International Journal of Theoretical Physics*, **45**(8), 1524–1551.

[49] Isham, C. J., & Butterfield, J. 1998. Topos Perspective on the Kochen-Specker Theorem: I. Quantum States as Generalized Valuations. *International Journal of Theoretical Physics*, **37**(11), 2669–2733.

[50] Isham, C. J., & Butterfield, J. 2000. Some Possible Roles for Topos Theory in Quantum Theory and Quantum Gravity. *Foundations of Physics*, **30**(10), 1707.

[51] Jackson, Patrick Thaddeus, & Nexon, Daniel H. 1999. Relations before States: Substance, Process, and the Study of World Politics. *European Journal of International Relations*, **5**(3), 291–332.

[52] Karakostas, Vassilios, & Zafiris, Elias. 2017. Contextual Semantics in Quantum Mechanics from a Categorical Point of View. *Synthese*, **194**(3), 847–886.

[53] Katzenstein, Peter J. 2018. The Second Coming? Reflections on a Global Theory of International Relations. *Chinese Journal of International Politics*, **11**(4), 373–390.

[54] Kavalski, Emilian. 2018a. Chinese Concepts and Relational International Politics. *All Azimuth*, **7**(1), 87–102.

[55] Kavalski, Emilian. 2018b. Guanxi or What Is the Chinese for Relational Theory of World Politics. *International Relations of the Asia-Pacific*, **18**(3), 397–420.

[56] Kessler, Oliver. 2018. The Mind-Body Problem and the Move from Supervenience to Quantum Mechanics. *Millennium*, **47**(1), 74–86.

[57] Khalkhali, Masoud. 2013. *Basic Noncommutative Geometry*. European Mathematical Society.

[58] Khrennikov, A. 2009. *Interpretations of Probability*. New York: Walter de Gruyter.

[59] Kochen, Simon, & Specker, E. P. 1967. The Problem of Hidden Variables in Quantum Mechanics. *Journal of Mathematics and Mechanics*, 17(1), 59–87.

[60] Lake, David A. 2009. Relational Authority and Legitimacy in International Relations. *American Behavioral Scientist*, 53(3), 331–353.

[61] Landsman, Klaas. 2017. *Foundations of Quantum Theory: From Classical Concepts to Operator Algebras*. New York: Springer Open.

[62] Long, Tom. 2017. It's Not the Size, It's the Relationship: From "Small States" to Asymmetry. *International Politics*, 54(2), 144–160.

[63] MacDonald, Paul K. 2018. Embedded Authority: A Relational Network Approach to Hierarchy in World Politics. *Review of International Studies*, 44(1), 128–150.

[64] Majid, Shahn. 2000. Quantum Groups and Noncommutative Geometry. *Journal of Mathematical Physics*, 41(6), 3892–3942.

[65] Mazzola, Guerino. 2002. *Yoneda Perspectives*. Basel: Birkhäuser Basel. Pages 175–189.

[66] McCourt, David M. 2016. Practice Theory and Relationalism as the New Constructivism. *International Studies Quarterly*, 60(3), 475–485.

[67] Michel, Torsten. 2018. Of Particles and Humans: The Question of "Human Being" in Alexander Wendt's Quantum Mind and Social Science. *Millennium*, 47(1), 114–127.

[68] Mitchell, George E. 2016. "Follow the Partners": A Relational Ontology for NGO Studies. *International Studies Review*, 18(2), 399–401.

[69] Nebbiosi, Gianni, & Federici, Susanna. 2014. The Relational Model: International Relations and Dissemination in Italy: A Historical Account. *Psychoanalytic Dialogues*, 24(5), 590–600.

[70] Nexon, Daniel H., & Pouliot, Vincent. 2013. "Things of Networks": Situating ANT in International Relations. *International Political Sociology*, 7(3), 342–345.

[71] Pitowsky, Itamar. 1989. *Quantum Probability–Quantum Logic*. Berlin; New York: Springer-Verlag.

[72] Powell, Christopher John, & Dépelteau, François. 2013. *Conceptualizing Relational Sociology: Ontological and Theoretical Issues*. New York: Palgrave Macmillan.

[73] Qin, Yaqing. 2009. Relationality and Processual Construction: Bringing Chinese Ideas into International Relations Theory. *Social Sciences in China*, 30(4), 5–20.

[74] Qin, Yaqing. 2018. A Multiverse of Knowledge: Cultures and IR Theories. *Chinese Journal of International Politics*, 11(4), 415–434.

[75] Querejazu, Amaya. 2016. Encountering the Pluriverse: Looking for Alternatives in Other Worlds. *Revista Brasileira de Política Internacional*, 59(2), 1–16.

[76] Radil, Steven M., Flint, Colin, & Chi, Sang-Hyun. 2013. A Relational Geography of War: Actor–Context Interaction and the Spread of World War I. *Annals of the Association of American Geographers*, 103(6), 1468–1484.

[77] Shih, Chih-Yu. 2016. Affirmative Balance of the Singapore-Taiwan Relationship: A Bilateral Perspective on the Relational Turn in International Relations. *International Studies Review*, 18(4), 681–701.

[78] Steiner, David. 1998. Politics of Relationality: From the Postmodern to Post-Ontology. *Philosophy & Social Criticism*, 24(4), 1–21.

[79] Sundén, Jenny, & Blagojević, Jelisaveta. 2019. Dis/connections: Toward an Ontology of Broken Relationality. *Configurations*, 27(1), 37–57.

[80] Svozil, Karl. 1998. *Quantum Logic*. New York: Springer-Verlag.

[81] Tsekeris, Charalambos. 2010. Relationalism in Sociology: Theoretical and Methodological Elaborations. *Facta Universitatis: Series Philosophy, Sociology, Psychology & History*, 9(1), 139–148.

[82] Van Heijenoort, Jean. 2002. *From Frege to Gödel: A Source Book in Mathematical Logic, 1879–1931*. Cambridge, MA; London: Harvard University Press.

[83] Van Oystaeyen, F. 2007. *Virtual Topology and Functor Geometry*. Lecture Notes in Pure and Applied Mathematics. CRC Press.

[84] Wendt, Alexander. 2015. *Quantum Mind and Social Science: Unifying Physical and Social Ontology*. Cambridge: Cambridge University Press.

[85] Whitehead, Alfred North, Griffin, David Ray, & Sherburne, Donald W. 1978. *Process and Reality: An Essay in Cosmology*. New York: Free Press.

[86] Wolters, Sander. 2013. A Comparison of Two Topos-Theoretic Approaches to Quantum Theory. *Communications in Mathematical Physics*, 317(1), 3–53.

[87] Zafiris, Elias. 2000. Probing Quantum Structure with Boolean Localization Systems. *International Journal of Theoretical Physics*, 39(12), 2761.

[88] Zafiris, Elias. 2004a. Boolean Coverings of Quantum Observable Structure: A Setting for an Abstract Differential Geometric Mechanism. *Journal of Geometry and Physics*, 50(1–4), 99.

[89] Zafiris, Elias. 2004b. Interpreting Observables in a Quantum World from the Categorial Standpoint. *International Journal of Theoretical Physics*, 43(1), 265–298.

[90] Zafiris, Elias. 2004c. On Quantum Event Structures. Part III: Object of Truth Values. *Foundations of Physics Letters*, 17(5), 403–432.

[91] Zafiris, Elias. 2004d. Quantum Event Structures from the Perspective of Grothendieck Topoi. *Foundations of Physics*, 34(7), 1063.

[92] Zafiris, Elias. 2006a. Category-Theoretic Analysis of the Notion of Complementarity for Quantum Systems. *International Journal of General Systems*, 35(1), 69.

[93] Zafiris, Elias. 2006b. Sheaf-Theoretic Representation of Quantum Measure Algebras. *Journal of Mathematical Physics*, 47(9), 092103.

[94] Zafiris, Elias. 2006c. Topos-Theoretic Classification of Quantum Events Structures in Terms of Boolean Reference Frames. *International Journal of Geometric Methods in Modern Physics*, 3(8), 1501–1527.

[95] Zafiris, Elias. 2007. Quantum Observables Algebras and Abstract Differential Geometry: The Topos-Theoretic Dynamics of Diagrams of Commutative Algebraic Localizations. *International Journal of Theoretical Physics*, 46(2), 319–382.

[96] Zafiris, Elias. 2010. Boolean Information Sieves: A Local-to-Global Approach to Quantum Information. *International Journal of General Systems*, 39(8), 873–895.

[97] Zafiris, Elias. 2012. Rosen's Modelling Relations via Categorical Adjunctions. *International Journal of General Systems*, 41(5), 439–474.

[98] Zafiris, Elias, & Karakostas, Vassilios. 2013. A Categorial Semantic Representation of Quantum Event Structures. *Foundations of Physics*, 43(9), 1090–1123.

12

On Quantum Social Theory and Critical International Relations

Michael P. A. Murphy

Introduction

Unlike the encounter between behavioral economics and International Relations (IR) decades ago, quantum social theory encounters a diverse field of IR, marked by established "camps" (Sylvester 2007, 2013), instead of a binary division of— to borrow Hedley Bull's (1966) descriptors—classical and scientific approaches. Within the broader pluralism of contemporary IR theory, the intellectually diverse body of thought known as "critical IR" further complexifies any attempt at categorization. Or, in the words of Richard Wyn Jones, rather than a singular framework, "critical IR theory is...best understood as a constellation" (2001, 9). While critical approaches to IR remain marginalized within the American academy, their collective footprint beyond the United States is sufficiently significant that the possibility of a general quantum revolution across the globalized discipline of IR demands consideration of how quantum and critical ideas can peacefully and productively coexist.

The exploration of common ground shared between quantum and critical approaches to IR theory is still in its early stages. Laura Zanotti's (2019) book *Ontological Entanglements, Agency, and Ethics in International Relations* charts a critical course through the waters of quantum ethics, but it is perhaps a recent forum on that book (e.g., Murphy 2021a; Zanotti 2021a) that stands as the broadest reflection on the critical/quantum question. Elisabeth Prügl (2021) explores how feminist accounts of IR stand to benefit from a quantum framing of gender, while Şengül Yıldız-Alanbay (2021) explores how quantum ideas can inform critical discourses around affect theory.[1] Christopher McIntosh (2021) brings entangled ontology into conversation with novel accounts of temporality in war, while my contribution (Murphy 2021b) outlines similarities between quantum and postcritical accounts of relationality. Laura Sjoberg's (2021) reflection on quantum ambivalence shares her encounter with quantum IR, intrigued by the idea but ultimately unconvinced and uncomfortable with a quantum-theoretic revolution. The forum on *Ontological Entanglements* serves as the first substantial conversation explicitly focused on the critical/quantum connection to appear in print, and—far from reaching definitive conclusions—the response thereto will likely only bring further perspectival diversity to the discussion.

Beyond *Ontological Entanglements,* other stand-alone projects in critical/ quantum IR explore different themes, such as entanglement (Fierke 2019; Fierke & Antonio-Alfonso 2018; Fierke & McKay 2020), decolonial ethics (Zanotti 2021b), and strategies for engaging quantum IR from a critical perspective (Murphy 2021c). While these inroads represent an important starting point, much of this dialogue remains to be written.[2] In this chapter, I will explore possibilities for future critical/ quantum study by outlining the three key relationships between critical IR and quantum IR—quantizing as critique, quantizing critique, and quantized critique.

Since an exhaustive review of all critical approaches to IR would far exceed the scope of one chapter, I will instead discuss the interface of quantum and critical thinking by discussing critique as a scholarly disposition. The first section attempts this task through a brief historical and conceptual review of critique in IR. The second section of the chapter reviews three strategies for integrating quantum and critical thought—quantizing *as* critique, quan*tizing* critique, and quan*tized* critique. As noted previously, the conclusion responds to concerns shared about the relationship between critical and quantum IR by reflecting on the significance of critical/quantum IR being a pluralistic one, much like the broader quantum community—which, in the words of James Der Derian and Alexander Wendt (2020, 409), consists of "quantum approaches (in the plural) rather than...a quantum theory (in the singular)."

As a final prefatory note, I acknowledge that this review dispenses with the conventional practice of the specific introduction of quantum ideas. While this is partially possible given the erudite contributions of my fellow collaborators to this volume, I seek also to challenge my colleagues in the quantum journey. With a series of introductory texts now available in quantum IR and proximate fields of social science and social theory (Barad 2007; Haven & Khrennikov 2013, 2018; Murphy 2021c; Orrell 2018; Wendt 2015; Zanotti 2019; Zohar 1990; Zohar & Marshall 1994), it is high time that reflections on quantum IR move from explanations of *why* to *how.* The groundwork has been laid, and the construction of rigorous frameworks can begin.

Disaggregating Critical and Mainstream
International Relations

The term "critical" in IR today is claimed by divergent camps, often mobilized rhetorically in the effort to differentiate the critical *us* from the mainstream *them.* Rather than a stable signifier, however, the term carries always an implicit opposition to a moving target identified as "the mainstream." While recent developments around the notion of "postcritique" have sought to reinvigorate the critical project with different internal logics—moving from the "herme-neutics of suspicion" toward a more sympathetic (Austin 2019), nontotalizing (Huysmans & Nogueira 2021), or companionship-based model (Austin et al 2019)—much self-styled critical scholarship remains focused on responding to the otherized mainstream.

One point often identified as an origin of critical IR is Robert W. Cox's 1981 article "Social Forces, States, and World Orders," which argues for a classifi-cation of theories of world politics into two categories: problem-solving and critical. While problem-solving theory "takes the world as it finds it" and seeks to make existing institutions function more smoothly, critical theory "stands apart from the prevailing order of the world and asks how it came to be" to call into question, rather than to strengthen, existing institutions (Cox 1981, 128–129). Drawing on the similar distinction between critical and traditional theories discussed by Max Horkheimer and the Frankfurt School, early self-styled critical theorists advocated for a critical approach to emerge as a "new focus within the discipline of International Relations that is post-realist and post-Marxist" with a correspondingly expanded mission beyond explanation of world-political events insofar as "to alter the world" (Hoffman 1987, 244). Against the protests of those who argue that critical theory requires both the questioning of current orders *and* the proposal of emancipatory alternatives to truly be a critical theory of IR (e.g., Hynek & Chandler 2013), "critical IR" has become the home for a number of different theoretical traditions (Rengger & Thirkell-White 2007) with different levels of commitment to the task of pro-posing alternative political futures.

Since (1) my primary concern in this chapter is of the practice of critique rather than the theorization of theory, and (2) emancipatory alternatives are not universally held but interrogating dominant structures and explanations are, I will operate under the following practically informed definition of crit-ical IR: *critical theories of IR are those approaches that stand outside a perceived mainstream and seek new ways to question the unquestioned.* Defining critical IR in terms of its sociology of knowledge, rather than the normative political claims of emancipatory or alternative futures, ensures that the definition reflects the practice of critique as it exists in the field. While a normatively driven defi-nition may be preferred by some scholars and a methodologically driven defi-nition by others, both would exclude large portions of the other. Thus, while the sociology-of-knowledge approach may be unsatisfactory to some in terms of their political commitments, my goal in this chapter is to build bridges rather than to keep gates. The significance in the difference between critique and postcritique is that the postcritical sensibility seeks to overcome the embedded antagonism of criticality—less an act of "us" standing outside to question "them" and more an act where we all come together to explore common concerns of meaning making.

Quantum and Critical: Three Strategies

The significance of Wendt's definition of Newtonian social science at the outset of *Quantum Mind and Social Science* can be understood in strategic terms with reflection on the position and tradition of critical IR. Just as Cox's strategic bifurcation of the field into critical and problem-solving camps placed on an equal footing the new research community and established paradigms of realist and liberal international theory,[3] by describing how the causal closure of classical physics serves as a boundary for research in IR, Wendt effectively sets the stage for a disciplinary bifurcation between Newtonian and quantum IR (2015, 11–14). While in practical terms this claims sufficient space for the kind of pluralist research community that Wendt and Der Derian have consistently proposed (see Der Derian & Wendt 2020), there is also a dispositional homology between Wendt (2015) and Cox (1981) in their desire to set as the foremost task the questioning of the unquestioned. Wendt's effort to clear space for quantum is thus similar to Cox's both in strategy and in sensibility.

Because quantum social theory is still in early stages of development, and the connection to IR earlier still, it is still rather easy to identify works of "quantum IR" by their introductory paragraphs on what "quantum IR" is.[4] Western social science arose in a context where Newton's account of physics was the "most successful and prestigious science of the day," and while explicit analogies, metaphors, and homologies faded as social science matured as a field of inquiry, the metaphysical assumptions of Newton carried through (Wendt 2015, 12). The power of invisibility that metaphysics inevitably possesses granted a pass for Newtonian assumptions (e.g., separability, locality, predictability, observability) to proceed with their source largely undetected—and, therefore, uninterrogated. The investigatory function of quantum social theory is—at least in a disciplinary sense—to highlight the existence of these Newtonian assumptions such that the barriers to thought that they impose can be overcome. This is not to say that *all* social scientific research is directly Newtonian. Many relational accounts, for example, suspend Newtonian metaphysics to include ideas of connectivity bearing stronger resemblance to quantum entanglement than Newtonian separability. Here too quantum social theory plays an investigatory role, showing

248 MICHAEL P. A. MURPHY

how a quantum ontology can provide a framework for critical accounts that previously employed ad hoc workarounds of Newtonian metaphysics in a sort of "ontological mish-mash."[5]

In the sections that follow, I will reflect on three strategies for bringing quantum social theory and critical IR together. As an attempt at disciplinary sociology rather than advocacy for one strategy or another, I bracket any evaluation of the preferability of one strategy or another.

- The first strategy—which I call "quantizing *as* critique"—commits to the quantum question's capacity to destabilize long-ignored metaphysical assumptions at the heart of IR theory, carrying the torch for all future quantum inquiry. Within this strategy, the call to a quantum IR is not merely a new project that extends the limits of IR from within its dominant paradigm—which Thomas Kuhn (2012) might describe as "normal science"—but instead a move that brackets and labels all nonquantum IR into a mainstream box and then presents an alternative model that is critical of that mainstream. To this end, *all quantum IR is critical IR*,[6] as quantizing is understood as a form of critique.
- The second strategy, "quant*izing* critique," brings quantum theory and critical theory together by quantizing existing critical approaches. As I first explored in *Quantum Social Theory for Critical International Relations Theorists* (Murphy 2021c), quantizing critique proceeds either by identifying quantum-like phenomena already operative in nonquantum Newtonian forms of critical IR and then translating into the common language of quantum social theory, or identifying points where Newtonian assumptions in critical theories produce conceptually substantial barriers that can be overcome through an application of quantum thinking.
- Finally, the third strategy for bringing together quantum IR sees quantum principles inform new modes of critical scholarship, in an entirely new model of "quant*ized* critique". Quantum ideas serve as the raw materials for theoretical interventions into the debates of critical IR. Here, quantum accounts of ethics, politics, and sociality form the bedrock upon which new critical projects are established. Given the relationality at the heart of quantum social theory, this is an especially welcome territory for postcritical moves.

In the next three subsections, I turn my attention to these strategies of bringing together quantum and critical thinking. The strategies begin from different starting points and address different audiences, but all share the common goal of quantizing inquiry into IR.

Quantizing as Critique

Following the working definition offered earlier, quantum models of social theory stand outside the perceived mainstream—here understood to be those approaches either explicitly or implicitly abiding a Newtonian causal closure of physics—and offer an alternative set of questions. While there are different explanatory claims that justify the move from a Newtonian to a quantum framework, common preliminary assumptions are that (1) existing social science is in some manner Newtonian, and (2) turning from Newtonian to quantum physics allows for a new set of questions and insights. To this end, quantizing as critique is critical insofar as it is quantum, and the process of *becoming quantum* should be understood as a critical act.

Part one of Karen Barad's *Meeting the Universe Halfway* presents a philosophical and analytical framework of entanglement and diffraction clearly in opposition to Newtonian assumptions of separability. This strategy is indeed central to Barad's answer to the proverbial "so what" question when it comes to quantum: "diffraction is a quantum phenomenon that makes the downfall of classical metaphysics explicit" (2007, 72). The assumptions of separability that classical/Newtonian metaphysics grants to all forms of research, for Barad, neglect the diffractive effects of measurement apparatuses and must therefore give way to a new—and explicitly quantum—way of thinking. Within IR, Laura Zanotti's approach to quantum IR similarly begins metatheoretically with a rejection of what she terms Newtonian substantialism, most visible in dominant traditions of realism and liberalism (and their antecedents), but nevertheless present in critical accounts informed by Foucault, Agamben, and others (Zanotti 2017; 2019, chap. 1 The quantum turn thus marks a significant detour from the substantialist mainstream. As mentioned previously, Wendt's (2015) strategy in *Quantum Mind and Social Science* begins by identifying the ubiquity of the causal closure of physics in social science and then arguing that since social science abides the causal closure of physics (largely) without engaging quantum ideas, the core assumptions of Newtonian physics serve as fundamental limitations to the conceptual bounds of social science. Shifting from a causal closure informed by *classical* physics to a causal closure informed by *quantum* physics then grants access to an entirely new set of possibilities.

The conceptual move that presents existing social science as a Newtonian pursuit and quantum thinking as a new repository of questions leads to a number of different theoretical projects. As I have suggested elsewhere, the "spectrum of quantum leaps" (Murphy 2021c, 39) extends from those clearly arguing for a quantum basis of physical reality to those who are explicit that their engagement is purely analogical. Rather than a clear divide, however, the generalized agnosticism of quantum IR toward the more experimental questions of quantum reality leads to the sketching of a number of different relationships in terms of analogy, metaphor, homology, model, actuality, structure, imaginary, framework, and so on. Mindful of this intellectual diversity, reviewing a series of quantum projects can help illustrate how critique can be achieved through quantum means.

At the most agnostic and analogical pole, we find the mathematical modelers of the quantum-like (QL) paradigm. Most productive in questions of finance, psychology, and decision theory (e.g., Arfi 2005; Busemeyer & Bruza 2012; Hanauske et al. 2010; Khrennikov 2018; Piotrowski & Sladkowski 2004), research in the QL paradigm seeks out phenomena that look or behave in ways similar to the signatures of quantum interactions, with quantum formulae then deployed in a predictive capacity. Andrei Khrennikov summarizes the QL approach in these terms:

> The *quantum-like paradigm* (QL) is based on an understanding that the mathematical apparatus of quantum mechanics (and especially quantum probability) is not rigidly coupled with *quantum physics*, but can have a wide class of applications. (Khrennikov 2010, 1)

While one prima facie critique is aimed at those who would rather leave the mathematical models of quantum mechanics within the narrowly constructed borders of "physics"—specifically, to the physics of the microworld—there is a more general critique of classical models as insufficient. For example, in *Quantum Social Science*, Emmanuel Haven and Andrei Khrennikov critique the incompleteness of econophysics as grounded in classical statistical models, and the QL model is proposed as a new way of questioning and explaining. To this end, their efforts broadly meet the practice-oriented definition of critique. But, contrary to claims of quantum realism, Haven and Khrennikov are from the outset abundantly clear that the application of quantum mathematical models does not require a fundamental quantum reality, stating that their QL models "do not have a direct relation to quantum physics" (2013, xviii).[7]

The contrary pole sees claims made about a real quantum foundation grounding social life—with the paradigmatic formulation here coming through in Alexander Wendt's already-famous claim that "we really are walking wave functions" (2015, 293 and *passim*). If we really are quantum, then our analytical tools should be similarly quantum. The critique of Newtonianism is quite straightforward given a foundation of quantum reality, as the conventional approach (in this reading) asks a *physically incorrect* set of questions that must be replaced. Indeed, the central argument of Wendt's book is precisely this clear—because Newtonian social science cannot understand the problem of consciousness, we must turn to the quantum/panpsychist model that is capable (and—following some strands of inquiry into cognition, decision, and psychology—plausible).

Turning from Newtonian to quantum social science, then, not only solves the foundational problem of consciousness but also explains different anomalies for which social science has struggled to account. Given the comprehensiveness of the quantum consciousness explanatory model, Wendt argues that "it is too elegant not to be true" (2015, 35). While quantum panpsychism may seem like a lot to swallow, the conceptual payoff for Wendt's hard case for a kind of quantum realism is immense.

A plethora of positions across the spectrum of quantum leaps leads to claims of analogy and actuality of varying thicknesses, with any possible superposition of the two. Mathias Albert and Felix Bathon (2020) identify how analogies between existing theoretical frameworks with quantum-like tendencies and quantum ideas can be put to complementary analytical use, whereas Leonardo Orlando (2020) takes a stronger stance to speak of an isomorphic relation between introspective psychology and quantum mind hypotheses. Chengxin Pan (2018) grounds a new account of relationality within the structural part/whole relationship of quantum holography in opposition to the Newtonian/classical agent/structure model, whereas David Orrell (2020) focuses on the duality of the value question in money as a quantum-like constituent of a macroscopic international economy. Like both critical theory and quantum theory, the messy middle of quantizing-as-critique has a seemingly infinite array of approaches to the explanatory justification for quantization. Bracketing the justification, all approaches in this section share the critical sensibility that new questions must be asked and that those new questions can be quarried from quantum.

Quantizing Critique

The second strategy for bringing together quantum and critical traditions is what I call *quantizing critique*, where existing frameworks in critical IR theory are quantized either through translation or application, depending on the nature of the critical theory in question. Rather than a critique-of-critique that takes on a threatening posture, the strategy of quantizing critique is one of bridge-building between quantum and critical communities. The project of quantizing critique shares with the first strategy a common aim of identifying the Newtonian limits to inquiry as a starting point but differs in that much of the conceptual apparatus is salvaged. Quantizing critique aims to bring critical IR from a Newtonian social-theoretic imaginary (or an uninterrogated mish-mash) into a quantum social-theoretic imaginary, leading to a superposition of two critical momenta. To expand on this strategic relationship where quantum theory strengthens the criticality of existing critique, I will outline the two methods of quantizing critique as developed in *Quantum Social Theory for Critical International Relations*

252 MICHAEL P. A. MURPHY

Theorists (Murphy 2021c), before reflecting in more general terms on the relationship between quantum and critique in the strategy of quantizing critique.

In the first method of quantizing through translation, critical approaches that express in nonquantum terminology characteristic elements of quantum social theory—for example, one approach may draw attention to the observer's role in cocreating the observed reality, while another may call attention to fundamental microconstituent/macrostructural dualities—are translated into the quantum vernacular (Murphy 2021c, chap. 4). Drawing on Carol Cohn's (1987) insights around the power of linguistic systems to limit the scope of the imaginable, I argue that a critical theory grounded in a Newtonian imaginary will similarly be bound by what is conceptually possible in a Newtonian social science. Just as Cohn identified that technostrategic language rendered inaccessible concerns of peace and humanity that could be spoken about through a feminist framework, a Newtonian imaginary lacks the linguistic and conceptual capacity to discuss key elements of quantum theory—duality, uncertainty, observer effects, collapse, entanglement, nonlocality, etc. Many critical theories pointing to these sorts of underlying realities beneath simplified conventional accounts receive, through their translation into quantum terms, a vocabulary that facilitates rather than fights the quest for further questioning. The vocabulary of quantum physics, can complement the conceptual tools already at work in critical IR. Rather than abide the fundamentally limiting Newtonian assumptions embedded into the vernacular of social science, a quantum vocabulary works *with*, rather than *against*, critical IR's quest to identify and interrogate complexity, relationality, and uncertainty.

The second method of quantizing critique, which I term quantizing through application, identifies critical theories that have hit a conceptual barrier—for example, a microsociological theory that cannot recognize structural effects—and applies principles of quantum ontology to open up new scales of inquiry (Murphy 2021c, chap. 5). While objections to this strategy are easily enough imagined—for example, "Theory X doesn't *need* quantum to explain Y, and we can just use a different theory to understand Z," or "Theory A doesn't have to explain *everything*"—the heart of the matter is that a quantum imaginary removes Newtonian barriers to the application and development of critical theories. Yes, the theory works with the metaphysical imaginary left in brackets—but if an alternative metaphysics permitted further insights and greater ontological consistency, *why not try*? Indeed, while critical theories of IR have proliferated and the formation of new critical "camps" has largely been treated as a welcome development in those circles, quantum IR has been met with a higher degree of skepticism. It is unclear the extent to which this reluctance is grounded in a well-founded concern with physics envy or a more personal suspicion of the constellation of scholars coming together to form the quantum IR community, but the end result in some areas of critical IR has been a shift from bridge-building to gatekeeping.

In *Quantum Social Theory for Critical International Relations Theorists*, I discuss the case of actor-network theory. This critical sociological theory challenges the tendencies of pregiven categories of analysis to determine what counts and what doesn't count in social inquiry, arguing that sociologists macrostructure reality through their pregiven assumptions (Callon & Latour 1981; Latour 1987). Drawing on insights from analysis of laboratory research, actor-network theory draws attention to the precise interactions between human and nonhuman *actants* to paint a more detailed picture of the construction of both scientific knowledge and social reality (Latour & Woolgar 1986; Callon 1986). But by focusing only on the visible interactions of microconstituents within a Newtonian social-theoretic framework, the existence of structural forces like patriarchy, racism, or economic inequality is simply *unimaginable* for actor-network theory.[8] Drawing a parallel between actor-network theory's close microsociological analysis and the collapse to particle found during the act of measurement in quantum physics, I argued that an application of a quantum ontology can expand the scope of the imaginable within actor-network theory, such that wave-like structural forces can be recognized in their pattern effects. Similar efforts taking structural analyses as a starting point might—through quantization—permit a conceptually consistent deconstructive methodology that retains structural recognition while providing microsociological detail of how events within the structure are constructed.

As a strategy, quantizing critique takes critical IR as both its starting point and central audience. The payoff for the critical audience is a quantum grammar that offers escape from the metaphysical limits of a Newtonian imaginary. Like the strategy of quantizing as critique, the pitch to nonquantum audiences includes the opportunity to move beyond the disciplining effects of Newtonian social science. However, because the audience of such efforts—critical IR—is presumably on board with questioning the mainstream, the project of quantization serves a project already in progress. The smaller membership of the audience will hopefully be offset by a reduced barrier to entry[9] (as skepticism of core tenets of the disciplinary mainstream pre-exists the quantum question). To take but one example, a critical feminist project, broadly defined, seeks to raise questions that highlight the patriarchal and sexist forces at play in a given social milieu, and also to critique the conventional explanations that failed to interrogate those inequities at work. Embedded within that scholarship is not only an empirical critique of the way that a particular patriarchal structure came into being but also a metatheoretical or disciplinary critique of the mainstream that failed to identify what the critical project highlights. Quantizing that critical feminist account—say, by employing the notion of interference to discuss how some elements of society have increased spectra opportunities while others have less as instances of constructive and destructive interference—adds to the original critique a quantum argument around the wave-like nature of social structures. Not only is the existing order questioned for its patriarchal effects, but also quantum interference provides a new model for explaining differential outcomes through that one structure's operation. Here too we can turn to Karen Barad's work, such as her use of quantum field theory to read queer theories of touching (Barad 2012) or offering an entangled ontology as a path beyond anthropocentric tendencies of analysis grounded in queer performativity (Barad 2011). Quantizing critique permits a completion of the act of radical questioning, because instead of confronting the limiting Newtonian vernacular, quantized critique moves beyond the dominant physical imaginary that has grounded dominant trends in Western social science from its inception (Murphy 2021c, 103).

Quantized Critique

As indicated in the introduction, the specific purpose of this chapter is to disentangle three strategies by which quantum IR engages with critical IR. One way to understand the differences between the strategies is the primary audiences. For both the second and third strategies, the main audience is critical IR—indeed, in addition to developing novel quantum accounts of different phenomena, both the second and third strategies seek to contribute to the literatures of critical IR, while the first strategy may be understood as separate because the intended readership is either broader (e.g., IR writ large or social theory) or different (e.g., game theory or decision theory). One way to model the distinction between quantizing critique and quantized critique as strategies of engagement would be that quantizing critique begins with an existing framework of critical IR (bringing critical IR to quantum IR), while quantized critique begins from a quantum position to speak to critical IR (bringing quantum IR to critical IR).

The strategy of quantized critique seeks to develop new theoretical models and tools while speaking to the audience of critical IR, producing a quantum form of critique that is often more relational than nonquantum forms of critical IR. While there may be disciplinary-sociological similarities between the calls to action of quantized critique and the postcritical movement in IR theory (see Murphy 2021b), the content of the various approaches falling into the quantum tradition are unique from existing forms of thought. As self-consciously critical efforts, theorists of quantized critique demonstrate a sense of questioning the unquestioned, and the new form of quant*ized* critique rethinks the critical project anew from foundational concepts of quantum social theory to forward explicitly critical accounts of existing systems. The point is not merely to identify or understand quantum-like phenomena, but to shift our thinking away from binaries of "Version 1.0" to "Version 2.0" toward a fundamentally new and quantum way of making sense of the superposed world (Der Derian 2013).[10]

Some forms of quantized critique draw inspiration from changes in the world related both to the quantum technology revolution and to the broader trends of connectivity and relationality. Of all the claims made across the spectrum of quantum IR, some of these precepts ought to be the least controversial. For example, with the proliferation of the reach of networks and smartphone connections, communications appear to approach instantaneity by human scales, thus facilitating the *experience* of entanglement and nonlocal causation in formerly unimaginable ways. If no human being is sufficiently temporally sensitive to discern the difference between the locality or nonlocality of communication, Newtonian metaphors merit serious suspicion. In this mode, critique must be reimagined from a new (and quantum) position because social inquiry bounded by Newtonian assumptions will never fully articulate a world that exceeds a Newtonian imaginary. Even critique of the conventional wisdom will be incomplete, because fundamentally Newtonian questions beg fundamentally Newtonian answers from a quantum world.

The idea that the speed of contemporary life reveals the insufficiency of Newtonian social science offers an example of how quantized critique contributes to established debates of critical IR from new, quantum, perspectives. As connectivity, globalization, and the omnipresence of images shift the nature of diplomacy (Der Derian 2011), war (Der Derian 2013), and security (Der Derian 2019), the binaries that structured both mainstream realist and liberal thought (in their construction) and constructivist and postmodern perspectives (in their deconstruction) cease to serve the same function. Quantum theory's core concepts—entanglement, nonlocality, duality, and so on—arise as key models for understanding a new way of living and connecting that exceeds the Newtonian approximation.

Other approaches to quantized critique begin from the position that an entangled ontological position poses a fundamental challenge to all forms of knowledge. The universality of these challenges leads to a constructive rather than a deconstructive critique, whether that is expressed epistemologically by building new frameworks for knowledge or politically by unpacking the potential for more emancipatory alternative political futures.[11] As discussed earlier, Barad's *Meeting the Universe Halfway* begins with a rejection of Newtonian assumptions and instead argues that diffraction and entanglement demand a new framework for social theory. Barad calls for an ontological prioritization of relations over relata and constructs a radical social theory premised on the claim that our reality is not one where separable actors *inte*ract with one another externally, but where *intra*-action occurs within entangled phenomena. We are not separate entities coming into relation, but our relations are always already there and experience can only occur within our entangled system. In her application of an entangled ontological model to IR, Zanotti (2019) takes specific aim at the role of applying abstract principles in guiding international intervention. The possibility of abstraction and intervention, she argues, relies on a Newtonian understanding of both state-centric politics and substantialist onto-epistemology. An alternative entangled ontology grounds a new quantum vision of world politics, where actions demand consideration of the full web of relations. This fundamental relationality has a radical ethical implication, insofar as we become responsible for all effects within our system when we act—rendering unimaginable the possibility of violence being written off as collateral damage. While both Barad and Zanotti draw on existing—at best nonquantum but quantum-like—literature from various traditions of critical theory, the conceptual move is undeniably quantum in nature, and therefore introduces a new form of quantized critique.

A final important form that quantized critique takes is to position quantum as the (meta)physical means for overcoming the nexus of Newtonian physics and colonial power. Just as Newtonian assumptions shape dominant trends in Western social science, quantum social theorists have argued that dominant ethical frameworks and modes of political domination are grounded in Newtonian metaphysics. Quantum ideas offer a path outside of not only Newtonian physics and conventional social science but also conventional (Newtonian) society. Norah Bowman's (2021) account of the Newtonian foundation of settler-colonial onto-epistemology highlights how quantum models can open space for Indigenous experiences. Similarly, Laura Zanotti's (2021b) critique of Kantian ethics demonstrates the decolonial potential of quantum ethical frames. Building on prior work noting the centrality of new ways of communication and community building to the postcolonial political project (Noxolo & Preziuso 2012, 133) is Patricia Noxolo's commentary on (post)diaspora as an entangled experience of being (Noxolo 2020). A similar argument has been made regarding Indigenous ways of living (Parry 2006; Peat 2002), highlighting the important parallels between Indigenous and quantum ideas, in contradiction to the destructive excesses of Newtonian/colonial society. These various interventions demonstrate the potential of the quantum turn to create space for approaches central to critical political praxis. Indeed, this may even indicate a manner by which quantum ideas can contribute to those critical projects that seek explicitly to propose alternative and emancipatory political futures.

Quantum Social Theor*ies* for Critical International Relations

Within the quantum IR community, answers to the "why quantum" question vary widely, and the panoply of relational definitions employed to capture the connection between quantum ideas and social life—metaphor, analogy, homology, reality, isomorphism, complementary analysis—demonstrates that pluralism is a fundamental characteristic of quantum social theory (and quantum IR). But that accurate description of quantum IR offered by Der Derian and Wendt (2020, 409)—plural approaches rather than singular unified theory—might just as easily be applied to the broadly defined research community of critical IR. The question of how to bring together quantum social theory and critical IR, then, can only be destined to fail if we presume two defined and discrete theoretical camps. Quantum social theory and critical IR are both broad spectra of potential engagements, and their superposition may well lead (through constructive interference) to a radical increase in the range of possible research questions to be asked.

Following Barad, I believe that understanding the potential connections between critical and quantum inquiry must prioritize the conceptual relations over the disciplinary relata. Rather than canvass all critical theories of IR and then move to understand how each narrowly defined point connects to a distilled core of quantum social theory, recognizing the plurality of both quantum and critique calls on us to begin with the relationality. *Quantizing as critique* speaks to any form of project that critiques the shortcomings of Newtonian science from a quantum perspective. *Quantizing critique* bolsters existing critical projects through translation into quantum language or application of quantum ontologies. *Quantized critique* develops novel contributions to the critical literature grounded in a quantum imaginary. Leaving specifics in superposition, focusing on the relationality facilitates an inclusive and conceptually diverse field of inquiry for all potential approaches that stand outside the Newtonian mainstream to ask quantum questions of the unquestioned.

Notes

1. See also Yıldız-Alanbay (2020) for broader context on how affect theory and quantum theory fit into posthumanist discourses.
2. Including not only the possibility of engaging critical IR from a quantum perspective but also—as Wendt (n.d.) explores—traditions of critical theory in philosophy and pedagogy.
3. This point is made by Hoffman (1987), and I revisit the strategic move made by Cox in Murphy (2021, 4).

4. It may well be the case in the future that quantum approaches to IR are sufficiently widespread that quantum authors need not restate the quantum-versus-Newtonian opposition and identify their position on the quantum side. That is not yet the case.
5. I thank Alexander Wendt for this descriptor.
6. With the exception of writings that are *about* quantum issues or the quantum IR moment, which are important voices in the debates around quantum IR, but not quantum per se. See Allan (2018), Grove (2020), Jackson (2016), Smith (2020), etc.
7. That it is less a rejection of the idea and more a matter of interests lying elsewhere is perhaps hinted at in a later work's preface, where they state: "A researcher applying the methods of quantum theory to, e.g., cognition need not search for quantum physical processes which might lead to the appearance of quantum-like features in behavior. The quantum formalism is treated as an operational formalism describing outputs of possible measurements.... Of course, this approach does not exclude the possibility that quantum physics is involved in some way into the generation of quantum-like behavior" (Haven & Khrennikov 2018, v).
8. This is not, of course, to accuse all actor-network theory scholars of rejecting structural forces as a matter of politics, but only that the price for considering such forces is sacrificing the ontological consistency of the conceptual framework.
9. Or, unfortunately, continued gatekeeping due to the narcissism of minor differences, skepticism of physics envy, or another factor.
10. While ultimately skeptical of the project, Kathryn Schaffer and Gabriela Barreto Lemos describe this kind of approach as one that concludes that "quantum physics changes 'everything,' because it tells us that the universe does not respect the basic preconceptions about reality that we develop as inhabitants of the macroscopic realm" (2021, 22).
11. These approaches to quantized critique would be particularly interesting to critical IR scholars who adhere to a definition of "critical IR" where the political project figures more prominently.

Bibliography

Albert, Mathias, and Felix Maximillian Bathon. 2020. "Quantum and Systems Theory in World Society: Not Brothers and Sisters but Relatives Still?" *Security Dialogue* 51(5): 434–449.
Allan, Bentley B. 2018. "Social Action in Quantum Social Science." *Millennium: Journal of International Studies* 47(1): 87–98.
Arfi, Badredine. 2005. "Resolving the Trust Predicament: A Quantum Game-Theoretic Approach." *Theory & Decision* 59: 127–274.
Austin, Jonathan Luke. 2019. "A Parasitic Critique for International Relations." *International Political Sociology* 13: 215–231.
Austin, Jonathan Luke, Rocco Bellanova, and Mareile Kaufmann. 2019. "Doing and Mediating Critique: An Invitation to Practice Companionship." *Security Dialogue* 50(1): 3–19.
Barad, Karen. 2007. *Meeting the Universe Halfway: The Entanglement of Matter and Meaning.* Durham, NC: Duke University Press.

Barad, Karen. 2011. "Nature's Queer Performativity." *Qui Parle* 19(2): 121–158.

Barad, Karen. 2012. "On Touching—The Inhuman That Therefore I Am." *differences* 23(3): 206–223.

Bowman, Norah. 2021. "Here/There/Everywhere: Quantum Models for Decolonizing Canadian State Onto-Epistemology." *Foundations of Science* 26(1): 171–186.

Bull, Hedley. 1966. "International Theory: The Case for a Classical Approach." *World Politics* 18(3): 361–377.

Busemeyer, Jerome R., and Peter D. Bruza. 2012. *Quantum Models of Cognition and Decision.* New York: Cambridge University Press.

Callon, Michel. 1986. "Some Elements of a Sociology of Translation: Domestication of the Scallops and the Fisherman of St. Brieuc Bay." In: *Power, Action, and Belief: A New Sociology of Knowledge?*, ed. John Law. London: Routledge, 196–223.

Callon, Michel, and Bruno Latour. 1981. "Unscrewing the Big Leviathan: How Actors Macro-Structure Reality and How Sociologists Help Them to Do It." In: *Advances in Social Theory and Methodology: Toward an Integration of Micro- and Macro-Sociologies*, eds. K. Knorr-Cetina and A. V. Circouel. London: Routledge & Kegan Paul, 287–313.

Cohn, Carol. 1987. "Sex and Death in the Rational World of Defense Intellectuals." *Signs* 12(4): 687–718.

Cox, Robert W. 1981. "Social Forces, States, and World Orders: Beyond International Relations Theory." *Millennium: Journal of International Studies* 10(2): 126–155.

Der Derian, James. 2011. "Quantum Diplomacy, German—US Relations, and the Psychogeography of Berlin." *Hague Journal of Diplomacy* 6: 373–392.

Der Derian, James. 2013. "From War 2.0 to Quantum War: The Superpositionality of Global Violence." *Australian Journal of International Affairs* 67(5): 570–585.

Der Derian, James. 2019. "A Quantum of Insecurity." *New Perspectives: Interdisciplinary Journal of Central & East European Politics and International Relations* 27(2): 13–27.

Der Derian, James, and Alexander Wendt. 2020. "'Quantizing International Relations': The Case for Quantum Approaches to International Theory and Security Practice." *Security Dialogue* 51(5): 399–415.

Fierke, K. M. 2019. "*Contraria sunt complementa*: Global Entanglement and the Constitution of Difference." *International Studies Review* 21(1): 146–169.

Fierke, K. M., and Francisco Antonio-Alfonso. 2018. "Language, Entanglement, and the New Silk Roads." *Asian Journal of Comparative Politics* 3(3): 194–1206.

Fierke, K. M., and Nicola Mackay. 2020. "'To See' Is to Break an Entanglement: Quantum Measurement, Trauma, and Security." *Security Dialogue* 51(5): 450–466.

Grove, Jairus. 2020. "Bringing the World Back In: Revolutions and Relations before and after the Quantum Event." *Security Dialogue* 51(5): 414–433.

Hanauske, Matthias, Jennifer Kunz, Steffen Bernius, and Wolfgang Konig. 2010. "Doves and Hawks in Economics Revisited: An Evolutionary Quantum Game Theory Based Analysis of Financial Crises." *Physica A* 389: 5084–5102.

Haven, Emmanuel, and Andrei Khrennikov. 2013. *Quantum Social Science.* New York: Cambridge University Press.

Haven, Emmanuel, and Andrei Khrennikov. 2018. *The Palgrave Handbook of Quantum Models in Social Science: Applications and Grand Challenges.* London: Palgrave Macmillan.

Hoffman, Mark. 1987. "Critical Theory and the Inter-Paradigm Debate." *Millennium: Journal of International Studies* 16(2): 231–250.

Huysmans, Jef, and Joao P. Nogueira. 2021. "International Political Sociology as a Mode of Critique: Fracturing Totalities." *International Political Sociology* 15(1): 2–21.

Hynek, Nik, and David Chandler. 2013. "No Emancipatory Alternative, No Critical Security Studies." *Critical Studies on Security* 1(1): 46–63.

Jackson, Patrick Thaddeus. 2016. "Fundamental Grounding." *Perspectives on Politics* 14(4): 1153–1157.

Khrennikov, Andrei. 2010. *Ubiquitous Quantum Structure: From Psychology to Finance.* Heidelberg: Springer.

Khrennikov, Andrei. 2018. "Social Laser Model: From Color Revolutions to Brexit and Election of Donald Trump." *Kybernetes* 47(2): 273–288.

Kuhn, Thomas S. 2012. *The Structure of Scientific Revolutions,* 50th Anniversary Edition. Chicago: University of Chicago Press.

Latour, Bruno. 1987. *Science in Action: How to Follow Scientists and Engineers Through Society.* Cambridge, MA: Harvard University Press.

Latour, Bruno, and Steve Woolgar. 1986. *Laboratory Life: The Construction of Scientific Facts,* 2nd Edition. Princeton, NJ: Princeton University Press.

McIntosh, Chris. 2021. "Writing Quantum Entanglement into International Relations: Temporality, Positionality, and the Ontology of War." *Millennium: Journal of International Studies* 49(1): 162–174.

Murphy, Michael P. A. 2021a. "Exploring the Crossroads of Critical and Quantum Thinking: An Introduction to the Forum." *Millennium: Journal of International Studies* 49(1): 117–125.

Murphy, Michael P. A. 2021b. "Quantising Post-Critique: Entangled Ontologies and Critical International Relations." *Millennium: Journal of International Studies* 49(1): 175–185.

Murphy, Michael P. A. 2021c. *Quantum Social Theory for Critical International Relations Theorists: Quantizing Critique.* London: Palgrave Macmillan.

Noxolo, Patricia. 2020. "I Am Becoming My Mother: (Post)Diaspora, Local Entanglements, and Entangled Locals." *African and Black Diaspora: An International Journal* 13(2): 134–146.

Noxolo, Patricia, and Marika Preziuso. 2012. "Moving Matter: Language in Caribbean Literature as Translation between Dynamic Forms of Matter." *Interventions: International Journal of Postcolonial Studies* 14(1): 120–135.

Orlando, Leonardo. 2020. "The Fabric of Agency: Navigating Human Potentialities through Introspection." *Security Dialogue* 51(5): 467–481.

Orrell, David. 2018. *Quantum Economics: The New Science of Money.* London: Icon.

Orrell, David. 2020. "The Value of Value: A Quantum Approach to Economics, Security, and International Relations." *Security Dialogue* 51(5): 482–498.

Pan, Chengxin. 2018. "Toward a New Relational Ontology in Global Politics: China's Rise as Holographic Transition." *International Relations of the Asia-Pacific* 18(3): 339–367.

Parry, Glenn Aparicio. 2006. "Native Wisdom in a Quantum World." *Shift* 9: 29–33.

Peat, F. David. 2002. *Blackfoot Physics: A Journey into the Native American Universe.* Boston: Weiser.

Piotrowski, Edward W., and Jan Sladkowski. 2004. "Quantum Games in Finance." *Quantitative Finance* 4(6): 61–67.

Prügl, Elisabeth. 2021. "The Gender Thing: Apparatuses and Intra-Agential Ethos." *Millennium: Journal of International Studies* 49(1): 140–150.

Rengger, Nicholas, and Ben Thirkell-White. 2007. "Introduction: Still Critical After All These Years? The Past, Present, and Future of Critical Theory in International Relations." *Review of International Studies* 33: 3–24.

Schaffer, Kathryn, and Gabriela Barreto Lemos. 2021. "Obliterating Thingness: An Introduction to the 'What' and the 'So What' of Quantum Physics." *Foundations of Science* 26(1): 7–26.

Sjoberg, Laura. 2021. "Quantum Ambivalence." *Millennium: Journal of International Studies* 49(1): 126–139.

Smith III, Frank L. 2020. "Quantum Technology Hype and National Security." *Security Dialogue* 51(5): 499–516.

Sylvester, Christine. 2007. "Whither the International at the End of IR." *Millennium: Journal of International Studies* 35(3): 551–573.

Sylvester, Christine. 2013. "Experiencing the End and Afterlives of International Relations/Theory." *European Journal of International Relations* 19(3): 609–626.

Wendt, Alexander. 2015. *Quantum Mind and Social Science: Unifying Physical and Social Ontology.* New York: Cambridge University Press.

Wendt, Alexander. n.d. "Quantum Theory as Critical Theory: Alienation, Entanglement, and the Politics of Social Physics." Unpublished manuscript.

Wyn Jones, Richard. 2001. Introduction to *Critical Theory and World Politics.* Boulder, CO: Lynne Rienner.

Yıldız-Alanbay, Şengül. 2020. "Posthumanist Perspectives on Causality, Agency, and Ethics in International Relations." *New Political Science* 42(2): 233–237.

Yıldız-Alanbay, Şengül. 2021. "The Matter of Affect in the Quantum Universe." *Millennium: Journal of International Studies* 49(1): 151–161.

Zanotti, Laura. 2017. "Reorienting IR: Ontological Entanglement: Agency, and Ethics." *International Studies Review* 19: 362–380.

Zanotti, Laura. 2019. *Ontological Entanglements, Agency, and Ethics in International Relations: Exploring the Crossroads.* London: Routledge.

Zanotti, Laura. 2021a. "A Response to the *Millennium* Forum." *Millennium: Journal of International Studies* 49(1): 186–193.

Zanotti, Laura. 2021b. "De-Colonizing the Political Ontology of Kantian Ethics: A Quantum Perspective." *Journal of International Political Theory* 17(3): 448–467.

Zohar, Danah. 1990. *The Quantum Self: Human Nature and Consciousness as Defined by the New Physics.* New York: Quill & William Morrow.

Zohar, Danah, and Ian Marshall. 1994. *The Quantum Society: Mind, Physics, and a New Social Vision.* New York: Quill & William Morrow.

13

Quantum Sovereignty + Entanglement

Mark B. Salter

Quantum theory provides a new lens through which to re-evaluate key assumptions about the mechanics of International Relations, starting with the assumption that the observer determines the phenomenon: it is only through observation that probabilistic wave functions collapse into particular states. Relationality or processualism, however much we might be sympathetic to the arguments of Jackson and Nexon (2019), preloads a separation between the entities that are relating. In the words of Bruno Latour: "whenever we talk of individual subjects that are supposed to engage in some sort of…relation [] whether you speak of a cell, a sheep, a worker, a nation, or an atom, the boundary that delineates its existence *before* it enters into relationships is its fortress…. [T]here is no question in this view of things that there first exists parts, and then interactions amongst those parts" (Latour 2016: 312),[1] whereas experimental evidence and theoretical explication from quantum mechanics demonstrate that *any* agency is a product of "intra-action" (Barad 2007: 136–137). If entities cannot be separated from each other or from the observer, this poses an enormous critical challenge to International Relations.

While one can appreciate the attempt to rationalize quantum theory within profoundly Newtonian International Relations theory, taking quantum seriously requires a much deeper reboot (Wendt 2015). Sovereignty, like Newtonian physics and Hobbes's politics, is the product of the long seventeenth century, which was profoundly concerned with the classification of political agency in terms of autonomy. In Bodin as in Hobbes, the international is always already part of the constitution of the sovereign, as the whole of which sovereigns are the part (Walker 2009).[2] The Hobbesian origins of thinking about sovereignty as an *inter-national* relation is also profoundly connected to historical conceptions of the Indigenous[3] and nature (Jahn 2000; Shaw 2008). When we challenge the Newtonian model of science, we must also challenge the Hobbesian model of sovereignty on the basis of "science" and the separation of science and politics (Latour 1993). "The Eurocentrism of International Relations is rooted in the alterities established with the 'discovery' of the 'New World,'" as Capan suggests, and *any* engagement with sovereignty must unpack that complicated history (2017: 3). A quantum sovereignty must be avowedly decolonial to symmetrically unpack Newtonian and Hobbesian assumptions about rule, authority, autonomy, facticity, and the role of human/nonhuman. But, as Latour so powerfully argues, "When anyone begins to speak of the relations inside which any entity is supposed to 'enter,' *it is too late*…to start with the interests of the nation-state and *then* try to see how it is 'influenced' by its global environment. The qualities that the relations bring to the entity were *there all along*, except that they had been cut off by the principle of *localisation*.… [T]o put it more starkly, an entity *plus* its relations remains a monster no matter what you do afterwards to retie it. International Relations always precede internal relations" (Latour 2016: 315–316).

Quantum sovereignty is not simply modeled as a series of nested binary relationships of sovereign and subject, sovereign and territory, Europeans and nature, Europeans and Indigenous peoples, or even as a set of relationships among sovereigns. Rather, quantum sovereignty must be modeled as an intra-active field of probabilities that are constantly being created and being collapsed. It is a common point among quantum theorists that these binaries are always already entangled with one another before being measured (Barad 2007; Kirby 2011; Zanotti 2019). Rather than focus on the creation and maintenance of boundaries, which has been an obsession of modern political theory and International Relations (Walker 2009), the quantum turn affirms that the relational connection already exists before the attempted dichotomization. As with quantum physics, we argue that the quantum model of sovereignty is not simply theoretically tighter than the Newtonian model but explains more empirical phenomena than can be captured or explained in traditional models. Rather than view sovereignty as "organized hypocrisy" (Krasner 1999) or a system that is populated by states and "quasi-states" (Jackson 1993), that is, as a series of hypocrisies, disjunctures, silences, or paradoxes to explain away, quantum sovereignty accepts that "sovereignty" is invoked and performed in an infinite number of ways and can exist in different modes in different places, and that connections between abstract discourses and specific practices are nonlocal and complex. The superpositionality of sovereignty is a feature of the international system, and not a bug.

Quantum sovereignty, then, is best understood also as a condition of superpositionality, a relationship of entanglement and a mechanism of measurement. Bordering decisions (inside/outside, member/outsider, legal/illegal, citizen/foreigner, ruler/subject) are multiple and in superposition until measured or tested, in which case the sovereign and its object collapse locally into one relation, and while those local relations may have spooky effects at a distance, they are nongeneralizable. The state is always testing its authority in relation to other states: the claim of territoriality is not made toward God, nature, or the universe, but toward other sovereigns. The migrant is in superposition before the border examination: inside and outside the jurisdiction of the state, until a decision is made about status, membership, or entry (Salter 2008; Fierke 2020). The truth of the crime is in superposition before the trial, and then a decision is made. The jurisdictional claim over a territory is in superposition before the adjudication, and the treaty is signed, or international action implies assent (Lyons 2010; Coulthard 2014; Salter 2019). The Indigenous person is in superposition before national membership is claimed and granted—or avoided (Simpson 2014; Nadasdy 2017). Before those states are measured, the land, the law, and the subject are multiplicitous and bound up in complementary and conflicting relations. Bowman was the first to successfully and compellingly demonstrate the application of these quantum concepts to Canadian-Indigenous governance (2021). What a theory of quantum sovereignty demonstrates, then, is a relational mode of analysis that focuses on the superpositionality of decisions and measurement devices—how multiple forms of territoriality, jurisdiction, membership, and conduct collapse into decisions of inclusion or exclusion in ways that are always mutually implicated. The measurement of territory implies jurisdiction, which then is interpellated with membership: the measurement of one of these aspects does not automatically resolve the other questions but brings their ontological relatedness into sharp focus.

While traditional theorizations of sovereignty are frequently formulated as if Indigenous peoples, laws, and lands were the unproblematic object of colonial governance, the quantum theory of entanglement illuminates how the performance of sovereign statehood by the provision of security is entangled with Indigenous conceptions of sovereignty and measured through particular mechanisms. Lyons and Rifkin both demonstrate empirically how European claims of sovereignty required Indigenous participation (Lyons 2010; Rifkin 2009). Todd warns that scholars too often "avoid engaging with contemporary Indigenous scholars and thinkers while [engaging] instead with eighty-year-old ethnographic texts or two-hundred-year-old philosophical tones" (2016: 8).

So, let us set out how one Inuit thinker has laid out a parallel critique of the Westphalian concept of sovereignty.[4] Qitsualik arrives at a similar critique of Western model sovereignty from an Inuit ontology. First, she critiques the lack of emphasis on the theological component of Westphalian sovereignty, in a way that excludes other cosmologies: "how can we possibly expect to find an accurate reflection—the truth of our species, whether repellent or majestic—via any device through which we hold ourselves apart and independent from the earth.... In truth, independence remains a concept alone, since we have yet to locate one independent phenomenon in our entire cosmos" (2013: 24). In her argument, Qitsualik demonstrates what Todd suggests, that Indigenous thinkers have active theorizations about more-than-human agency, the Anthropocene, and politics that exceeds the normal anthropological caricature. Within the official government English-French-Inuktitut dictionary, *aulatsignnarniq* would be transliterated as "the ability to make things move" (Qitsualik 2013: 26), which is of course appealing to Foucauldians (Salter 2019). Her more expansive definition, which pays attention to Inuit cosmology, notes, "sovereign, then, is *truth....* Inuit, who know the *Nuna* (Land) so well, cannot define sovereignty via mastery of their home, but rather of their hearts...sovereign over self, respectful of the self-sovereignty of others. It is the human whose awareness not only renders self-sovereignty possible, but comprehends how self-sovereignties—those of others in society—synergize towards a system of self-perpetuating health" (Qitsualik 2013: 32). Here is the active, competing model of sovereignty that Canadian sovereignty is interpellated by—both in the historical example that follows and in the contemporary period. A statist sovereignty that is concerned with jurisdiction over territory and population, with producing the truth via the mechanism of the court, and connected to the nation and the international is in active entanglement with an Inuit sovereignty that is concerned with the interdependence of humans and the land, who assume that the truth is not a choice but an individual duty (Flaherty 1988: 275), and about a relation between the self-mastery of the individual and the survival of the group. The first murder trials of Inuit under Canadian law demonstrate how a quantum sovereign connection between law and subject is always collapsed by the measurement apparatus of the court, and how Canadian and Indigenous conceptions of sovereignty are profoundly entangled.

We focus on Canadian sovereignty in relation to the Inuit because of its important liminality: sovereign boundaries are continually asserted, tested, and defended on land, at sea, in relation to other states, in relation to Indigenous peoples, and in relation to its own capacity, particularly in this early period before state consolidation in the mid-twentieth century. The weak Canadian claims to Arctic sovereignty were not thought to be accepted by the international community well into the mid-twentieth century (Grant 2010). Inuit themselves had a radically different lifeworld and relation to the land, and were nomadic until forced into settlements in the 1950s. This leads to radically different theories of Inuit sovereignty (Qitsualik 2013). Because there was no treaty with a precontact polity (like the numbered treaties, 1871–1921), Inuit have always been understood as Canadian citizens but were not given the right to vote until 1951 and were enfolded slowly and differentially into the welfare state (Stephenson 2014).

We focus here on two murder trials: the 1917 trial of Sinnisiak and Uluksuk and the 1923 trial of Nuqallaq. In each of these cases, the claim of the Canadian state to be sovereign over the territory and the people of the Arctic was measured by a court trial that collapses the multiple political potentialities into a series of decisions. The quantum correction is absolutely necessary because dominant representations of Arctic sovereignty assume that the primary audience for

Canadian claims is (1) other states, like Russia, the United States, or Denmark, but that the object of that assertion is always (2) domestic actors—as if the domestic and the international were distinct and separate (Zellen 2009; Christie 2011). However, these early assertions of Canadian sovereignty over Arctic spaces and Arctic peoples, which is happening at precisely the same historical moment as the development of early quantum theory, demonstrate the degree to which the Indigenous, the "national," and the international audiences for these decisions are always already entangled.

Kirby makes the point that both quantum theorists and poststructuralists share a similar disposition. "What binds all of us is a sense that the way the world works isn't at all straightforward, and that counterintuitive approaches to questions about communication between senders and receivers, or more comprehensively, individuals of whatever sort, whether atoms, measuring instruments, human subjects—'phenomena' more generally—might have more explanatory power than what seems unequivocally and banally self-evident" (2011: 76). In this project, we are going to stay with the trouble. Rather than parse all of quantum theory and its variants (Wendt 2015; Murphy 2021), for the purposes of this chapter, I will focus on the concepts of entanglement. Bowman sets out clearly: "Quantum phenomenon such as superposition (in which a particle exists simultaneously in two distinct forms until it is observed, at which point it collapses into one of such forms; an entangled state (superposition of two or more possibilities for a composite entity); and non-locality (the entanglement effects of an entangled state) are not ontological *metaphors*" (2021: 178). Entanglement and superpositionality are physical and social phenomena, in no small part because the social is always already the material in terms of either language, discourse, concretized relations (like Callon and Latour's black boxes), or simply neurological patterns in the minds of the humans engaged in that society (Wendt 2015). "Entanglement suggests that the very ontology of the entities emerges through relationality: the entities do not pre-exist their involvement" (Kirby 2011: 76). Or, as Barad describes it: "to be entangled is not simply to be intertwined with another, as in the joining of separate entities, but to lack an independent, self-contained existence" (Barad 2007: ix).

Quantum Politics

We want to make a strong argument here for a quantized International Relation (IR). Decisions are the quanta of politics—that which cannot be further decided. Symbolic, cultural, political, and economic capital must be understood as wave functions, defined fields of possibility, which collapse into individual decisions. While decisions are discrete, the systems in which they exist as concretized moments of potential remain entangled with all other possible decisions and all other systems. One of the most productive models of contemporary sovereignty has been the extensions of social theory, particularly feminist and queer theories, on the notion of performativity, that identities are never constructed from whole cloth but rather are iteratively and interactively created by individual and society, sovereign and subject. We seek entangled sovereignty as it emerges as one particular set of relations, that is, all of those coordinated and uncoordinated moments in which the notion of sovereignty (independence, authority, control, stewardship, management) is invoked to create relations, create knowledge, and draw boundaries—in short, to structure the conditions of possibility for particular forms of life. This means dispensing with scales of analysis, much as the actor-network theorists before us have done. The concept of the state has been a methodological liability of political science since inception as a distinct social science, and doubly so for IR. The field of IR asserts that sovereign politics are fundamentally different than other kinds of politics. At base, the argument put forward by Walker is that the institution of sovereignty separates inside from outside and consequently defines a realm of law and realm of anarchy, which certainly benefits particular power structures and makes some transboundary political projects impossible. The "borders, boundaries, and limits" of states become the same borders, boundaries, and limits of politics itself and the possibility of the good life (Walker 2009). By accepting this frame, the ontology of sovereignty is always pregiven: it is the sine qua non of any other political virtues. Without independence, equality, and noninterference (at least formally), there can be no situation in which peace is possible, even though peace is not guaranteed between sovereign states because of the anarchical quality of the relations between juridically equal states. This predisposition toward "the state" blinds analysts to the multiple invocations of sovereignty and its accordant values of independence, authority, control, stewardship, and management.

This is why so much important theorizing about actual global politics comes from sociologists, and particularly international political sociologists, who investigate really existing relations among actors and agencies, crisscrossing, hopping, or ignoring state boundaries and institutions. What any micro-level analysis will illustrate is that there are no clear, perfect, pregiven boundaries (between states, between nations, between cultures, between individuals, between particles, between objects, between ideas). There are only diffractions— the intra-action of decisions causing amplification and nullification, creating never-clear insides and outsides—that are never pregiven and always intra-active, and always constituting both sides of the line at once, while drawing the line as a suture, dividing and connecting at once (Barad 2007: 148). As we see in quantum behavior, there are no absolute boundaries, only diffractions. If, at that core level, there are no boundaries, no limits, no borders, then we must ask how borders come to matter—in both senses of the term. This to me is the essence of sovereignty: bordering—to decide through the ban what counts as inside and what counts as outside—not as a line or a chasm, but as a suture, as a diffraction. Sovereignty, then, is constituted by decisions—the quanta of politics, but as a particular set of decisions to describe limits.

Bowman makes an empirical and ontological critique of Canadian "settler-colonial state epistemology" that "systematically ignores Indigenous testimony about land, oil, water, economics, health and nationhood....Indigenous knowledge of a living, entangled world has been rejected by a state wedded to a notion of a deterministic world" (2021: 172). In addition to demonstrating the way that Canadian settler-colonial state epistemology is wedded to a Newtonian, deterministic ontology that is politically problematic, she makes a claim that because the Indigenous epistemology is inherently more plural and open, "Indigenous knowledge systems can successfully accommodate western deterministic science and Indigenous onto-epistemologies that allow for entanglement and superposition; the settler-colonial Canadian state does not accommodate such complementarity" (Bowman 2021: 174). In this, as with quantum mechanics itself—which demonstrates its value added by explaining more than traditional Newtonian physics—Bowman claims that Indigenous knowledge systems can explain more than Canadian settler-colonial state epistemology.

We see this Indigenous perspicacity when applied to sovereignty itself. The 2009 Inuit Circumpolar Council's declaration of sovereignty demonstrates that the quantum view of sovereignty is much more robust and precise than a realist or Newtonian view. The declaration of sovereignty is couched in contemporary debates about sovereignty. Art. 2.1 declares: " 'Sovereignty' is a term that has often been used to refer to the absolute and independent authority of a community or state both internally and externally. Sovereignty is a contested concept, however, and does not have a fixed meaning. Old ideas of sovereignty are breaking down as different governance models, such as the European Union, evolve. Sovereignty overlap and are frequently divided within federations in creative ways to recognize the right of peoples." But it is in the assertion of principles that I find the most leverage of those notions of entanglement between semiotic and material contexts, the intersubjectivity of boundary claims, and the indeterminacy of decisions. They start by asserting multiple justifications for a claim of sovereignty that is irreducible to a state's authority:

Art. 1.1 Inuit live in the Arctic.
  Art. 1.2 Inuit have been living in the Arctic from time immemorial. Our use and occupation of the Arctic Islands and waters predates recorded history.
  Art. 1.3 Inuit are a people....[A]s a people we enjoy the rights of all peoples.

Art. 1.4 Inuit are an indigenous people with rights and responsibilities of all indigenous peoples. These include the rights recognized in and by the international legal and political instruments and bodies.... [S]tates are required to respect and promote the realization of our right to self-determination.

Art. 1.6 Inuit are citizens of Arctic states.

Art. 1.7 Inuit are indigenous citizens of Arctic states.

These multiple, overlapping, and material claims to a multiplicitous sovereignty, sometimes autonomy, sometimes responsibility and stewardship, sometimes united, and sometimes multiple, have profound international ecological and legal entanglements. Quantum sovereign claims are not just being made by political scientists for us to apply and evaluate; Indigenous thinkers are bending the rules of politics to demonstrate that sovereignty itself derives its meaning from measurement. Indigenous and Canadian sovereignties were entangled: they were separately unmeasurable. Inuit and qallunaat[5] justice spin in opposite directions, much like entangled particles when measured: collective survival vs. individual rights, consensus-based conflict avoidances vs. adversarial representation, focus on harmony and balance vs. focus on agonism and punishment. Historically, the thin British legal claims to dominion over the Arctic were transferred to the new Canadian state, claims that were dependent on Inuit use and occupation—but the Inuit themselves did not necessarily accede to the larger territorial claims made about their land. The Inuit notion of Nula (land) simply does not comprehend ownership over the land, but rather dependence on it, and so the originary claims about territory, citizenship, and belonging were not interpreted in the same frame as sovereignty, or self-mastery and group survival (Qitsualik 2013). Functionaries of the Canadian state were anxious to demonstrate sovereignty—primarily to an international audience, because of an interpretation of international legal doctrine that the Canadian claim to the High Arctic would not stand up in international law, because the state had not demonstrated occupation (Grant 2002: 96), but also to the Inuit, who did not have a framework for parsing this geopolitical order (and did not have the inclination to do so).[6]

A crucial part of the Inuit story is precisely the fact that Inuit have survived in the harsh Arctic "since time immemorial" based on traditional knowledge (Inuit quajimajatuqangit: "that which Inuit have always known to be true") (Karetak and Tester 2017). Thus, the Inuit theories of justice, of sovereignty, and of conflict resolution had a great deal of authority, and radically different ontology. Inuit maligarjuat ("big things that must be followed") is composed of four principles: "1. working for the common good and not being motivated by personal interest or gain; 2. Living in respectful relationships with every person and thing that one encounters; 3. Maintaining harmony and balance; and 4. Planning and preparing for the future" (Karetak and Tester 2017: 3). Given the success of *maligarjuat* in sustaining life in the harsh Arctic, the Canadian government's claim to sovereignty had to work hard to explain the need for change. The Canadian government's claim to sovereignty was entangled with the Inuit claim to permanent occupation, but that appropriation of not just territory but also time would only function when measured if there could be evidence that the Canadian state now had authority over the Inuit.

Performing Sovereignty through Murder

The questions of violence, law, and order, then, became central to demonstrating Canadian sovereignty (Morrison 1986). "The significant purpose of police activities and eventual trials was the symbolic assertion of control over native people that it represented.... [N]orth of the 60th parallel, the North West Mounted Police were (and for long years thereafter remained) the only effective or even visible arm of the government" (Schuh 1979: 14). Inuit, thus, are intimately entangled with a community of sovereigns (the international audience for a demonstration of effective occupation and control over the Arctic) and an alternate understanding of violence, law, and order embedded in Inuit thought (an opportunity to demonstrate the "civilized" nature of Canadian/British justice) (Cameron 2015). The two trials of Sinnisiak and Uluksuk in 1917 and of Nuqallaq in 1923 became signal machines for measuring and testing those entangled sovereignties.[7]

Both trials illustrate competing ontologies of sovereignty, order, and justice. For Inuit, the survival of the collective is paramount, and individuals are "insane" if they cannot demonstrate self-mastery and show respect for the survival of the group, and the insane must be killed. The decision to remove the dangerous person is made collectively, and the responsibility is shared by the community. Grant summarizes: "If an Inuk's actions became deviant and menaced others, and if that individual did not respond to other means of control [counseling, derision, gossip, and public confession], then he or she was considered to be insane, providing just cause that his or her life be terminated" (Grant 2002: 19). Inuit political thought, in this sense, differs greatly from Foucault's model of discipline, or the biopolitical sovereign who "made die and let live" or biopower's schema "to make live and let die." This is also a much different discourse of sovereignty than the Canadians were actively trying to promote, which entailed obedience to the king's law and visibility of punishment (Grant 2002: 49). We can, in fact, point to the very moment that the Inuit of Pond Inlet were first told about their new status as Canadians, and the assertion of sovereignty over them. In 1906, as part of the first official government expedition to claim sovereignty over the Arctic Archipelago, Cpt. Bernier wintered at Pond Inlet, hosted a Christmas dinner for 120 Inuit, and informed them of the new dominion.[8] He recounts his tale to an Ottawa audience: "In annexing those lands we have annexed probably in the neighborhood of [a] thousand Esquimaux....I told them that they had become Canadians and therefore they were subject to our laws. Well they could not see that, but I tell you they saw it when they came on board my vessel to a dinner to which I had invited them, and they had everything they wanted, and then they commenced to realize that it was a good thing to be a Canadian" (Harper 2017: 29). The mere assertion of annexation of the Inuit is, unsurprisingly, not compelling in the moment, but, in that demonstration, Inuit and Canadian notions of sovereignty are entangled with one another (and of course of notions of hospitality, welfare, and survival). Bernier attempts to link the assertion of Canadian sovereignty over territory (proclamations buried in stone cairns across the archipelago) to obedience to a unpromulgated and unfamiliar law. This is later reinforced in a 1925 poster, which demonstrates how much work must be done to explain the monopoly of legitimate violence:

Know Ye The King of the Land commands you, saying "THOU SHALT DO NO MURDER." Why does he speak thus? Long ago our God made the world and He owns the world. The people He also made, and He owns them. The King of the land is commanded by God to protect the people well. The white people and Indians and Eskimos have him for their ruler. He is their ruler, therefore he commands saying "THOU SHALT DO NO MURDER." But if a man kills a man, the King sends his servants, the police, to take and kill the murderer. But ye do not kill the murderer, nor cause him to be killed. This only the King's servants, the police, ought to do. But when a man commits murder, at once they tell the King's servants, the police, and they will take and bind the murderer and the ruler will judge him. Thus our God commands us so that you are to follow the King's command. (Harper 2017: 318; Grant 2002: 226)

Political theologians will no doubt delight in the clear cosmology of divine right that permeates this reading—but it is also clear that the proscriptions of violence and the sketches of procedural justice are in clear dialogue with what the authors (Royal Canadian Mounted Police [RCMP]) understood to be Inuit senses of justice. We will parse the two cases to follow as mechanisms for measuring the quantum sovereignty in the Arctic.

1917: Sinnisiak and Uluksuk

In the fall of 1913, Sinnisiak and Uluksuk killed two Catholic priests who were sent to proselytize the Inuit in the North West Territories. Neither Fr. Rouvière nor Fr. Le Roux could speak any Inuktitut and were unprepared for survival in the Arctic. After a dispute over the ownership of one of their two guns with a local village, the two priests fled into a snowstorm. Sinnisiak and Uluksuk followed them, purportedly to assist another family on the same trail, and caught up with the priests, who offered the Inuit hunters animal traps in exchange for assistance. The two Inuit built an igloo for the night, but in the morning, the priests forced the two Inuit at gunpoint to physically haul their sled through the deep snow. After hours of threats, Sinnisiak tricked Le Roux and stabbed him in the back, then used the rifle to shoot the fleeing Rouvière. Given the remoteness of the community and the event, the crime was not discovered until 1914, and due to the incredible difficulty of investigation, the two Inuit were not apprehended until 1916. The first trial of Sinnisiak alone ended with a not-guilty verdict, and so, the same judge and prosecutor transferred the case from Edmonton to Calgary, a new jury was selected, and both Sinnisiak and Uluksuk were retried. The judge's instructions were clear: the jury must find them guilty—they have confessed to the act, but the jury should be reassured that the accused will not receive the mandatory death sentence. The dual performance of punishment and mercy produced a guilty verdict and a sentence of life imprisonment. However, since there were no prisons in the North, the two were released within three years and hired by the RCMP themselves as guides, becoming in time special constables.

There is no doubt that in addition to the individual guilt of the two Inuit, Sinnisiak and Uluksuk in the strict sense, the participants in the 1917 trial understood themselves to be making a wider case for *qallunaat* sovereignty itself. As the Crown prosecutor sets out in his opening statement:

> These remote savages, really cannibals, the Eskimo of the Arctic have got to be taught to recognize the authority of the British Crown, and that the authority of the Crown and of the Dominion of Canada, of which these countries are a part, extends to the furthermost limits of the frozen North. It is necessary that they should understand that they are *under the Law*...that they must regulate their lives and dealings with their fellow men, of whatever race, white men or Indians, according to, at least, the main outstanding principles of that law, which is part of the law of civilization. This is one of the outstanding ideas of the Government, and the great importance of this trial lies in this: that for the first time in history these people, these Arctic people, pre-historic people, people who are as nearly as possible living today in the Stone Age, will be brought in contact with and will be taught what is whiteman's justice (Moyles 1979: 9).

Despite a goal of demonstrating sovereign power over Inuit peoples, the need for a second trial, the need for prebaked clemency, and the inefficacy of the actual

punishment led the Inuit themselves to be confounded by the lesson. As one po-
liceman reported of their return home, the object lesson of these murderers was
not convincing: "they came back with rifles, ammunition, trunks full of white
man's clothing and enough pale-faced cussedness to high-hat the rest of the
tribe. Now they're big men among the natives and some of the others think all
they've got to do to have a good time is to stick a knife in someone" (Moyles
1979: 88). While the *qallunaat* and Inuit theories of justice are entangled, the
comparative weakness at the heart of the Canadian justice system was measured
in this trial. Between the two entangled senses of justice, *qallunaat* sovereignty
was not found in the measurement of this case. To understand these trials as
simply the messy and incomplete imposition of sovereign law over Indigenous
peoples and territory misses the point: Inuit notions of justice and sovereignty
persisted in that community, and they did not understand themselves to be
under the *qallunaat* law.

1923: Nuqallaq

Nuqallaq killed *qallunaat* fur trader Robert Janes on March 15, 1920, on the
ice of Admiralty Inlet, Baffin Island. While Janes had Arctic experience and
spoke some Inuktitut (although he required a translator), after a series of un-
successful seasons he was desperate to return south. While historically an ag-
gressive man who had previously threatened to shoot Inuit trading partners, he
was totally hopeless when the Inuit at the camp near Cape Crauford collectively
decided to hide Janes's gun and all go hunting (a strategy of conflict avoidance).
He threatened to kill the Inuit at the camp and their dogs unless they provided
him furs (to buy passage south) and sled dogs (to go to Igloolik, where he might
find a boat), and so the group came together and agreed that he must be killed.
Nuqallaq agreed with the group and shot Janes three times. The rest of the group
gave Nuqallaq furs and other tokens of their appreciation. While Janes's body
was buried, his personal possessions were taken back to the trading post, and the
Hudson's Bay trader then communicated the crime down south. A sole police
officer was sent to investigate, conduct a coroner's inquiry, and then act as justice
of the peace to charge the responsible—a literal one-man show of sovereignty
and justice. He arrested three Inuit, but only Nuqallaq, who pulled the trigger,
was found guilty. As part of the assertion of sovereignty, the RCMP and the
government felt a trial was a necessary sign of occupation and a necessary machine of colonization. The formalities of the court seemed out of place in Pond
Inlet: starched collars and long black robes, a francophone jury from the government ship, and RCMP dressed in scarlet uniforms unsuited for the weather. The
gathered Inuit had no lexicon to read these cultural signs of authority, and many

understood that the audience might all be killed if found guilty by the judge. The Canadian government was extremely concerned about competing international territorial claims in the Arctic at this moment: American commercial expansion, an atlas that represented Alaska and the Canadian Arctic in the same color, Norway's exploration of the Sverdrup islands, and Danish/Greenlandic Inuit hunting on Ellesmere Island. The RCMP commissioner argued for police stations throughout the High Arctic, including Pond Inlet, that would be able to investigate this particular murder, conduct "administrative acts to confirm authority and possession over that territory," and surveil the activities of the Americans and Danish (Grant 2002: 96–98).

When given the verdict, it was not immediately clear that Nuqallaq or any of the other Inuit understood the lesson of justice and punishment. He was told he would be taken south where he would be housed, fed, clothed, and kept warm without needing to hunt. The Inuit were relieved that neither Nuqallaq nor the rest of the crowd gathered would be killed. The lesson of *qallunaat* justice was lost on the perpetrator and his community. Nuqallaq served his sentence in a special prison in Winnipeg reserved for Indigenous peoples and new immigrants, where he contracted tuberculosis. In a similar demonstration of "clemency" to the other case, Nuqallaq was returned to Pond Inlet, despite his known, active case of tuberculosis. Community spread was almost immediate, and a public health crisis emerged that persists to this day (Stephenson 2014). The sovereign urge to enact bodily punishment on the individual resulted in the epidemiological decimation of Inuit on Baffin Island.

Frontier Justice

In both cases, we see Inuit expressing this notion of the murdered men failing to demonstrate self-mastery (threatening to kill in anger), the failure to live in harmony with the land (in both cases being unequipped or ill-prepared to survive), and the failure to respect the self-mastery of others in the group (Frs. Rouvière and Le Roux treating Sinnisiak and Uluksuk as draught animals and forcing them to pull their sled at gunpoint; Janes threatening to kill the dogs and the men if he was not given furs and supplies). This Inuit understanding was well understood by Inuit and Canadian police alike. "Nuqallaq believed he had done no wrong. He had accepted the responsibility conferred on him by other hunters and believed that he had saved the camp from possible starvation" (Grant 2002: 89). In both cases, the performative nature of the judicial sentence was the primary point for the Canadian actors, not the particular crime. It was important to the prosecutors that the Inuit be found guilty, but also that they *not* be punished according to the law. Sinnisiak and Uluksuk's prosecutor made this point: "my instructions had made it quite clear that the Government had not the slightest intention, if the prisoners were found guilty of murder, of allowing the death penalty to be carried into effect" (Moyles 1979: 37). Nuqallaq's prosecutor makes the same kind of case. Grant concludes, "Mr. Falardeau for the prosecution was similarly sympathetic in his summation, stating that 'in civilization, he would ask for a verdict of murder,' but because of 'the ignorance of the prisoners,' he recommended that a conviction be entered for manslaughter. He also informed the *qallunaat* jury 'that they could, if they desired, recommend the accuseds to the clemency of the court'" (Grant 2002: 176). Thus, the administration of local justice, which would demonstrate nonlocally (internationally) that Canada was exercising jurisdiction, required a necessary accommodation of Inuit notions of justice, order, and responsibility.

Grant and Harper's admirable histories of Nuqallaq's murder trial at Pond Inlet balance Canadian historical, written archives with Inuit oral histories, leading to a complex, symmetrical story of colonial justice. In each history, Inuit experiences are given as much ontological weight as the formal bureaucratic record, demonstrating how to undo the tendency of the settler-colonial state to discount Indigenous ways of knowing. However, the model for sovereignty in both of these historical works is entirely Westphalian and unproblematized, and the encounter is portrayed as a solid Inuit culture meeting a solid *qallunaat* culture (see also Grant 2010). Both Grant and Harper are careful to frame Inuit notions of justice with the complicated performance of the Canadian judicial process, but they also fall into the trap of assuming a separation between the two—that Canadian justice and Inuit justice are pre-existing parts that come into contact, in which Canadian justice "wins" the controversy. As Bowman argues, "Western legal testimony is structured so as to recognize the metaphysics of monads; individuals presenting evidence deemed credible by external measurement, rather than collective knowledge, shared across time and space, a priori entangled," and as such "these negative epistemic biases eliminate potential for Indigenous testimonial credibility to be heard *as such*" (Bowman 2021: 184).

A quantum sovereignty frame provides more analytical leverage and does not presume the strength of the settler-colonialists because of the post facto success of Canadian colonialism. Inuit justice had been operating in a relatively stable way for hundreds of years, based on a radically different model of balanced individual and collective responsibility, conflict avoidance, consensus-based decision-making, and a relationship to the other-than-human (*Nula*: the land). Canadian justice needed to prove itself as superior, inevitable, and true and profoundly failed in its enactment on its own terms, and on Inuit terms. As Flaherty points out, the trials demonstrated to the Inuit that telling the truth or lying was a choice—rather than being a moral duty and survival strategy (1988). The court worked precisely opposite to that Foucauldian frame as a truth machine: it worked to create the possibility of lies. But, from the *qallunaat* perspective, the trials were successful in both arriving at "truth" and demonstrating judgment, fairness, punishment, and mercy. The very content of sovereignty—jurisdiction and authority—was understood very differently from Inuit and *qallunaat* observers.

Some Indigenous theorists like Alfred caution that "in making a claim to sovereignty—even if they don't really mean it [Indigenous politicians] are making a choice to accept the state as their model and to allow indigenous political goals to be framed and evaluated according to a 'statist' pattern. Thus, the common criteria of statehood—coercive force, control of a territory, population numbers, international recognition—come to dominate discussion of indigenous peoples' political goals as well. This is not only a movement away from traditional indigenous philosophies, but transparently disingenuous in terms of the sovereignty model itself" (Alfred 2006: 323). But Inuit themselves are again directly contesting the statist view of sovereignty. As we argued earlier, the 2009 Inuit Circumpolar Council's declaration of sovereignty demonstrates that the quantum view of sovereignty is much more capacious and accommodating than a realist or Newtonian view. Inuit elder Aupilarjuk makes a similar point: "*Taakua katikpanik sannginiqarniqsauqquu'migjugat*," which McGrath translates as "If both (Inuit and *qullunaat*) ways were brought together we would possibly have more strength" (McGrath 2018: 198–199). Quantum sovereign claims are not just being made by political scientists for us to apply and evaluate; Indigenous thinkers are bending the rules of politics to demonstrate that sovereignty itself derives its meaning from measurement.

Acknowledgments

My thanks to James Der Derian and Alexander Wendt for inclusion in this long-term project. Versions of this argument have been presented at the International Studies Association, the Q Project, the Mershon Center of International Security Studies, and the Millennium Conference. My specific thanks to Michael Murphy, Nisha Shah, and Jairus Grove for their critical engagements with this slow-gestating project.

Notes

1. Kirby (2011) engages critically with Latour on the question of binarism (chap. 4).
2. "Wherefore let this be the first and chief mark of a sovereign prince, to be of power to give laws to all his subjects in general, and to every one of them in particular, (yet is not that enough, but that we must join thereunto) without consent of any other greater, equal, or lesser than himself" (Bodin 1962: 159).

3. In the Canadian context, Indigenous peoples refer to First Nations, Métis, and Inuit peoples.
4. Inuit refer to those Indigenous people who inhabit Inuit Nunagat. Historically referred to as Eskimo or Esquimaux, Inuit comprise those who live or have historically lived in Inuvialuit, Nunavut, Nunvaik, and Nunatsiavut. Following convention, Inuit will be used except in historical sources; Inuktitut words will be italicized.
5. *Qallunaat* is the Inuktitut word for white people.
6. See Zacharias Kunuk's 2019 *One Day in the Life of Noah Piugattak* (Isuma) for a cinematic portrayal of that moment.
7. One could also point to the trial of Tatamigana at Herschel Island in 1923, which involves the prosecution of an Inuit for the murder of other Inuit, which follows the same narrative as Nuqallaq (Komar 2019: 85–93). Previous murders were identified by the Northwest Mounted Police in 1903 but not prosecuted (Schuh 1979: 6–7).
8. Bernier returned to Ottawa and requested from the government 960 acres of land at Pond Inlet, making him the first and only private land owner on Baffin Island (the fifth largest island in the world) (Harper 2017: 30).

References

Alfred, Gerald Taiaiake. 2006. Sovereignty—an inappropriate concept. In *The Indigenous Experience: Global Perspectives*, Roger Maaka and Chris Anderson, eds. Toronto: Canadian Scholar's Press: 322–336.

Barad, Karen. 2007. *Meeting the Universe Halfway: Quantum Physics and the Entanglement of Matter and Meaning*. Durham, NC: Duke University Press.

Bodin, Jean. 1962. *The Six Bookes of a Commonweal*. Richard Knolles, trans.; Kenneth Douglas McRae, ed. Cambridge, MA: Harvard University Press.

Bowman, Norah. 2021. Here/there/everywhere: quantum models for decolonizing Canadian state onto epistemology. *Foundations of Science* 26(1): 171–186.

Cameron, Emilie. 2015. *Far Off Metal River: Inuit Lands, Settler Stories and the Making of the Contemporary Arctic*. Vancouver: University of British Columbia Press.

Capan, Zeynep Gulsah. 2017. Decolonising international relations? *Third World Quarterly* 38(1): 1–15.

Christie, G. 2011. Indigeneity and sovereignty in Canada's Far North: the Arctic and Inuit sovereignty. *South Atlantic Quarterly* 11: 329–346.

Coulthard, Glen Sean. 2014. *Red Skin White Masks: Rejecting the Colonial Politics of Recognition*. Minneapolis: University of Minnesota Press.

Fierke, Karin Marie, and Nicola McKay. 2020. To 'see' is to break an entanglement: quantum measurement, trauma and security. *Security Dialogue* 51(5): 450–466.

Flaherty, Martha. 1988. I fought to keep my hair. In *Northern Voices: Inuit Writings in English*, Penny Petrone, ed. Toronto: University of Toronto Press, 274–278.

Grant, Shelagh D. 2002. *Arctic Justice: On Trial for Murder, Pond Inlet, 1923*. Montreal; Kingston: McGill-Queen's University Press.

Grant, Shelagh D. 2010. *Polar Imperative: A History of Arctic Sovereignty in North America*. New York: Douglas & McIntyre.

Harper, Kenn. 2017. *Thou Shalt Do No Murder: Inuit, Injustice and the Canadian Arctic*. Iqaluit: Nunavut Arctic College Media.

Inuit Circumpolar Council. 2009. *A Circumpolar Inuit Declaration of Sovereignty in the Arctic.*   https://iccalaska.org/wp-icc/wp-content/uploads/2016/01/Signed-Inuit-Sovereignty-Declaration-11x17.pdf

Jackson, Patrick T., and Daniel H. Nexon. 2019. Reclaiming the social: relationalism in anglophone international studies. *Cambridge Review of International Affairs* 32(5): 582–600.

Jackson, Robert H. 1993. *Quasi-States: Sovereignty, International Relations and the Third World.* Cambridge: Cambridge University Press.

Jahn, Beate. 2000. *The Cultural Construction of International Relations: The Invention of the State of Nature.* Basingstoke: Palgrave Macmillan.

Karetak, Joe, and Frank Tester. 2017. Inuit Qaujimajatuqangit: Truth and Reconciliation. In *Inuit Qaujimajatuqangit: What Inuit Have Always Known to Be True*, Joe Karetak, Frank Tester, and Shirley Tagalik, eds. Halifax: Fernwood: 1–17.

Kirby, Vicki. 2011. *Quantum Anthropologies.* Durham, NC: Duke University Press.

Komar, Debra. 2019. *The Court of Better Fiction: Three Trials, Two Executions, and Arctic Sovereignty.* Toronto: Dundurn.

Krasner, Stephen D. 1999. *Sovereignty: Organized Hypocrisy.* Princeton, NJ: Princeton University Press.

Latour, Bruno. 1993. *We Have Never Been Modern*, trans. Catherine Porter. Cambridge: Harvard University Press.

Latour, Bruno. 2016. *Onus Orbis Terrarum:* About a possible shift in the definition of sovereignty. *Millennium* 44(3): 305–320.

Lyons, Scott Richard. 2010. *X-Marks: Native Signatures of Assent.* Minneapolis: University of Minnesota Press.

McGrath, Janet Tamalik. 2018. *The Qaggiq Model: Toward a Theory of Inuktut Knowledge Renewal.* Iqaluit: Nunavut Arctic College Media.

Morrison, William R. 1986. Canadian sovereignty and the Inuit of the Central and Eastern Arctic. *Études/Inuit/Studies* 10(1/2): 245–259.

Moyles, R. G. 1979. *British Law and Arctic Men: The Celebrated 1917 Murder Trials of Sinnisiak and Uluksuk, First Inuit Tried under White Man's Law.* Saskatoon: Western Producer Prairie Books.

Murphy, Michael P. A. 2021. *Quantum Social Theory for Critical International Relations Theorists: Quantizing Critique.* Basingstoke: Palgrave Macmillan.

Nadasdy, Paul. 2017. *Sovereignty's Entailments: First Nation State Formation in the Yukon.* Toronto: University of Toronto Press.

Qitsualik, Rachel A. 2013. Inummarik: Self-sovereignty in classical Inuit thought. In *Nilliajut: Inuit Perspectives on Security, Patriotism and Sovereignty*, Scot Nickels, Karen Kelley, Carrie Grable, Martin Lougheed, James Kuptana, eds., Kevin Kablutsiak, Sadie Hill, Rachel A. Qitsualik, Zebedee Nungak, trans. Ottawa: Inuit Tapiriit Kanatami: 23–34.

Rifkin, Mark. 2009. Indigenizing Agamben: rethinking sovereignty in light of the 'peculiar' status of Native peoples. *Cultural Critique* 73(2): 88–124.

Salter, Mark B. 2008. When the exception becomes the rule: borders, sovereignty and citizenship. *Citizenship Studies* 12(4): 365–380.

Salter, Mark B. 2019. Arctic security, territory, population: Canadian sovereignty and the international. *International Political Sociology* 13(4): 358–374.

Schuh, Cornelia. 1979. Justice on the northern frontier: early murder trials of Native accused. *Criminal Law Quarterly* 22(74): 1–23.

Shaw, Karena. 2008. *Political Theory and Indigeneity: Sovereignty and the Limits of the Political*. New York: Routledge.

Simpson, Audra. 2014. *Mohawkus Interruptus*. Durham, NC: Duke University Press.

Stephenson, Lisa. 2014. *Life beside Itself: Imagining Care in the Canadian Arctic*. Berkeley: University of California Press.

Todd, Zoe. 2016. An Indigenous feminist's take on the ontological turn: "ontology" is just another word for colonialism. *Journal of Historical Sociology* 29(1): 4–22.

Walker, R. B. J. 2009. *After the Globe, before the World*. New York: Routledge.

Wendt, Alexander. 2015. *Quantum Mind and Social Science: Unifying Physical and Social Ontology*. New York: Cambridge University Press.

Zanotti, L. 2019. *Ontological Entanglements, Agency, and Ethics in International Relations*. New York: Routledge.

Zellen, B. S. 2009. *On Thin Ice, the Inuit, the State, and the Challenge of Arctic Sovereignty*. New York: Lexington Books.

14

Quantum and Systems Theory in World Society

Not Brothers and Sisters but Relatives Still?

Mathias Albert and Felix M. Bathon

Introduction

The present chapter offers a sympathetic, yet also somewhat critical, engagement with "quantizing" International Relations from a particular vantage point.[1] This vantage point starts from the observation that much of both the charm, and the difficulty of the quantizing move stems from quantum theory's radical break with intuitively plausible ways of seeing the world that are associated with the "classical" worldview of physics, and that this classical worldview is mirrored in many of the basic social science assumptions of seeing the social world. However, there is a real danger that a quantum view is merely laid on to what remains a classical view of the social world, irrespective of the fact that there are a range of theories and theoretical traditions out there that have gone to great lengths already in fundamentally challenging that worldview and providing quite radical alternatives to it. Put differently, we see one of the great challenges and promises of a quantizing move not in challenging classical problems of, for example, actorhood, mind/body, or causality, but in entering a dialogue with alternative nonclassical theories.

Using modern systems theory in the Luhmannian tradition, the present contribution probes one such possibility for dialogue. If this was only about deviating from a classical worldview, other bodies of theory could have been chosen, most notably post-/neostructuralist theories, and there is arguably a wealth of ideational commonalities in terms of, particularly Leibnizian, philosophical traditions that might be worthwhile to explore here. The choice of modern systems theory in this context, however, is rooted in the observation that there exist, even at first sight, a wealth of analogies between systems and quantum views that are too obvious to be ignored, particularly when it comes to the central categories of "observation" and "meaning." While the question of whether, and to what degree, these analogies are in fact rooted in specific traits of philosophical tradition is beyond the scope of a single chapter, we set ourselves a double task that nonetheless seems quite ambitious already: we explore the central concepts of observation and meaning in both quantum and systems theory in order to probe the degree to which obvious analogies in fact could be read as overlaps and similarities that could be put to complementary analytical use. We come to the conclusion that such a complementarity indeed exists, and that it does so in a rather strong sense. In the end, systems theory provides a strong account of social and historical change that quantum approaches lack, while the latter allow for bringing in relations between social and natural systems that systems theory tends to bracket out. It remains a strange complementarity when it comes to International Relations, however, as arguably both systems and quantum theory leave little of the classical pillars—which serve as points of differentiation for International Relations as a separate field/discipline in the system of science—intact.

In the following, we will proceed in four steps: In a first step, we offer a condensed and stylized reading of quantum and systems theory that forms the basis of our argument; given that many aspects of quantum theory are covered in the other contributions to this volume, the emphasis here is somewhat more on systems theory. In a second step, we explore the concepts of observation and meaning in both theories in turn, before, in a third step, we ask whether, and to what degree, "more" than mere analogy is involved here. The fourth step will then outline some of the possible consequences to the world of International Relations of recruiting these two theories as bedfellows.

An Outline of Systems and Quantum Theory

Systems Theory

While certainly a challenge to social scientific thought in its many guises, we take "systems theory" here to refer to the type of "modern" systems theory most notably developed by the German sociologist Niklas Luhmann. Despite many roots in older forms of systems theory, and particularly Parsonian structural functionalism, it presents a quantum (!) leap in terms of theory development. It is important to notice as well that, strictly speaking, a theory of social systems is only one aspect and a theoretical building block of what has become known as "systems theory" in shorthand. Luhmann's project and ambition was a theory of society that was built on a theory of social systems yet always included as important elements both a theory of social differentiation (Luhmann, 1977, 1982a, 1987a, 1992b) and a theory of social evolution (Luhmann, 1987b, 1990a, 1992c, 2012 [1997]; Albert, 2016a). In terms of its challenge and radical departure from other kinds of social theorizing, it seems worthwhile to highlight the following features:

First of all, systems theory is a theory about the social world that sees that world to be constituted by communication, and *only* by communication (Luhmann, 1981, 1996). People are not the "parts" or "elements" of a society that would somehow emerge from interaction. Rather, as persons they can be addressed, and thus be included into, or excluded from, specific social systems (Luhmann, 1995 [1984]: 137–176, 1980). While psychic systems, in addition to social systems, are the only systems that operate on the basis of processing meaning (Luhmann, 1995 [1984]: 52–103), they are parts of the environment of social systems, not parts of those systems themselves (Luhmann [1984], 1995: 176–210, 255–278). This perspective fundamentally changes the guiding question of any kind of social theory, and particularly any theory of society, from the classical sociological question of how society hangs together and is integrated to the question of how communication can continue. How, to put it simply, can the myriad communication offers, under the condition of double contingency (Luhmann, 1995 [1984]: 103–137), lead to the emergence of structured complexity (i.e., order) in social systems, rather than to some kind of "communicative entropy" (i.e., in a sense, universal and unstructured "babbling"). "Double contingency" here refers to the fact that even two (let alone a couple billion) psychic systems in any encounter are "black boxes" for each other. There is no direct way of linking one to the other (Luhmann, 1994). The creation of meaning beyond single psychic systems can only take place in a social system that, in the case of two people encountering each other, is a simple interaction system. However, even such a "simple" system will only be established successfully if it can draw on communication that has already taken place within an established structure of society, with its forms of social differentiation and according symbolically generalized media of communication (such as power or money [Luhmann, 1976]), systemic codes, and programs. Creating simple social interaction systems without that background is not impossible but bound to be a rather uncertain, demanding, or even violent affair (witness numerous examples from Robinson Crusoe to Captain Cook).

The continuation of society, that is, the structured continuation of myriads of communication, is neither fixed or mechanical nor completely arbitrary. It proceeds as social evolution (cf. Brunkhorst, 2014). Every communication introduces a variation to the status quo, and every variation is either selected or not, leading to a restabilization of the system. The crucial point here is selection. While in principle a variation can always be selected or not, the likelihood of selection is strongly conditioned. Put simply, claims of a peasant who farms the land against the person who owns it (variation) are much more likely to be selected in case of a functionally differentiated society where both are bound together contractually in the legal system (through mediating organizations) as tenant and landlord, compared to a stratified society where their mutual relation is primarily defined by status (e.g., peasantry versus nobility).

Processing meaning is, however, an even more complex affair. Generally, the processing of meaning can be depicted on the basis of abstract forms. This is why Luhmann introduces Spencer Brown's (1969) calculus of forms into his theory, as it

> allows one to analyze the processing and operation with meaning in a deeper fashion than is possible with the notion of meaning alone.... Luhmann ...takes the central figure of the analysis of forms, the distinguishing-and-designating, to be a variation of the general mechanism of meaning, which consists in providing for a surplus of possibilities of connectivity, with the consequences of having to choose between those possibilities. (Schützeichel, 2003: 48)[2]

We will return to this issue later, as the introduction of the analysis of forms into the theoretical analysis of meaning also leads to the inclusion of an inherent difference between actuality and potentiality into meaning that, together with the notion of observation, might provide a bridge to quantum theory.

While all these remarks necessarily are theoretical, it seems important to note at this point already that an obvious analytical consequence for the study of International Relations stems from the view that only communication constitutes society, and that there can be no communication outside of society. This basically means that there can be only one society—world society—and that at least on planet Earth only one such society has existed for a couple of centuries (separate "world societies" simply require a lack of knowledge about the existence of one another [Luhmann, 1982b, 1997]). This, in a sense, changes everything, and does so in a very fundamental sense (although not necessarily in the practice of its application!), immunizing systems theory from any kind of "methodological nationalism": *every* kind of formation and transformation of social orders and structures takes place *within* world society; it can only take place on the basis of, for example, the symbolically generalized media of communication that are available, and under the conditions of the forms of social differentiation in existence.

Quantum Theory

While systems theory is concerned with the description and explanation of social phenomena based on communication, and on this basis deals with world society as the most comprehensive social system that includes all communication, quantum theory deals with microscopic physical objects in the subatomic domain (e.g., the structure of atoms). We approach its world relation through the question of which part of the measuring process triggers the interruption in the wave function. According to John von Neumann (1955 [1932]), who consolidated the mathematical foundation of quantum mechanics by combining Schrödinger's equation and matrices mechanics into a single formalism, this question *cannot* be answered in principle. He assumes that quantum theory does not merely apply to quantum events on the subatomic level, but to the *whole world*. This means that measuring devices are not things somehow external to, and ontologically different from, a quantum object to be measured. Rather, the measuring devices themselves are also to be seen as entangled quantum objects and are therefore represented by a combined wave function. Following von Neumann, the wave function collapses by choosing an arbitrary position, by making the measurement. Before that, the electron itself appears as nothing else but a set of possibilities that do not know at which location they will be. In a major break with the classical worldview that would allow for the prediction of future system states when all the relevant parameters are known, a quantum system exists in a superposition of different possibilities until it is measured.

Quantum theory challenges central assumptions of classical physics. Among other things (see Wendt, 2015: 58–70): (1) Quantum physics shows that there is an emergent level of reality at larger scales, that is, that objects do not have definite and fixed characteristics (uncertainty principle), and that objects are not separate from each other but that their identity is determined by internal structures as well as by their place in space and time. This challenges atomism, preferring a "holism" over an "atomism" view of the world. (2) Determinism is challenged because quantum physics is a probabilistic theory. (3) The mechanist view of classical physics includes local causality between material phenomena, while quantum physics demonstrates that cause and effect are bound together nonlocally and instantaneously through measurement without a cause. (4) The view of classical physics that time and space are absolute categories that exist objectively in reality is challenged because quantum physics assumes that there simply *is no* locality until it is measured and that time and space "happen" in and between entangled systems. In this sense, space is discrete and not continuous—it cannot be divided arbitrarily. The wave function does not evolve *in time* but *into time*. (5) The classical assumption that knowledge is independent from the observer is challenged through the notion that the observer itself is a part of the system.

Translation Devices: Observation and Meaning

Having laid out the main issues of "what is at stake" in systems and quantum theory in terms of their views of the world, we now turn to the concepts of observation and meaning. Rather than positing substantive overlaps, we at this point limit our argument to identifying analogies as translation devices between the two theories.[3] In relation to both systems and quantum theory, the "observer" is the culminating point of the relation between knowledge and reality. While "classically" this relation is conceived as a problem of knowledge being well founded (as truth and through justification), conceiving of what is being perceived as dependent on how it is perceived *changes the problem of what exists and can be known to the question of the distinctions that are used in observation.*[4] Closely related, but different, is the issue of which of the possibilities that exist in "virtuality" either as "horizon" in the phenomenological sense (in the case of systems theory) or as "superposition" (in the case of quantum theory) become "actualized" and how. Both systems and quantum theory differ here from the "classical" solution of causal mechanisms.

Observing Observers: Luhmann's Operative Constructivism

Luhmannian systems theory is a radically constructivist theory or, more specifically, an "operative constructivist" theory (see Scholl, 2012; also Riegler and Scholl, 2012). The distinction between operation and observation is crucial in this respect, as it replaces the classical distinctions between subject and object and thought and being, as well as between the transcendental and empirical (Luhmann, 1992a: 78–79): as an effect produced by the observer, a phenomenon is what appears in the observation, while an observation is an operation that cannot simultaneously be observed as a phenomenon. Everything that comes after the operation of "observation" is first of all generated by it. The observer does not stand above the things that it observes—there is no subject outside the object. It is itself a part of the observation it creates because it can only observe the operations if it operates and creates those operations (Luhmann, 1992a: 506–507). The ontology of Luhmann's constructivism therefore is an ontology of operations. Luhmann (1990b: 37) speaks of a "de-ontologization of reality" in this respect. Reality is not denied, as otherwise there would be nothing that operates, that is, nothing that could be observed and distinguished (Luhmann, 1990b: 41). What is denied, however, is that an ontological representation of reality, in the form of the distinction between being and not-being, bears any epistemological relevance.

For Luhmann, the concept of the observer refers to the formation of systems in which (cognitive) operations take place. A system forms when operations are not only single events but also concatenated sequences that can be distinguished from an environment (Luhmann, 2004: 142). Each operation, as an element of the autopoietic system, reproduces the system. Therefore, the observation is an operation and the observer is a system that observes the operations.[5] The observer theorem becomes self-referential and recursive (Luhmann, 1995 [1984]: 111f; 2012 [1997]: 1128, 1142). The observing system can observe the environment only in its own and system-specific way, so other systems arrive at different observation results of the "same" phenomenon observed.

The operation "observing" is defined as the unity of distinction and indication. Without a distinction, nothing could be indicated. This distinction needs to be asymmetric and mark one side of the distinction, even though the other, "unmarked" side is always presupposed and carried along (Luhmann, 1992a: 73; this is what Spencer Brown [1969] calls a "form"). The distinction used operatively in the observation is not observable itself as one side needs to be marked, and while marking one side it is not possible to mark the distinction itself in the same operation. This is the observer's "blind spot" (von Foerster, 1981), an "excluded included third" (Luhmann, 1990b: 31). Each observation therefore produces invisibility and finally it is the observer that makes itself invisible. An observation of the operation as observation can only take the form of *second-order observation*, that is, the observation of the distinction that an observer uses. Regarding the question of what an observer can see and where its blind spots are, second-order observation is an observation that observes how an observer using a certain distinction observes itself or the environment. It is here that the last bit of ontological certainty regarding data, essential forms, or world content vanishes completely. The blind spots just shift but can never be eliminated.

The Measurement Problem and the Discovery of Observation in Quantum Physics

"Does the moon exist even when no one is looking?" This was the polemic question that Albert Einstein posed to Nils Bohr. The question expresses the seemingly absurd consequences of taking quantum theory seriously in its challenges to classical thought: quantum mechanical systems lack definite objective properties before they are observed. Thus, when examining the properties of a wave, it is possible to precisely calculate its momentum *or* its location, but *never* both at the same time.

The discovery of the observer in quantum physics can be reconstructed through three major experiments and their outcomes (Wendt, 2015: 43–58):

(1) The double-slit experiment demonstrated that matter only has particle characteristics once it is measured and does not even exist before that measuring. As long as there is no information of the particle, there is only probability distribution regarding where the particle could be found. In the

moment of measurement the wave interference pattern is destroyed, the wave function collapses, and the particle changes its "behavior" to a certain point.

(2) The formalism of quantum mechanics states that particles that interact or have entered into each other, and are thus entangled in a quantum-like manner, also *remain* connected to each other once separated spatially (Einstein [1971 ([1947])] calls this the "spooky action at a distance"). This quantum entanglement (Bohr, 1928) was attacked by Einstein, Podolsky, and Rosen ("EPR") (1935). The EPR paper sought to demonstrate an incompleteness of quantum theory, arguing that there would be an underlying theory that could deterministically explain the probabilistic character of quantum outcomes. It was John Bell (1964) who demonstrated experimentally that Einstein was wrong and showed that the physical world is not compatible with local realism. This means that there is instantaneous action, while reality does not exist independently of measurement.[6]

(3) The delayed-choice experiment (Wheeler, 1978; Jacques et al., 2007) proved that the nonlocality that Bell showed in his experiments is to be understood both spatially and temporally: instantaneous correlations can occur between two events that are extremely remote from each other in *both* space and time.

The outcomes of these experiments suggest that the observer (i.e., for example, the researcher) and the arrangements of the experiment (i.e., for example, the specific settings applied) *determine* the results. Phenomena and observation do not exist independently but complement each other in forming a local reality. The results can only be explained if, on the one hand, it is assumed that particles can observe themselves and can also detect whether they are being observed. On the other hand, it must be assumed that they can somehow "communicate" over greater distances and through time (inducing the notion of "backward causality").

Systems Theory and Meaning—Phenomenological Horizons

Systems theory sees the relationship of the physical and the social in the context of uncertainty connected in the medium meaning. For Luhmann, "meaning" is not related to intentionality; it cannot be understood as information or significance. Rather, it is a prerequisite for that, a medium, and therefore a fundamental form of social order. Luhmann bases his concept of meaning on Edmund Husserl's phenomenology. Meaning, then, is *a reference context ("Verweisungszusammenhang") of the world* (Luhmann, 1995

[1984]: 59–103). This reference context is stretched out between actuality and potentiality. Each experience and action fixes a possible experience and action and carries with it further possibilities of experiencing and action. Accordingly, there is a double selectivity of what is chosen and the frame from which it is selected (Luhmann, 1995 [1984]: 135). From each "update" of meaning follows a surplus of references and then a simultaneous presence of two levels of possibility and reality that are maintained with each observation (Luhmann, 1995 [1984]: 93).

This means that, always, more possibilities of experience and action exist than can possibly be realized. Meaning, therefore, forces the selection of one of these possibilities, saving the other possibilities to be potentially selected in the future. This, on the one hand, makes meaning fundamentally unstable as the "actuality core" of each determination shifts again and again, as each update opens up new actualities and potentialities. On the other hand, meaning becomes self-referential as it provides for its own ability to be updated again. It always refers to meaning and can therefore be understood as being without difference, as there is no negation of it. Meaning, then, has a functional component, since it processes information but keeps it present as world complexity. This reduces indefinite complexity (selection) yet builds up specific complexity (horizon) (Luhmann, 1995 [1984]: 94).

Only meaning assigns information values to events. This information value is located in the communication in three dimensions that each inscribe their own differences (horizons) into the difference between what is currently given and what is possible (Luhmann, 1995 [1984]: 75–82): The factual dimension (*Sachdimension*) arranges information with regard to the topics of communication by means of the distinction between "this" and "something else." The temporal dimension (*Zeitdimension*) orders information with regard to the irreversible distinction of past and future but dissolves it in the distinction between "before" and "after." The social dimension (*Sozialdimension*) relates information between different perspectives of participant egos and alter egos that produce themselves in competing provisions of meaning in the distinction between "dissent" and "consensus."

This is, so to speak, the strictly systems theory part of systems theory. The interesting question for a theory of society, of course, is not only how meaning is produced and processed but also which forms are, and historically have been, actualized. This is the point where other major components come in, namely the theory of social differentiation and the theory of social evolution. Put simply, the starting point here is that the world *is* structured in many ways. Like quanta, communications do not exist in an entropic state of chaos. Social systems may pop up and disappear ("forgotten" by society, as most interaction systems are); some possibilities may be actualized, others not. However, this process is not

completely arbitrary as the forms of social differentiation (segmentation, strat-
ification, functional differentiation) condition possibilities at any given point
in history. Nor is determination involved: forms of social differentiation might
say something about the likelihood of some variations being selected in social
evolution. However, every variation in principle entails the possibility of being
selected or not.

Quantum Theory and Meaning—Superposition and Decoherence

While the phenomenological concept of meaning in systems theory serves as
an ongoing information process via the theorem of double selectivity, the wave
function represents a similar difference between actuality and potentiality. At
the quantum scale, particles can exist in different states, for example, different
positions, energies, or speeds. However, they do not "switch" between those states
but rather exist across them at the same time; they can be in two places at once.
This overlap is known as the superposition of states: Schrödinger's (1935: 823)
probability wave represents the potentially unlimited states that are in a superposition of all being possible.

On a macro-scale, superpositions cannot actually be observed. We cannot see
an atom being in an indeterminate state. All we can see are the consequences of
its existence. Determination happens once a measurement is made. The measurement acts as an interaction of the formerly isolated quantum system with an
environment. Any kind of interaction with the environment causes the quantum
system to de-cohere, resulting in the collapse of the wave function and therefore the destruction of superposition, reducing it to a single state. Quantum
decoherence means that the wave functions of different particles are not the
same, but they are entangled because they can be described as one system with
the same Schrödinger equation.

Decoherence therefore describes the problem of how the indeterministic
quantum world merges into the classical world (Zeh, 1970; Joos and Zeh, 1984).
Schrödinger discussed the seemingly absurd consequences of quantum physics
when dealing with large objects in his famous thought experiment, known as
"Schrödinger's cat": A cat is in a closed box. The states "dead" or "living" depend
on the state of a radioactive atom, whether it has decayed and radiated radiation
or not. These states can be described as a wave function. The Copenhagen interpretation now says that the cat is both "dead" and "alive" until the condition
is observed. Obviously that sounds bizarre. Quantum theory applies not only
to the subatomic world simply because quanta like cats are never isolated from
an environment. Trillions of photons always leap off every object. Therefore, in

practice we never observe quantum systems directly. But there is still a small degree of indefiniteness of the things observed. With decoherence and superposition, quantum physics introduces an "inescapable contingency factor" (Vogt, 2011: 220) and thus introduces its central epistemological implication into the world *regardless of scale* (Heisenberg, 1986).

Superposition can be demonstrated by sending electromagnetic waves to a quantum object. If that wave is at an appropriate frequency, then the atom alternates between states. If this is done frequently, an average can be calculated. Since atoms are never isolated in reality and always collide with each other, superposition and oscillation disappear. The time it takes for the superposition to disappear is called decoherence time. It provides information about the interaction between quantum objects and their environment. In this sense, decoherence appears as a loss of information of the system to its environment. Decoherence then provides an explanation for the observation of the wave collapse, since at the moment of observation the system changes into its environment or evolves with it. This does not explain the measurement problem, but the *transition from the system to a tangled state with the observer*. This is where quantum meaning comes into existence. The most far-reaching interpretation following from this that would seem to open the door for a rather elegant translation between the quantum and the social world then is to view quantum entities as *concepts*:

> Similar to the "conceptual way" we used to explain the double-slit experiment, the elementary microscopic entities, whilst not describable as particles, waves of fields (since they are not representable in the three-dimensional space, or four-dimensional spacetime), would nevertheless behave as something that is very familiar to us all, and that we continually experience in a very intimate and direct way: *concepts*. (Aerts and Sassoli de Bianchi, 2017: 118)

The Meaning of Analogy: Complementarity Rather Than Priority

The previous section outlined an analogy between the concept of meaning as the difference of potentiality and actuality and the concept of wave decoherence and wave collapse. We want to take this as a starting point to ask whether more than mere analogy might be involved here, and if so, whether quantum and systems theory can be seen as complementing each other, or whether actually one somehow takes "precedence" over the other. The latter suspicion is fueled by the observation that systems theory designates itself as social theory, and the social could be seen as but a subset of the entire world for which quantum theory provides the most fundamental theory available.

In relation to the concept of meaning, both the potentiality/actuality and the wave decoherence/wave collapse dualism refer to the observer dependency of social and physical reality (Stetter, 2016: 192–193). Both concepts refer to the same theme, namely that every observation is a demarcation, out of which the world comes into being (cf. Luhmann, 2001: 254). Actualization is the transfer of the medium meaning into concrete, yet contingent, forms, while there is always a horizon of potentiality, which Luhmann, following Spencer Brown, calls the "unmarked space" (Luhmann, 2001: 224, 242). It is about the domestication of the improbable and its probability (Luhmann, 1992a: 256).

We take this to indicate that systems and quantum theory share the thought of a common ontology of the physical, biochemical, psychic, and social (Stetter, 2016: 192). Systems theory sees this relationship in the context of uncertainty connected in the medium meaning, while quantum theory, although starting with the subatomic world, *does not exclude anything*: although it is not a simple micro–macro issue that is at stake here; this is where the argument that, for large parts of the world, the quantum view is irrelevant as quantum effects (mathematically!) "wash out" at macro-levels is not wrong, but simply misses the point: "washing out" does not mean "simply going away"!

Both systems theory and quantum theory assume that the world is not objectively "given," but determined by the unmarked space (systems theory) or by superposition (quantum theory) as the world's background of indeterminacy, in the forefront of which objects appear. This appearance necessarily requires an observation, as measurements or distinctions that construct reality. While very similar to one another, quantum and systems theory approach this construction from different ends: For quantum theory, John von Neumann (1955 [1932]) tried to solve the puzzle of where and when an observation creates reality by decomposing the process (in the so-called "von Neumann chain"). Here, the collapse of the wave function happens at the *end* of the chain, when the outcome is registered by the observer's mind. For Luhmann, the construction of reality starts with the need for the observer to *begin* somewhere, which is the imperative to (in terms of Spencer Brown's calculus of forms) "draw a distinction"!

In an analogy to quantum physics, Luhmann developed a complementary notion of the observer (Luhmann, 1992a: 68–122, 505–507, 694, 699–701): the observer itself stands for an operation, while the operation (process) causes phenomena that the observer cannot see, being able to only observe the effects of the observer's operations. This, in turn, changes the local reality to which the observer belongs. Put bluntly, this is the uncertainty principle outside quantum physics: operation and observation, like spin and location, together represent a unitary description of the reality, yet both cannot be observed at the same time (Heisenberg, 1971: 70–82, 117–125).[7]

We take this *formal similarity* between quantum and systems theory, through the translation devices of the form of the observer, as well as through the forms of superposition and distinction, as a clear indicator that both are recursive theories that produce a world overlap between them. The crucial point here is that through the operation of observation, *both* are about the world in a necessarily contingent and open sense, without in the end facing the problem of bridging seemingly different natural and social worlds. The observer observes, and no ether, or, as in Wendt, "elan vital," is needed for the continuation of the observer observing. To reiterate a point made earlier already: quantum and systems theory share the thought of a common ontology of the physical, biochemical, psychic, and social (see Stetter, 2016: 192). This allows us to speak of *meaning* in both cases as a nontrivial way that opens the door toward seeing similarities that go beyond mere analogies, yet also preserve system-specific characteristics that are different for social, psychic, and natural systems.

Quantum theory is about the universe. There is always more and more of it, as it continues, but it remains singular (we leave aside the concept of the multiverse here). Systems theory is about society constituted by communication. There is always more and more of it, as it continues, but it remains singular (we leave aside the issue of extraterrestrial lifeforms at this point). In toto, through the lens of either theory, one looks at the history and form of one single universe/society. In and through it, myriads of observations create what is ultimately a structured reality (without this requiring any kind of ontological account). What this means for us is that we see the relation between quantum and systems theory to be one of strong complementarity, and one might even speculate whether and to which degree it might be seen as a symbiotic one. Despite different evolutionary trajectories, they are not enclosed sets of theory between which one needs to somehow choose. One could actually rather claim that systems theory to a quite significant degree "does" quantum theory for the natural, while quantum theory "does" systems theory for the social world. In so doing, they fully complement each other in observing what the respective other doesn't observe. What we would reject, however, is the idea that behind that complementarity there is a hierarchy, according to which quantum theory would be the physical basis of systems theory, and thus the more "fundamental" of the two. We think that this hierarchy issue simply does not arise in theories that do not concern themselves much, or at all, with questions of ontology (in the sense that the distinction between being and non-being is not seen as relevant for knowing: it is distinctions and observations that "are"!). Of course, there is a physical reality that is the basis of everything social. But then, by being a theory, every *theory* about that physical reality, including quantum theory, *as theory* is always already an inextricable part of the social world (Fuchs, 2009). After all, theories themselves do not float as particles in the vacuum of space; rather, every theory is, and is constituted as well as situated, in a universe of communication!

It should be mentioned, however, that the "flat" ontology shared between systems and quantum theory does *not* mean that one could not distinguish between different "worlds," that is, most notably between a social and a natural world. However, the relevant distinctions are not "naturally" given. As hinted at previously, systems theory's "trick" here is to simply start somewhere: the maxim "Draw a distinction," taken from the Spencer Brownian calculus of forms, means to start somewhere, anywhere, and then look at how systems are constituted by system/environment distinctions that can (and do) reappear within the systems themselves. This, incidentally, is also where the mind-body problem comes into play and disappears as a "problem." On the one hand, it is historicized as a linguistic or semantic distinction "which relates to the changing relations of early modernity. Understood as a linguistic form, it is no longer important to 'solve' the mind-body trilemma, but to reconstruct the preconditions and particular perspectives that this *distinction* gives rise to" (Kessler, 2018: 80, emphasis added). On the other hand, systems theory as a theory of society is radically anti-humanist in that it posits social systems as autopoietic systems of a type completely different from natural and psychic systems that constitute the world dualism on which the mind-body problem is based in the first instance.[8]

To be more precise: systems theory's ontology is "flat" not because different worlds are not distinguished ontologically. It is "flat" in the sense of lacking contours in that these worlds are de-ontologized. They only come into "existence" through distinctions that might be seen as unfolding singularities. While this line of thought arguably has a distinct ring of Leibnizian monadology to it, it is worth noting that such an approach does not *require* to ensure the "flatness" of ontology through a metaphysical principle, such as most notably the causal closure of physics (CCP) (either in its classical or quantum form).[9] This is not an argument about whether CCP holds true or not, but simply to say that as a *metaphysical* principle (see Buhler, 2020) it has no place in systems theory. Distinctions take place and unfold and constantly make the world. They are not "grounded" in anything, and causal closure is simply not required in this case.[10] Social systems are operatively closed (this being the core behind the notion of "autopoiesis"), meaning that all causal claims, for example, about the social effects of natural or intentional causes, within social systems can only be communicative events, that is, observations based on the distinction of cause and effect, which an observer employs to reduce complexity.

Both systems and quantum theory are well equipped for "dealing with changing ontologies and relations of observation. Different to the present philosophical tradition...[they exhibit]...a *richness of structure* that allows grounding a theory in the groundless, without leading to the arbitrary" (Vogd, 2014: 28). They are both similar in the sense that they do not take a specific fixed entity as their starting point and they are both theories about the world. They share between them a radical departure from many aspects of a "classical" world-view, notably about the limits to the possibility of knowing the world. Although it is possible to draw links to poststructuralist philosophy in both cases (and particularly to the notion of *différance* in Derrida), quantum and systems theory have developed their concepts of theory-immanent radical limitations to the possibilities of knowledge largely independent from (and often earlier than) that body of thought. The equivalent concepts are (double) contingency, in the case of systems theory, and uncertainty, in the case of quantum theory. What these concepts share is that they are not simply characteristics or attributes of the world, but that they are built into both theories as *generative* and *reflexive* concepts: both concepts account for how social and physical realities emerge and make claims as to the possibilities (and limitations) of knowing and describing them.

Quant- and Systemizing: Something Left of International Relations?

Contextualizing systems and quantum theory, and their relation to each other, in International Relations cannot involve a simple "application" of a body of theory to an "International Relations reality out there." From our reading emerges a view that sees quantum and systems theory as theories that aim at the very fundaments of how an academic field's subject matter is conceived, and how it is observed. The most relevant issue in this respect is the one about the significant differentiations between a system and an environment that constitute "International Relations" as a discernible social system in the first place. This issue pertains to what essentially is a historical process, in and through which, out of myriads of observations, emerges what is ultimately a structured reality (without this requiring any kind of ontological account) that is accompanied by specific historical semantics. What are, in other words, the relevant social systems within world society that International Relations looks at? One could, for example, argue that International Relations could be described strictly in terms of the historical evolution of the internal differentiation of the political system of world society, including the emergence of a distinct subsystem of world politics (see Albert and Buzan, 2017). The quantum approach would take such a systems-focused approach even further as it helps to see that there is no categorical distinction between world society and the world; in a world that only operates, the relation between the natural and the social world is simply not one of *categorical* differences in many respects (although it is certainly one of many structural and formal differences). But then, both systems and quantum theories do not look at established worlds: they reflect how these are co-constituted through observation. It is probably easiest to say what does not emerge from this: concepts of International Relations or world politics that see that these, in one way or another, are fixed realities external to the observer (or even, as some forms of realism might have it, "eternal" in relation to it).

International Relations, very broadly speaking (with many exceptions confirming the rule here), has a rather established way of thinking about the world. This is arguably less the case for the question pertaining to the delimitation of its subject matter but is rather solidly the case when it comes to the modes of seeing this subject matter, most notably in terms of temporal and spatial structure. Particularly regarding the latter, the International Relations world is a micromacro world; the levels of this world are thought of more in exclusive rather than in inclusive terms, and there is a strong tendency to equate macro with "global" and micro with "local." As we have tried to argue throughout our contribution, "quantizing" International Relations will remain an intellectually nice, but rather harmless, exercise if it leaves this classical worldview of International Relations intact: "In contrast to...a theory of evolution-based thoughts on differentiation *and* unity, Wendt's social theory remains strongly rooted in the tradition of social scientific 'consensual theories'..., which however is problematic from a sociological point of view since Simmel, Durkheim and Weber" (Stetter, 2016: 1989). It is in this sense that we argue that the quantizing needs the systemizing in order not to simply be the classical International Relations emperor's new clothes.

Again: "what's in it for International Relations?" Not much, if one's expectation is to stay anywhere close to what may count as established "disciplinary confines"—however, the issue here is that systems-cum-quantum theorizing arguably challenges the disciplinary organization of scientific knowledge, so this is by no means a problem specific to International Relations. Turned on its head, this observation, however, also means that there is no limit for rephrasing disciplinary questions here either. In addition to offering fundamentally different (in the sense of paradigmatic) ways of seeing the world, systems-cum-quantum theorizing offers to International Relations the reminder that recursivity fundamentally involves an inseparability of "inquiry" and "object." It is, in this sense, ineluctably *critical* in that it neither allows for nor requires the basic move of distancing required of any "classical," including (post)modern, instantiation of critique (κριτική).

We take quantum and systems theory to be related and complementary theories that help us make sense of the operative universe in which International Relations take place and are observed. Quant- and systemizing International Relations at the same time is very difficult: doing only one of the two might sound quite radical at first but still leaves the comfort zone of a classical world-view against which this radicalness can be asserted. Where it gets really challenging, and promising, is when that comfort zone is left.

Both quantum and systems theory are highly counterintuitive in relation to everyday experiences—although certainly those everyday experiences are to a large degree also shaped by worldviews that are contingent, yet deeply historically entrenched. They both test the patience of the theorist as they tend to exhibit, and often even produce, difficult issues that refuse to go away (yet had better do this for the sake of the theory's cohesiveness), and they remain stubbornly at odds with other "big" accounts of (social) reality. However, arguably more than any other scientific theories before them, both bodies of theory engender the possibility that the many issues they leave open—and the permanent theory-immanent questioning of some of their central features—not only are expressions that these theories are parts of paradigms that ultimately will give way to new paradigms but also rather express quite fundamental disjunctures, contradictions, and paradoxes in the "fabric of reality" that simply elude coherent theoretical completeness.

There can be little doubt that both systems and quantum theory present quite radical challenges to most of the ways in which the world has been framed in International Relations. In both cases, however, it seems noteworthy that these challenges, on the one hand, derive from rather basic ways of thinking about the world in different terms than most of International Relations scholarship—the respective starting points are nothing less than different assumptions about the basic fabric of the world, in the case of quantum theory, or at least the social world, in the case of systems theory. On the other hand, the challenges derive from features of both theories that might, at first, let both appear to be very *problematic* bodies of theory when it comes to "applying" them to the "substantive" matters traditionally associated with International Relations: issues of war and peace, the relations between states, the global political economy, international regimes, the role of transnational actors, and so on.

It should be immediately clear from these condensed stock takings of systems and quantum theory that both provide quite comprehensive descriptions of the world that are far removed from the "classical" worldviews characteristic of much of both the modern natural and social sciences. Both are a long way off from what counts as International Relations or even the most abstract forms of International Relations theory. While of course exceptions might confirm the rule here, International Relations and International Relations theory as a whole remain pegged to a classical worldview in its broadest sense.

What is at stake is the possibility to say something meaningful about International Relations' purported subject matter(s), if the starting points are quite different worldviews about the basic characteristics of the (social) world's fabric, as well as the guiding questions of (social) theory that arise from that. Both quantum and systems theories require thinking about this fabric, including its basic textures such as levels and micro–macro distinctions, and how it is always contingently, yet not arbitrarily, continued out of myriad potentialities. Through the concepts of the observer and meaning, and through the recursivity built into them, quantum and systems theory can account for this fundamentally self-referential and partially paradox reality. It is because of this that both are counterintuitive: at the end of the tunnel, neither promises theoretical closure nor a view of the world as complete.

Notes

1. This chapter first appeared under the same title in 2020 *Security Dialogue* 51(5); it has been revised for the purpose of publication in this volume.
2. All translations in this text are our own.
3. See Swedberg (2014) on the theory-building function of translation devices.
4. Within the concept of Alexander Wendt, this reality exists in the form of a wave function, while Luhmann (1995 [1984]: 12) starts with a setting: "The following considerations assume that there are systems."
5. Which is why we think that the observers' genus is of no relevance here, hence the "it" (this is rather easy in English, using the neuter in German would sound completely wrong; Luhmann uses the masculine "der Beobachter").
6. Bell's theorem states that there is no local hidden variable that could serve as an explanation for all the predictions that quantum mechanics makes, although nonlocal hidden variables remain a possibility (Bell, 1993 [1986]).
7. Concerning the problem that the occurrence of a particular cause cannot explain the function as an effect, Luhmann in his method of equivalence functionalism states that between the two there is a "Unbestimmtheitsrelation" (Luhmann, 1962: 628), thus explicitly using the German term for Heisenberg's uncertainty principle. The use is metaphorical in this context and refers to the observation that whenever one is concerned with the effect, causes cannot exactly be determined, and vice versa. Therefore, a clear determination of a cause and an effect at the same time is not possible (Wagner, 2012: 61).
8. One could argue (without a trace of polemic, but rather reflecting on the reactions on the very first and very preliminary draft of this contribution at the quantum workshop at Ohio State in April 2018) that it is this "insult" of a refutation of humanism (see Moeller, 2012: 19) that—for all its departures from classical worldviews—Quantum Mind–inspired theorizing finds somewhat hard to swallow. To be fair (this being pointed out by Alex Wendt in a communication on this footnote), Quantum Mind is distinctly not humanist in the traditional sense, in that it rather bestows subjectivity on all organisms—yet this is still quite different from being "anti-humanist" in the sense of seeing the social world as constituted by communication (with any organism being an environment for social systems).

9. This pertains particularly to the specific reading of monadology by Deleuze: "We begin with the world as if with a series of inflections or events: *it is a pure emission of singularities*" (Deleuze, 1993: 60; emphasis in original). It is worth noting, and probably a point for further discussion, that Alexander Wendt in *Quantum Mind* sees Leibnizian monadology as a possible track to follow, but he does not follow it very far (see Albert, 2016b, for an earlier elaboration of this observation).

10. Following on the remark made in the last endnote, a big irony of CCP, of course, is that the "laws" that govern the causally closed universe become rather flexible (or might be said to disappear altogether) the closer one gets to a *singularity* (in this case: the big bang or black holes). In a cosmological perspective, one could say that CCP's main problem is that it pertains to "physics of local or small phenomena, scaled up to the largest scales.... [P]hysics has been the study of subsystems of the universe. This approach is incapable of providing answers to the central questions of cosmology, such as the nature of time and space and the origins or explanations of the laws and initial conditions of the universe (Unger and Smolin, 2015: xx).

References

Aerts, Diederik, and Massimiliano Sassoli de Bianchi. 2017. *Universal Measurements. How to Free Three Birds in One Move.* Singapore: World Scientific.

Albert, Mathias. 2016a. *A Theory of World Politics.* Cambridge: Cambridge University Press.

Albert, Mathias. 2016b. "Theoretischer Quantensprung oder ein Quäntchen IB? Alexander Wendt's 'Quantum Mind and Social Science.'" *Zeitschrift für Internationale Beziehungen* 23(2): pp. 177–189.

Albert, Mathias, and Barry Buzan. 2017. "On the Subject Matter of International Relations." *Review of International Studies* 43(5): pp. 898–917.

Bell, John. 1964. "On the Einstein Podolsky Rosen Paradox." *Physics* 1(3): pp. 195–200.

Bell, John. 1993 [1986]. "John Bell Interview." In: *The Ghost in the Atom: A Discussion of the Mysteries of Quantum Physics,* edited by Paul Charles William Davies and Julian R. Brown, pp. 45–58. Cambridge: Cambridge University Press.

Bohr, Niels. 1928. "The Quantum Postulate and the Recent Development of Atomic Theory." *Nature* 121(Supplement 14 April): pp. 580–590.

Brunkhorst, Hauke. 2014. *Critical Theory of Legal Revolutions.* London: Bloomsbury Academic.

Buhler, Keith. 2020. "No Good Arguments for Causal Closure." *Metaphysics* 21(2): pp. 223–236.

Deleuze, Gilles. 1993. *The Fold. Leibniz and the Baroque.* London: Athlone Press.

Einstein, Albert. 1971 [1947]. "Letter to Max Born." In: *The Born–Einstein Letters: Correspondence between Albert Einstein and Max and Hedwig Born, from 1916 to 1955,* edited by Albert Einstein and Max Born, pp. 156–158. Houndsmills: Macmillan.

Einstein, Albert, Boris Podolsky, and Nathan Rosen. 1935. "Can Quantum-Mechanical Description of Physical Reality be Considered Complete?" *Physical Review* 47(10): pp. 777–780.

Fuchs, Peter. 2009. *Die doppelte Verschränkung—Das Konzept der Beobachtung in der Quantenphysik und in der Allgemeinen Theorie der Sinnsysteme (ATS)—Ein Essay.* http://www.fen.ch/texte/gast_fuchs_quantenphysik.pdf (Accessed November 25, 2020).

Heisenberg, Werner. 1971. *Physics and Beyond: Encounters and Conversations*. Pomerans, Arnold Julius (Trans.). New York: Harper & Row.

Heisenberg, Werner. 1986. *Quantentheorie und Philosophie*. Stuttgart: Reclam.

Jacques, Vincent, E. Wu, Frédéric Grosshans, François Treussart, Philippe Grangier, Alain Aspect, and Jean-François Roch. 2007. "Experimental Realization of Wheeler's Delayed-Choice Gedanken Experiment." *Science* 315(5814): pp. 966–968.

Joos, Erich, and Heinz-Dieter Zeh. 1984. "The Emergence of Classical Properties through Interaction with the Environment." *Zeitschrift für Physik B: Condensed Matter* 59(2): pp. 223–243.

Kessler, Oliver. 2018. "The Mind-Body Problem and the Move from Supervenience to Quantum Mechanics." *Millennium: Journal of International Studies* 47(1): pp. 74–86.

Luhmann, Niklas. 1962. "Funktion und Kausalität." *Kölner Zeitschrift für Soziologie und Sozialpsychologie* 14(4): 617–644.

Luhmann, Niklas. 1976. "Generalized Media and the Problem of Contingency." In: *Explorations in General Theory in Social Science: Essays in Honor of Talcott Parsons*, edited by Jan J. Loubser, Rainer C. Baum, Andrew Effrat, and Victor Meyer Lidz, pp. 507–532. New York: Free Press.

Luhmann, Niklas. 1977. "Differentiation of Society." *Canadian Journal of Sociology* 2(1): pp. 29–53.

Luhmann, Niklas. 1980. "The Actor and the System: The Constraints of Collective Action." *Organization Studies* 1(2): pp. 193–195.

Luhmann, Niklas. 1981. "The Improbability of Communication." *International Social Science Journal* 23(1): pp. 122–132.

Luhmann, Niklas. 1982a. *The Differentiation of Society*. Holmes, Stephen, and Larmore, Charles (Trans.). New York: Columbia University Press.

Luhmann, Niklas. 1982b. "World Society as a Social System." *International Journal of General Systems* 8(3): pp. 131–138.

Luhmann, Niklas. 1987a. "Modern Systems Theory and the Theory of Society." In: *Modern German Sociology*, edited by Volker Meja, Dieter Misgeld, and Nico Stehr, pp. 173–186. New York: Columbia University Press.

Luhmann, Niklas. 1987b. "The Evolutionary Differentiation between Society and Interaction." In: *The Micro-Macro Link*, edited by Jeffrey Alexander, Bernhard Giesen, Richard Münch, and Neil J. Smelser, pp. 112–131. Berkeley: University of California Press.

Luhmann, Niklas. 1990a. "The Paradox of System Differentiation and the Evolution of Society." In: *Differentiation Theory and Social Change*, edited by Jeffrey Alexander and Paul Colomy, pp. 409–440. New York: Columbia University Press.

Luhmann, Niklas. 1990b. "Das Erkenntnisprogramm des Konstruktivismus und die unbekannt bleibende Realität." In: *Soziologische Aufklärung 5 Konstruktivistische Perspektiven*, edited by Niklas Luhmann, pp. 31–59. Opladen: Westdeutscher Verlag.

Luhmann, Niklas. 1992a. *Die Wissenschaft der Gesellschaft*. Frankfurt am Main: Suhrkamp.

Luhmann, Niklas. 1992b. "The Concept of Society." *Thesis Eleven* 31(1): pp. 67–80.

Luhmann, Niklas. 1992c. "The Direction of Evolution." In: *Social Change and Modernity*, edited by Hans Haferkamp and Neil J. Smelser, pp. 279–293. Berkeley: University of California Press.

Luhmann, Niklas. 1994. "How Can the Mind Participate in Communication?" In: *Materialities of Communication*, edited by Hans Ulrich Gumbrecht and Karl Ludwig Pfeiffer, pp. 371–387. Stanford, CA: Stanford University Press.

Luhmann, Niklas. 1995 [1984]. *Social Systems*. Bednarz, John Jr., and Baecker, Dirk (Trans.). Stanford, CA: Stanford University Press.

Luhmann, Niklas. 1996. "On the Scientific Context of the Concept of Communication." *Social Science Information* 35(2): pp. 257–267.

Luhmann, Niklas. 1997. "Globalization or World Society: How to Conceive of Modern Society?" *International Review of Sociology* 7(1): pp. 67–79.

Luhmann, Niklas. 2001. "Erkenntnis als Konstruktion." In: *Aufsätze und Reden*, edited by Oliver Jahraus, pp. 218–243. Stuttgart: Reclam.

Luhmann, Niklas 2004. *Einführung in die Systemtheorie*. Heidelberg: Carl-Auer Verlag.

Luhmann, Niklas. 2012 [1997]. *Theory of Society* (2 Vols.). Barrett, Rhodes (Trans.). Stanford, CA: Stanford University Press.

Moeller, Hans-Georg. 2012. *The Radical Luhmann*. New York: Columbia University Press.

Riegler, Alexander, and Armin Scholl, eds. 2012. "Luhmann's Relation to and Relevance for Constructivist Approaches." Special Issue. *Constructivist Foundations* 8(1). www.univie.ac.at/constructivism/journal/8/1 (Accessed November 25, 2020).

Scholl, Armin. 2012. "Between Realism and Constructivism? Luhmann's Ambivalent Epistemological Standpoint." *Constructivist Foundations* 8(1): pp. 5–12.

Schrödinger, Erwin. 1935. "Die gegenwärtige Situation in der Quantenmechanik." *Die Naturwissenschaften* 23(48–50): pp. 807–818, 823–828, 844–849.

Schützeichel, Rainer. 2003. *Sinn als Grundbegriff bei Niklas Luhmann*. Frankfurt am Main: Campus.

Spencer Brown, George. 1969. *Laws of Form*. London: Allen & Unwin.

Stetter, Stephan. 2016. "Säen und Ernten: Quantentheorie sozial- und (welt-) gesellschaftstheoretisch weitergedacht." *Zeitschrift für Internationale Beziehungen* 23(2): pp. 188–206.

Swedberg, Richard. 2014. *The Art of Social Theory*. Princeton, NJ: Princeton University Press.

Unger, Roberto Mangabeira, and Lee Smolin. 2015. *The Singular Universe and the Reality of Time. A Proposal in Natural Philosophy*. Cambridge: Cambridge University Press.

Von Foerster, Heinz. 1981. *Observing Systems*. Seaside, CA: Intersystems Publications.

Von Neumann, John. 1955 [1932]. *Mathematical Foundations of Quantum Mechanics*. Princeton, NJ: Princeton University Press.

Vogd, Werner. 2014. *Von der Physik zur Metaphysik. Eine soziologische Rekonstruktion des Deutungsproblems der Quantentheorie*. Weilerswist: Velbrück.

Vogt, Peter. 2011. *Kontingenz und Zufall. Eine Ideen- und Begriffsgeschichte*. Berlin: De Gruyter.

Wagner, Gerhard. 2012. *Die Wissenschaftstheorie der Soziologie. Ein Grundriss*. Munich: Oldenburg Verlag.

Wendt, Alexander. 2015. *Quantum Mind and Social Science Unifying Physical and Social Ontology*. Cambridge: Cambridge University Press.

Wheeler, John Archibald. 1978. "The 'Past' and the 'Delayed-Choice Double-Slit Experiment.'" In: *Mathematical Foundations of Quantum Theory*, edited by A. R. Marlow, pp. 9–48. New York: Academic Press.

Zeh, Heinz-Dieter. 1970. "On the Interpretation of Measurement in Quantum Theory." *Foundations of Physics* 1(1): pp. 69–76.

15

The Value of Value

A Quantum Approach to Economics, Security, and International Relations

David Orrell

Introduction

> The structure of the international political economy is determined
> as much by the distribution of wealth and of economics power as it is
> by the distribution of military and political weight and power.
> —Susan Strange, speaking at Chatham House in 1976[1]

Like a quantum particle, a word's meaning cannot usually be reduced to a single
definition, but exists in a superposition of states whose measurement is context dependent. According to one well-known online dictionary,[2] three main
meanings of the word "value" are:

1. The regard that something is held to deserve; the importance, worth, or
   usefulness of something
2. Principles or standards of behavior; one's judgment of what is important
   in life
3. The numerical amount denoted by an algebraic term; a magnitude, quantity, or number

The first and third aspects of the word—a sense of worth or utility and a
numerical amount—have very different properties (we return to the second
meaning later). For example, numbers are stable and unchanging (the number
3 was the same in ancient Greece as it is today); are linear and additive (2 +
2 = 4); are virtual and cannot be owned or possessed; and represent an exact
objective quantity. Our sense of worth or utility, in contrast, is variable and
context dependent; does not obey simple mathematical laws; is associated
with real ownership (as in a valued object); and is fuzzy, subjective, and im-
precise. The money system can be viewed as a way of mediating between these
two senses—of finding the value of value. In particular, money objects—be

they real coins or virtual bitcoins—are unique in that they are ownable objects with a fixed numerical value.

The complementary nature of the dual aspects of value, which compares with the dual wave/particle nature of quantum entities, is what leads to the dualistic and sometimes conflicting properties of money (Orrell, 2016; Orrell and Chlupatý, 2016). This chapter will argue that the money system in general shows the same kind of behavior that so puzzled physicists when they encountered it in their studies of subatomic particles at the start of the twentieth century. Rather than being either loosely analogous to quantum physics, or somehow reducible to quantum processes, it is better understood as exhibiting its own version of quantum properties, which not only affect individual behavior but also scale up to the global level, with very real implications for International Relations and security.

An outline of the chapter is as follows. Following this introduction, the second section illustrates the relevance of money to the field of International Relations by discussing the role of a risk-free security. The third section explores the meaning of "quantum" in the context of economics, and the fourth gives a summary overview of the quantum nature of the money system. The fifth section discusses how quantum social science was first applied to explore the roles of cognition and consciousness, while the sixth section describes applications in finance and argues that fields such as quantum cognition and quantum finance need to engage with the topic of money to present a genuine alternative to classical theory. The final section examines some of the objections to the quantum approach and argues that in order for the quantum viewpoint to influence economics and other areas including International Relations, a first step is to bring money back into the picture.

Quantum Security

While money is obviously important to International Relations and security—a major test of a country's sovereignty, after all, is its ability to control its own money supply—it might seem that the topic of monetary value, and in particular a quantum theory of money, is more tangential. Indeed, even in economics, finance is usually treated as a somewhat specialized subject. However, to bring out the dictionary another time, the two main meanings (or eigenmeanings, in the sense discussed later) of the word "security" are "the state of being free from danger or threat" and "a thing deposited or pledged as a guarantee of the fulfilment of an undertaking or the repayment of a loan, to be forfeited in case of default."[3] As Boy (2015: 537) notes, there is a direct relationship between these two meanings, since the definition of a risk-free asset (so something with a constant intrinsic value) "is not only a critical element in the pricing of stocks and derivatives, but serves as a benchmark for valuing any financial asset: its inconspicuous existence, subsumed by the general focus of modern finance theory on asset pricing and the calculability of the future, has only begun to attract attention through the sovereign debt crisis in the wake of the global financial crisis."

Throughout history our views of what counts as money have oscillated between two poles, which correspond to money as an abstract system of credit and money as an owned thing (e.g., gold or silver). As Schumpeter (1954: 53) noted, the debate between "the two fundamental theories of money" goes back to ancient Greece, when Aristotle argued that money needed to be a valuable commodity in itself, while Plato saw it as a virtual symbol. These theories have in turn defined our measures of financial risk.

During the gold standard, which was initiated in England in 1821 and persisted in one form or another (and with a few breaks for war) for almost 150 years, the risk-free asset was a physical weight of gold. Today, while the gold standard still has its admirers, our financial system is based more closely on Plato's ideas than on Aristotle's, and a risk-free asset is considered to be a US government bond. However, each of these theories reduces money down to a single dimension—to metal that can be physically possessed (what might be called the real aspect) or an abstract rational calculation on a ledger (the virtual aspect)—while, as argued here, money is better seen as a dualistic entity that combines these properties in a single package. And if the financial system was previously shaped by theories of money, it may be more accurate to say that today it is shaped by the absence of such a theory, or rather that money has been treated as unimportant, and the concept of risk subsumed into a mathematical calculation. This is best illustrated through the notion of financial entanglement, which eludes conventional economic analysis.

In mainstream economics, debt tends to be seen as something that just cancels out in the aggregate (Krugman, 2012: 112), while risk can be hedged away by an appropriate mix of investments. As Das (2006) wrote just prior to the financial crisis of 2007–2008, "financial risks, particularly credit risks, are no longer borne by banks. They are increasingly moved off balance sheets. Assets are converted into tradable securities, which in turn eliminates credit risks. Derivative transactions like interest rate swaps also serve the same purpose." In this picture, any asset or loan can be a risk-free asset if appropriately hedged. The result, as Brown (2012: 348–349) notes, is a different kind of "black magic" that creates seemingly secure assets "by redefining the basis of value from cash or gold in the vault to risk equations.... Quants know how to create true capital, and you don't need a printing press or sovereign powers. The keys are derivatives and securitization."

However, as discussed in the fourth section later, loan agreements or financial derivatives represent financial entanglements, in which a decision to default immediately affects the status of the loan (even if the creditor doesn't find out until later). Furthermore, such decisions are not made in isolation but are influenced and triggered by external events, leading to phenomena such as mass defaults and financial contagion. Far from being an inert chip or record in a ledger, money is a psychoactive substance that resonates with and amplifies the complex properties of the human mind (see the fifth section). Asset prices depend as much on trader psychology—and cognitive phenomena of the sort studied by cognitive scientists—as they do on the underlying assets. And in the quantum finance view (see the sixth section) "mass" refers not to a weight of metal, but to a term that varies inversely with an asset's volatility, and thus measures a kind of provisional stability (Baaquie, 2007; Orrell, 2020a, 2021a; Schaden, 2002).

To summarize: theories of money are relevant to security and International Relations because they both define and help enforce the financial standards that underpin many aspects of international order. For the gold standard, the risk-free asset was a "real" weight of metal, while for a fiat currency, it is the "virtual" promise of the state. In either case, the secure standard had to be backed by military power to be successful, which reveals the inherent link between money and power. However, classical theories of money give only partial views of money because money is a nonclassical phenomenon, which doesn't fit in the dictionary of standard economics.

In 1944, the Bretton Woods conference extended a version of the gold standard into the postwar period, with the US dollar acting as a reserve currency pegged to gold. As Sheng (2019: 364–365) noted in an article for the Bretton Woods Committee on its seventy-fifth anniversary, a new approach is called for today:

> To put it simply, we can no longer use the reductionist neoclassical economic paradigm, because the invisible hand of the market cannot deal with climate change, nor the inequities of war and disruptive technology....The neoclassical blindness arose because its framework was founded on the classical mathematics and physics of Descartes and Newton....A quantum paradigm of finance and the economy is slowly emerging, and its nonlinear, complex nature may help the design of a future global economy and financial architecture....Financial assets and virtual liabilities have quantum characteristics of entanglement with each other that are not yet fully understood....All of these developments suggest that using a new "quantum" imagination, the Bretton Woods framework can be reengineered.

Before proceeding to describe the quantum view of money, and its relation to other areas of quantum social science, in more detail, we first turn to another word that eludes precise definition, namely "quantum."

Quantum Information

The meaning of the word "quantum" is, like that of "value," both unstable and debated. In physics, as Lemos and Schaffer (2019) point out, there is no single quantum ontology, but instead a range of different interpretations. In the social sciences, the situation is of course even more contested. While readers will bring their own interpretations, this section will describe the approach used here to describe economic phenomena.

One common interpretation, when "quantum" is used outside of physics, is that the word is being employed as a metaphor; we say that the behavior of social systems in some respects resembles that of subatomic particles. However, this seems to be the wrong way around, because the usual purpose of a metaphor is to explain something that is difficult or abstract in terms of something that is more simple and concrete. When Shakespeare had an actor read "All the world's a stage" in *As You Like It*, he was comparing the vastly complex world to a wooden platform on which the actor was actually standing. In quantum physics, we might think of a wave function as real because it can be expressed using mathematical equations, at least for the most simplified of situations. But no one has actually seen or felt an electron's wave function (for one thing, it involves imaginary numbers). So at the risk of anthropomorphizing nature, it would actually make more sense as a metaphor to go the other way and say that subatomic particles behave like social systems.

Another interpretation is the physicalist approach, which asserts that the brain and consciousness in general are based on quantum processes (see, e.g., Penrose, 1989), so we are literally "walking wave functions" (Wendt, 2015: 3). As Wendt points out, this approach is bolstered by experimental evidence (see Lambert et al., 2013) that quantum effects play a role in biological phenomena such as photosynthesis or avian navigation.

Finally, there is the quantum-like modeling approach, popular among researchers working in quantum cognition, which is to make clear that they are using quantum models only for their mathematical properties and are not asserting that brain processes are quantum (see, e.g., Khrennikov, 2015; Accardi et al., 2008). Some authors relate this approach to the quantum information interpretation of quantum mechanics (Nielsen and Chuang, 2000; Wheeler, 1990), but, as Bagarello et al. (2017) note, this connection is not typically emphasized.

The terrain is made even more complicated by the fact that use of the word "quantum" outside of physics is generally viewed by physicists as problematic, in part because of things like "quantum healing," in part because of physicists being protective of their turf, and in part because of the Platonic tendency in science to confuse models with reality (Orrell, 2012). The physicalist and the quantum-like approaches can be viewed as two responses to this: the first sees the social sciences as embedded in physics, while the latter makes it clear that the intention is only to exploit a set of mathematical instruments and often treats any connection as unexplained, coincidental, or simply out of scope.

As seen in the next section, the approach in this chapter is a little different, because it says that the money system is quantum in the same way that the subatomic world was seen as quantum by physicists and mathematical modelers in the early twentieth century, in that it exhibits properties such as interference and entanglement that elude classical analysis and demand a quantum treatment. One difference between the money system and physics, of course, is that the money system operates at the macroscopic scale; another is that the money system is a quantum social technology, which we have designed ourselves.

The physicalist interpretation therefore does not apply, because the assertion that money is quantum does not rely on complex physical experiments to prove it true or false: we invented the system and so can check for ourselves. Conversely, showing that brain processes exploit quantum properties would certainly change the conversation around quantum effects in the social sciences but would not prove that money has such properties too; nor would it affect the way we model the financial system, which is the topic here, any more than knowing that birds exploit quantum effects to navigate—or for that matter that GPS systems in cars exploit relativistic effects to determine location—would mean that birds or traffic are best handled using quantum field theory. As physicist Robert Laughlin notes, the laws of hydrodynamics cannot be deduced from first principles—"The reason we believe them, as with most emergent things, is because we observe them" (Laughlin, 2005: 40)—and the same is true of economic phenomena. We return to this topic in the final section.

The approach here more closely resembles the quantum-like paradigm, except that (and this is more a matter of style or emphasis) this chapter dispenses with the qualifier "like": it does not treat quantum methods as tools that are borrowed from physics, but as a set of mathematical techniques that as computer scientist Scott Aaronson (1999) notes are adapted to handle "information and probabilities and observables, and how they relate to each other." Quantum probability is the simplest framework that allows for negative probabilities, and therefore interference. Many key elements of quantum mechanics such as the Hilbert space were developed by mathematicians before they ever found use in quantum physics. The primary application for quantum models is therefore not subatomic particles, but information. In this view, quantum social properties are not inherited from those of subatomic particles, but should be taken at face value. And the fact that the same tools work for both subatomic systems and the money system is not coincidence, but a sign that the common currency of the social and physical worlds treated by these models is information. Note that this is not the same as saying that reality itself is information, because the model is not the system. The reason we associate these tools with physics is purely historical—because they were applied there first.

Quantum Money

While as mentioned earlier this approach, which might be described as an informationalist approach, is based more on applied mathematics than physics (and is more epistemic than ontological), comparisons with quantum physics are at the same time certainly helpful and worth exploring, if only for illustration. Starting with perhaps the most obvious, the key discovery that led to the development of quantum physics was that energy is transmitted in discrete amounts, or "quanta," rather than continuously (Einstein, 1905).[4] Money, of course, is exactly the same. When you receive your pay packet, there isn't a little needle that shows the money draining into your account. Instead, it goes as a single discrete lump. It is the same as when you use your credit card at a store, or when a bank creates new funds by issuing a loan. And it is impossible to make payments smaller than a certain amount, such as a cent.

In physics, this discovery eventually led to the idea that matter has complementary wave/particle attributes. In the standard Copenhagen interpretation, attributes such as position and momentum are indeterminate and are revealed only upon measurement (according to some versions, by a conscious observer), with a mathematical wave function specifying the probability of each possible value being observed. Again, the money system is similar. The value of something like a house is fundamentally indeterminate and only takes on a precise value when the house is exchanged for money, in the economic version of a measurement procedure. In finance, the price and momentum of a stock can also only be measured through transactions, which in turn affect these variables. Of course, most items come with a price tag, but even here the price is subject to change and is only confirmed at the moment of purchase. Offering a product for a particular price gives little information about its worth if there are no buyers.

One of the more mysterious aspects of quantum physics is the fact that particles can become entangled, so that a measurement on one can instantaneously inform an experimenter about the state of another, even if it is located on the other side of the universe—a phenomenon Einstein mocked as "spooky action at a distance" (Kumar, 2008: 348). Despite his skepticism, entanglement was shown to be real in a series of ingenious experiments that teased out mathematical correlations between the spin states of entangled particles. With money, entanglement is less controversial or difficult to test. A loan agreement, for example, constitutes a single system that includes both the debtor and the creditor. If the debtor's decision to default is modeled using the quantum formalism as in quantum cognition (next section), then the loan agreement can be expressed as a single wave function, in which the states of the debtor and creditor are indeterminate but linked (Orrell, 2018a, 2018b).

Perhaps the biggest form of entanglement, which played a key role in both the financial crisis and the ensuing eurozone crisis, consists of financial derivatives, whose nominal value has been estimated at over a quadrillion dollars (Wilmott and Orrell, 2017: xiv). These allow businesses or investors to hedge against, or bet on, things like currency fluctuations or company defaults. It may have been hyperbole when Warren Buffett called derivatives "weapons of mass destruction," but they can certainly destroy lives and economies, and pose a threat to financial stability and therefore national security. Yet these instruments were developed with little regard for the complex social dynamics of credit systems (LiPuma and Lee, 2004), on the part of economists or social scientists in general. Since most money is today created through loans from private banks, similar entanglements characterize the money supply in general.

Another basic property of quantum systems is that they show interference. The most famous example is the double-slit experiment (Taylor, 1909), in which photons produce an interference pattern even when they pass through the slits individually. Money objects do not, of course, show such effects themselves; we know a ten-dollar bill is worth exactly ten dollars, and it doesn't interfere or cancel out if we put it next to a five-dollar bill in our wallet. But while their fixed nature means that money objects can't interfere with one another, they can certainly produce interference effects in the human mind, as seen next. The reason is that money objects are used to measure subjective value, which is something that can only be felt or experienced by a conscious individual.

Quantum Cognition

In recent years there has been growing interest among psychologists and others in the area of quantum cognition, which has proved useful at explaining not just our numerous departures from perfect rationality but also the nature of thought processes in general. An example is the well-known experiment where psychologists offered subjects a game in which they had an even chance of either winning $200 or losing $100 (Tversky and Shafir, 1992). After playing once, they were offered the chance to play again. If they were told that they won the first game, 69 percent decided to gamble their winnings, perhaps because they thought they had a hot hand or were playing with free money. If they knew they lost, then 59 percent played another round. But if they were not told the result, then only 36 percent opted to repeat. According to expected utility theory, the answer should be the average of the first two possibilities, which is 64 percent—a striking difference from the observed number.

This so-called disjunction effect applies to many other situations where one is trying to choose between a number of options with uncertain outcomes. From a quantum perspective, the decision to play a second time is affected by the result of the first game; and when this is unknown, the uncertainty between a positive reason (having a hot hand) and a negative reason (desire to win back losses) creates a kind of mental interference pattern that affects the decision-making process. As Busemeyer and Bruza (2012: 267) note, the situation is "analogous to wave interference where two waves meet with one wave rising while the other wave is falling so they cancel out." A related phenomenon is the "order effect" where responses to survey questions depend on the order in which they are asked, because the first question establishes a context for the following one (Wang et al., 2014).

The well-known game of the prisoner's dilemma (see Wendt, 2015: 172), where two prisoners are given a choice to act as informants in return for a reduced sentence, gives one answer if the prisoners are assumed to follow classical logic (they both snitch on the other) and another if they are assumed to follow a quantum logic (their behavior is affected by entanglement through things like social norms). James Der Derian taught the game to convicts from Gardner State Prison in a world politics class he was holding there "and in turn learned a lesson or two about Prisoner's Dilemma" when it turned out that they based their decisions on established criminal norms such as "traditional codes of silence, pre-scripted stories, and intersubjective rituals of honor," which makes sense in the quantum picture (Der Derian, 1998: 117).

Another example is the phenomenon known as preference reversal, where we change our mind about a question depending on the context (Tversky and Thaler, 1990). As a real-life illustration, consider the observed rate of strategic default during the US housing crisis. According to objective utility maximization, owners should default if the projected costs associated with staying in a home exceed the costs associated with selling it, and surveys did indicate that homeowners were ready to do so if this were the case (Guiso et al., 2013). However, when homeowners were actually faced with a real decision, their preferences reversed, to the point that the median borrower only defaulted when they were underwater by 62 percent (Bhutta et al., 2010: 21). This reversal is hard to explain from a classical utility-maximizing perspective but is consistent with an estimate derived from a quantum approach, which takes interference between objective and subjective factors, such as fear and guilt, into account (Orrell, 2021a).

Other studies have shown that a broad range of cognitive phenomena, discovered initially by behavioral psychologists, can be modeled in a parsimonious manner using the quantum approach, because of the natural way that it can account for effects such as context, interference, and entanglement (Wang et al., 2014; Busemeyer et al., 2015). While the mathematics may appear daunting to nonspecialists, it can often be easily expressed in terms of a quantum circuit, of the sort used in quantum computing; see Figure 15.1 (Orrell, 2021a, 2022a). The same quantum formalism extends naturally to economics: a person's decision, for example, to buy a stock, or default on a loan, or sell their company, can be modeled as the collapse of a context-dependent wave function (Orrell, 2018a, 2020a). When combined with the quantum properties of money, this implies that the money system as a whole can be viewed as a quantum system in its own right, with interference effects arising from the role of conscious participants. In particular, money acts as a vector that transmits and amplifies the quantum characteristics of human cognition to the global level, with significant implications for International Relations. It is the social equivalent of an atomic device—a quantum technology with the ability to help power us or destroy us. In the Preface to this volume Stephen Del Rosso points out that quantum IR "lacks a mushroom cloud equivalent" but—when one considers the energy encoded in the financial system (Garrett, 2014)— money provides a less tangible but even more powerful kind of bomb (Orrell, 2022b).

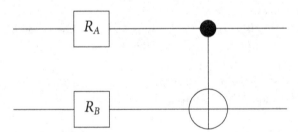

Figure 15.1 A simple but versatile quantum circuit. The input on the left is two initialised qubits. These are acted on by the gates R_A and R_B respectively. The qubits are then entangled with a C-NOT gate, which flips the lower qubit depending on the state of the upper qubit, before being measured. Gates R_A and R_B can represent a context and a decision (the disjunction effect, preference reversal); responses to two questions in order (the order effect); a strategy, and subjective beliefs about the other player's strategy, in the prisoner's dilemma; and so on. It can also represent a debt relationship, where the top qubit represents a debtor and the lower qubit a creditor.

Quantum Finance

Given the rather obvious and direct connections between money and quantum reality, it is curious that the money system's remarkable properties such as complementarity, indeterminacy, entanglement, and interference have received so little attention in economics. The only one of these characteristic properties that has been influential is that of indeterminacy, which was accommodated by allowing for stochastic uncertainty in otherwise deterministic models—part of the so-called probabilistic revolution in science (Krüger et al., 1990). In finance, the stochastic approach (see Cootner, 1964) formed the basis for key results including the efficient market hypothesis (Fama, 1965) and the Black-Scholes equation for valuing options (Black and Scholes, 1973). The connection with quantum physics was later rediscovered—and taken further—by researchers working in the field of quantum finance, which applies the quantum formalism to the modeling of financial assets such as stocks and bonds (as opposed to money per se).

It was found, for example, that the Black-Scholes equation is a close relation of Schrödinger's wave equation, for the special case where markets are assumed to be efficient (Haven, 2003). Under certain conditions, the markets even get their own version of an uncertainty principle, expressed this time in terms of the uncertainty in the price multiplied by uncertainty in momentum (Baaquie, 2007: 99). The random walk model, which is central to many algorithms in finance, finds a quantum challenger in the quantum walk (Orrell, 2021a, 2021b; Anonymous, 2021). And financial transactions in something like a stock market can be described in a very natural way using the formalism of quantum field theory. Schaden (2002) showed, for example, how investor portfolios can be interpreted in terms of wave functions in a Hilbert space. The purchase or sale of securities is modeled using the same operators as those used to simulate the creation or annihilation of bosons in a multibody quantum system.

The difference between quantum finance and traditional quantitative finance is best illustrated by the concept of a security's "intrinsic value." The point of a "risk-free" security after all—whether it is a gold sovereign in the era of the gold standard or a Treasury bond today—is that it has a fixed and dependable intrinsic value, and this sense of intrinsic value feeds into prices through markets. One standard definition of an efficient market, for example, says that "the price of an asset reflects all relevant information that is available about the intrinsic value of the asset" (Jones and Netter, 2017). The quantum version would state that the price corresponds to an *eigenvalue* of the system, in the sense of a possible value. The word "eigenvalue" comes from the German *eigen* for "own" or "inherent," and thus means something similar to "intrinsic value," though there can be more than one such value (indeed, there may be infinitely many).

To summarize, researchers have separately found that both human cognition and the behavior of markets are amenable to a quantum treatment. The point again is not that the financial system bears some superficial resemblance to quantum physics; instead, it is that, as a particular form of information transfer, it can be viewed as a quantum system in its own right. This has implications for the kinds of mathematical models used, but also the way we think about the economy in general. Experiments of human cognition often involve the use of money as a reward, and finance uses money as a metric, but its properties tend to be taken for granted. However, money objects are the link that connects economic decision-making with price changes in the market. Existing in the gap between economics, quantum social science, and International Relations, money is like a kind of connecting tissue that is invisible to conventional scans yet plays a vitally important role. It is the entangling properties of money and credit that weave the complex—and ever-growing—system of connections that have long played a key role in International Relations. And as with any quantum system, it is affected by context, which as already seen includes our theories of money.

Most money today is produced not directly by the state but by private banks—in the United Kingdom, for example, the amount is about 97 percent (McLeay et al., 2014)—and financial standards are enforced not just by international agreements but also in large part by complex financial derivatives that mediate between different currencies and financial products, at the same time that the traditional simple relation between national currency and nation-state has become blurred (Cohen, 2000). Calculations of risk premiums for individual countries are far from impartial but are affected by numerous preconceptions and cultural biases (LiPuma and Lee, 2004: 57) in a large-scale version or relative of the disjunction effect, where our perception of risk depends on context and the stories we tell. Bond traders are subject to their own version of the prisoner's dilemma where the "first redeemer advantage" impels them to redeem bonds at the first hint of a crash, thus increasing the chance of a crash (Guthrie, 2016). The aforementioned preference reversal on the part of US mortgage holders prevented a potential mass default on debts, which, according to one bank's estimate, were collectively worth some $745 billion (Streitfeld, 2010). Derivatives similarly rely for their function on the highly complex, coupled social phenomena of trader psychology and financial entanglement.

Based as they are on a classical view that treats the economy as a kind of mechanistic barter system (Samuelson, 1973: 55), mainstream economic models have a blind spot when it comes to all such phenomena that involve the complex, quantum properties of money and debt (Häring, 2013; Werner, 2016). As Vítor Constâncio, vice president of the European Central Bank, pointed out in a 2017 speech, one reason dominant economic models couldn't predict the crisis of 2007–2008 was because they "ignored the fact that banks create money by extending credit *ex nihilo*." More generally, "In the prevalent macro models, the financial sector was absent, considered to have a remote effect on the real economic activity." Indeed, a working assumption in macroeconomic models has long been that the possibility of default, let alone mass default, can be ignored (Goodhart et al., 2016). It is hard to predict a financial crisis—or understand its effects on the global economy—when the models don't include money creation, debt, default, banks, or a quadrillion dollars' worth of derivatives.

Neglect of these effects leaves a curious void in our treatment of international financial affairs, which quantum social science can help to fill. To return to the question of a financial security, one of the main contributions of quantum social science is to highlight the importance of effects such as uncertainty and entanglement, which find perhaps their most powerful and direct expression in finance. It is probably the case that the sophisticated derivatives that supposedly underpin the international financial order are simply too complex to properly value.

The quantum approach also emphasizes the role of power and energy in things like money creation. Just as it takes energy to create matter from the void, money isn't ushered into existence without a substantial input of effort. A medieval tally stick was accepted as money because it was backed by the sovereign's power to collect the debt (Orrell, 2021a); today the world's reserve currency is backed by the world's largest military.

Finally, as one more connection with the fields of security and International Relations, it should also be noted that if the financial system is quantum, then the advent of quantum computers as tools to interpret it will both drive adoption of quantum methods (Orrell, 2020b) and bestow a first-mover advantage on those state organizations and firms that are investing in the area (Asmundsson, 2017; Orús et al., 2019; Anonymous, 2021).

Quantum Insecurity

Quantum physics is usually described as being somehow alien: Einstein said it reminded him of "the system of delusions of an exceedingly intelligent paranoiac, concocted of incoherent elements of thoughts" (Fine, 1996: 1). As the physicist Steven Weinberg said in an interview (Hossenfelder, 2018: 124), quantum mechanics "has a number of features we find repulsive.... What I don't like about quantum mechanics is that it's a formalism for calculating probabilities that human beings get when they make certain interventions in nature that we call experiments. And a theory should not refer to human beings in its postulates." Yet as we have seen, concepts such as complementarity, indeterminacy, and entanglement seem quite reasonable when applied to the macrophysical world of money (even if the economic result is sometimes equally confounding). And the idea, which so repulsed some physicists, that consciousness might be a necessary part of the mix is again obvious with money, since only conscious beings can value something.

One objection to treating the economy as a quantum system is that, even if we accept that transactions are quantum in nature, that doesn't mean the economy as a whole need behave in a quantum manner. After all, Bohr's principle of correspondence shows that quantum mechanics should converge at large scales to its classical counterpart, and the same might be true of the economy (Hubbard, 2017). But in physics quantum properties *do* scale up by design in technologies such as computer chips, lasers, superconductors, magnetic resonance imaging, nuclear devices, and so on (see Der Derian and Wendt's introduction and the chapters by Frank Smith and Jarius Grove in this volume). Money too is a designed technology, and its quantum properties scale up and affect the economy as a whole, in phenomena such as money creation, entanglement through financial instruments, or mass defaults.

This does not imply that the economy can be reduced to quantum equations. The idea that a system can be broken down into parts is the hallmark of reductionist, deterministic science, but complex systems show emergent properties that need not be reducible to equations of any sort (Laughlin, 2005; Wolfram, 2002). From a quantum perspective, prices are similarly best seen as an emergent property of the money system (Orrell, 2017). They cannot therefore be reduced to measurements of labor, utility, or anything else (though they may reflect these qualities). Nor is it possible to explain economic transactions according to some micro-founded set of laws. Finally, the assertion that the financial system is quantum does not, of course, necessitate the use of quantum models for every case, any more than the assertion that matter is quantum implies that weather forecasters should quantize their models of the atmosphere.

Mainstream economics, with its emphasis on independence, rationality, and optimal equilibrium, is based on a classical paradigm. More than a decade on from the financial crisis, the problems of mainstream economics have been widely acknowledged, but changes have so far been mostly cosmetic. The purpose of the money system is to put numbers on the fuzzy concept of value (worth), in a way similar to the measurement procedure in physics, and treating the economy as a quantum system offers a natural framework for modeling effects such as money creation, financial entanglement, interference effects, and so on, all of which mainstream models struggle to address.

The quantum view of money and value has direct implications for the areas of International Relations and security simply because these form the basis of our economic system; and to understand relations and conflicts between countries and regions—from the United States with its privileged reserve currency, to Europe with its fragile eurozone, to China with its increasingly important (and digital) renminbi and massive holdings of American debt, to Venezuela with its hyperinflating bolivar—we need to account also for financial entanglements. By incorporating money into the analysis, quantum social science can explore how cognitive effects scale up in phenomena such as financial contagion or mass defaults, shed new light on the social construction of systems of value, offer an alternative to the conventional analysis of our financial system by including social factors, and question how changing ideas of money relate to the very idea of the nation-state.

To summarize, the main conclusions of this chapter are:

- Money exists at the nexus between value and power, and throughout history our treatment of it has been an important factor in shaping International Relations and security.
- Mainstream economics treats money as an inert medium of exchange, and its models ignore or downplay things like the financial sector or the role of debt, with very real implications for global society.
- The quantum theory of money, in contrast, treats money as a substance with complex, dualistic properties that scale up through the workings of the financial system to affect the economy as a whole.
- This quantum approach connects fields such as quantum cognition and quantum finance to the conscious human economy and provides a more accurate view of the money system and our interactions with it.
- A quantum reassessment of money will again have implications for International Relations and security, at a time when the financial sector, and its complex web of entanglements, has more power than ever over people and nations.

Only by understanding the money system's dualistic, entangling, dynamic, and potentially explosive effects—and by exploring its relation to value, in every sense of the word—can we accurately account for its influence over our behavior and more safely harness its creative and transformative power. It is hoped that this chapter will serve as an early foray that will encourage further investigations into the quantum nature of money and its entanglement with International Relations.

Acknowledgments

The author would like to thank James Der Derian, Alexander Wendt, and the anonymous reviewers for their useful comments on the article.

Notes

1. Retrieved from https://twitter.com/ChathamHouse/status/1339135202828967936.
2. Value (n.d.). In Oxford English Dictionary. Retrieved from https://en.oxforddictionar ies.com/definition/value.
3. https://www.lexico.com/definition/security.
4. Here discreteness refers to what (Lemos and Schaffer, 2021) call the "core fact" of quantum physics, which is that "at the smallest scale, nature is 'digital' not 'analog.'"

References

Aaronson S (1999) PHYS771 Lecture 9: Quantum. https://www.scottaaronson.com/dem ocritus/lec9.html (accessed December 12, 2019).

Accardi L, Khrennikov A, and Ohya M (2008) The problem of quantum-like representation in economy, cognitive science, and genetics, in Freudenberg W, Ohya M, and Accardi L(eds.), *Quantum Bio-Informatics II: From Quantum Information to Bio-Informatics.* Conference proceedings, Tokyo University of Science, Japan, March 12–16, 2008, 1–8.

Anonymous (2021). Schrödinger's markets. *The Economist.* November 6.

Asmundsson J (14 June 2017) Quantum Computing Might Be Here Sooner Than You Think. https://www.bloomberg.com/news/features/2017-06-14/the-machine-of-tomorrow-today-quantum-computing-on-the-verge

Baaquie BE (2007) *Quantum Finance: Path Integrals and Hamiltonians for Options and Interest Rates.* Cambridge: Cambridge University Press.

Bagarello F, Basieva I, and Khrennikov A (2017). Quantum field inspired model of decision making: Asymptotic stabilization of belief state via interaction with surrounding mental environment. *Journal of Mathematical Psychology*, 82, 159–168.

Bhutta N, Dokko J, and Shan H (2010) The depth of negative equity and mortgage default decisions. *FEDS* Working Paper No. 2010–35. Washington, DC: Federal Reserve Board.

Black F and Scholes M (1973) The pricing of options and corporate liabilities. *Journal of Political Economy*, 81(3): 637–654.

Boy N (2015) Sovereign safety. *Security Dialogue* 46(6): 530–547.

Brown A (2012) *Red-Blooded Risk: The Secret History of Wall Street.* Hoboken, NJ: Wiley.

Busemeyer J and Bruza P (2012) *Quantum Models of Cognition and Decision.* Cambridge: Cambridge University Press.

Busemeyer JR, Wang Z, and Shiffrin RS (2015) Bayesian model comparison favors quantum over standard decision theory account for dynamic inconsistency. *Decision* 2: 1–12.

Cohen B (2000) *The Geography of Money.* Ithaca, NY: Cornell University Press.

Constâncio V (2017) Macroprudential policy in a changing financial system. Remarks at the second ECB Macroprudential Policy and Research Conference, Frankfurt am Main, May 11. https://www.ecb.europa.eu/press/key/date/2017/html/ecb.sp170511. en.html (accessed December 12, 2019).

Cootner PH (1964) *The Random Character of Stock Market Prices.* Cambridge, MA: MIT Press.

Das D (2006) Globalization in the world of finance: An analytical history. *Global Economy Journal* 6(1): 1–25.

Der Derian J (1998). Review: The scriptures of security. *Mershon International Studies Review* 42(1): 117–122.

Einstein A (1905) Über einen die Erzeugung und Verwandlung des Lichtes betreffenden heuristischen Gesichtspunkt (On a heuristic viewpoint concerning the production and transformation of light). *Annalen Der Physik* 17(6): 132–148.

Fama EF (1965) *Random Walks in Stock-Market Prices.* Chicago: Graduate School of Business, University of Chicago.

Fine A (1996) *The Shaky Game.* Chicago: University of Chicago Press.

Garrett T (2014) Long-run evolution of the global economy Part I: Physical basis. *Earth's Future* 2: 127–151.

Goodhart C, Romanidis N, Tsomocos D, and Shubik M (2016) Macro-modelling, default and money. FMG Discussion Paper DP755. London: London School of Economics and Political Science. http://www.lse.ac.uk/fmg/assets/documents/papers/discussion-papers/DP755.pdf (accessed December 12, 2019).

Guiso L, Sapienza P, and Zingales L (2013). The determinants of attitudes toward strategic default on mortgages. *Journal of Finance* 68(4): 1473–1515.

Guthrie J (2016) Prisoner's Dilemma reveals bond fund risks. *Financial Times*, March 6.

Häring N (2013) The veil of deception over money. *Real World Economics Review* 63: 2–18.

Haven E (2003) A Black-Scholes Schrödinger option price: "Bit" versus "qubit." *Physica A* 324(1–2): 201–206.

Hossenfelder S (2018) *Lost in Math: How Beauty Leads Physics Astray.* New York: Basic Books.

Hubbard WH (2017). Quantum economics, Newtonian economics, and law. *Michigan State Law Review* 3: 425–480.

Jones SL and Netter JM (2017) Efficient capital markets. Library of Economics and Liberty, October 28. http://www.econlib.org/library/Enc/EfficientCapitalMarkets.html (accessed December 12, 2019).

Khrennikov A (2015) Quantum-like modelling of cognition. *Frontiers in Physics* 3(77):1–12.

Krüger L, Daston LJ, and Heidelberger M (1990) *The Probabilistic Revolution, Volume 1: Ideas in History.* Cambridge, MA: MIT Press.

Krugman P (2012) *End This Depression Now!* New York: W.W. Norton & Co.

Kumar M (2008) *Quantum: Einstein, Bohr and the Great Debate About the Nature of Reality.* London: Icon Books.

Lambert N, Chen Y-N, Cheng Y-C, Li C-M, Chen G-Y, and Nori F (2013) Quantum biology, *Nature Physics* 9(1): 10–18.

Laughlin RB (2005) *A Different Universe: Reinventing Physics from the Bottom Down.* New York: Basic Books.

Lemos GB and Schaffer S (2021) Obliterating thingness: An introduction to the "what" and the "so what" of quantum physics. *Foundations of Science* 26(1): 7–26.

LiPuma E and Lee B (2004) *Financial Derivatives and the Globalization of Risk.* Durham, NC: Duke University Press.

McLeay M, Radia A, and Thomas R (2014) Money creation in the modern economy. *Quarterly Bulletin 2014 Q1.* London: Bank of England. https://www.bankofengland.co.uk/-/media/boe/files/ quarterly-bulletin/2014/money-creation-in-the-modern-economy.pdf (accessed December 12, 2019).

Nielsen MA and Chuang IL (2000) *Quantum Computation and Quantum Information*. Cambridge: Cambridge University Press.

Orrell D (2012) *Truth or Beauty: Science and the Quest for Order*. New Haven, CT: Yale University Press.

Orrell D (2016) A quantum theory of money and value. *Economic Thought* 5(2): 19–36.

Orrell D (2017) A quantum theory of money and value, part 2: The uncertainty principle. *Economic Thought* 6(2): 14–26.

Orrell D (2018a) Quantum economics. *Economic Thought* 7(2): 63–81.

Orrell D (2018b) *Quantum Economics: The New Science of Money*. London: Icon Books.

Orrell D (2020a) A quantum model of supply and demand. *Physica A: Statistical Mechanics and its Applications* 539: 122928.

Orrell D (2020b) Quantum-tative finance. *Wilmott* 2020(106): 16–23.

Orrell D (2021a) *Quantum Economics and Finance: An Applied Mathematics Introduction* (second edition). New York: Panda Ohana.

Orrell D (2021b) A quantum walk model of financial options. *Wilmott* 2021(112): 62–69.

Orrell D (2022a) Quantum financial entanglement: The case of strategic default, in Chakraborti A et al. (eds.), *Quantum Decision Theory and Complexity Modelling in Economics and Public Policy*. Cham: Springer.

Orrell D (2022b) *Money, Magic, and How to Dismantle a Financial Bomb: Quantum Economics for the Real World*. London: Icon Books.

Orrell D and Chlupatý R (2016) *The Evolution of Money*. New York: Columbia University Press.

Orús R, Mugel S, and Lizaso E (2019) Quantum computing for finance: Overview and prospects. *Reviews in Physics* 4: 100028.

Penrose R (1989) *The Emperor's New Mind: Concerning Computers, Minds and the Laws of Physics*. Oxford: Oxford University Press.

Samuelson PA (1973) *Economics* (9th ed.). New York: McGraw-Hill.

Schaden M (2002) Quantum finance. *Physica A* 316(1): 511–538.

Schumpeter J (1954) *History of Economic Analysis*. New York: Oxford University Press.

Sheng A (July 2019) A new Bretton Woods vision for a global green New Deal, in *Revitalizing the Spirit of Bretton Woods: 50 Perspectives on the Future of the Global Economic System*. Washington, DC: Bretton Woods Committee, 360–367.

Strange S (1998) What theory? The theory in *Mad Money*. CSGR Working Paper No. 18/98. https://warwick.ac.uk/fac/soc/pais/research/researchcentres/csgr/papers/workingpapers/1998/wp1898.pdf (accessed December 23, 2019).

Streitfeld D. (2010) No help in sight, more homeowners walk away. *New York Times*, February 2.

Taylor GI (1909) Interference fringes with feeble light. *Proceedings of the Cambridge Philosophical Society* 15: 114.

Tversky A and Shafir E (1992) The disjunction effect in choice under uncertainty. *Psychological Science* 3: 305–309.

Tversky A and Thaler RH (1990) Anomalies: preference reversals. *Journal of Economic Perspectives* 4: 201–211.

Wang Z, Solloway T, Shiffrin RS, and Busemeyer JR (2014) Context effects produced by question orders reveal quantum nature of human judgments. *Proceedings of the National Academy of Sciences* 111(26): 9431–9436.

Wendt A (2015) *Quantum Mind and Social Science: Unifying Physical and Social Ontology.* Cambridge: Cambridge University Press.

Werner RA (2016) A lost century in economics: Three theories of banking and the conclusive evidence. *International Review of Financial Analysis* 46: 361–79.

Wheeler JA (1990) Information, physics, quantum: The search for links, in Zurek WH (ed.), *Complexity, Entropy, and the Physics of Information.* Reading, MA: Addison-Wesley, 112–131.

Wilmott P and Orrell D (2017) *The Money Formula: Dodgy Finance, Pseudo Science, and How Mathematicians Took Over the Markets.* Chichester: Wiley.

Wolfram S (2002) *A New Kind of Science.* Champaign, IL: Wolfram Media.

PART 4.

BRINGING THE HUMAN BACK INTO SCIENCE

16

Introspection Redux

Incorporating Consciousness into Social Research

Leonardo Orlando

Introduction

In *Quantum Mind and Social Science: Unifying Physical and Social Ontology*, Alexander Wendt (2015) tries to break "the 'taboo' of subjectivity" that he claims pervades most of contemporary social science by giving an ontological and epistemological place to consciousness through quantum theory—the proper path, according to him, for solving the mind–body problem. His project appears to be of great relevance for social research not only on strict metaphysical grounds but also regarding the philosophy of social science and—particularly for International Relations scholars—the practice of research in different disciplines that deal with human intentionality. The question that he raises regarding the place of consciousness within social research forces social scientists to take sides. Either we discard Wendt's argument, thereby accepting that there is no ontological or epistemological place for consciousness and carrying on with our research as before (meaning with no consideration of it), but must therefore accept that humans are zombies or robots and give up on agency and free will, or we accept that consciousness has its place in the study of the social and we act accordingly and start incorporating it in our research—because to do otherwise would entail treating humans as though they were zombies or robots. If the first option seems unacceptable from a humanistic point of view, the second is, at this stage, underserved by emerging methodologies for social sciences that try to incorporate consciousness. Accordingly, the highly important question that Wendt raises poses the challenge of identifying how consciousness can make an effective entrance into social research. Such a task is extremely relevant for political science and International Relations, as the inclusion of consciousness into research could lead to a radical new understanding of the dynamics of conflict, cooperation, strategic defense, political polarization, radicalization, violent extremism, and terrorism, as well as of the processes of social transformation required to cope with climate change. In this chapter, I intend to provide an answer to Wendt's question through a technique inherent in human consciousness: introspection.

First, I will begin by establishing the reasons why social science research, in its current "business as usual" version, can be conducted without any consideration of consciousness. Second, I will show how this dominant approach has been proven wrong, by introducing a sophisticated method of guided introspection developed by French psychologists, philosophers, and neuroscientists. Then, I will explain why introspection can only be incorporated into social science research through a quantum paradigm (rather than the classical, Newtonian one) and how, simultaneously, its inclusion allows for a better understanding of that same paradigm. Finally, I will conclude by advancing some core issues of political science and International Relations where the presented introspective technique could revolutionize our understanding of agency. My ultimate goal will be to provide a roadmap for incorporating consciousness into social research that fulfills (and enhances) Wendt's quantum paradigm, but that makes it possible to conduct this kind of research without making it necessary to directly engage with that paradigm—in other words, to stop worrying about quantum theory and start doing quantum social research.

The Futility of Consciousness

The definition of *consciousness* is just as problematic as the topic itself. However, it is possible to bring the term's multiple meanings to a single concept that encompasses most of the problem and its ramifications: *consciousness as experience* (Wendt, 2015, p. 15). This latter term is used in line with the concept of *phenomenal consciousness* as provided by Ned Block (1995, p. 228): "what makes a state phenomenally conscious is that there is something 'it is like' to be in that state." Consciousness as experience opposes, in Block's understanding, "access consciousness"—that is, "information-processing" consciousness. It is also different from self-consciousness or the awareness that one is conscious (Wendt, 2015, p. 15 and *passim*). What Block means by *consciousness as experience* follows what Thomas Nagel introduced in his seminal article "What Is It Like to Be a Bat?," namely, how it is for the subject himself to be himself:

> The fact that an organism has conscious experience at all means, basically, that there is something it is like to be that organism. There may be further implications about the form of the experience; there may even (though I doubt it) be implications about the behavior of the organism. But fundamentally an organism has conscious mental states if and only if there is something that it is like to be that organism—something it is like for the organism. (Nagel, 1974, p. 436)

Nagel (1974, p. 436) calls this "the subjective character of experience." If we intend to treat human actors as conscious beings whose actions contain intentionality, it is this form of subjectivity that we would like to bring into social research. However, this subjective experience is not self-evident: Is it the perception itself, as pure experience of what is there? Or is it the experience and its expression for the agent himself and/or for others? As Michel Bitbol (2014, p. 55) points out: "without the reflexive consciousness, there would be nothing like a visible and audible view of the world, but only an ecstatic adherence to appearing." Subjective experience, then, becomes perception intertwined with awareness of that perception, or "the entanglement of thinking and thinking about that thinking" (Bitbol, 2014, p. 71). This kind of subjectivity rejoins a tradition that goes at least as far back as John Locke, who claimed that "consciousness is the perception of what passes in a man's own mind" (Locke, 1689, quoted in Bitbol, 2014, p. 65). This notion was further refined by Freud when he established that it is through "consciousness that each one of us knows their own mental states" (Freud, 1915, quoted in Bitbol, 2014, p. 65). Hence, what is brought to the scene through this tradition is consciousness as introspection, or as the "inspecting perception of the interior" (Bitbol, 2014, p. 65)—namely, a process that "enlightens [mental states] and extracts them, in a resistible way, from their unconscious night" (Bitbol, 2014, p. 65). This brings us to the tension regarding whether consciousness should be included into or excluded from social science research: Are humans able to accurately describe their decision-making processes? Or do these processes occur at an unconscious level that is inaccessible to us, therefore making introspection irrelevant to social research? As a result of extensive psychological research conducted over the twentieth century, the introspective account of choice and decision-making processes was excluded from the investigation of human actions for what appear to be very sound reasons. Actually, in one of the most cited articles in the social sciences, "Telling More Than We Can Know," Richard Nisbett and Timothy Wilson (1977) set the basis for the impossibility of relating one's own mental processes. The authors assert that "we may have no direct access to higher order mental processes such as those involved in evaluation, judgment, problem solving, and the initiation of behavior," further concluding, on the basis of a set of experiments that they conducted, that the "accuracy of subjective reports is so poor as to suggest that any introspective access that may exist is not sufficient to produce generally correct or reliable reports" (Nisbett and Wilson, 1977, p. 233). These results have been recently validated through much more sophisticated research. In a replicated study conducted by Petter Johansson and his team (Johansson et al., 2005, 2006), the findings of Nisbett and Wilson were confirmed through the following experiment:

The experimenter shows the participants two pictures of women's faces and asks them to choose which one they find the most attractive. Immediately after, he shows the chosen picture again and asks them to explain the reasons for their choice. But in some cases, the picture which is re-presented is the one that was not chosen (through the use of a double-card ploy, the subject does not realize the manipulation). Surprisingly, the participants detect the substitution in only 27% of cases, and in 73% of cases, provide an explanation for the choice they did not make. (Petitmengin et al., 2013, pp. 654–655)

A detailed analysis of the verbal reports provided by subjects after they were asked why they chose the way they did showed no differences in emotionality, specificity, and certainty between those explaining the manipulated and those explaining the nonmanipulated choices (Johansson et al., 2006). These conclusions seem to be a devastating blow toward any possibility regarding the usefulness of introspection. Moreover, they are consistent with what neuroscientists have established in regard to the relationship between the actions that humans undertake and the explanations that they provide. As proved through research involving subjects who had undergone split-brain surgery,[1] the consensus that neuroscientists seem to have reached is that people are unaware of their decision-making processes, and the explanations that they provide for them cannot be understood as reasons. In the words of the leading living scholar in this field, Michael Gazzaniga (2011, p. 78): "listening to people's explanations of their actions is interesting—and in the case of politicians, entertaining—but often a waste of time."

Thus, everything seems to lead to the conclusion that consciousness, no matter how interesting or relevant it may be as a metaphysical question for the philosophy of social science, should not be the concern of social scientists. Actually, if we cannot access our mental processes, then consciousness, for all practical purposes, is irrelevant for social research. However, there is one problem with this approach: according to recent developments in the sciences of consciousness, it is almost certainly wrong.

Introspection Redux

Claire Petitmengin and a team of cognitive scientists in France reproduced Johansson et al.'s experiment but introduced "expert guidance" to the description of the choices made by the participants (Petitmengin et al., 2013). This modification led to an incredible outcome: it allowed the subjects to detect the deceit in 80 percent of the cases! While still proving that actors are usually unaware of their decision-making processes, Petitmengin and her team found that we can actually access those processes through specific mental acts. This finding is of utmost importance for the place of consciousness in social science research as it demonstrates that the exclusion of introspection has been done on the basis of a confusion: being unaware of a mental act does not necessarily mean that it is inaccessible. Thus, phenomenal consciousness and access consciousness (Block, 1995) are relied on through the bridge of *conscious attention*. It is not memory but retroactive awareness that activates the "passive memory" of Edmund Husserl, namely, the constant, involuntary memorization of the lived experience without noticing that experience:

> Whether we are touching, seeing, listening, imagining, remembering, under-standing or deciding, whether we are performing a concrete or an abstract ac-tivity, a large part of our activity, although "lived through" subjectively, is not immediately accessible to reflective consciousness and verbal description. We experience it, but in an unrecognized or "pre-reflective" way. The most sur-prising thing is that we are not aware of this deficit of awareness, which is the first obstacle in the way of becoming conscious of them: why should I make an effort to acquire an awareness I do not know I lack? (Petitmengin et al., 2013, pp. 656–657).

To achieve that awareness, what is necessary is to bypass the level of explanations and confront subjects with their own cognitive processes and the way they carry them out. And this is exactly what Petitmengin and her team achieved through the "elicitation interview method," recently renamed the "micro-phenomeno-logical interview method" (Petitmengin et al., 2019). This method, whose roots go back to the "neurophenomenological project" of Francisco Varela (1996), is a very specific technique developed by psychologist Pierre Vermersch (1994, 1999, 2009, 2012) and perfected by cognitive scientist Claire Petitmengin. Through the use of a carefully studied and widely tested protocol that considers an im-portant set of variables (including direction of the eyes, flow of speech, body position, and words), and by constantly avoiding the question "why?," which is never asked because it "deflects the subject's attention to the description of explanations and abstract considerations," the subject is guided throughout the interview by the question "how?," which leads him "towards the description of more and more detailed elements of his evoked choice process" (Petitmengin et al., 2013, p. 658).[2] The interview uses three main parts or "keys" to achieve its goal. Given the originality and specificity of the method, it is necessary to briefly present these "keys" in detail:

1. The first key to the elicitation interview consists of helping the subject to choose a particular occurrence of the cognitive process to be described,

which is precisely situated in space and time, and bringing the subject back to this singular experience when he moves away from it toward the expression of comments, justifications, explanations, and beliefs corresponding not to what he is experiencing but to what he thinks or imagines or believes about his lived experience (and thus interpreting it rather than describing it).

2. The second key to the interview is thus to help the subject to retrieve or to "evoke" the experience, whether it is in the past or only just over.... [T]he interviewer helps the subject to retrieve precisely the visual, auditory, tactile and kinaesthetic, and possibly olfactory sensations associated with the very start of the process: "What were you seeing, hearing, feeling...at this moment?" The subject "evokes" this moment when he recalls it to the point that the past situation becomes more present for him than the present situation is.

3. The third key to the interview consists of helping the subject to redirect his attention from the content, the "what" of his evoked cognitive activity, towards the involved process, the "how."...The diachronic dimension of the process corresponds to the stages of its unfolding in time: the succession of actions, perceptions and inner states which are lived. The synchronic dimension of the process corresponds to its configuration at a given moment in time, which cannot be described under the form of a succession: it includes in particular the type of attention and the sensorial modalities which are mobilized. (Petitmengin et al., 2013, p. 657)

The result of the careful application of these three "keys" is that the method becomes a "remedy" to the "ordinary blindness to living experience" (Petitmengin et al., 2013, p. 668). Hence, the use of the "micro-phenomenological interview" brings into awareness the decision-making processes and equally provides a precise description of them. Actually, the findings of Petitmengin and her team are not isolated but relate to the new trend in "introspective sciences," the main characteristic of which is to guide the subjects toward a regaining of contact with the lived experience, rather than diffusing their attention by asking questions that are abstract or general (Bitbol, 2014, pp. 603–662). This has the effect of making the objections raised by Nisbett and Wilson to introspection disappear, as we can clearly understand now that their subjects were not truly introspecting. In fact, their subjects never left the level of representations and beliefs: they were rather led into diving deeper into the trap of providing post hoc reasons for their cognitive processes, and the exploration of their choices through the guidance of the interviewer via the question "why?" alienated them from delving into the actual experience of the decision-making process.

However, several questions arise regarding how introspection could actually work and whether it should really be brought back from academic oblivion. The main objection that is raised against introspection is that it alters the mental process that it intends to know (Bitbol, 2014, pp. 603–662)—an objection that takes several forms. First of all, all introspection appears to be "retrospection" (Petitmengin and Bitbol, 2009, p. 368), meaning that a very serious obstacle arises: the correctness of memory. If our purpose is to use this method in the social sciences in general, and political science and International Relations in particular, this problem is of utmost importance, as we run the risk, through a rebuilding of memories, of opening Pandora's box and creating "a retrospective falsification of conscious history, by the processes that Dennett (1991) calls 'Orwellian' and 'Stalinesque' " (Petitmengin and Bitbol, 2009, p. 368).[3] This objection intersects with another one: that of "interpretative distortion"—that is, that the preconceptions of the subject may have a distorting effect or even substitute for the experience (Petitmengin and Bitbol, 2009, p. 369). This brings us to the most important challenge regarding the validity of this method in itself and for its use for research in the social sciences: "What do these strange fables told by the subjects about their own experience teach us about the objective world? Is not their reach limited to the people who pronounce them, and to when they are pronounced?" (Bitbol, 2014, p. 641). In other words, introspection seems to be doomed by what could be its impossibility to faithfully link the experience as it appears to the subject with the objective world of that actual experience. However, as we will see, this challenge is easily overcome when we switch paradigms and move from the classical, Newtonian understanding of reality to that of quantum physics.

Quantizing Introspection

As Michel Bitbol points out, the epistemological situation of introspection is isomorphic to the epistemological situation of quantum physics (Bitbol, 2000, 2008, 2011, 2014; Petitmengin and Bitbol, 2009). The argument goes like this: quantum phenomena "adhere to the contraptions in which they arise; they are not independent of the experimental situation which makes them manifest" (Bitbol, 2008, p. 67). Actually, following the Copenhagen interpretation of quantum physics, "each phenomenon is co-defined by the experimental conditions of its manifestation; in the sense of Bohr, each phenomenon is constituted and not disturbed by the instrumental device" (Bitbol, 2014, p. 625). Thus, according to a quantum paradigm, it is no longer possible to "complain of the distortion of phenomena by the processes used to know them, since there is nothing like phenomena independent of these processes" (Bitbol, 2014, p. 625). The scientific quest of quantum physics, then, could be characterized as "an operative project of extraction of invariant or covariant structures within a complex of appearances" (Bitbol, 2014, p. 625). This is achieved through the following quantum development:

> We begin by giving up the objectivation at the level of specific phenomena occurring in space-time....Afterwards, we undertake an ascension towards a less detailed statistical description, relying on the fact that the strict reproducibility and indifference to the order of the measurements, which cannot be reached at the level of the individual values, will be easily recovered at the average distributions of large numbers of values. At the end of the procedure, we go up to a higher level of abstraction: that of formal tools, or state vectors in a Hilbert space, capable of generating as many statistical distributions as types of measurements, and legally formalized as part of the Schrödinger equation. The state vectors are basically the maximally invariant structures used by quantum physicists; they play the role of objectivized entities without, however, maintaining the slightest resemblance to our archetypal image of the objects of physics, namely, material bodies extended in ordinary space. (Bitbol, 2014, pp. 642–643)

This principle is analogically applied to introspection by combining "a descent and an ascent" that happens through two steps:

1. Descent to minimally interpreted descriptions of the fine texture of lived events, asking subjects not to try to reconstruct their own cognitive processes, nor to explain in abstracto their "reasons" for acting...
2. Ascension a posteriori, undertaken by the researchers who analyze introspective reports treated as data, to transversal structures that do not depend on subjects and circumstances. (Bitbol, 2014, p. 643)

This process of descent and ascension is exactly what has been achieved through the "micro-phenomenological interview," whose structure corresponds to this epistemological framework. As we have seen, the first step of the researchers was to "guide the subjects towards an intimate contact with their experience, while dissuading them from elaborating rational reconstructions that would interfere with their task of description," and, the second, to "delineate data formatted from their disciplined descriptions, and undertake to extract generic structures" (Bitbol, 2014, pp. 647–648). The practice of introspection thus becomes epistemologically isomorphic to quantum theory, and it is therefore through a quantum paradigm that this method can be undertaken, as the objections that were raised against it correspond to an understanding of science that does not fit into modern physics.

However, a quantum approach to introspection not only is a methodological stand but also coincides with a wider anchoring of the human psyche in a quantum paradigm. Actually, it is indeed by virtue of quantum grounding that a promising new understanding of human actions is arising among cognitive approaches to decision-making processes (Wang et al., 2013) as well in relation to conscious attention (Jiang and Prakash, 2014). As explored in detail by Wendt (2015, pp. 149–188), a "quantum model of man" has proven to be extremely fruitful for rational-choice studies of human behavior, as quantum indeterminism is a more appropriate fit for the probabilistic character of social action. As Harold Atmanspacher (2017, p. 305) argues, "There is accumulating evidence in the study of consciousness that quantum concepts like complementarity, entanglement, dispersive states, and non-Boolean logic play significant roles in mental processes." These approaches lead to "well defined and specific theoretical models with empirical consequences and novel predictions" around psychological phenomena such as decision and judgment processes, bistable perception, learning processes, or semantic networks and concept decompositions (Atmanspacher, 2017, pp. 306–307).

Certainly, the quantum model of man that these approaches are depicting appears only metaphorical: the psychological dynamics exposed by Busemeyer and Bruza (2012), Haven and Khrennikov (2013), or Lambert-Mogiliansky et al. (2009) are, according to them, "quantum-like" cognitive processes. Nevertheless, current developments in quantum biology entertain the prospect that "brain activity correlated with those mental processes is in fact governed by quantum physics" (Atmanspacher, 2017, p. 305). Therefore, the possibility of an *actual* quantum brain should be also seriously envisioned in spite of the apparent unlikeliness of that hypothesis at the current stage of scientific research (Searle, 2010). Moreover, beyond the particular neurophysiological mechanisms that they advance, an interesting commonality of "quantum brain" theories such as those of Freeman and Vitiello (2008, 2010), Hameroff and Penrose (1996, 2014), Stapp (2009), or Wendt (2015) is the possibility that they open to considering mental states as superpositions of potentialities that eventually collapse into actions. Consequently, as per its ability to bypass the unconscious dimension of language (Pinker, 1994, 1997), guided introspection could explore the perceptual moment before the (mental) wave collapses, namely, mental states as representational states of desires and beliefs that agents can introspect without deceiving themselves (Skokowski, 2019). Therefore, and even if we cannot know what it feels like to be in a quantum superposition (Albert, 1992; Gao, 2017; Lehner, 1997), introspection appears as a promising path through which to dive into the "wider sea of possibilities" where "potentialities seem to float" and out of which they are chosen (William James, quoted in DeWitt and Graham, 1973, p. vi).

Furthermore, and even if one remains entirely agnostic about the plausibility of the "quantum brain" hypothesis, the potential of introspection for exploring the indeterminism of mental states before they collapse into actualities becomes a tool for navigating one of the key aspects of a quantum social paradigm: the matrix of probabilities. Actually, if human action is the result of both conscious and unconscious processes, it is conscious thinking that creates alternative possibilities, thus activating agency and volition (Baumeister et al., 2018a, 2018b). Hence, to consider that decision-making is the exclusive result of unconscious processes is virtually to rule out free will, as extensive psychological research shows that "the unconscious operates on the basis of a largely deterministic worldview" (Baumeister et al., 2018b, p. 235). It is consciousness that is required to open the "matrix of maybe" and relate agents to the multiplicity of outcomes of their actions, perceived not as a set of predetermined results but as a dynamic process of envisioning alternative possibilities (Baumeister et al., 2018b). Introspection is the procedure that allows actors to gain access to this process, becoming, then, a method that puts consciousness at the core of human activity, understood as the actualization of uncountable potentialities rather than the result of a mechanistic process.

We thus arrive at a major conclusion regarding introspection and its application to knowing more about mental processes: its quantum grounding is not only epistemological but also—and perhaps more importantly—ontological. As posited by Henry Stapp (1999, p. 26), if we intend "to hold our thoughts to be causally efficacious," then we cannot do it at the current stage of scientific research but through quantum physics. The quantum paradigm has superseded all the previous ones, reproducing "all of the empirical successes of classical physical theory" while also succeeding "in every known case where the predictions of classical physical theory fail" (Stapp, 1999, p. 4). Quantum theory provides the most robust and well-proved explanation of physical reality. Thus, beyond the epistemological framework, a quantum approach to introspection constitutes the ontological condition of possibility for a proper understanding of the connection between consciousness and physical states, meaning between mental processes and agency. We can therefore assert that to "quantize" introspection reveals itself not only as the path to bringing consciousness into social sciences but also as the bridge between agency, free will, and action: quantum social theory represents both the precondition and the fulfillment of this triad.

A Revolutionary Road for Security Studies

If the goal of International Relations research is to understand global politics within a framework that considers actors as beings endowed with free will, and the most suitable path for achieving this is to undertake a quantum turn, then the next logical step would be to adopt a method that incorporates consciousness into research. This method could be one of guided introspection such as the "micro-phenomenological interview," which could prove enriching if applied to International Relations. When tested in different areas, this method has demonstrated its success in making subjects gain awareness of their decision-making processes, consequently helping them to improve these processes while facing critical choices. In fact, over the last decades the method has been employed successfully in "educational sciences and psychopedagogy, cognitive sciences, the control of industrial facilities, major companies, sports (athletics, rugby, football, refereeing, swimming), justice, health, bodily awareness and arts including performing arts [ballet dancers]" (Maurel, 2009, p. 85), as well as with first responders of the French National Emergency Medical Help Service (Mouchet and Bertrand, 2018). Moreover, other guided introspective techniques have been able to provide core insights into fundamental aspects of human interactions, such as empathy (Lumma et al., 2019). Building on this, we can claim that an introspective method for navigating actors' conscious experience of mental processes would allow not only for a better understanding of core issues and problems of International Relations but also for a new way to approach key assumptions about social research.

Introspection redux through quantum theory could provide a new research agenda for security studies, as it entails a significant shift in our understanding of the decision-making processes involved, for example, in conflicts, strategic defense, political polarization, radicalization, violent extremism, or terrorism. Through its ability to bypass the level of reasons, guided introspection would give us entrance into a new dimension of study that was hidden until now: the fabric of agency—that is, actors' conscious experience of their mental processes. This is not just an incremental step in our understanding of social phenomena but challenges what is at its core, namely, our assumptions about the attribution of reasons for action.

As Joseph O'Mahoney has argued, the problem of reason attribution is a fundamental one for International Relations, as "most explanations of behavior in political science rely, whether implicitly or explicitly, on some attribution of motive, intention, or some reason for action to actors" (O'Mahoney, 2015, pp. 231–232). In other words, social science research anchors its explanation in the premise that "providing a reason for action explains the action" (O'Mahoney, 2015, p. 237), while at the same time precluding the possibility of directly accessing those reasons, for others as well as for ourselves. Hence, for social research, "making an action comprehensible, or 'make sense,' involves redescribing the reason for the action in a way that intuitively makes sense to the observer" (O'Mahoney, 2015, p. 234). Several methodological strategies exist for solving the conundrum of reason attribution, such as assuming "a possible reason and explain[ing] behavior in terms of that reason," or avoiding "the direct attribution of reason to individuals and locat[ing] explanatory leverage at an analytical level beyond the individual actor reason for action," or even "us[ing] empirical evidence to adjudicate between possible reasons" (O'Mahoney, 2015, p. 233). All these strategies have in common the underlying assumption that it is impossible to access actors' mental processes, consequently excluding them entirely. Agency is framed by exclusively focusing on the actions and their interplay with different sets of properties (of the environment, the actors, etc.). However, this kind of strategy cannot provide a full account of the social phenomena under study because, as Wendt points out, to get to "the real explanation we need to get inside the heads and discourse of decision makers and see what is motivating their behavior" (Wendt, 2001, quoted in O'Mahoney, 2015, p. 242).

What seems to be an unsolvable aporia could actually find a possible solution through the use of guided introspection as a tool for diving into the mental processes of actors. This entails a consequence of utmost importance for political science and International Relations, as an introspective approach could constitute a pathway for mapping the structure of agency. Such an endeavor could possibly revolutionize our understanding of reasons and their entanglement with goals, attention, consciousness, and unconsciousness. Actually, diving into the conscious experience of the actor establishes a distinction between action as the result of deliberate choice and action as the outcome of a process that responds to reasons beyond our understanding, though that doesn't preclude us from accessing the latter. In other words, the phenomenal dimension of mental states disentangles "what somebody is thinking" from the decision-making processes themselves. This could change the entire panorama of aspects that are involved in what we conceive as a research project around political and international issues.

First of all, it would be possible to approach novel dimensions, such as the sensory, the kinesthetic, and the affective. If a new established cartography finds solid correlations between one of those dimensions and a specific decision-making outcome, it would open intriguing and fruitful paths of research. Moreover, the affective dimension could be explored in a completely novel way: that of the actors approaching the granularity of their actual affects rather than the explanatory reports of what they felt. Furthermore, the method would allow for two levels of analysis: that of individual actors and that of collective agents. This does not imply breaking the "flat ontology" that quantum social theory invites us to adopt (Wendt, 2015). On the contrary, it means that we could approach through this method the different decision-making processes of, for example, policymakers, political leaders, and military officers, on one hand, and of the social aggregations that operate in a "we mode," such as institutions, states, social movements, and digital crowds, on the other. Afterward, the researchers could undertake the quest for common structures that signal the mutual links between these levels, further proving the entanglement of the individual minds that leads to the collective (Wendt, 2015).

The picture that introspection draws would certainly not be a clear and defined one, but more like a puzzle whose parts are spread along the whole spectrum of actors, and it would be a picture that researchers would have to put together to understand the elements involved in the phenomena under study. Moreover, limitations exist at the current stage of development of the introspective interview methods. For instance, the subjects must be collaborative with the interviewers, meaning that we could hardly conduct this kind of research with actors that are unwilling to dive into their consciousness—and, paradoxically, the most interesting subjects for security studies could be the most uncooperative ones. Nonetheless, in spite of these difficulties, the method seems worth the investment. Recent research shows that "goals can be activated unconsciously by features of the environment" (Dijksterhuis and Aarts, 2010, p. 471). In the international political arena, we have an extremely rich body of descriptions of multiple environments and their possible combinations: economic, political, institutional, etc. However, we lack a map pinpointing the relations between phenomenal consciousness and the actions undertaken in those very same environments. Such a map could turn out as a rich pattern for those cases where environmental conditions do not correlate with the outcome of actions undertaken by different actors facing similar situations. Here, the common structures of the lived experience of the actions as told by the actors and extracted by the researchers could potentially present common internal structures that allow for connecting the missing dots. Establishing such a cartography could help travelers crossing similar lands to navigate their way through the unexpectedness of human action, by mapping sets of possibilities for probable outcomes being actualized from similar potentialities.

Last but not least, another crucial aspect of bringing consciousness into social research through introspection is that this endeavor could foster ongoing biological, evolutionary, and neuroscientific approaches to political science and International Relations. Evolution has selected the human brain for "cognitive mechanisms that are specialized for reasoning about social exchange" (Cosmides and Tooby, 2005, p. 585). Consequently, it is at the level of the brain and the mind that the different evolutionary characteristics and strategies of human beings occur (Barkow et al., 1992; Pinker, 1997; Kurzban, 2010; Christakis, 2019), and it is the human cognitive structure that underlies both the neurobiology of violence (Panksepp, 1998) and adaptations for cooperation such as morality and emotions (Trivers, 1971; Haidt, 2001). Within human nature we find "motives that impel us to violence, like predation, dominance, and vengeance, but also motives that—under the right circumstances—impel us toward peace, like compassion, fairness, self-control, and reason" (Pinker, 2012, p. 581). Hence, the fountainhead of political processes is to be found within the brain and the mind: it is the individual mental processes underlying social dynamics that will have primacy, ultimately, over how human ideas and decisions are presented and adopted or rejected (Turner, 2007; Hatemi and McDermott, 2011; Johnson, 2015). Biological, evolutionary, and neuroscientific approaches to political science and International Relations such as those undertaken by Azar Gat (2006, 2009, 2019), John Friend and Bradley Thayer (2011, 2012, 2013, 2017), Peter Hatemi and Rose McDermott (Hatemi and McDermott, 2011, 2012; McDermott and Hatemi, 2014, 2018), or Michael Bang Peterson (2016) constitute some of the most promising and scientifically rigorous endeavors within the field. However, their study of the human brain and mind in relation to political processes could be diminished owing to the lack of attention to the phenomenal consciousness of the actors. Thus, in the same way that the neurophenomenological project of Francisco Varela (1996) intends to bring the dimension of phenomenal consciousness into neuroscientific research, guided introspection could fill the same gap for those biological, evolutionary, and neuroscientific approaches to political science and International Relations. If human consciousness is "evolution perceiving itself by reflecting upon itself," as Pierre Teilhard de Chardin (1955, p. 221) argues, then the "micro-phenomenological interview" could turn social researchers into geographers mapping the evolutionary mental processes involved in risk-taking or risk aversion, conflict, cooperation, bargaining, negotiation, and all other dimensions of agency where the brain and the mind intertwine with political outcomes.

Conclusion

Introspection, I suggest, can become a roadmap for integrating consciousness into social science research. The validity of first-person reports gains solidity if social research is conducted within a quantum framework, as the former is epistemologically isomorphic to the latter. Moreover, an introspective dive into mental states considered to be in superposition is consistent with quantum brain theories and probable hypotheses about how agency unfolds. Hence, to do quantum social theory is to turn methodological, epistemological, and ontological attention to techniques such as the "micro-phenomenological interview." This allows subjects to gain awareness of their decision-making processes, and researchers to obtain insight into the *structures* of these processes. The possibilities that such a research project could open are endless, as the discipline of International Relations could move to more solid ground in its exploration of change in global politics: rather than focusing on the outcomes and stimuli of different social processes, it could be possible to dive into the mental dimension of those dynamics. This could fulfill the quantum paradigm proposed by Alexander Wendt in two ways. First, it would be possible to explore not only experience and cognition but also will (Wendt, 2015), accessing the fountainhead of human action and allowing a better understanding of how the superpositions of potentialities collapse into actualities. Second, the nonlocal experience of time could be better understood, and the "addition effect" and "replacement effect" (Wendt, 2015, pp. 202–205) explored by a better first-person experience, thus providing a more appropriate study of how the present intertwines with the past and alters it, opening toward unexpected futures. Last but not least, introspection constitutes what, from Leibniz to Strawson through Schopenhauer, James, and Whitehead, could be called the "argument from experience of causation" in support of panpsychism (Mørch, 2019), namely, the experience of will as proof of the omnipresence of consciousness. This latter point further expands the quantum reach of introspection: its implications go beyond Niels Bohr and apply also to David Bohm, Henry Stapp, and different theories of quantum consciousness (Wendt's included). Introspection then appears, finally, as an optimal path for quantizing International Relations. And if skepticism about its utility or the proper foundation of its theoretical validity remains, that could be easily overcome by an analogy that Michel Bitbol (2014, pp. 661–662) establishes between introspection and one of the key inventions of human history: the telescope. As he points out, at the beginning of modern astronomy, when the telescope was first introduced, scientists refused to use it, as they claimed it didn't provide a faithful image of the objects and phenomena that it intended to study, but was transforming them through its lens. Not even when further theories (namely, geometrical optics) started to become available did scientists accept it as a valid research tool. However, some fearless pioneers used it all the same, making amazing discoveries that, eventually, caused the old paradigm to collapse and the new one to flourish. In times of bewildering ecological, technological, and political threats that we can hardly navigate, social research urgently requires this kind of bold pioneer.

Notes

1. A procedure that involves severing the corpus callosum, that is, the large tract of nerves that connects the two hemispheres of the brain (Gazzaniga, 2005, 2011), and that consequently "blocks the interhemispheric transfer of perceptual, sensory, motor, gnostic and other forms of information in a dramatic way, allowing us to gain insights into hemispheric differences as well as the mechanism through which the two hemispheres interact" (Gazzaniga, 2005, pp. 653–654).

2. For their reproduction of the Johansson et al. experiment, Petitmengin et al. conducted the interviews as follows:

> The experimenter/interviewer starts by encouraging the subject to retrieve the moment where the pictures were presented to him: "I suggest you go back a few seconds ago, to the moment when I showed you the pictures. To do this, I propose that you listen again to my voice when I ask the question, 'Which of the two faces do you prefer?', and that you see again the pictures as you saw them then." When the subject shows that he has arrived at this moment (a nod, a smile), the interviewer helps him to retrieve the different phases of his choice process, through questions that "'point to' the different moments of the process, without inducing any content, such as: 'When you see the pictures, what happens?... What happens after this?'" The same type of questions are repeated for each phase, in order to elicit a description of a finer and finer diachronic granularity. For example, if the subject says: "First I look at the face on my right," the interviewer asks: "When you look at the face on your right, what do you look at first? How do you go about looking at it? And then?" The interviewer draws the subject's attention more specifically to the moment of the decision and the criteria of choice through questions such as: "At the time when you finally pointed at this face, how did you know that you had made your choice? What had happened just before?" (Petitmengin et al., 2013, p. 658)

3. "Retrospective alteration of history can be obtained in two ways, according to Dennett (1991). In the Orwellian way, somebody first makes one conclusion based on partial evidence, and then changes her memory of having made this previous conclusion in order to accommodate further evidence. In the Stalinesque way, somebody does not make any intermediate conclusion but entirely reconstructs the whole sequence ex post facto, when all the evidence is available" (Petitmengin and Bitbol, 2009, p. 368).

References

Albert, D.Z. 1992. *Quantum Mechanics and Experience*, Cambridge, MA: Harvard University Press.

Atmanspacher, H. 2017. "Quantum approaches to brain and mind." In Schneider, S. and Velmans, M. (eds.), *The Blackwell Companion to Consciousness*, pp. 298–313. Hoboken, NJ: John Wiley & Sons.

Barkow, J.H., Cosmides, L., and Tooby, J. 1992. *The Adapted Mind: Evolutionary Psychology and the Generation of Culture*, Oxford: Oxford University Press.

Baumeister, R., Lau, S., Maranges, H., and Clark, C. 2018a. "On the necessity of consciousness for sophisticated human action." *Frontiers in Psychology*, 9, p. 1925.

Baumeister, R., Maranges, H., and Sjåstad, H. 2018b. "Consciousness of the future as a matrix of maybe: Pragmatic prospection and the simulation of alternative possibilities." *Psychology of Consciousness: Theory, Research, and Practice*, 5 (3), pp. 223–238.

Bitbol, M. 2000. "Physique quantique et cognition [Quantum physics and cognition]." *Revue internationale de philosophie*, 212, pp. 299–328.

Bitbol, M. 2008. "Is consciousness primary?" *NeuroQuantology*, 6 (1), pp. 53–71.

Bitbol, M. 2011. *Physique et philosophie de l'esprit* [Physics and Philosophy of Mind], Paris: Flammarion.

Bitbol, M. 2014. *La conscience a-t-elle une origine? Des neurosciences à la pleine con-science: une nouvelle approche de l'esprit* [Does Consciousness Have an Origin? From Neuroscience to Mindfulness: A New Approach to the Mind], Paris: Flammarion.

Block, N. 1995. "On a confusion about a function of consciousness." *Behavioral and Brain Sciences*, 18 (2), pp. 227–247.

Busemeyer, J.R. and Bruza, P.D. 2012. *Quantum Models of Cognition and Decision*, Cambridge: Cambridge University Press.

Christakis, N.A. 2019. *Blueprint: The Evolutionary Origins of a Good Society*, New York: Hachette Book Group.

Cosmides, L. and Tooby, J. 2005. "Neurocognitive adaptations designed for social ex-change." In Buss, D.M. (ed.), *The Handbook of Evolutionary Psychology*, pp. 584–627. Hoboken, NJ: John Wiley & Sons.

Dennett, D. 1991. *Consciousness Explained*. New York: Little, Brown & Co.

DeWitt, B.S. and Graham, N. 1973. "Preface." In DeWitt, B.S. and Graham, N. (eds.), *The Many-Worlds Interpretation of Quantum Mechanics*, pp. v–vi. Princeton, NJ: Princeton University Press.

Dijksterhuis, A. and Aarts, H. 2010. "Goals, attention, and (un)consciousness." *Annual Review of Psychology*, 61, pp. 467–490.

Freeman, W.J. and Vitiello, G. 2008. "Dissipation and spontaneous symmetry breaking in brain dynamics." *Journal of Physics A: Mathematical and Theoretical*, 41 (30), p. 304042.

Freeman, W.J. and Vitiello, G. 2010. "Vortices in brain waves." *International Journal of Modern Physics B*, 24 (17), pp. 3269–3295.

Friend, J.M. and Thayer, B.A. 2011. "Brain imaging and political behavior." In Peterson, S.A. and Somit, A. (eds.), *Biology and Politics*, pp. 231–255. Bingley: Emerald Group Publishing.

Friend, J.M. and Thayer, B.A. 2012. "Evolution and foreign policy: Insights for decision-making models." In Peterson, S.A. and Somit, A. (eds.), *Biopolicy: The Life Sciences and Public Policy*, pp. 97–117. Bingley: Emerald Group Publishing.

Friend, J.M. and Thayer, B.A. 2013. "Neuropolitics and political science: Providing a foun-dation for the study of politics." In Peterson, S.A. and Somit, A. (eds.), *The World of Biology and Politics: Organization and Research Areas*, pp. 71–90. Bingley: Emerald Group Publishing

Friend, J.M. and Thayer, B.A. 2017. "Biology and international relations." In Peterson, S.A. and Somit, A. (eds.), *Handbook of Biology and Politics*, pp. 165–180. Cheltenham: Edward Elgar.

Freud, S. 1915. *The Unconscious*, London: Hogarth Press.

Gao, S. 2017. *The Meaning of the Wave Function: In Search of the Ontology of Quantum Mechanics*, Cambridge: Cambridge University Press.

Gat, A. 2006. *War in Human Civilization*, Oxford: Oxford University Press.

Gat, A. 2009. "So why do people fight? Evolutionary theory and the causes of war." *European Journal of International Relations*, 15 (4), pp. 571–599.

Gat, A. 2019. "Is war in our nature?" *Human Nature*, 30 (2), pp. 149–154.

Gazzaniga, M.S. 2005. "Forty-five years of split-brain research and still going strong." *Nature Reviews Neuroscience*, 6 (8), pp. 653–659.

Gazzaniga, M.S. 2011. *Who's in Charge? Free Will and the Science of the Brain*, New York: Harper Collins.

Haidt, J. 2001. "The emotional dog and its rational tail: A social intuitionist approach to moral judgment." *Psychological Review*, 108 (4), pp. 814–834.

Hameroff, S.R. and Penrose, R. 1996. "Conscious events as orchestrated spacetime selections." *Journal of Consciousness Studies*, 3 (1), pp. 36–53.

Hameroff, S.R. and Penrose, R. 2014. "Consciousness in the universe: A review of the 'Orch OR' theory." *Physics of Life Reviews*, 11 (1), pp. 39–78.

Hatemi, P.K. and McDermott, R. 2011. *Man Is by Nature a Political Animal: Evolution, Biology, and Politics*, Chicago: University of Chicago Press.

Hatemi, P.K. and McDermott, R. 2012. "The genetics of politics: Discovery, challenges, and progress." *Trends in Genetics*, 28 (10), pp. 525–533.

Haven, E. and Khrennikov, A.I. 2013. *Quantum Social Science*, Cambridge: Cambridge University Press.

Jiang, Y. and Prakash, R. 2014. "Some vital and unrecognized roles of attention in quantum theories of consciousness." *NeuroQuantology*, 12 (4), pp. 406–416.

Johansson, P., Hall, L., Sikström, S., and Olsson, A. 2005. "Failure to detect mismatches between intention and outcome in a simple decision task." *Science*, 310 (5745), pp. 116–119.

Johansson, P., Hall, L., Sikström, S., Tärning, B., and Lind, A. 2006. "How something can be said about telling more than we can know: On choice blindness and introspection." *Consciousness and Cognition*, 15 (4), pp. 673–692.

Johnson, D.D. 2015. "Survival of the disciplines: Is international relations fit for the new millennium?" *Millennium*, 43 (2), pp. 749–763.

Kurzban, R. 2010. *Why Everyone (Else) Is a Hypocrite: Evolution and the Modular Mind*, Princeton, NJ: Princeton University Press.

Lambert-Mogiliansky, A., Zamir, S., and Zwirn, H. 2009. "Type indeterminacy: A model of the KT (Kahneman–Tversky)-man." *Journal of Mathematical Psychology*, 53 (5), pp. 349–361.

Lehner, C. 1997. "What it feels like to be in a superposition. And why." *Synthese*, 110 (2), pp. 191–216.

Locke, J. 1689. *An Essay Concerning Human Understanding*, London: Thomas Ballet.

Lumma, A.L., Hackert, B., and Weger, U. 2019. "Insights from the inside of empathy: Investigating the experiential dimension of empathy through introspection." *Philosophical Psychology*, 33 (1), pp. 64–85.

Maurel, M. 2009. "The explicitation interview: Examples and applications." *Journal of Consciousness Studies*, 16 (10–11), pp. 58–89.

McDermott, R. and Hatemi, P.K. 2014. "The study of international politics in the neurobiological revolution: A review of leadership and political violence." *Millennium*, 43 (1), pp. 92–123.

McDermott, R. and Hatemi, P.K. 2018. "Biology, evolution, and international security." In Gheciu, A. and Wohlforth, W.C. (eds.), *The Oxford Handbook of International Security*, pp. 193–209. Oxford: Oxford University Press

Mørch, H.H. 2019. "The argument for panpsychism from experience of causation." In Seager, W. (ed.), *The Routledge Handbook of Panpsychism*, pp. 269–284. New York: Routledge.

Mouchet, A. and Bertrand, C. 2018. *Décider en urgence au Samu-Centre 15* [Deciding Urgently at the Emergency Medical Services], Toulouse: Octares Éditions.

Nagel, T. 1974. "What is it like to be a bat?" *Philosophical Review*, 83 (4), pp. 435–450.

Nisbett, R. and Wilson, T. 1977. "Telling more than we can know: Verbal reports on mental processes." *Psychological Review*, 84 (3), pp. 231–259.

O'Mahoney, J. 2015. "Why did they do that? The methodology of reasons for action." *International Theory*, 7 (2), pp. 231–262.

Panksepp, J. 1998. *Affective Neuroscience: The Foundations of Human and Animal Emotions*, Oxford: Oxford University Press.

Petersen, M.B. 2016. "Evolutionary political psychology." In Buss, D.M. (ed.), *Handbook of Evolutionary Psychology*, Vol. 2, pp. 1084–1102. Hoboken: Wiley.

Petitmengin, C. and Bitbol, M. 2009. "The validity of first-person descriptions as authenticity and coherence." *Journal of Consciousness Studies*, 16 (10–11), pp. 363–404.

Petitmengin, C., Remillieux, A., Cahour, B., and Carter-Thomas, S. 2013. "A gap in Nisbett and Wilson's findings? A first-person access to our cognitive processes." *Consciousness and Cognition*, 22 (2), pp. 654–669.

Petitmengin, C., Remillieux, A., and Valenzuela-Moguillansky, C. 2019. "Discovering the structures of lived experience." *Phenomenology and the Cognitive Sciences*, 18 (4), pp. 691–730.

Pinker, S. 1994. *The Language Instinct*, New York: William Morrow & Co.

Pinker, S. 1997. *How the Mind Works*, New York: W. W. Norton & Co.

Pinker, S. 2012. *The Better Angels of Our Nature: Why Violence Has Declined*, New York: Viking Books.

Searle, J.R. 2010. "Consciousness and the problem of free will." In Baumeister, R., Mele, A., and Vohs, K. (eds.), *Free Will and Consciousness: How Might They Work?*, pp. 121–134. Oxford: Oxford University Press.

Skokowski, P. 2019. "Introspection and superposition." In De Barros, J. and Montemayor, C. (eds.), *Quanta and Mind: Essays on the Connection between Quantum Mechanics and the Consciousness*, pp. 173–186. Cham: Springer.

Stapp, H. 1999. "Attention, intention, and will in quantum physics." *Journal of Consciousness Studies*, 6 (8–9). https://escholarship.org/uc/item/5xr366vq (accessed June 19, 2020).

Stapp, H. 2009. *Mind, Matter, and Quantum Mechanics*, Berlin: Springer.

Teilhard de Chardin, P. 1955. *Le phénomène humain* [The Phenomenon of Man], Paris: Éditions du Seuil.

Trivers, R.L. 1971. "The evolution of reciprocal altruism." *Quarterly Review of Biology*, 46 (1), pp. 35–57.

Turner, S. 2007. "Social theory as a cognitive neuroscience." *European Journal of Social Theory*, 10 (3), pp. 357–374.

Varela, F. 1996. "Neurophenomenology: A methodological remedy for the hard problem." *Journal of Consciousness Studies*, 3 (4), pp. 330–349.

Vermersch, P. 1994. *L'entretien d'explicitation* [The Explication Interview], Paris: ESF.

Vermersch, P. 1999. "Introspection as practice." *Journal of Consciousness Studies*, 6 (2–3), pp. 17–42.

Vermersch, P. 2009. "Describing the practice of introspection." *Journal of Consciousness Studies*, 16 (10–11), pp. 20–57.

Vermersch, P. 2012. *Explicitation et phénoménologie: Vers une psychophénoménologie* [Explicitation and Phenomenology: Towards Psychophenomenology], Paris: Presses universitaires de France.

Wang, Z., Busemeyer, J., Atmanspacher, H., and Pothos, E. 2013. "The potential of using quantum theory to build models of cognition." *Topics in Cognitive Science*, 5 (4), pp. 672–688.

Wendt, A. 2001. "Driving with the rearview mirror: On the rational science of institutional design." *International Organization*, 55 (4), pp. 1019–1049.

Wendt, A. 2015. *Quantum Mind and Social Science: Unifying Physical and Social Ontology*, Cambridge: Cambridge University Press.

17

To "See" Is to Break an Entanglement

Quantum Measurement, Trauma, and Security

K. M. Fierke and Nicola Mackay

> When a pair of entangled particles is observed, the entanglement
> will be broken.
>
> —Mahood (2018: 198)

Memory represents an entanglement with the past. When President Assad invokes the Armenian genocide or Prime Minister Orban refers to incoming refugees by reference to "Ottoman invasions," they invoke a traumatic past that has political implications. Arguments about collective trauma highlight the extent to which the narration of trauma expresses the concerns of successor generations, which may or may not be linked to an underlying traumatic experience (Alexander 2012; Alexander et al. 2004; Sztompka 2000).[1] In this respect, memory is put in service of a present and future political project, which may be a source of community building (Hutchison 2016) and/or aggression (Fierke 2004; Scheff and Rezinger 1991). As Edkins (2002) notes, while trauma is "unspeakable," given the rupture of everyday safety, it is often domesticated in political discourse.

The political uses of memory often refer to events that long precede the living, which raises a question of why they would continue to exercise an affective pull on contemporary populations. Lerner (2019) argues that the resonance is in part a function of the severity of the trauma or its recurring experience by communities over time. The political discourse may express multiple traumas and layers of entanglement that continue to resonate with populations. For instance, the literature on historical trauma emphasizes the continuing impact of past traumas of a political nature on the present health of Indigenous communities in particular, arising from interrelated genetic, social, and environmental factors (Matthews and Phillips 2010; Walters et al. 2011), as well as the continuing impact of structural violence on successor generations (Kirmayer et al. 2014: 311).

Starting with a claim that trauma represents an entanglement with the past, this chapter seeks to explore the quantum notion that to "see" an entanglement is to break it, as well as the implications of this claim for the politics of security. While it is often assumed that the quantum debate in International Relations remains at the level of theory (Lamb-Books 2016), we explore the meaning of measurement, seeing, and breaking an entanglement in the context of an experiment regarding the ongoing impact of traumatic political memory on the present. How does quantum measurement differ from classical? What does it look like and what are the implications for the analysis of security practice? What does it mean to say that when an entanglement is "seen" it is broken? The analysis that follows arose from collaboration over the past four years between the two authors, one a scholar of International Relations, and the other a therapeutic practitioner with training in medical physics.[2] Our "experiment" was motivated by an interest in exploring methods that approach problems of security from a different angle, thereby opening up new potentials in light of increasing questions about the efficacy of existing practices and a "crisis" in the field (Nyman and Burke 2016).[3]

In this chapter, our objective is to explore a conceptual problem rather than the experiment itself, or the results arising from it, not least due to the difficulty of communicating an experiential method in language. In the first section, we explore a broad contrast between classical and quantum measurement, asking what this might mean at the macroscopic level. In the second section, we categorize Wendt's claim about language as a form of *expressive* measurement and explore the relationship to discourse analysis. In the third section, we explore the broad contours of our experiment and the role of a somewhat different form of nonlinear expressive measurement. In the final section, we elaborate on the relationship between *redemptive* measurement and breaking an entanglement, which involves a form of "seeing" that witnesses to unacknowledged past trauma.

Classical and Quantum

In classical physics a particle can only be a particle and thus an independent entity, which gives rise to assumptions of materialism, locality, and determinism. One of the central discoveries of quantum physics, as demonstrated in the famous two-slit experiment, is that a particle can become a wave and a wave can become a particle in certain circumstances. Elementary particles are not objective material objects, but rather phenomena that arise from an interaction of some kind, or indeed can be seen as the interaction itself. The latter contrasts with classical assumptions that a particle has a path, position, and velocity that exists independently. Instead, as the American quantum physicist, Henry Stapp (1971: 1303) stated, it is "in essence a set of relationships that reach toward other things."

In classical physics, the separateness of objects with pre-existing properties and boundaries makes it possible to measure their interactions. There is an assumed intrinsic separation between the knower and the known, as well as the apparatus of measurement itself. The scientist stands outside of the objects of observation, which are assumed to exist as discrete entities, with a fixed location in time and space. In simple terms, the measurement consists of quantifying the distance between objects. In quantum physics the object of measurement is not fixed; the boundary that separates the object from the "agencies of observation" will be heavily dependent on the physical arrangement of the apparatus, and thus indeterminate. As Karen Barad (2007: 113–115) notes, the apparatus is a crucial part of the measuring process. The choice of apparatus for each measurement creates the condition "to give meaning to a particular set of variables at the exclusion of other essential variables." The apparatus and the measurement are entangled, and thus not entirely separable. The apparatus and the observed phenomenon change alongside one other. The measuring apparatus itself enacts a "cut," which is an "intra-action" from which separation and difference emerge (Barad 2007: 140).[4] The intra-action between object and apparatus are a part of the phenomenon, which means that measurement practices also constitute the results, and are thus indispensable to them. The analyst cannot be separated from the apparatus of measurement, and the measurement itself arises from an act of seeing.

The question is, what form would the apparatus take in relation to human intra-actions? Barad conceptualizes the apparatus in broad material-discursive terms, which can take a variety of forms. Wendt (2015) specifies that language itself is an apparatus; language use is a form of measurement that impacts on what is observed. He states that "in language what brings about a concept's collapse from potential meanings into an actual one is a speech act, which may be seen as a measurement that puts it into a context, with both other words and particular listeners" (Wendt 2015: 217). The collapse starts with communicative intent, which depends also on the listener, whose understanding will depend on how what is said interacts with a memory of words and their association. As such, "memory structures relate to concepts in the same way that measurement devices in physics relate to particles," which suggests that quantum entanglement and interference are manifested in actual language use (Wendt 2015: 217). Memory is the repository of meanings from which the specific measurement arises, as wave functions collapse into language, materializing one potential rather than another.

In Wendt's argument language use is both an expression of entanglement and the point of departure for the enactment of multiple potentials. What does this look like in practice? For instance, as discussed elsewhere (Fierke 2017), the concepts of migrant, refugee, or terrorist are, from this perspective, relational and defined in contrast to those who "belong." None of these categories maps neatly onto a subject with an intrinsic identity; rather, these are thin identity categories, which replace the thicker sense of self as it emerged in a place of origin. In the confrontation between host society and incomers, the use of language is a measurement that places people along a status hierarchy, which determines the extent of their "humanness." The language already *contains* a measurement of the identity of particular groups of people as human "like us" or less than human and a potential source of danger. This then also becomes a measure of how we should feel, whether compassion or fear, and how "we" should act toward "them," that is, whether they should be welcomed or refused entry, held behind barbed wire or a wall, stripped of their possessions, tortured, or even killed.

Expressive Measurement

Language expresses a form of "seeing" by the observer as wave functions collapse. The seeing is "partial." The thin concepts of "migrant," "refugee," or "terrorist" define the boundaries within which the "other" is seen, and any one "cut" creates a particular separation between "us" and "them." Another example highlights the role of memory, making it possible to explore the "partiality" of the cut and measurement from a somewhat different angle. In a lengthy interview in 2014, President Bashar al-Assad made an unexpected reference to the massacres of 1.5 million Armenians and identified the perpetrator as Ottoman Turkey. During the interview, Assad compared the Armenian Genocide of 1915 to the brutal killings of civilians in Syria today:

> The degree of savagery and inhumanity that the terrorists have reached reminds us of what happened in the Middle Ages in Europe over 500 years ago. In more recent modern times, it reminds us of the massacres perpetrated by the Ottomans against the Armenians when they killed a million and a half Armenians and half a million Orthodox Syriacs in Syria and in Turkish territory. (Sassounian 2014).

Assad's words were articulated in the context of a dispute with Turkey and were intended to lash back at the Turkish government's hostile actions against the Syrian regime.[5]

The example highlights several points. First, Assad's use of language is a *measurement* of the war that enacts a particular kind of separation between terrorists and states, which is magnified by reference to a particular memory of brutality. Memory, in this reading, is an observational instrument by which a particular "cut" is made. Assad's reference to "terrorists," associated with Turkey, places them outside of Syria, thereby reinforcing his legitimacy as the leader of Syria, as well as his actions in defense of Syria's security. A discourse of terrorists and legitimate leaders represents a different measure than, for instance, that of a Syrian "civil war." As suggested by Ricouer (1990: x), the identification of a resemblance between things that would at first glance seem to have nothing to do with each other "grasps together" and integrates scattered events into a single whole. This involves a degree of forgetting, and thus elements that are not seen. The narrative excludes other possible alternatives and is itself selective. Second, the memory constitutes a future that is only "there" as a project to be realized (Kratochwil 2018: 420). Assad claims the memory as his own and frames it in a particular way that enables him to heighten his own use of violence, thereby drawing power from it. The implicit logic not only becomes a form of forgetting, in light of its selectivity, but also justifies his present and future project to eliminate "terrorists." "Seeing" happens from a particular position in time and space, which is partial. The measurement *expresses* a particular "cut" that shapes a relational world in the present, one of Ottoman terrorists and legitimate state actors. An earlier perpetration fuels a perpetration in the present. Assad's use of language is itself a form of *expressive* measurement by which he "sees" the world. Third, the measurement of past, present, and future obscures the more complex, open field within which the memory remains alive—in all those who were forcefully displaced, died, or are otherwise unseen in their suffering, both past and present.

Discourse Analysis

One might question the added value of associating discourse with abstract ideas about the activity of waves. The quantum argument is that physical systems do not have definite properties *until* they are measured through memory, and it is at this point of observation that something comes to life. Assad's terrorists become agents of genocide as he invokes a memory that then has further physical or material consequences. The act of giving meaning is a collapse into the physical properties of language. While interesting, discourse analysts have engaged in language analysis for decades without reference to wave function.

The quantum angle is important for beginning to think differently about what it means to measure, and how this relates to "seeing." Measurement is usually associated with quantification, which rests on classical assumptions of atomism, as well as an understanding of language as a mirror that more or less accurately reflects truth in the world. Approaching language and measurement from a quantum angle turns this logic on its head. In Wendt's (2015: 217) argument, language use involves a speech act that is a measurement that puts words in context, by which they are collapsed from a potential meaning into an actual. Discourse analysis is the empirical study of relational worlds embedded in meaning structures that have been manifested in the words of political agents.

While discourse analysis is not dependent on a quantum framework, the latter highlights aspects of seeing. Discourse analysis provides a means to "see" the discourse not as a description of reality "as it is," but as expressing a structure of power and exclusion. The use of language by, for instance, political leaders is also a form of "seeing" that constitutes political reality. To take another example, which involves an even more problematic conflation, Hungary's prime minister Viktor Orban stated that incoming migrants represent an "Ottoman invasion."[6] The claim relates to two contrasting forms of "seeing." In the first, Orban, like Assad, manifests a particular reality by invoking a specific memory. In this "seeing," a population, composed primarily of people fleeing violence and persecution, becomes an invading army. The single claim is embedded in a larger relational world that is meaningful precisely because of the memory it brings to life. To "see" in this use is to go beyond a descriptive understanding of language to its embeddedness in relational structures of power. A further form of "seeing" arises from the *analysis* of the political statements of, for example, Orban. From this position we also begin to see not only the multiplicity of relational potentials but also the silences contained in discourse including the absence of the voices of the refugees themselves (Chouliaraki and Stolic 2017: 1170). The analysis makes it possible to begin to "see" the unseen, along with the suffering constituted by the discourses that surround refugees and migration, thereby breaking the hold of an entanglement.

Placing discourse analysis in a quantum framework reinforces several arguments that have been more or less successfully employed by critical scholars in the past. Discourse analysis does not by definition deal with memory, but it has been employed by analysts concerned with memory. A fourth generation of memory studies in the field of history, focused on "entangled memory," represents a shift toward an emphasis on entanglement in discourse across time (see Feindt et al. 2014; Pestel et al. 2017).

The latter, nonetheless, remains limited by the availability of texts and, particularly when looking across time, the absence or destruction of documents or archives, not least relating to those who suffered and are unseen. For instance, a recent BBC documentary (Haymen 2018) contrasted the myth of Scottish innocence in the slave trade, as well as Scotland's status as victim of England, with the many ways in which Glasgow, no less than Liverpool or Bristol, profited from the slave trade. This history, it was suggested, was written with the intention of not "seeing" and expresses a national amnesia that was willful and deliberate, written from the perspective of elite white men who controlled the archives, diaries, and ledgers. National amnesia and forgetting worked at the level of a system that sought to erase, complemented by a public narrative in which all could participate in the obfuscation of "reality." In what follows, we suggest a method that both is compatible with discourse analysis and goes further to explore the affective resonance of memory. In other words, in addition to understanding memory as an observational instrument by which a particular "cut" is made, memory can be examined as itself an entangled phenomenon. How is it possible that traumas experienced centuries ago have a continuing resonance in the present? Is this resonance on some level prior to discourse and entangled with an experiential past? In the next section, we highlight another form of the expressive measurement that is dependent on quantum effects, and thus the relationship between collapsing wave functions and language.

Measuring Transgenerational Trauma

The experiential *and* experimental aspects of our project are difficult to communicate in words, not least owing to the nonlinear nature of the phenomenon and the divergence from conventional social science practice. The emphasis on the experiential as well as the experimental highlights the quantum assumption that the analyst or any participants cannot be separated from either the apparatus of measurement or the outcomes. "Experience" in this case can be contrasted with both third-party "objective" experience and "subjective" first-person experience (see Scott 1991). Instead, it can be thought of as a form of second-person experience that arises from an *inter-action* with what Barad (2010: 260) refers to as memory that is "written into the fabric of the world." Our concern was less with the historical detail of what happened than with a diffracted relational pattern of affect that is entangled in memory, which we sought to map. The individuals involved engaged with the affect surrounding a temporal phenomenon—that is, an experience that occurred in past time—rather than an entity, individual or otherwise.

Given space limitations, we briefly present what the method is about and the relationship between the apparatus and forms of measurement involved. In doing so, we draw on insights and data from the experiment anecdotally to make conceptual points. While we recognize that the account may raise more questions than it answers, the unpacking of further concepts will have to wait for another time.

The method relies on several quantum assumptions. First, as already suggested, entangled phenomena are by definition *nonlocal* and *nonlinear*. Barad draws on the imagery of light behaving as a fluid that, upon encountering an obstacle, breaks up and moves outward in different directions (Barad 2014: 171). Time itself is diffracted, she argues, insofar as it is "broken apart in different directions, non-contemporaneous with itself. Each moment is an infinite multiplicity"

(Barad 2014: 169). Patterns of diffraction, as noted by Donna Haraway (1997), do not mark where differences occur but rather where the effects of difference appear. Our experiment shifts focus slightly to patterns of *affective* difference that emerge from the mapping of a relational whole, in which past and present are not fully separable.

Second, following on from the last point, entanglements express *emotions and affect.* As Sparrer (2007) notes, emotions do not "belong" to us as stable attributes but can be both nonlocal and entangled with others, both present and past. Our method begins with an assumption that war, forced displacement, and violence, suffered or perpetuated in one generation, crosses over to other generations, in such a way that a younger generation may bear the burdens of its parents' or grandparents' generations, thereby assuming the latter's unsanctioned behaviors and related guilt (Dietrich 2013: 139). The main point is illustrated in a simple example at the individual level, where two men from different belief systems are embroiled in a deeply emotional fight, with each of them carrying the anger and experience of their father, grandfather, great-grandfathers, etc. The entanglement with the past thus adds to the toxicity of current conflict.

A notion of transgenerational trauma points to a field of affective resonance that is beyond language. As Bessel Van Der Kolk (1998: 52) noted:

> A century of study of traumatic memories shows that (i) semantic representations may coexist with sensory imprints; (ii) unlike trauma narratives, these sensory experiences often remain stable over time, unaltered by other life experiences; (iii) they may return, triggered by reminders, with a vividness as if the experience were happening all over again; and (iv) these flashbacks may occur in a mental state in which victims are unable to precisely articulate what they are feeling and thinking.

While Van Der Kolk's emphasis was individual memory, we explore the entanglement of collective memories of trauma with sensory imprints—that is, the memory is itself an entangled phenomenon that can be triggered by political changes that bring past traumas to the surface.

Third, it is possible to map sensory imprints of transgenerational trauma—or what we refer to as fields of resonance. As we began our experiment, we relied on the basic principles and theory of systemic constellations therapy, which has established a central place in German therapeutic culture.[7] The basic idea of systems therapy more generally is that individual problems can't be viewed in isolation from a larger relational system. While family systems therapy is often concerned with role playing, systemic constellations go further to the groundbreaking observation that it is possible, in certain circumstances, for substitutes or proxies—which we refer to as representatives—to experience the physical and affective dynamics of a system during a constellation exercise, thereby bringing insight to its deeper and often hidden affective dynamics (Carvalho and Klussman 2010). Those who occupy positions within a relational system are able to represent the bodily sensations, feelings, and impulses of someone they do not know or, in our experiment, associated with categories of memory that are larger than the individual. The phenomenon arises from an intra-action between diffraction patterns of affect, which express a collective experience of suffering in the past, and representatives within the experiment, who experience the affective resonance surrounding this past.

Similar to what many physicists have said about quantum physics more generally, Splinter and Wustehube (2011: 118) state that the effectiveness of the systemic constellations approach "can be regarded as empirically proven, but a broadly approved scientific explanation of *why* it works is missing." The German psychologist and engineer Peter Schotter demonstrated in a scientific study, involving 3,000 individual experiences, that the perceptions of proxies, who knew nothing of the parties they represent, were not random and were reproducible (Carvalho and Klussman 2010). One objective of our project was to determine whether, when moving from individual to collective memory, patterns would emerge from the interactions of the representatives during the mapping process. The maps were set up *blind*, to minimize interpretation by the individuals involved and to establish that any patterns could be attributed to a field of resonance.[8]

Fourth, the social or political dimensions of memory are the prior condition for individual memory. As Kratochwil (2018: 328) notes, individual memory is built up through participation in communication processes, which involve common reflections on who "we" are, which is shaped by where we think we come from, none of which can be separated from identities and collective memories that make "society" an ongoing and transgenerational concern among its members. While constellation work revolves around individuals, any one of whom will be entangled with diverse collective memories in their family lineage, the current project seeks to explore collective memory as prior to any one individual. Some work has been done by others to apply systemic constellations to political conflict, working directly with actors on the ground (see, e.g., Carvalho and Klussman 2010; Mayr 2003, 2012; Splinter and Wustehube 2011; Dietrich 2013). The present experiment began with an assumption that, as entangled memories are nonlocal and arise from the experience of past generations, it is possible to represent categories of actors in a mapping exercise without going to a physical site of, for instance, conflict.

As we worked further with the method, the frequent recurrence of memories of *forced displacement* led to a further distinction. The constellations are concerned with belonging and who belongs to a system, which in the case of political constellations is concerned with large groups (Dietrich 2013: 134). The central importance of belonging, and of attachment to and having a place within a group, highlights the extent to which forced displacement—as distinct from conflict, which tends to solidify group boundaries—represents the hard case. While forced displacement involves movements of large numbers of people, it represents a shattering of place and belonging within a society. This suggested the usefulness of shifting away from a focus on individuals or conflict per se to memories of migration and forced displacement in the past, to ask how these contribute to the reification of contemporary divisions of belonging and nonbelonging.

Discourse analysis provides a method for looking at the representation of phenomena in political discourse. What we refer to as *Dynamic Entangled Memory Mapping* (DEMM), by contrast, involves the representation and mapping of relational patterns of transgenerational traumatic memory that remain entangled with the past and fuel the affect surrounding contemporary migrations, among others. This brings Wendt's general observations about language back to the context of an experiment, in which, much like quantum mechanics, measurement brings about a wave function collapse, which is a byproduct of asking a particular question and preparing the experiment in such a way that it can be answered. The quantum effects that arise from the relational map, or more specifically the patterned expressions of affect that emerge out of the mapping process, point to a nonlocal field of resonance that is microscopic, while having macroscopic effects.[9]

The method doesn't measure a thing with intrinsic properties but relational positions within a system, the shape of which is heavily dependent on how the intentional question is asked. The intentional question, as the apparatus in our experiment, animates and became a lens through which, for instance, to understand why the refugee/migrant is seen or not seen, and may be distorted because viewed through a lens of past trauma. The discourse analyst examines *representation in political language*. By contrast, within our experiment, the *representatives*, who occupy positions within the memory map, *express the relational field* surrounding a traumatic past as they engage with one another, thereby *manifesting a physical presence* of the past *in language*. Specific maps explore forms of entanglement within a field or intersecting fields in more depth, including the hidden dimensions, which are less obvious in contemporary political articulations, thereby providing an affective measure of a relational whole, including the relationship between the seen (the political articulation) and the unseen (the victims, past or present).

The intentional question is the apparatus for setting up an initial map to examine the relationship between the different elements of a system. Representatives who occupy positions within that system express, through words, bodily movements, or gestures, the affect they experience while "standing in" for any one position. These articulations express a form of wave function collapse and a pattern of diffracted entanglement, by which the attributes of the system become visible or "seen" as the vibrational frequencies surrounding a particular space, and the affect that arises from it, are transformed into language, and thus became available for analysis. If language use is a measure of wave function collapse, the language arising from a relational system becomes a measure of a nonlinear historical trauma field.

The multidimensional memory maps can be contrasted with the one-dimensional field expressed in political discourse. For instance, our EU refugee/migration crisis pilot study began with an overarching question about what was standing in the way of a compassionate response to the refugees. The mapping method made it possible to explore the interplay of entangled memories, some of which were less visible, in constituting the dynamics of the relational field. For instance, as in the public discourse in Hungary, the memory of the Ottoman invasions had an active presence in the maps. Despite real-time images of refugees packed into trains or being thrown food like animals, which were reminiscent of the Holocaust, the Ottoman invasions had a more prominent place in the mapping. While the Holocaust did come into play, its role was recessive, and pulled back to a much earlier memory, specific to Hungary, that is, the 1848–1849 Hungarian revolution against the Habsburgs and Russia, during which tens of thousands of Hungarian civilians participated in anti-Semitic actions. This memory then became the focus of a separate map.

The reconstruction of multiple interfacing memories goes beyond Orban's one-dimensional account of the Ottoman invasions to identify the recessive influence and continuing power of memories of perpetration in fueling the emotional response to incoming migrants and refugees, even while the surface narrative is one of being a victim. The memories made it difficult for representatives of different states or groups to "see" the refugees. Orban's repeated comparison of the arrival of large numbers of refugees in Hungary to the Ottoman invasion is an acknowledgment of past suffering but one that reinforces a division of pain that highlights Hungary's past as a victim. Memories of perpetration are more likely to occupy a recessive space and, precisely because they are hidden, to fuel present perpetration. In this respect, one can see a complementary relationship between perpetrator and victim, in which the two, across time, are entangled. The spaces for migrants, the dead, the migrants' land of origin, and those left behind were also encumbered with separate historical trauma fields. There were layers of memory upon memory, of which we only touched the surface. The added toxicity provided by these memories, and the distortion of the present they provided, will not have been helpful or positive for the healthy integration of incomers and would indeed severely hamper successful integration.

Language functions like the apparatus in a physics experiment, both for political agents in real time and for the representatives in trauma time. The language of the intentional question, as formulated by the facilitator and case provider (e.g., What is standing in the way of a compassionate response to the refugees? What is standing in the way of delivery of aid to Aleppo? Who can see slavery?), provides a cut that shapes the relational field of exploration, making it possible to discern relationships of belonging and not belonging. The direct transcription of the words spoken by the representatives provides a nonlinear record of a *conversation* between different parts of the observed system that expresses an entanglement with past experience. While the various conversations corresponded broadly to the historical record in question, they also revealed hidden dimensions that were contrary to the "truth" as expressed in more accepted histories, which, as stated earlier, have often been written for purposes of "not seeing."

Redemptive Measurement

A further form of measurement provides a more human take on the quantum principle that an act of seeing breaks an entanglement, as well as the claim that measurement transforms the object of observation. What we refer to as a redemptive measurement involves beginning to see that which is hidden or unseen and to *give it a place of belonging* within a relational field. In this respect, there is a distinction between *expressive measurement*, that is, discourse analysis or the measurement of the nonlinear conversation between representatives, and *redemptive measurement*, which, with the guidance of the facilitator, involves seeing, acknowledging, and giving place to the unseen elements such that an entanglement is broken and a more positive relationality can begin to be restored. Redemptive measurement transforms a historical trauma field into a historical trauma *narrative*, in which the suffering is seen and the trauma loses some of its power.

Two distinct forms of language use constitute DEMM. The first is the spontaneous language expressed by the representatives within the map; the second is the more directed language narrative introduced by the facilitator. Unlike discourse analysis, which examines the partial view of political agents from the perspective of their present, the spontaneous language of the representatives expresses the relational whole, including the entanglements with historical trauma that shape the field of resonance. The more directed language of the facilitator, also informed by the intentional question, works with the

Quantum Measurement and Memory Mapping

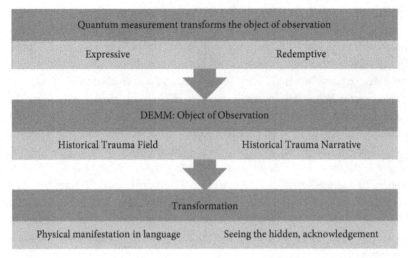

Figure 17.1 Quantum measurement and memory mapping (Smart Art Graphic, words added by authors).

representatives to change the narrative, thereby provoking wave function collapse around different potentials. The first expresses a field of habitual memory surrounding a past trauma; the second involves acknowledging and beginning to step outside the trauma, thereby paving the way for a different conversation.

DEMM starts with the mapping of a trauma field and in the process of measuring (i.e., seeing and expressing the field in language) begins a dynamic process of transforming it into a historical trauma narrative that is redemptive, which, in theory, opens space for a different and less toxic conversation.

The potential impact of redemptive measurement is difficult to judge in the absence of a sustained experiment over several years that would also explore any relevant ethical questions in more depth. The issue here is whether in measuring and acknowledging the roots of traumatic memories in past suffering, an entanglement is broken and something changes in the world itself. The most obvious answer, from the perspective of classical physics, is that it definitely would not have an impact of this kind. However, based on the quantum principle that measurement changes the object of observation, DEMM could hypothetically have this impact—and indeed, this is the purpose of the constellation method when applied in family and organizational therapy. The redemptive measurement of political memory opens a space for replacing the competition between conflicting memories with a broader conversation.

"Seeing"

But what is then meant by "seeing" in this case? The contrast between the two forms of measurement highlights a number of issues. The first regards the *non-local dimensions* of both the transgenerational entanglements and the method. Expressive measurement transforms the dynamics of an unobservable field of resonance into an analysable form. In the context of the experiment, the emergence of patterns from a *blind* process suggested that something powerful was going on, even while there is no clear explanation for why it works.[10]

Redemptive measurement is far more slippery insofar as it is difficult, if not impossible, to ever know for certain whether the measurement actually changes the object of observation and thus has broken the entanglement. For instance, one of the central themes that arose during the US Politics of Hate pilot study was the inability to "see" a history of enslavement. During several days of working with a series of distinct maps, the representatives, consistently, across separate maps, turned away from the occupant of the "slavery" square, as if he or she wasn't there. With guidance from the facilitator, the representatives began to acknowledge both the historical suffering and its continuing toxicity in the US context, and to engage in a way that would not have been possible when we began. While any educated person knows about the history of enslavement in the United States, this knowledge is not the same as "seeing." To "see" in this case means to acknowledge previously unseen suffering and entanglement within it. To "see" is to witness. To witness is not merely a passive act of observation; it is rather an embodied act that makes the absence of memory present.

The quantum concept of complementarity suggests that acknowledgment requires a recognition of the capacity for evil as well as good, in any one self or community. From this perspective, the mutual implication of perpetrator and victim is more clearly evident where, as in the Hungarian case, memories of perpetration relating to anti-Semitism in Europe interfaced with memories of being a victim during the Ottoman invasion. Or in the case of the United States, its identity as a "shining city on a hill" and a force for good in the world contains within it the barbarity of enslavement (see Lepore 2018). Free and equal US citizens, many of whom carried memories of persecution as immigrants from Europe, were the subjects of a constitution that emerged alongside laws regarding enslaved, who had been forcefully displaced from Africa. Once we begin to view the world from a different angle, recognizing ourselves as a part of life that is entangled across generations, as well as the planet, rather than outside and above it, the ethical bar for how we act toward others becomes much higher.

Balance in this conceptualization is not a mechanism, such as the balance of power, but an orientation to life, to self and other in all its forms; it encompasses "seeing" the humanity or more broadly "seeing" life in the other, and having a conversation with the other (see Fierke and Jabri 2019). While it may be tempting to regard this potential as utopian, particularly in relation to the international, this misses the point. What is suggested is an ethical re-orientation, and here a contrast is important. Many Western ethical systems rely on a metaphysics of atomistic rational individuals, for whom emotions are or should be absent, who are locally situated in time and space, in which the world is a mechanism and time is a quantitative measure, conceived in terms of clocks. By contrast, complementarity rests on quantum assumptions that the world is life, time is entangled, and affect is fundamental to life, in-cluding our humanity, and cannot be separated from reason. Insofar as the latter highlights the claim that harm done to others is ultimately harm done to the self as well, it is consistent with not only Buddhist or African Ubuntu philosophy but also a feminist ethic of care. But here we want to emphasize what this suggests about acknowledgment and the potential for redemption, and why both would be important. To redeem in this case is to acknowledge the reproduction of harm within a particular relational system or structure, which is a first step toward re-establishing balance and rethinking our secu-rity in relation to entangled others.

The second question regards *who precisely is better able to "see"* as a result. The most straightforward and understandable answer would be that those who participate in the mapping process begin themselves, as a result of their representation of parts within a whole, to "see" the previously unseen. They act as witnesses within the mapping and, as individuals, carry this away from the exercise. But the potential may extend further. For instance, in the weeks following the conclusion of the US Politics of Hate pilot study, the dramatization of far right toxicity in Charlottesville, Virginia in 2017, made it impossible to ignore the continuing impact of a history of not "seeing" the impact of a legacy of enslavement on contemporary politics in the United States. There was a corresponding emphasis in the media on the need for a conversation around the history of enslavement. Was this increased ability to see slavery at all related to our experiment in a living room in Scotland? Any kind of causal claim about the relationship between redemptive meas-urement within the mapping exercise and changes in the world would be premature. The correlation suggests that beginning to "see" slavery within the context of the mapping may facilitate "seeing" in a larger societal con-text, as the acknowledgment reverberates through entangled space.

A third issue regards the *nature of a broader impact* on the world, were this to be the case. A larger impact would take the form of greater attention to the ongoing effects of structural violence and, in theory, a reduction in fear and the toxicity attached to the possibility of engaging in conversation about it. The greater ability to "see" as a result of redemptive measurement may relate to those who participate in the mapping, thus making it a potential educational tool or a tool for engagement around policy, for example, examining the transgenerational entanglements between the descendants of European immigrants to the United States, including enslavers, and those forcefully displaced from Africa. Or, there may be more nonlocal and difficult-to-gauge changes such as the example of Charlottesville earlier or the enhanced "seeing" that followed George Floyd's death, which placed his experience in a longer history of US racial relations and transatlantic slave trade. As the physicist John Wheeler noted, in a quantum world we are "participants in creating the universe" (Folger 2002). Redemption points to our humanity and the ability to see the human in the other, not only in the present but also the past, and the other in the self. Redemption is less about changing the past (see Wendt 2015) than acknowledging it such that we are changed in the now.

Conclusions

DEMM does not measure the distance between "things" but rather the relationship between positions within a trauma field that is heavily dependent on the apparatus or how the intentional question is asked. The method makes it possible to "cut" into the relational dynamics of specific historical dislocations, to make visible the otherwise invisible affective resonance of transgenerational memory and its continuing impact on the present. There remains a question of whether this is primarily useful as a tool of analysis, for gaining insight into some of the hidden dimensions of memory on contemporary politics, or whether the nonlocal witness to and acknowledgment of historical patterns of displacement and perpetration change something in the world itself. The mapping process makes it possible to measure a historical trauma field in expressive terms. Out of this process the hidden dimensions of suffering relating to past trauma, which continue to impact on the present, begin to surface. The corresponding concept of redemptive measurement suggests that in the process of "seeing" and acknowledging this suffering, an entanglement is broken and something in the world itself changes, which is consistent with the quantum principle that observation changes the object of measurement. To "see" is to break an entanglement. Beginning to see the other in the self, and the self in the other, including as this relates to victim-perpetrator dynamics across time, provides the basis for an ethical reorientation toward both the study and practice of security.

Notes

1. This chapter was originally prepared for a special issue of *Security Dialogue* on "Quantizing International Relations," edited by James Der Derian and Alexander Wendt. It was written by K. M. Fierke but is a product of collaboration with Nicola Mackay. The authors would like to thank the Human Family Unity Foundation, and the Netherlands Institute for Advanced Studies for support for various aspects of this project, as well Sofiia Bairamukova, Olga Burkhardt-Vetter, Roxane Farmanfarmain, Caron Gentry, Frazer McDonald Hay, Naomi Head, Tony Lang, Mike Shanks, and Nadine Voelkner.

2. We sought to apply a method that is widely used in the analysis of family and organizational systems, particularly in Germany, to political phenomena. While Mackay has been a practitioner of the former for seventeen years, Fierke's interest in the method was sparked by the quantum effects that arise from the dynamics of the systems analysis, which have no explanation in classical physics.

3. The word experiment is used loosely to refer to the attempt to explore the usefulness of a method, developed for one purpose, for another. The process began out of curiosity, with no idea where we were going, but turned into three pilot studies regarding the delivery of humanitarian aid to Aleppo in 2016, the emergence of the US politics of hate following the elections in 2016, and the EU refugee/migration "crisis."

4. Interaction assumes an exchange between separate parts, in which they remain unchanged. Intra-action, by contrast, begins with the whole constitution of separability as boundaries are drawn in an active process.

5. See Sassounian (2014).

6. Orban here refers to Hungary's experience of conquest by the Ottoman Empire, going back to the sixteenth and seventeenth centuries. The decisive battle in the conquest of Hungary was the Battle of Mohacs in 1526, led by Sultan Suleyman the Magnificent, who defeated the medieval Kingdom of Hungary, which was far larger than the country's current size.

7. The method, while influenced by forms of systems therapy, such as gestalt or Virginia Satir's family sculpting, originated with Bert Hellinger (see, e.g., 1999) and has become one of the most popular forms of therapy in Germany (see Bilger 2016), although not without controversy, and has spread to some twenty-five countries.

8. In this respect, our project was more of a "pre-experiment," to establish the validity of proceeding with a larger, more structured project.

9. This is contrary to frequent claims that quantum effects "wash out" at the macroscopic level and are thus irrelevant for the social sciences. See, for example, Waldner (2017).

10. While this may seem like "spooky action at a distance," other forms of "spooky action at distance," from mobile phones to the internet to Skype, which at one time seemed a bit scary, are now a part of daily life. Like the memory mapping, these are all nonlocal phenomena but, unlike it, rely on technology.

Bibliography

Alexander, J.C. 2012. *Trauma: A Social Theory*. Cambridge: Polity.

Alexander, J.E., R. Eyerman, and B. Giesen, eds. 2004. *Cultural Trauma and Collective Identity*. Berkeley: University of California Press.

Barad, Karen. 2007. *Meeting the Universe Halfway. Quantum Physics and the Entanglement of Matter and Meaning*. Durham, NC: Duke University Press.

Barad, Karen. 2010. "Quantum Entanglements and Hauntological Relations of Inheritance: Dis/continuities, SpaceTime Enfoldings, and Justice-to-Come." *Derrida Today*, 3 (2): 240–268.

Barad, Karen. 2014. "Diffracting Diffraction: Cutting Together Apart." *Parallax*, 20 (3): 168–187.

Bilger, Burkhardt. 2016. "Where the Germans Make Peace with their Dead." *New Yorker*, September 12.

Carvalho, Marco de and Jorgen Klussman. 2010. *Konfliktbearbeiten in Afghanistan, De Systemische Konflikttransformation in praktischen Einsatz bei einem Grossgruppen-konflikt*. Berlin: Friedrich-Ebert Stiftung.

Chouliaraki, L. and T. Stolic. 2017. "Rethinking Media Responsibility in the Refugee 'Crisis': A Visual Typology of European News." *Media, Culture and Society*, 39 (8): 1162–1177.

Dietrich, Wolfgang. 2013. *Elicitive Conflict Transformation and the Transrational Shift in Peace Politics*. London: Palgrave.

Edkins, Jenny. 2002. "Forget Trauma: Responses to September 11." *International Relations*, 16 (2): 243–256.

Feindt, G., F. Krawatzek, D. Mehler, F. Pestel, and R. Trimcev. 2014. "Entangled Memory: Toward a Third Wave in Memory Studies." *History and Theory*, 53 (1): 24–44.

Fierke, K.M. 2004. "Whereof We Can Speak, Thereof We Must Not Be Silent: Trauma, Political Solipsism and War." *Review of International Studies*, 30: 471–491.

Fierke K.M. 2017. "Consciousness at the Interface: Wendt, Eastern Wisdom and the Ethics of Intra-action." *Critical Review*, 29 (2): 141–169.

Fierke, K.M. and V. Jabri. 2019. "Global Conversations: Relationality, Embodiment and Power in the Move towards Global IR." *Global Constitutionalism*, 8 (3): 506–535.

Folger, Tim. 2002. "Does the Universe Exist If We're Not Looking?" *Discover*, 23 (6): 44–49.

Haraway, D. 1997. *Modest_Witness@Second_Millennium.FemaleMan© Meets_OncoMouse™: Feminism and Technoscience*. New York: Routledge.

Haymen, David. 2018. "Slavery: Scotland's Hidden Shame." *BBC Two Scotland*, November 6, 9:00.

Hellinger, B. 1999. *Acknowledging What Is*. Phoenix, AZ: Zeig, Tucker and Co.

Hutchison, Emma. 2016. *Affective Communities in World Politics: Collective Emotions after Trauma*. Cambridge: Cambridge University Press.

Kirmayer, Laurence J., Joseph P. Gone, and Joshua Moses. 2014. "Rethinking Historical Trauma." *Transcultural Psychiatry*, 5 (3): 299–319.

Kratochwil, Friedrich. 2018. *Praxis: On Acting and Knowing*. Cambridge: Cambridge University Press.

Lamb-Books, Benjamin. 2016. "Book Review: *Quantum Mind and Social Science*." *Perspectives: Newsletter of the Theory Section*. Accessed on January 14, 2016, at http://www.asatheory.org/current-newsletter-online/book-review-quantum-mind-and-social-science

Lepore, Jill. 2018. *These Truths: A History of the United States*. New York: W.W. Norton.

Lerner, Adam. 2019. "The Uses and Abuses of Victimhood Nationalism in International Politics." *European Journal of International Relations,* 26 (1): 62–87.

Mahmood, Katy. 2018. *Entanglement.* London: Harper Collins.

Mahr, Albrecht. 2003. *Konfliktfelder-wissende Felder: Systemaufstellungen in der Friedens- und Versöhnungsarbeit* [Conflict Fields-Knowing Fields: Systemic Constellations in Peace and Reconciliation World]. Heidelberg: Carl Auer-Systeme-Verlag.

Matthews, Stephen G. and David I. W. Phillips. 2010 "Minireview: Transgenerational Inheritance of the Stress Response: A New Frontier in Stress Research." *Endocrinology,* 151 (1): 7–13.

Mayr, Fabian Patrick. 2012. *Consciousing Relatedness: Systemic Conflict Transformation in Political Constellations.* Saarbrucken, Germany: Lambert Academic Publishing.

Nyman, Jonna and Anthony Burke. 2016. *Ethical Security Studies.* London: Routledge.

Pestel, F., R. Trimcev, G. Feindt, and F. Krawatzek. 2017. "Promise and Challenge of European Memory." *European Review of History,* 24 (4): 495–506.

Ricouer, Paul. 1990. *Time and Narrative,* vol. 1. Chicago: University of Chicago Press.

Sassounian, Harut. 2014. "Syrian President Finally Recognizes the Armenian Genocide." *Asbarez.* Accessed December 24, 2019, at http://asbarez.com/118921/syrian-president-finally-recognizes-the-armenian-genocide/

Scheff, Thomas and Suzanne Rezinger. 1991. *Emotions and Violence: Shame and Rage in Destructive Conflicts.* Lanham, MD: Lexington Books.

Scott, Joan. 1991. "The Evidence of Experience." *Critical Inquiry,* 17 (4): 773–797.

Sparrer, Insa. 2007. *Miracle, Solution and System.* Cheltenham, UK: Solutions Books.

Splinter, Dirk and Llubyana Wustehube. 2001. "Discovering Hidden Dynamics: Applying Systemic Constellation Work to Ethnopolitical Conflict." In Daniela Korppen, Norbert Ropers, and Hans J. Giessmann, editors. *The Non-Linearity of Peace Processes: Theory and Practice of Systemic Conflict Transformation.* Opladen: Verlag Barbara Budrich, pp. 111–125.

Stapp, H.P. 1971. "S-Matrix Interpretation of Quantum Theory." *Physical Review D,* 3 (6): 1303–1320.

Sztompka, P. 2000. "Cultural Trauma." *European Journal of Social Theory,* 3 (4): 449–466.

Van der Kolk, Bessel A. 1998. "Trauma and Memory." *Psychiatry and Clinical Neurosciences,* 52 (S1): S52–S64.

Waldner, David. 2017. "Schrodinger's Cat and the Dog that Didn't Bark: Why Quantum Mechanics Is (Probably) Irrelevant to the Social Sciences." *Critical Review,* 29 (2) (June): 1–35.

Walters, Karina L., Ramona E. Beltran, David Huh, and Teresa Evans-Campbell. 2011. "Dis-placement and Dis-ease: Land, Place and Health among American Indians and Alaska Natives." In Linda M. Burton, Susan P. Kemp, ManChui Leung, Stephen A. Matthews, and David T. Takeuchi, editors. *Communities, Neighborhood, and Health: Expanding the Boundaries of Place.* Philadelphia, PA: Springer Science+ Business Media; pp. 163–199.

Washington, K. 2010. "Zulu Traditional Healing, African Worldview and the Practice of Ubuntu: Deep Thought for African/Black Psychology." *Journal of Pan African Studies,* 3 (8): 24–39.

Wendt, Alexander. 2015. *Quantum Mind and Social Science.* Cambridge: Cambridge University Press.

18

The Moral Failure of the Quest
for Certainty

Laura Zanotti

Introduction

This chapter explores the connections between Newtonian physics and Kantian ethics' ontological assumptions and performs a critique of the Kantian position. I explore this ontology's implications for international intervention and the possibility of reconceptualizing ethics beyond Kantian strictures. Is it possible to reimagine ethics without embracing the Kantian dualistic idea of nature and reason? Could we imagine subjects differently, not merely as monads programmed to pursue self-interest against others, the primary presupposition of both realism and economic liberalism?

Kant fears the abyss in which we may plunge if we cannot grasp a universal, constant, and stable truth. Conversely, in this chapter, I argue that the need for certainty in his ethical project is frightening. What if, instead of imagining the universe as the manifestation of a master plan already written, we think of the universe as unfolding and of ourselves as responsible for the cascade effects we produce in the context of the possibilities that are available for us as finite human beings? What if we embrace *uncertainty* as an ontological trait of the world, instead of *certainty* warranted by a deity as the foundation of ethics? Ultimately, what kind of implication would reorienting International Relations' (IR) ontological imaginary have for the justification of practices of international intervention? In this chapter, I argue that by embracing deep relationality and uncertainty, quantum physics' ontological imaginary opens alternative possibilities for justifying agency, devising political change, and engaging in international intervention.

Before I proceed, I need to define the theoretical scope of my argument. I do not aspire to propose a theory of matter or to make truth statements about how quantum applies to microscopic or macroscopic phenomena. I am interested instead in performing an ontological critique, that is, in exploring the political and ethical possibilities entangled with ontological imaginaries. As Maurizio Meloni (2016) argued, science and politics are in relations of generative entrenchments.

Theories are always elaborated with reference to political factors and "once elaborated, every scientific position becomes a force affecting morality and politics"
(Meloni 2016, 15). Quantum theory's ontology of entanglements, relationality,
and nonlinear causality depicts a radically different cosmology from Newtonian
physics and Kantian philosophy. In doing so, it opens the way for rethinking
what the universe is made of and how we inhabit it.[1]

Exploring the Dark Side of Kantian Ethics: Substantialism, Certainty, Coloniality, and Theocracy

The prevalent ontological imaginary within Western political thought broadly
relies upon three theoretical foundations: the Kantian dichotomy of reason
and nature, the Cartesian dualism of mind and matter, and the ontological
assumptions of Newtonian physics. Newtonian physics explains the world as
consisting of entities with stable characteristics, standing in a relation of exter-
nality to one another. Causality is limited to law regularity and can be represented
through mathematical equations. Furthermore, causality, reduced to relations
of push and pull, is reversible. Both in the Kantian and the Cartesian ontological imaginary, the human subject is ontologically separated and detached from
inert matter. In this framework, agency is conceptualized as the manifestation of
the rational free subject's power, as is *his* ability to shape the natural world and
society through planning rationalities. This view is, in turn, deeply intertwined
with representations of masculinity and with the attributes of sovereignty. This
ontological imaginary shapes how we conceptualize agency and ethics, the ways
we validate our political actions and political change, and how we imagine possibilities for living together.

For instance, understanding causality as a matter of law regularities endorses
the notion of the world as a homogenous space where the same causal inferences
may be drawn everywhere, regardless of context. The Kantian categorical imperative, "act that you can will your maxim to become a universal law," is based
upon the assumptions that the world is homogenous and constitutes a radical
excision of the ethical relevance of practices and situational diversity. Here, universal applicability is the test for the validity of principled actions. This way of
adjudicating moral validity can only stand in the context of a world in which
linear causality and the stability of cause/effect relations obtain. The categorical
imperative is patterned upon the Newtonian imaginary regarding the certainty
of the laws of nature. For Kant, "since the universality of the law according to
which effects are produced constitutes what is properly called nature in the most
general sense (as to form), that is, the existence of things so far as it is determined by general laws, the imperative of duty may be expressed thus: Act as if

the maxims of your action were to become through your will a universal law of nature" (2008 [1785], 10).

Furthermore, Kantian ethics is grounded within substantialist assumptions regarding the ontological character of the human subject, which is constituted in a struggle between "nature" and "reason." Cognitive faculties are ranked in a hierarchical order, from lower to higher. Not surprisingly, the lower faculties are the sensuous ones, while the higher faculties of cognition deal with ideas. "Nature" is the source of selfish instincts, while ethical behavior only results from being able to detach oneself from nature and the belligerent tendencies we are born with. Reason is what potentially frees human beings from such constraints and brings them closer to God, while bodily instincts, desire, and what Kant views as human beings' selfish character lead to conflict and moral decay. In what follows, I will showcase Sean Molloy's (2017) exploration of Kantian ethics as a starting point for further elaborating a possible alternative to Kant's position based upon different ontological assumptions.[2] Molloy's central contention is that Kantian ethics *requires* belief in Kant's deity. As I will show in the following section, my fundamental predicament with the Kantian theoretical implant is not solely, like Molloy's, with its unsustainability absent the concept of divine providence. My critique focuses instead on the questionable implications of a political ethos based upon substantialist ontological assumptions regarding who humans are as subjects, its conceptualization of reason, its aversion to uncertainty, and its obsession with abstractions and universality.

Molloy (2017) argues that because perpetual peace can be achieved only if there is a rational plan initiated by God, contemporary cosmopolitanism's claim to be rooted in Kantian tradition is untenable. While contemporary cosmopolitans base their theory of universal rights and justice on foundational concepts of human nature, Kantian ethics relies on overcoming said nature through reason and upon the presupposition of the existence of a deity who, through divine providence, is the only possible warrantor of peace. For Kant, the order of providence is opposed to the order of nature, with human beings' material nature, characterized by selfishness and passions, the primary impediment to their ethical development.

Substantialist assumptions about subjectivity (i.e., that we are ontologically separate monads whose preferred maximizing function is power or greed) continue shaping dominant reflections about the root causes of conflict, the functioning of the economy, and the way peace, justice, and development may be achieved. The assumption that selfishness is the defining trait of human "nature" is one of the unquestioned pillars of Western schools of thought dating at least from Hobbes, straddling political realism, economic liberalism, and philosophical utilitarianism. In line with Kant, the self is imagined as ontologically separated between the bad animal-like characteristics of humans and the goodness of abstract reason. The latter may bring humanity closer to God by taming human "nature." Kant's position regarding the benevolent outcomes of selfishness is isomorphic to the functioning of the market in the liberal political imaginary, where the free market, in a distant future, produces a condition of equilibrium and functions as a social equalizer and as a multiplier of the general wealth. Ultimately, in this picture, God and the market function in the same way. Providence guarantees progress, as the market guarantees efficient allocation of resources out of competition and selfishness. Both political imaginaries embrace strong ontological assumptions about the "nature" of human beings and project positive outcomes in a distant future, in a utopian temporality where the hidden and benevolent design of God (or the effects of the market) will manifest.

The political implications of Kant's theoretical implant are both interesting and troubling. Perpetual peace may be achieved by instituting "an ethical community composed of well- disposed human beings working toward 'a universal republic based on the laws of virtue.'…In short, the legislator/ruler of such an ethical community is God" (Molloy 2017, 126). The duty of human beings is to pursue the creation of a society conceived as a *church invisible,* "the unchanging and all-unifying church *triumphant*" (Molloy 2017, 127). The characteristics of such a church are "universality, purity of moral intent, relation under freedom, and unchangeableness of constitution" (Molloy 2017, 127). This political ethos is based upon the presupposition that a group of human beings can legitimately claim to embody a true, immutable virtue; offer a truthful interpretation of God's will and plan; and, finally, translate it into politics. Kant's apparatus of enunciation emphasizes certainty and immutability: "Perpetual Peace," "universal history," and "moral law" must be "rooted in a noncontingent and perfect source," and duties, for Kant, must be "as certain as a mathematical demonstration" (Molloy 2017, 132–133). In summary, Kant's political ethos is rooted upon the possibility of four, mutually enforcing foundations: the excision of the contingent; the existence of a master plan envisaged by God; the ability of a few, wise *men* to interpret said plan; and robust assumptions about human nature intended as selfish and driven by passions, coupled with a firm rejection of this nature. Such a rejection is guided by a notion of "reason" that is constructed as capable of taming the sinful ontology of humanity.

Kant's onto-epistemological imaginary, I argue, leads to a troubling solution to the problem of the political. His aspiration to ground ethics in certainty and truth, warranted by God, excises the inherent instability and reversibility of human relations and leads to potentially authoritarian solutions to the problem of living together. In summary, while Kant is regarded as the founder of modern critical thought, the troublesome implications of his political ethos remain rather unexplored. Kant's onto-epistemology of certainty, grounded in assumptions about human nature and the existence of a divine plan of which a few virtuous men are the interpreters, has contributed to the conceptual apparatus of coloniality. Kant imagined the world as divided between "civilized" and "uncivilized." Civilized people organized in liberal states were to be entrusted with the task of rescuing the "savages" from their "lawless freedom" (Kant 1771, in Pourmokhtari 2013). This position informs the three dominant peace discourses (democratic peace, humanitarian intervention, and Responsibility to Protect) as well as the "duty-civilizing-colonial tension that underpins IR studies" (Pourmokhtari 2013, 1788, note 33). It also excises from view the historical responsibilities and conditions that lead to inequalities in the world and justifies the West's "civilizing mission" and Western norms for how political communities should be organized. As Andreas Behnke (2008) has also argued, Kantian Perpetual Peace established the ontological foundations of Western liberalism's attempt to establish peace through the eradication of difference.

In the pages that follow, I will highlight the connections between physics' ontological imaginaries, political ontologies, and praxis and argue that quantum ontologies offer tools for performing an onto-epistemological critique of the grounding assumptions of a Kantian ethos (and Western political thought more broadly). Such critique also destabilizes justifications of international intervention (and political actions more generally based on principled universalities instead of careful contextual assessments.

The Dark Side of Kantian Frames
for International Intervention

The ontological, epistemological, and normative matrix of Kantian ethics bears important practical and political implications since it legitimizes initiatives predicated upon the presupposition that the world is a Newtonian space, where the same conditions and causal regularities obtain everywhere. For instance, in making decisions about international intervention and in justifying them politically, states and international organizations alike rely upon abstract norms and principles while paying little attention to contextual situations and to the means through which action is carried out or its distributive effects. The categorical imperative is a formal principle, excising contingency and prescribing universal applicability as the criterion for ethical adjudication, which also relieves subjects from assuming responsibility for the practical consequences of their actions. In summary, the very distinction between the "material" and the "ideal" feeds into Western moral and political failures. In line with this view, for instance, the political rationality of inter-national intervention and development and their justificatory narratives rely upon assumptions that reality can be driven mainly by aspirations, regardless of specific conditions or circumstances.[3] Development strategies and inter-national interventions alike are justified mostly through aspirations toward capacities able to bring about an ideal society, whose traits correspond to a static and oversimplified narrative of peace, democracy, and development. Such an imaginary is rooted within a Newtonian/Kantian representation of the world as a homogenous space where the similar causal forces produce the same effects regardless of contingency. Since the 1990s, abstract, standardized programs for establishing good governance have been adopted as the tools for stopping violence. The United Nations' doctrine of institution building as a way of making peace is based upon the (often unrecognized and undiscussed) assumption that the dissemination throughout the world of institutional reforms is a universally valid way for solving political and economic problems in conflict zones (Zanotti 2011, 2013).

This underlying rationality also assumes that the "how" questions that go along with implementing abstract aspirations are simply corollaries and only marginally relevant in determining ethical and political justification for ac-tion. As I have argued elsewhere, the massacres that occurred in Srebrenica and Rwanda in the 1990s constitute examples of how UN peacekeepers failed to prevent atrocities by uncritically following institutionalized rules. However, by doing so, UN officials and members of the Security Council have fallen short of considering the entanglements of such rules in specific practices and adjudicated action with little consideration for the possible consequences of upholding ab-stract prescriptions in those particular situations. Nevertheless, the language of international peacekeeping often blames the lack of success not on lack of sound assessment of existing conditions, but on "unintended consequences," "collateral damage," and the like, thus constructing an apparatus of enunciation conducive to self-appeasement.[4]

As we have seen, Kant's solution to the problem of living together is to institute what amounts to a theocracy, where enlightened human beings claim to pos-sess the correct interpretation of God's will and are therefore responsible for the earthly implementation of *his* design. By simultaneously claiming truth, univer-sality, stability, and perfection, this political imaginary, and the ethos that derives from it, demonstrates familial resemblances with the aspirations and language of totalitarianism. The notion that peace is based upon the existence of a com-munity of true interpreters of God's will, along with the excision of uncertainty, also contributes to the construction, justification, and self-appeasing features of a normative language of just war, international intervention, peacebuilding, and development that sees Western ways as the model.

Escobar (2018) argues that seemingly benevolent aspirations of development, for instance, actually point to the arrogance of development planning, as it appears, in a document of the UN Department of Social and Economic Affairs. A relevant passage reads as follows:

> There is a sense in which rapid economic progress is impossible without painful adjustments. Ancient philosophies have to be scrapped; old social institutions have to disintegrate; bonds of caste, creed and race have to burst; and large numbers of persons who cannot keep up with progress have to have their expectations of a comfortable life frustrated. Very few communities are willing to pay the full price of economic progress. (UN Department of Social and Economic Affairs 1951, 15)

These kinds of pronouncements are attuned to the Kantian ontology that there exists only one path to a good life (a path that embraces a neoliberal way to development) and that those who have expertise, status, and, above all, power do in fact know what a perfect society should look like, regardless of the feelings and views of those who are compelled to embed themselves in such models.

Recently, critical scholars of community development have recognized the need for ontological critiques in order to redefine such practices. Westoby and Dowling, for instance, argue for "deconstructive movements," which "provide an opportunity to remain open to complexity, refusing to practice the tyranny of simplifying social phenomena" (Westoby and Dowling 2013, 16). Further, following Derrida as well as Foucault, Westoby (2019) argues that the notion of universal truth needs to be substituted with the constant interrogation of the practices that are institutionalized in the name of justice. Thus, "deconstruction is an episteme—a way of reading, a way of viewing, or being in the world, a practice, a sensibility—that insists, or summons the reader or practitioner to be disrupted or disrupt" (Westoby 2019 8).

In the pages that follow, I will engage with quantum ontologies and specifically with the notion of the *apparatus* to sketch an ethos that is based, not on abstractions, universality, or assumptions about the nature of the self, but on uncertainty and practical engagements. I explore the possibility that quantum offers an alternative to the Kantian ontology of the subject and to the Newtonian view of the physical world, the idea that we need certainty to operate ethically, and the idea that there is already a script that gives meaning to human action. I argue that together the Foucauldian notion of apparatus and feminist quantum physicist Karen Barad's intra-agential ethos allow us to place *practices* at the center of moral adjudication and evaluation. These onto-epistemological starting points reposition how we imagine who we are as humans, how we live together, and how we may bring about change in the world.

Ontologies of Entanglements, Apparatuses, and Practical Ethics

Prevailing conceptualizations of the subject and Kantian justifications of moral choices based upon universal normativity have been widely questioned from an array of schools of thought.[5] In contrast to Kantian positions, Jacques Derrida (1992) frames ethics as a sphere that "exceeds the law" in a way that situates ethical decision-making in the sphere of uncertainty and personal responsibility. Richard Rorty (1989), on the other hand, argues that the basis for moral behavior is not abstract reason, but "felt" solidarity that develops within particular communities. Morality is a *sentiment*, not an abstraction, and can be improved through empathy. Others have followed this path and pointed to the relevance of practices for sound ethical decisions (see Amoureux and Steele 2014; Kennedy 2004, 2006; Mac Ginty and Williams 2009; Onuf 2009; Zanotti 2019).

De-colonial, feminist, and critical materialist theorists also challenge ethical rationalism. De-colonial scholar Walter Mignolo (2002) questions the aspiration to universality of rationalist ethics by emphasizing its ultimately "local" character. In the meantime, Roxanne Doty (2006) defended the relevance of "interim moral responses," such as placing water stations in the desert to save immigrants from dying of thirst, that do not imply any essential grounding. Foundations of ethics based upon the presupposition of separability and closure of meaning have also been challenged by Wittgensteinian feminist philosophers such as Alessandra Tanesini (2004) and Peg O'Connor (2008), as well as by proponents of an "ethics of care" like Fiona Robinson (2011) and Maria Puig de la Bellacasa (2017). Diana Coole and Samantha Frost (2010) explore the implications of new materialism for agency and politics, while Jane Bennett (2010) invites IR scholars to go beyond juridical models of moral responsibility in favor of a broader consideration of what she refers to as an "agency of assemblages," where agentic capacities are distributed across human and nonhuman actors.

Recently, the debate on the relevance of complexity theories, nondualistic ontologies, human/nonhuman entanglements, and posthumanist reflections for the discipline of IR has intensified (Connolly 2013; Cudworth and Hobden 2011; Cudworth et al. 2018; Salter 2015). James Der Derian and Alexander Wendt (2020) edited a special issue of *Security Dialogue* dedicated to exploring the relevance of quantum technology, quantum theory, and quantum science for IR theories and security practices. Quantum theories, they argue, propose a worldview that challenges the assumption of separability as the foundation of atomism in philosophy and of methodological individualism in social sciences. Entanglement, for Der Derian and Wendt, "makes quantum theory fundamentally holistic: the properties, even existence, of the parts depend in top-down fashion on the whole, rather than the other way around" (Der Derian and Wendt 2020, 6).

Alexander Wendt (2015) initiated a reflection on quantum ontology within IR. Wendt asks us to understand the human brain as a quantum phenomenon. In relying upon the "vitalist" philosophical tradition, Wendt questions the metaphysical assumption of modern physics that matter is "dead" and, in doing so, critiques the limits of classical physics' understanding of what matter is and the associated causal relations that obtain in the world. Contra Newtonian physics, and in line with what he refers to alternatively as "neutral monism" and panpsychism, Wendt argues that we must think of matter as "intrinsically minded." For Wendt, humans are walking quantum waves, existing in a state of indeterminacy interrupted by acts of free will. Wendt focuses on human consciousness and its connections with other beings, other humans in particular, viewing acts of free will as sites of ontological closure. An important conclusion that he draws from this argument is a critique of rational choice theory as well as one of the central presuppositions of Western political philosophy, that is, that humans are naturally programmed to engage in conflict. For Wendt, rationality is contextual, with the entanglements of quantum physics suggesting that the default position for human beings is not necessarily conflict, but cooperation.

Alexander Wendt insightfully questions some of the ontological presuppositions of Newtonian physics (as well as, implicitly, Kantian ethics), such as human separation from nature and ontological individualism. Here I will further explore the relevance of ontologies of entanglement through a different lens: the notion of *apparatus* or *dispositif*. For my argument, which focuses on the centrality of matter and practices, the theoretical repertoires of Karen Barad and Michel Foucault are central. As Karen Fierke (2019) argued, both Barad and Wendt "express the central point of entanglement" and "move from an individualistic to a relational ontology," while focusing the one on the entanglement of matter and the other on the physicality of consciousness (Fierke 2029, 151). By putting in conversation quantum onto-epistemologies with Eastern philosophies, Fierke argues that these positions suggest that reality is fluid and relational, and advocates for greater attention to our role in constituting it. Like Wendt, Barad sees the world as characterized by ontological indeterminacy. However, while Wendt focuses on studying how indeterminacy is resolved through the collapse of brain quantum waves as the result of free will, Barad views such indeterminacy as resolving from within the intra-action of the observer and the observed, the human and the nonhuman, through the *apparatus*. In doing so, Barad brings to the forefront the relevance not only of consciousness and language but also of social and material artifacts.

Building upon Judith Butler, Karen Barad (2007) argues that knowledge is performative, not reflective, and that matter is vital. This approach paves the way for devising an ethos rooted in practices and centered on the notion of responsibility. I have argued that Kantian ethics doctrine is based upon a substantialist ontological imaginary that envisions the world as driven by abstract laws, warranted by a deity that has already established a plan for the universe. In the remaining sections of this chapter, I argue that if we embrace an ontology of entanglement and causal uncertainty, our conceptualizations and justification of ethical agency radically change in a way that embraces practices and raises the bar for adjudication of ethico-political choices, while at the same time broadening the possibilities for human agency to bring about change. Barad embraces Foucault's notion of *dispositif*, which argues that apparatuses not only are observational instruments but also are themselves "productive (and part of) phenomena" (2007, 142). Foucault's Panopticon is an example of such an apparatus. The Panopticon embodies ways of knowing, of exerting social control, and of organizing space that, in turn, reinforce and enable a variety of different social practices through which modern subjectivity has been shaped. Similarly, Barad argues that the *experimental apparatus* sets the condition of determinability of the properties of entities. Importantly, apparatuses are neither "mere ideations" nor "Kantian conceptual frameworks: they are physical arrangements" (Barad 2007, 129). This position, in fact, changes the way we relate to the physical world and the way we imagine our agency in it. As Barad insightfully puts it, there is no such thing as "absolute freedom in our choice of apparatus, and, on the other hand, a strict deterministic causal relationship whereby objects simply 'do their things' once the apparatus has been chosen" (2007, 130). Focusing on the *apparatus*, a material contraption that has no necessity but which constitutes how we engage with the world, introduces the relevance of material entanglements in a way that is not deterministic but relational, and so, deeply relevant for questions of human agency. Indeterminacy is resolved through apparatuses, which imply an ontology that takes human beings as deeply enmeshed with the material reality and practices within which they exist and act.

Karen Barad's ontological position affirms that phenomena, not entities, are the primary ontological referents, "pre-existing relations: relations without pre-existing *relata*" (2007, 139). For Barad, while interaction presupposes the existence of independent entities (i.e., an atomistic ontology), intra-action maintains that "the boundaries and properties of the components of phenomena become determinate" only within the context of intra-actions (2007, 139). Matter is not passive but reveals itself to us in these continuously intra-active processes. Her posthumanist position shifts the attention from representation and human mastery over nature to "mattering practices." Because we are *of* the world, not *above* it, our actions contribute to manifesting ontology, while the world "out there" shapes our being. *Indeterminacy*, for Barad (and Bohr), is not an epistemological issue but an ontological one. It is also not an *obstacle* to be overcome, as for

Kant, in the name of a universal truth and the implementation of a pre-existing godly design. *In a quantum ontological imaginary, the universe is not the manifestation of an already written divine master plan. Uncertainty is the ontological condition of the universe within which humans acting through specific apparatuses bring about ontological effects.*

Apparatuses are what make possible the determination of boundaries and properties of objects (Barad's intra-agential cuts). In this ontological imaginary, there is no divine master plan to be followed; there are no interpreters of God's will, nor are there assumptions about *human nature* as the foundations of ethics. There are only *practices*, whose effects of inclusion/exclusion need to be carefully and responsibly assessed in the contexts within which they are enacted. In extending Foucault's radical nonsubstantialist position to the nonhuman through Bohr's quantum physics, Barad links a reflection of our being-in-the-world to a reflection on the way we know what we know and the way we subsequently act upon it.

In summary, a quantum onto-epistemological position has a direct bearing on how conceptualizations of agency, ontology, and epistemology intersect with and mutually construct each other. In a quantum framework, reimagining ontologies, epistemologies, and agency are urgent and necessary political actions. Quantum ontological imaginary repositions us vis-à-vis the universe. We do not act *upon* the world. Instead, we have agency as part of it. This is a central contribution of imagining the world through quantum. In an entangled ontological horizon, practical processes and the assumption of responsibility for thorough contextual assessments of the possible outcomes of our initiatives, rather than abstract principles of reasoning, must constitute the basis for ethical decisions. "Right intentions," absent competent analysis that includes "how" questions, do not constitute sufficient ways for validating international intervention (and political action more broadly). Claiming "unintended consequences" should be used very sparingly as appeasement for failure.

Discursive practices and material phenomena are ontologically imbricated, while experimental *dispositifs* are not only heuristic but also performative instruments that have a bearing upon resolving ontological indeterminacy. What-is, and the way we know it, cannot be conceptualized in isolation. Importantly, however, phenomena are not solely the *result* of human agency. Instead, "the world is a dynamic process of intra-activity and materialization in the enactment of determinate causal structures which determine boundaries, properties, meaning, and patterns of marks on bodies"(Barad 2007, 140). Both for Barad and for Foucault, specific arrangements of "things" and particular physical settings do produce ontological effects and enable processes of subjectification as well as possibilities for "knowledge." In this ontological imaginary, humans cannot overdetermine outcomes but do take part in processes of mattering by modifying the apparatuses through which they engage with what-is and so maintain a bearing within the enfolding of a universe whose end goals are not already set in a divine master plan. In Barad's words, "post-humanism eschews both humanist and structuralist accounts of the subject that position the human as either a pure cause or pure effect.... [P]ost-humanism doesn't presume the separateness of any-'thing,' let alone the alleged spatial, ontological, and epistemological distinction that sets humans apart" (Barad 2007, 136).

In addition to shifting the methods we use for adjudicating ethical behavior, quantum ontologies invite us to rethink who we are as subjects and the foundations of ethics. They challenge the validity of theorizing ethics based upon assumptions regarding the characteristics of human subjects. In other words, the Kantian divided subject is not the starting point for ethical adjudication. As subjects, we are ontologically shaped and defined through our intra-actions within practices or, to use Barad's vocabulary, within phenomena. Subjectification takes the place of an imaginary that assumes humans as ontologically endowed with characteristics of rationality, freedom, power, and selfishness.[6] In this regard, Foucault (1984) indicates that Kant's most important contribution is his reflections on the very notion of human subjectivity, that is, *his critical attitude, not his positive politics* (Foucault 1984). Foucault embraced a different concept of "reason" from Kant's: not a reason that claims for itself the ability to understand God's plans, a universal truth that must constitute the rule of behavior for an abstract humanity, but a reason that exercises a critical exploration of how "things" come to be in the world. Subjectivity itself is the result of a practice, as Foucault gestures toward, a "work of art." In this framework, ethics is rooted in the *acceptance* of human finitude, not its rejection. And the central criterion for the adjudication of the validity of any action is rooted in practical and contextual assessments of its consequences for people's lives, rather than the possibility of its universalization. Differently from Kant, the basis for adjudicating ethical decisions does not rely on abstractions regardless of effects, presuppositions about the nature of human beings and the work of divine providence, *but rather on the careful assessments of the apparatuses of which we are part and that we deploy to bring about political outcomes. Thus, special attention should be paid to "how" questions, that is, the specific means to an end available, and to the situational configurations that obtain in specific circumstances. Such assessments are a key and integral part of acting responsibly toward real human beings, instead of an abstract humanity. The end goal of human history is not determined in advance by a divine plan or inescapable structural or physical determinism. Ethical endeavors are situated within a human temporality instead of a divine, eternal time. Such temporality is irreversible in the sense that the past produces cascade effects and forms of materialization of matter that cannot be undone. Still, it is not oriented toward a preordained end goal. Cascade effects have consequences that often exceed their scope. Therefore, action must be assessed responsibly and prudently.*

Asserting an Ethos of Practice

While Kant imagines ethics as situated within an abstract realm of universals aloof from practice, a quantum ethos reclaims *practice* as the very space for ethics. Because it reclaims the ontological relevance of practices through the notion of apparatus, a quantum ontological imaginary invites to reconsidering how we make decisions, how we justify action, and how we make ourselves accountable for consequences. For Kant, the correct way of adjudicating ethical action is rooted in reason's ability to abstract from material conditions in the name of an abstract humanity. Instead, an intra-agential ethos is deeply rooted in *contextual assessments. Practices are not the residual of theories. They are the entanglements through which ontological closure occurs within complex processes that include, but are not limited to, knowledge and aspirations.* As ethical subjects, we produce ontological cuts and, hence, cascading effects.

Differently from Kant, sound ethical decisions are deeply rooted in our humanity, not hampered by it. Thus, the main question to ask in adjudicating the validity of an action is not whether the criteria we use to make any given decisions could be held as universally valid. Instead, it is what kind of materialization of matter and ontological cuts would the deployment of specific apparatuses, including the means to achieve any given end, likely entail. This way of deciding ethical action puts under scrutiny the political rationale of international interventions, often based upon simplified assumptions regarding the causal clusters that obtain in conflict zones, a position that overlooks the morphogenetic properties of practices. A quantum ontological imaginary raises the bar for deciding the ethical validity of our actions and offers an alternative to the self-appeasing effects of an ethos of abstractions. It requires assuming radical responsibility for the effects that result from our actions and suggests a prudent use of universal prescriptions as well as of the justification of failure as "unintended consequences."

Furthermore, an ethos of entanglement invites us to look with suspicion at any political program that claims to be based upon the certainty of its own view of justice or truth. Foucault argued that he did not see political engagements as a way of bringing about an immanent idealized and utopian social order that reverses all that exists but as a life practice of questioning and interrogation that opens new possibilities into what is otherwise assumed to be unchangeable and ontologically closed (Foucault 1979). Instead of being based upon a preplanned idea of a perfect social order or on the interpretation of a divine script, political agency for Foucault is rooted above all in creativity, alertness, and asking questions about why what-is is the way it is. This position is exemplified by the Greek philosophers' *parrēsia*, a life practice that interrogates what is made to appear as inevitable and natural. Similarly, David Campbell (1999), building on Derrida, has argued that the political salience of deconstruction resides in questioning the logic that has made violence and oppression appear natural. Judith Butler (2020) also bases her argument on the force of nonviolence upon a radical critique of individualistic ontologies and an ontological reimagination that sees us as part of a community first. I would add that if the universe is unfolding instead of predesigned, we bear responsibility for the footprint we leave. Such footprints (or micropolitical acts) may produce (irreversible) cascade effects.

A quantum perspective offers an ontological imaginary that debunks the unspoken assumptions of how the world is and how we inhabit it. Such assumptions constitute the starting point of international intervention, development, and ethics more broadly. As an ontology, quantum invites us to critique underlying assumptions of how we do social science and to embrace central concepts of poststructural theory, such as performativity, as an ontological feature of how we inhabit the universe. In this view, Newtonian substantialism as the sole paradigm for sound knowledge loses traction. Quantum political ontology paves the way for a reconceptualization of a political ethos grounded in responsible consideration of the entanglements that obtain, the apparatuses we deploy to address them, and the outcomes deriving from our engagement with what exists.

Ultimately, quantum ontologies invite an attitude of caution, modesty, curiosity, and relentless attention to the transformative possibilities that may open up in the practices within which we intra-act and affirm the centrality of *how* aspirational goals are implemented. *Because what-is is performative and not an inert mass, the possibility that planning rationalities based upon simplified assumptions regarding causality may provide useful tools for predicting and governing all chains of events necessary for the realization of any given aspiration comes under serious question.* This consideration is central for suggesting *prudence* as a key political virtue. A prudent political attitude asks "how" questions, focuses on competent assessments of situational contexts and refrains from adopting simplified solutions to complex political problems. It also regards with suspicion justifications for action relying on godly plans, or on the interest of an abstract "humanity." Kantian abstractions stifle creative political transformation and harbor the specter of totalitarianism. Furthermore, in a world of causal indeterminacy, mathematically calculated rules do not offer valid guidelines for action.

The central point of an ethics of entanglement is that abstractions are not sufficient to make sound ethical adjudications, especially if such abstractions are used to relinquish responsibility for the wrongdoings and sufferings our actions produce. Indeed, in history there are many examples of atrocities that were framed as legal. Norms do not cause action in a linear way. Instead, accepted abstract norms and laws may be hijacked and twisted to justify the very deeds they in principle forbid. For instance, Claudia Koontz (2003) has shown that the Nazi racist regime emerged as a process that progressively institutionalized and legalized actions that excluded and othered the Jewish people while Hitler paid lip service to condemnations of the blatant atrocities he de facto permitted and encouraged.[7] In a different context, Anthony Lang (2009) has argued that the relabeling of torture as "harsh interrogation" under the Bush administration and its accompanying attempts to define carefully the degree of pain admissible before questioning becomes torture, are examples of the substitution of anodyne language and apparently precise technical guidelines that obscure the horror evoked by the word "torture" and replace it with images of bureaucratic efficiency.

In summary, in an entangled universe made of relations without *relata*, where practices have morphogenetic properties, sound justifications of ethical choices are not grounded within universals but within a careful analysis of the particular.

Conclusions

Molloy concludes his volume on Kant with the following question: "in an era when the belief prescribed by Kant is no longer persuasive, alternative answers may have to be forged to the Kantian question: what can I know, what ought I do, for what may I hope?" (Molloy 2017, 164). In this chapter, I argued that to answer the Kantian question with which Molloy concludes his book, we need to carefully scrutinize Kant's ontological starting points and reimagine how the world is made and how it holds together. I have also outlined the possible answers that are offered by ontologies of entanglements. These ontologies lead us to embrace uncertainty and responsibility rather than certainty and universality as central criteria for ethical adjudication. Questioning Kant's metaphysics (and ontological substantialism more generally) paves the way for reimagining ethics without having to presuppose ontological closure, God, or universal truths.

As I have argued earlier, quantum ontological imaginaries radically reposition our being in the world. In this framework, we are ontologically *entangled with* what exists, not ontologically *above it*. And we act in the world not as masses impressing movement on other masses in an inert and homogenous space, but through complex apparatuses that we deploy and of which we are part. By radically questioning the very notion of separability that underlines notions of individuality, rationality, and universal normativity, quantum traces the ontological and methodological horizon for devising an ethics that embraces uncertainty and complexity. Imagining the world as entangled points at the political relevance of *how* we inhabit it and at the (yet nonlinear) causal power of micropolitical processes. Alexander Wendt argued that, in contrast with atomism's tendency to promote individualism and competition, an ontology of entanglement may favor cooperation. In a quantum ontology, while there is no guarantee that "individuals will put their agency to progressive causes, at least...they have the option" (Wendt 2015: 282). In addition, I argue, the very notion of entanglement points at the ethical relevance of practices. Thus, it raises the bar for adjudication of ethical action. In this way, it opens the way for imagining an ethos based upon situational analysis and radical assumption of responsibility for the morphogenetic processes we enable. In this ontological horizon, micropolitical interventions, while not revolutionizing the status quo, may be relevant to trigger desirable, and maybe unexpected, changes. The destiny of the world is not already decided by divine design. On the contrary, we are deeply responsible for the morphogenetic effects we may produce through the deployment of the apparatuses we enact. Apparatuses are material assemblages of knowledge and power that shape space, constitute subjects, and make ways of living together possible. In other words, apparatuses are not only heuristic tools but also performative instruments. If we make the notion of the apparatus central to the adjudication of moral choices, the attention shifts from abstractions to contextual assessments of the possible effects any given arrangement may produce. Ethical behavior is connected with an attitude of prudence. It remains concerned with the ontological cuts we operate and with *how* the apparatuses we put in place produce consequences for real human beings in real life.

Quantum ontologies invite to take responsibility for analyzing the material entanglements that produce political effects (beyond appeasing abstractions), and for the consequences of our acts. Even though we do not *control* the entire chain of events that will ensue from our decision, we have a duty to always assess the means to end, and how causal forces may operate in specific practices. Responsibility and prudence do not lead to acquiescence, inaction, or empty relativism. On the contrary, as Wendt, Fierke, and Barad have also argued, the notion of entanglement challenges individualism. It also nurtures an idea of political engagement that does not exclude a priori any type of tool to produce political effects, but that first and foremost invites a careful consideration of the contexts within which such initiatives are situated. Because reality is complex and entangled, similar tools do not produce the same effects across situations and circumstances. Therefore, claims that justify action based upon abstract aspirations or justifications, be they "following the law," bringing about democracy, an alternative societal model, peace, etc., must be based on careful evaluation of what conditions obtain in specific environments and consideration of "how" questions. The obsession with universality may be ethically counter-productive. As humans, our horizon is finite. We do not live in an eternal time. All we have is a world of practices, and we should take responsibility for enabling or foreclosing specific ways of materializing matter.

Acknowledgments

A previous version of this article was published as "De-Colonizing the Political Ontology of Kantian Ethics: A Quantum Perspective," in *Journal of International Political Theory*, August 18, 2020, https://doi.org/10.1177/17550 88220946777. It is entangled with many colleagues and students who joined in discussing "the quantum thing." The discussions with my graduate students at Virginia Tech enticed me to reflect on Kant and to push my reflections on the implications of quantum ethics a step forward. I am indebted to Alexander Wendt for his comments on this chapter and for engaging with me in chal-lenging conversations. I am grateful to Michael Murphy for nurturing debates on quantum at the American Political Science Association and at the International Studies Association. James Der Derian's invitation to be part of the Q Project Symposium in 2019 and the diverse scholars I met there reinforced my fascina-tion with quantum imaginaries and their political relevance. I am also grateful to Anthony Szczurek and Sabrina Harris for their editorial suggestions. The usual disclaimer applies, as I am solely responsible for the contents (and shortcomings) of this chapter.

Notes

1. For a discussion of the political relevance of concepts and cosmologies for International Relations see Kurki (2020). See also Allan (2018).
2. This reflection is rooted upon a dissatisfaction I developed as a practitioner. I worked for about a decade at the United Nations as a peacekeeper. As a practitioner, I increas-ingly came to the realization that relying mainly upon abstractions is not a valid foun-dation for making ethical decisions; indeed, it is often a recipe for making the wrong ones. The work of diplomats like Jean Marie Guehénno (2015), former under-secretary general for peacekeeping operations, and US ambassador R. Nicholas Burns (2019) has also shown that the failure of practical assessment of the context and means of in-tervention is conducive to problematic outcomes of international intervention.
3. Relying on overarching assumptions instead of contextual competence has led to dis-astrous initiatives, such as, for instance, the war in Iraq, as Jack Amoureux and Brent Steele (2014) have documented.

4. I explore this topic more extensively in *Ontological Entanglements, Agency and Ethics in International Relations* (2019). It is worthwhile to note here that this analysis does not intend to personify the United Nations or cast blame on any specific individual. The United Nations is a field of forces where the political agendas of many actors, especially powerful member states, contribute to shape and limit what the organization may be able to accomplish.

5. What follows builds upon Zanotti (2019).

6. Substantialist ontological assumptions have deeply informed ontological security studies. As Browning and Joenniemi (2017) have argued, ontological security studies rely on the assumptions that identities are somehow fixed instead of relationally constituted, thus limiting the conversation about ontological security to identity preservation and to avoiding violence. Elisa Randazzo and Ignasi Torrent (2020), in critiquing some streams of governmentality studies, argued that the agency of peacekeepers is adaptive in the context of processes of interactions, rather than driven by the establishment of specific liberal agendas.

7. For a critique of legalistic justifications of Nazi atrocities see Zanotti (2014).

References

Allan, Bentley. *Scientific Cosmology and International Orders.* Cambridge Studies in International Relations 147. Cambridge; New York: Cambridge University Press, 2018.

Amoureux, Jack L., and Brent J. Steele. "Competence and Just War." *International Relations* 28, no. 1 (March 2014): 67–87. https://doi.org/10.1177/0047117813507735.

Barad, Karen Michelle. *Meeting the Universe Halfway: Quantum Physics and the Entanglement of Matter and Meaning.* Durham, NC: Duke University Press, 2007.

Behnke, Andreas. "'Eternal Peace' as the Graveyard of the Political: A Critique of Kant's Zum Ewigen Frieden." *Millennium: Journal of International Studies* 36, no. 3 (May 2008): 513–531. https://doi.org/10.1177/03058298080360030701.

Bellacasa, María de la. *Matters of Care: Speculative Ethics in More than Human Worlds.* Minneapolis: University of Minnesota Press, 2017.

Bennett, Jane. *Vibrant Matter: A Political Ecology of Things.* Durham, NC: Duke University Press, 2010.

Browning, Christopher S., and Pertti Joenniemi. "Ontological Security, Self-Articulation and the Securitization of Identity." *Cooperation and Conflict* 52, no. 1 (March 2017): 31–47. https://doi.org/10.1177/0010836716653161.

Burns, William J. *The Back Channel: A Memoir of American Diplomacy and the Case for Its Renewal.* 1st ed. New York: Random House, 2019.

Butler, Judith. *The Force of Nonviolence: An Ethico-Political Bind.* Brooklyn: Verso Books, 2020.

Campbell, David. "The Deterritorialization of Responsibility: Levinas, Derrida, and Ethics after the End of Philosophy." In *Moral Spaces: Rethinking Ethics and World Politics*, edited by Michael J. Shapiro. Minneapolis: University of Minnesota Press, 1999: 29–56.

Connolly, William E. *The Fragility of Things: Self-Organizing Processes, Neoliberal Fantasies, and Democratic Activism.* Durham, NC: Duke University Press, 2013.

Coole, Diana H., and Samantha Frost, eds. *New Materialisms: Ontology, Agency, and Politics.* Durham, NC; London: Duke University Press, 2010.

Cudworth, Erika, and Stephen Hobden. *Posthuman International Relations: Complexity, Ecologism and Global Politics*. London: Zed Books, 2011. http://site.ebrary.com/id/ 10520625.

Cudworth, Erika, Stephen Hobden, and Emilian Kavalski, eds. *Posthuman Dialogues in International Relations*. London; New York: Routledge, 2018.

Der Derian, James, and Alexander Wendt. "'Quantizing International Relations': The Case for Quantum Approaches to International Theory and Security Practice." *Security Dialogue* 51, no. 5 (October 2020): 399–413. https://doi.org/10.1177/0967010620901905.

Derrida, Jacques. "Force of Law: The 'Mystical Foundation of Authority.'" In *Deconstruction and the Possibility of Justice*, edited by Drucilla Cornell, Michel Rosenfeld, and David Carlson. New York, London: Routledge, 1992: 3–67.

Doty, Roxanne Lynn. "Fronteras Compasivas and the Ethics of Unconditional Hospitality." *Millennium: Journal of International Studies* 35, no. 1 (December 2006): 53–74. https:// doi.org/10.1177/03058298060350010701.

Escobar, Arturo. *Designs for the Pluriverse: Radical Interdependence, Autonomy, and the Making of Worlds. New Ecologies for the Twenty-First Century*. Durham, NC: Duke University Press, 2018.

Fierke, Karen M. "Contraria sunt Complementa: Global Entanglement and the Constitution of Difference." *International Studies Review* 21 (2019): 146–169. doi:10.1093/isr/viy043.

Foucault, Michel. "Truth and Power: An Interview with Michel Foucault." *Critique of Anthropology* 4, nos. 13–14 (January 1979): 131–137. https://doi.org/10.1177/0308275 X7900401311.

Foucault, Michel. "What Is Enlightenment? ('Qu'est Que Les Lumières?')." In *The Foucault Reader*, edited by Paul Rabinow, 1st ed., 32–50. New York: Pantheon Books, 1984.

Guéhenno, Jean-Marie. *The Fog of Peace: A Memoir of International Peacekeeping in the 21st Century*. Washington, DC: Brookings Institution Press, 2015.

Kant, Immanuel. "Essay on the Maladies of the Head." In *Anthropology, History, and Education*, edited by Robert B. Louden and Günter Zöller. Cambridge Edition of the Works of Immanuel Kant in Translation. Cambridge; New York: Cambridge University Press, 2007.

Kant, Immanuel. "Groundwork of the Metaphysic of Morals." In *Critical Theory and International Relations: A Reader*, edited by Steven C. Roach. New York: Routledge, 2008 [1785]: 5–15.

Kennedy, David. *The Dark Sides of Virtue: Reassessing International Humanitarianism*. Princeton, NJ: Princeton University Press, 2004.

Kennedy, David. *Of War and Law*. Princeton, NJ: Princeton University Press, 2006.

Koonz, Claudia. *The Nazi Conscience*. Cambridge, MA: Belknap Press of Harvard University Press. 2003.

Kurki, Milja. *International Relations in a Relational Universe*. New York: Oxford University Press, 2020.

Lang, Anthony. *Punishment, Justice, and International Relations: Ethics and Order After the Cold War*. London, New York: Routledge, 2009.

Mac Ginty, Roger, and Andrew J. Williams. *Conflict and Development*. Routledge Perspectives on Development. London; New York: Routledge, 2009.

Meloni, Maurizio. *Political Biology. Science and Social Values in Human Heredity from Eugenics to Epigenetics*. New York: Palgrave Macmillan, 2016.

Mignolo, W. D. "The Geopolitics of Knowledge and the Colonial Difference." *South Atlantic Quarterly* 101, no. 1 (January 1, 2002): 57–96. https://doi.org/10.1215/00382 876-101-1-57.

Molloy, Seán. *Kant's International Relations: The Political Theology of Perpetual Peace*. Ann Arbor: University of Michigan Press, 2017.

O'Connor, Peg. *Morality and Our Complicated Form of Life: Feminist Wittgensteinian Metaethics*. University Park: Pennsylvania State University Press, 2008.

Onuf, Nicholas. "Structure? What Structure?" *International Relations* 23, no. 2 (June 2009): 183–199. https://doi.org/10.1177/0047117809104634.

Pourmokhtari, Navid. "A Postcolonial Critique of State Sovereignty in IR: The Contradictory Legacy of a 'West-Centric' Discipline." *Third World Quarterly* 34, no. 10 (November 2013): 1767–1793. https://doi.org/10.1080/01436597.2013.851888.

Randazzo, Elisa, and Ignasi Torrent. "Reframing Agency in Complexity-Sensitive Peacebuilding." *Security Dialogue*, 52, no. 1: 3–20. https://doi.org/10.1177/096701062 0904306.

Robinson, Fiona. *The Ethics of Care: A Feminist Approach to Human Security. Global Ethics and Politics*. Philadelphia: Temple University Press, 2011.

Rorty, Richard. *Contingency, Irony, and Solidarity*. Cambridge; New York: Cambridge University Press, 1989.

Salter, Mark B., ed. *Making Things International. 1: Circuits and Motion*. Minneapolis: University of Minnesota Press, 2015.

Tanesini, Alessandra. *Wittgenstein: A Feminist Interpretation*. Cambridge, UK; Malden, MA: Polity Press, 2004.

UN Department of Social and Economic Affairs. "Measures for the Economic Development of Under-Developed Countries," Department of Economic Affairs, New York, 1951.

Wendt, Alexander. *Quantum Mind and Social Science: Unifying Physical and Social Ontology*. Cambridge; New York: Cambridge University Press, 2015.

Westoby, Peter. "'A Community Development Yet-to-Come': Jacques Derrida and Re-Constructing Community Development Praxis." *Community Development Journal*, 56, no. 3: 375–390. https://doi.org/10.1093/cdj/bsz013.

Westoby, Peter, and Gerard Dowling. *Theory and Practice of Dialogical Community Development: International Perspectives*. Abingdon, Oxon: Routledge, 2013.

Zanotti, Laura. "Governmentality, Ontology, Methodology: Re-thinking Political Agency in the Global World." *Alternatives*, 38, no. 4 (2013): 288–304. doi:10.1177/ 0304375413512098.

Zanotti, Laura. "The Danger of Following Rules: Reflections on *Eichmann in Jerusalem*." *Spectra* 3, no. 2 (2014). http://doi.org/10.21061/spectra.v3i2.305.

Zanotti, Laura. *Governing Disorder: UN Peace Operations, International Security, and Democratization in the Post-Cold War Era*. University Park: Pennsylvania State University Press, 2011.

Zanotti, Laura. *Ontological Entanglements, Agency and Ethics in International Relations: Exploring the Crossroads*. London, New York: Routledge, 2019.

Index

Note: Tables and figures are indicated by *t* and *f* following the page number